The Fight for the High Ground

The U.S. Army and Interrogation during Operation Iraqi Freedom I,
May 2003 - April 2004

Major Douglas A. Pryer
U.S. Army

Keep up the good fight!!

foreword by
Col. Stuart A. Herrington
U.S. Army, Ret.
Counterintelligence Officer, Interrogator & Author

CGSC Foundation Press • Fort Leavenworth, Kansas

Keep up the good fight!! [handwritten inscription]

Published by the CGSC Foundation Press
100 Stimson Ave., Suite 1149
Fort Leavenworth, Kansas 66027

Copyright © 2009 by CGSC Foundation, Inc.

All rights reserved.

www.cgscfoundation.org

Portions of this book were originally submitted by Army Major Douglas A. Pryer in 2009 as part of a Masters Thesis to satisfy the Masters of Military Arts and Sciences degree at the U.S. Army Command and General Staff College at Fort Leavenworth, Kansas.

Publication of *The Fight for the High Ground* was made possible by a grant from Pioneer Services, a division of Mid-Country Bank. We are grateful for their support.

ISBN 978-0-615-33274-1

Book design by
Mark H. Wiggins
MHW Public Relations and Communications

Printed in the United States of America by Allen Press, Lawrence, Kansas

The past few days when I've been at that window upstairs, I've thought a bit of the 'shining city upon a hill'. . . . I've spoken of the shining city all my political life, but I don't know if I ever quite communicated what I saw when I said it. But in my mind it was a tall proud city built on rocks stronger than oceans, wind-swept, God-blessed, and teeming with people of all kinds living in harmony and peace, a city with free ports that hummed with commerce and creativity, and if there had to be city walls, the walls had doors and the doors were open to anyone with the will and the heart to get here. That's how I saw it and see it still.

President Ronald Reagan

Contents

Table of contents vii
Illustrations ix
Tables ix
Acronyms x
Foreword xii
Prologue: Through the looking glass xxi

Chapter 1   A terribly hot summer 1

Chapter 2   "It's just not right" 8
                 Detainees, the Law of War, and U.S. National law 9
                 Detainees and military law, regulations, and doctrine ... 11
                 Interrogation approaches and U.S. Army doctrine 12
                 Ambiguities and inconsistencies 15
                 Conclusions 18

Chapter 3   The city upon the hill 19
                 The Bush Administration and interrogation policy 20
                 Gitmo adopts SERE interrogation techniques 22
                 Enhanced interrogation techniques migrate to Iraq ... 24
                 Conclusions 28

Chapter 4   CJTF-7's long list of not nearly enoughs 29
                 Too few MI soldiers 31
                 Too few military policemen 34
                 The mother of all fragos 35
                 Too few lawyers 39
                 CJTF-7's austere interrogation facilities 39
                 "Short-lived and poorly drafted" interrogation policies ... 45
                 Conclusions 48

Chapter 5	Tragic blunders	50
	Enhanced interrogations in Al Anbar	51
	Macabre dances at two "Discos" in Mosul	55
	Troubles in Tikrit	61
	Conclusions	63
Chapter 6	Old Ironsides	66
	The road to stability operations	66
	Seizing the high ground	68
	Out front!	70
	An MI community takes charge	71
	The TF 1AD Division Interrogation Facility	72
	MI shortfalls	74
	Conclusions	78
Chapter 7	Three brigades	80
	The "Ready First" Brigade	80
	The Bulldog Brigade	90
	The Iron Brigade	96
	Conclusions	105
Chapter 8	The ascent from Abu Ghraib	107
	Publishing new doctrine	107
	Growing the interrogation force	111
	Improving professional education and training	115
	Conclusions	116
Chapter 9	A tale of two cities	118
	Key conclusion	120

Acknowledgments	122
Notes	123
Sources	165
Chronology	182
Glossary	187
Index	192
Photos	200
About the author	202

Illustrations

Figure 1	Combined Joint Task Force 7 Area of Operations 3
Figure 2	Interrogation Policies in Guantanamo, Afghanistan and Iraq 26
Figure 3	205th MI Brigade Task Organization, August 2003 32
Figure 4	U.S. Detention Facilities as of August 2003 35
Figure 5	CJTF-7 Detention Process 38
Figure 6	Interrogation Approaches Posted at Abu Ghraib, Oct-Dec 2003 45
Figure 7	Synopsis of Witness Statements 57
Figure 8	TF 1AD Area of Operations 67
Figure 9	1AD Detainee/Information Flow 72
Figure 10	TF 1AD Division Interrogation Facility 73
Figure 11	501st MI Battalion Information Flow 77
Figure 12	1BCT, TF 1AD, Detainee Holding Area 84
Figure 13	3BCT, TF 1AD, Detainee Holding Area 91
Figure 14	2BCT, 1AD Intel Organization 99
Figure 15	2BCT, TF 1AD, Detainee Holding Area 102
Figure 16	MI versus MP Responsibilities 108
Figure 17	Increased MI Capability 112

Tables

Table 1	U.S. Army Doctrinal Interrogation Approaches during OIF I 13
Table 2	CJTF-7 Detainee Classifications 36

Acronyms

1AD	1st Armored Division
2BCT	2nd Brigade Combat Team
2LCR	2nd Light Cavalry Regiment
3ACR	3d Armored Cavalry Regiment
4ID	4th Infantry Division
AO	Area of Operations
AIT	Advanced Individual Training
AR	Army Regulation
BCT	Brigade Combat Team
BFSB	Battlefield Surveillance Brigade
CFSO	Counterintelligence Force Protection Source Operations
CG	Commanding General
CI	Civilian Internee or Counterintelligence
CID	Criminal Investigation Division
CIA	Central Intelligence Agency
CJSOTF-AP	Combined Joint Special Operations Task Force-Arabian Peninsula
CJTF-7	Combined Joint Task Force 7
CJTF-180	Combined Joint Task Force 180
CSA	Chief of Staff of the Army
COL	Colonel
CONEX	Container Express
CW	Chief Warrant Officer
DIF	Division Interrogation Facility
DAIG	Department of the Army Inspector General
DIVARTY	Division Artillery
DOCEX	Document Exploitation
DoD	Department of Defense
EPW	Enemy Prisoner of War
FBI	Federal Bureau of Investigation
FOIA	Freedom of Information Act
FOB	Forward Operating Base
FRAGO	Fragmentary Order
FM	Field Manual
G2	Deputy Chief of Staff, Intelligence
GSR	Ground Surveillance Radar
Gitmo	Guantanamo Bay, Cuba
GWOT	Global War on Terrorism

HCT	HUMINT Collection Team
HOC	HUMINT Operations Cell
HUMINT	Human Intelligence
ICE	Interrogation Control Element
IG	Inspector General
IMINT	Imagery Intelligence
J2	Joint Staff Directorate, Intelligence
JIDC	Joint Interrogation and Debriefing Center
JSOC	Joint Special Operations Command
JPRA	Joint Personnel Recovery Agency
LTC	Lieutenant Colonel
LTG	Lieutenant General
MAJ	Major
MG	Major General
MI	Military Intelligence
MP	Military Police
MWD	Military Working Dog
MSO	Military Source Operations
MTOE	Modified Table of Organization and Equipment
NCO	Noncommissioned Officer
OD	Other Detainee
OIF	Operation Iraqi Freedom
OMT	Operational Management Technician
PMO	Provost Marshal Officer
ROE	Rules of Engagement
RP	Retained Person
S2	Staff Officer, Intelligence
SEAL	Naval Sea, Air, Land Special Warfare Specialist
SERE	Survival, Evasion, Resistance, and Escape
SIGINT	Signals Intelligence
SIR	Summary Interrogation Report
SJA	Staff Judge Advocate
SMU	Special Mission Unit
TACON	Tactical Control
THT	Tactical HUMINT Team
TF	Task Force
TF 1AD	Task Force 1st Armored Division
UCMJ	Uniform Code of Military Justice
WO	Warrant Officer

Foreword

When retired Colonel Bob Ulin, CEO of the Command and General Staff College Foundation, asked me to contribute a foreword for a new book on interrogation, my interest was immediately piqued. Interrogating prisoners and detainees had been one of my personal and professional specialties during a thirty-year career as a military intelligence officer. Like many Americans, I suffered with each disappointing report of detainee abuse by American operating forces. The years have taught me that the only way to deal with such scandals is transparency—establish what happened, get it into the open—and deal with it. Major Doug Pryer's excellent account in *The Fight for the High Ground* thus struck a responsive chord in me. If I could help by lending my voice to the work, I told Bob Ulin, I would gladly do so. Major Pryer and I had a lot in common.

*****

In late 2003, five years after retiring from a thirty-year career, I received an invitation from the Office of the Army G2 in the Pentagon. Brigadier General Barbara Fast, the senior intelligence officer of Combined Joint Task Force 7 in Baghdad, wanted me to come to Iraq. Seven months had elapsed since the dramatic entry of American forces into Baghdad and the electrifying images of Saddam Hussein's statue toppling onto the pavement in Firdos Square. Hussein's powerful and ruthless sons had been killed in Mosul, but the Dictator himself continued to elude capture, and an insurgency was brewing.

This was my second post-retirement mission at the behest of the Army leadership. In March 2002, two months after it opened, the Army requested that I visit the detention facility at Guantanamo to evaluate the new operation. If correctly organized, resourced, and run, the site was a critical intelligence collection opportunity. By my visit, the operation was in its infancy, as the intelligence community struggled to find qualified personnel to man it. It was, in those early days, a place where controlling the detainees was the priority, not interrogating them. Not surprisingly, the operation was already receiving a very bad press.

It didn't take long to conclude that the hastily-established effort there was improperly organized and ill-equipped to successfully exploit the marvelous pool of sources that had fallen into our hands as a result of the lightning-like invasion of Afghanistan. There were 300 detainees on hand, with another 200 or more due to arrive within weeks. Of the twenty-six interrogators on hand, many were young and inexperienced. Only a few spoke Arabic, fewer still spoke other languages common to Taliban and al-Qaeda prisoners, which necessitated the use of contract interpreters, never a good idea if it can be avoided. Of 25 vital analyst positions planned for the Task Force, only 12 were filled.

Under the command of a Marine brigadier, a strict, "one size fits all" treatment of detainees was the order of the day at Gitmo. Since its establishment in January 2002, it had been run as a maximum security cage to maintain control over prisoners whom the Secretary of Defense labeled "the worst of the worst." Each inmate, guards were reminded, was a trained killer. The problem was, with this kind of an assumption, harsh treatment was the lead card in dealing with the closely-packed detainees, which, in turn, contributed to their militancy and solidarity (just as American pilots bonded in the harsh confines of the "Hanoi Hilton").

"Interagency" representatives on site (principally CIA and FBI), accustomed to handling sources out of safe-houses, not cells, were unhappy with the military's by-the-book handling of prisoners and the ability of the detainees to converse with one another, to observe who was being interrogated, and to know which of their comrades seemed to be spending long hours in the interrogation booth. They implored me to do everything possible to persuade the Army that a human intelligence collection operation would best succeed if a rapport-building approach were adopted, and if the facilities could be modified to decrease the ability of the detainee population to organize and conspire.

The interrogation of al-Qaeda fighters and terrorist captives, I wrote in my report, was a difficult challenge that required that the Gitmo facility be run by intelligence personnel in a manner consistent with proven principles of human intelligence operations. This meant that "Treatment, rewards, punishment, and anything else associated with a detainee should be centrally orchestrated by the debriefing team responsible for obtaining information from that detainee." Intelligence officers, not security types, should therefore be at the helm. My report contained many recommendations; most of them intended to remake the operation into a sophisticated human intelligence collection site modeled after successful interrogation operations in Vietnam, Panama, and Desert Storm with which I had first-hand experience. Under that model, decent, humane treatment plays a central role.

By the fall of 2002, two Army generals had come and gone at Gitmo, after which the Army assigned MG Geoffrey Miller, a hard-charging Field Artillery Officer, to command Joint Task Force 170—as the Guantanamo operation was called. Now, at least, the intelligence side of the house was in the driver's seat, even if Miller himself had no experience in running an interrogation operation. By all reports, he presided over a "get tough" agenda over which considerable controversy developed, with allegations (many substantiated, some levied by the FBI) of interrogator misconduct. It took years, tens of millions of dollars, and more than a few ugly scandals, before Gitmo re-emerged from its descent into the "dark side," and transformed itself into a professional intelligence collection facility along the lines I had recommended. By this time, though, its name was so tainted that the issue had become how to close the state-of-the-art facility, with critics pointing out that closing costs could approach $200 million.

Now, Baghdad-bound, I wondered if I would have better luck influencing events in Iraq.

*****

General Fast was concerned about two issues: the interrogation of detainees, a key command priority whose state of health she doubted, and the increasingly-unmistakable signs that a full-blown insurgency was taking hold—which meant that the command would have to wage a new kind of war. The general asked me to visit key interrogation and intelligence nodes, take a look at these two issues, and report back to her.

In the week that followed, I visited more than a dozen intelligence organizations, often after hair-raising trips in a speeding SUV. The exit briefing to BG Fast was blunt, as was the lengthy written report of findings and recommendations that I submitted to her and the Army G2 on December 12, 2003.

The burgeoning insurgency was real trouble. Observing events, it was impossible not to think about Vietnam, and the lessons we had learned at considerable cost of

American and South Vietnamese blood. In Vietnam, our conventionally-oriented military leadership had not understood the insurgency and what was required to defeat it until too late. Our Army and Air Force's use of firepower in the Vietnamese countryside had exacerbated the situation, often making enemies of the very people we were trying to save from Communism. Ultimately, after the departure of General William Westmoreland, the focus shifted to securing and protecting the South Vietnamese population. The Viet Cong movement soon began to falter.

But it had taken too many years to learn this lesson. American public opinion had turned against the war, and my last glimpse of Vietnam was in predawn Saigon, April 30, 1975, from the bay of an evacuation helicopter as it extracted me from the roof of our Embassy.

Now Iraq was being consumed by an insurgency, but it was obvious that the basic importance of securing the population and winning their loyalty had been forgotten. Many Iraqis had valid reasons to welcome our removal of Saddam, but the first order of business after the Ba'athist regime was score-settling time. Human life had become cheap. Sectarian violence was brutal, supplemented by the fact that al-Qaeda had decided that Iraq was a good place to kill Americans and humble Washington. American soldiers and ordinary Iraqi citizens, Sunni, Kurd, and Shi'ia, were subject to vicious and bloody fates. Overstretched coalition forces simply could not provide security. As in the darkest days of the Vietnam War, our hard-pressed Army and Marines only controlled the ground they occupied. Outside the gates of their compounds, danger lurked. Particularly hard hit were those decent Iraqi citizens who voted, and who volunteered to serve in the military, the police, or in government. Bodies laid out on the highways each morning testified to these grim risks.

Because we had too few forces, the borders with Iran and Syria were open—sanctuaries for the enemy, conduits for weapons and foreign fighters—shades of Laos and Cambodia. Worse yet, the paucity of coalition forces left much of California-sized Iraq as a sanctuary for any group that wanted to oppose the coalition.

To further complicate matters, yesterday's liberators were well on their way to becoming today's occupiers. In many cases, those who might have wished to assist us were alienated by heavy-handed coalition operating forces that were charging around the country, kicking down doors at midnight in search of Saddam and his loyalists, sweeping up suspects for incarceration as threats to the security of the coalition. We were, I reported to the general, "making gratuitous enemies."

In the detainee interrogation arena, there was little positive to report. My tour began at Abu Ghraib, months before it became a place more infamous than My Lai. The prison was a grim reminder of the past, a blood-soaked symbol of Saddam's oppression. Its gallows and adjacent death row cells, their walls scarred with the graffiti of the doomed, evoked brutality and excess, but tone-deaf coalition authorities had decided to use the hated prison.

The prison was dank, seemingly afloat on a sea of mud and toxic waste. Security was a myth. Insurgent mortar teams regularly attacked the sprawling facility, killing guards, interrogators, and prisoners alike. Within the walls, security was also weak. Unvetted Iraqi police personnel assigned to assist the American MPs included some who were in collusion with the insurgency. Shortly before my visit, one Iraqi police officer smuggled a weapon into the facility and gave it to a prisoner, who engaged in a firefight with guards from inside his cell.

Abu Ghraib was a time bomb awaiting detonation. There were too few interrogators, too few MPs, and a growing sea of detainees. At the time of my visit (early December 2003), some 6000 Iraqis were housed within its walls. Approximately 10% were regarded as worthy of intelligence exploitation, but there were far too few interrogators, linguists, and support facilities to conduct 600 or more properly-planned and administered interrogations. As a result, detainees and their captors were crouched in place, struggling to survive until someone sorted it all out. Many detainees were common criminals; others had the misfortune to be in the wrong place at the wrong time. Throngs of inmates were so-called "security detainees," picked up by our operating forces and deemed a threat to the coalition. They were housed in large tents pitched in a muddy courtyard, cheek-to-jowl, awaiting interrogation, making it easy for them to collude with one another. It was a recipe for failure.

Every morning, fresh lots of detainees, swept up in midnight raids by American units hunting for Saddam and his loyalists, were dumped at the prison, in spite of MP protests that the facility was bursting at the seams and at risk of a prisoner revolt that could take American lives.

One Abu Ghraib detainee whose case came to my attention was an 85-year old man who had been picked up in July by a unit searching for an alleged captain in the Fedayeen Saddam. The American sergeant and lieutenant who detained him reported that their target was not present during the raid of his home. They detained the older man because he lived at the target's address and his name was similar. The hapless octogenarian had appealed his detention weeks earlier, claiming that he was 85, deaf, and certainly not an officer in Uday Hussein's fanatical Fedayeen Saddam. But by December, the coalition bureaucracy had still not managed to figure out how to release him. One can imagine what he and his family thought about our liberation of their country.

The MI unit that was supposed to conduct interrogations was under-resourced and demoralized, its soldiers convinced that they had been forgotten at the far end of the supply chain. Their officer-in-charge was a civil affairs officer, not an experienced human intelligence operator. Nonetheless, they toiled gamely trying to get the job done, in spite of shortages of linguists, reports officers, computers, paper, electrical power, radios, and vehicles. Effective leadership, be it on the MP or the MI side, was lacking, with bad blood between the two sides over who should do what.

Worse than all of this was the most obvious deficiency: the facility was completely unsuitable for the professional exploitation of high-value detainees. This was not a place where patient human intelligence professionals could employ the sophisticated, developmental methods with which I was familiar from successful interrogation experiences in Vietnam, Panama, and Operation Desert Storm. Within the walls of Abu Ghraib, there might have been a bonanza of possible sources, but they were warehoused in the worst possible facility, and no one seemed to have a clue about who they were, let alone how to exploit them. The interrogation "rules of engagement" shown to me were heavily weighted on the harsh side.

At another interrogation/detention facility, Camp Cropper, the camp's military police custodians, more than 100 strong, handled a more manageable number of detainees. Some were "Top 55" Saddamists, such as Deputy Premier Tariq Aziz, who was languishing in a tiny cell that made me wince. Had he been my prisoner, he would have been accorded VIP treatment and an ego-stroking approach. No less than his recruitment would have been the goal. Other detainees were thought to have knowledge of weapons of mass destruction or of other key strategic matters. To our surprise, on a day-to-day basis, the Military Police, not Military Intelligence, operated the facility. The military intelligence team that was supposed to conduct interrogations was located in a separate facility, not even on the site. Although better than Abu Ghraib, once again, the facilities were inadequate for professional exploitation. On the day of our visit, 102 detainees were in custody, many of whom were living communally in two large, barracks-sized rooms (facilitating communications and resistance). Those who were isolated lived in cells that afforded them visibility of the path to the interrogation trailers. Their Saddam-era cells were cramped and austere, certainly not appropriate for high-ranking military or civilian detainees.

The senior intelligence officer for the interrogation project admitted to me that the Special Operations Task Force tasked to round up "Top 55" fugitives was regularly turning over bruised and battered captives to the Camp Cropper facility. The camp's medical team advised that newly-arrived captives showed clear signs of beatings and abuse. The harsh treatment, we later learned, was taking place at the Task Force's separate, infamous location, called "Camp Nama." ("Nama," insiders joked, stood for "Nasty-Assed Military Area.") When I asked if I could visit Nama, I was told by my escort that, even with my high-level invitation to Iraq, it would be impossible to obtain clearance for me to visit the secret site. We also learned that the Special Ops troopers of the Task Force sometimes showed up at Camp Cropper and signed out detainees, who would be taken away for a day or two of follow-on exploitation. When the unfortunate detainees were returned to Camp Cropper, camp medical personnel reported that they showed unmistakable evidence of having been again physically abused.

Asked if he had reported this illegal conduct, the officer who ran the Camp Cropper interrogation effort squirmed in discomfort and replied evasively, "Everyone knows it." Pressed, he admitted that he had not formally reported the problem in writing to the chain of command.

I left Camp Cropper convinced that the world was upside down, mystified at how our forces could have so lost their way—unaware at the time (December 2003) that guidance for such treatment was coming out of Washington from the Office of the Secretary of Defense—or higher. At Camp Cropper, even more so than at Abu Ghraib, we had control of a potential gold mine of sources, a treasure-trove of information begging to be unlocked by skilled, developmental interrogators, yet the camp was being run by the MPs, with the intelligence element not on site, and detainees were housed in inadequate facilities and subject to abuse. A year earlier, we would have salivated at the prospect of having just a couple of Saddam Hussein's generals and confidants in our possession. Now we had dozens of them, yet some (high ranking) amateur had determined that they were "the worst of the worst" who should be treated in a harsh and uncompromising manner by personnel ready to "take off the gloves" and venture into "enhanced interrogation techniques," a code name for abuse.

Experience and history taught that this methodology flew in the face of generations of interrogation savvy, which virtually all experienced and professional interrogators understood. The proven way to exploit captives required hard work, subtlety, and guile, woven together with deep knowledge of the subject, his country, his religion, and his movement. Interrogation was not about physical mistreatment, but about outwitting and even recruiting the subject. Everyone knew that, or at least I had so thought. How could anyone think that abusing prisoners was effective, let alone wise, moral, advisable, or good for our country's image? Didn't these people know that one of the longest lists in the world consisted of lies told by prisoners being abused and tortured?

Only at the Division Interrogation Facility of the First Armored Division did we encounter a refreshing example that not all interrogation operations had fallen for the terrible wrong turn that had been hatched in Washington, force-fed to operators in Afghanistan and Guantanamo, and ultimately imported into Iraq. Operated by the 501st Military Intelligence Battalion, and supported by personnel from the 501st Military Police Company, the Division Interrogation Facility was a model of organization—clean, well-run, humane, and certain to have easily withstood any inspection by the Red Cross. Procedures for handling evidence, for screening and in-processing detainees, and a system to account for their personal effects, were in place and understood by the facility's staff. There was a documented and sound set of procedures that could lead to a detainee's release. Detainees were treated respectfully; abuse was out of the question.

The facility's Commandant, Captain Amy McConville, was a squared-away intelligence officer (not an MP) whose smart appearance and confident demeanor conveyed that she was pleased to receive a visitor from the States and lay open the Division's operation for inspection. Our team consisted of myself, two lieutenant colonels from the Pentagon, and a civilian from General Fast's office, arguably an intimidating combination, but the captain's superiors did not find it necessary to hover nervously as the young officer hosted our team. Obviously, the 501st was proud of its efforts, and confident that its Division Interrogation Facility was in proficient hands.

Captain McConville pointed out that her team and its guard force of thirty soldiers was capable of housing forty detainees—a far more favorable ratio that Abu Ghraib, where 350 demoralized and frightened MPs were guarding 6000 detainees. Other than suggesting to the captain that detainees be provided Arabic-language reading material about developments in post-Saddam Iraq to educate them and to assist in sparking a dialogue between captors and detainees, I could make no suggestions to improve the operation.

I recall thinking as I departed the First Armored Division facility that it was a shame that leaders at the theater's higher echelons, those responsible for Abu Ghraib and Camp Cropper, had not had the foresight, resources, or wisdom to have tackled the mission as intelligently as this division had done. As Major Pryer points out, had my team visited additional tactical interrogation facilities, we would have found some that were equally impressive, and others that had gone down the darker path. From his research, Pryer concluded that "the systemic use of enhanced interrogation techniques only made it down to those tactical-level interrogation facilities where interrogators were led by someone who had SERE/GTMO/Afghanistan experience and an ends-justify-the-means mentality."

Still, the First Armored Division Interrogation Facility was more of a tactical operation. However well-organized and run it might be, it was still not the sort of sophisticated strategic interrogation facility that had worked so well for me and the Army in Vietnam, Panama, and during Operation Desert Storm. Unaccountably, such a facility simply did not exist in Iraq.

I reported in writing the admissions of mistreatment and brutality made by the officer at Camp Cropper and waited for weeks—in vain—for signs that they were being investigated. Months after my report, a half-hearted and incompetent investigation was undertaken, and closed when the investigator stated that too much time had passed to determine if the allegations were true. To quote the words of the Staff Judge Advocate, Combined Joint Task Force 7, in a letter to me dated April 7, 2004, "Due to the lack of contemporariness (sic)," the colonel wrote, "she (the investigating officer) was unable to recreate those conversations upon which your report is based."

Shortly thereafter, as a result of the glare of publicity triggered by the Abu Ghraib scandal, I and the American people would learn that the excesses of the Special Operations Task Force that I had reported were sanctioned activity—sanctioned by the Secretary of Defense, if not by the Office of the Vice President, or higher, and buttressed by a series of enabling memoranda authored by a coterie of inside-the-beltway attorneys, none of them interrogators, one can be certain.

Small wonder that the officer who investigated the allegations of abuse contained in my report did so at a snail's pace, and found no evidence.

*****

Fresh from trips to Guantanamo and Iraq, it was a mystery to me how the Army and its military intelligence branch could have so seriously dropped the ball in the critical arena of interrogation operations. Just twelve years earlier, American and co-alition forces had triumphed against this same Iraqi Army in the deserts of Kuwait and southern Iraq, capturing some 70,000 enemy prisoners, including dozens of colonels and generals. I had led a special team to that war. On orders from General Norman Schwarzkopf, we set up a secret "guest facility" for captured Iraqi senior officers, at which they were provided good food, medical care, newspapers, clean rooms with private baths, spiritual aids, and, of course, a chance to unburden themselves of their anger and frustration at having been set up for humiliation by Saddam Hussein. All of my team members were under the strictest orders that we would treat Saddam's humiliated generals with unconditional dignity and respect, that we would house them comfortably, salute them, and provide them with quality medical care and tasty Middle Eastern meals, not Army combat rations. We did this, and our "guests" poured out their innermost frustrations, anger, and fears to us—not to mention countless military secrets—in the process satisfying most of the intelligence requirements we were under pressure to fulfill. Not for a moment would it have occurred to us that we should "take off the gloves" and mistreat our "guests." The very notion that an enemy prisoner was a candidate for abuse and torture was alien to us, to our Army's core values, and to our country. No one had to tell us this. Such treatment was a specialty of the Gestapo, the North Koreans, and the brutal torturers at the "Hanoi Hilton," but certainly not the United States Army.

*****

What had changed? Answers to this question may be found in the burgeoning literature of our misadventure in Iraq, but Major Douglas Pryer's *The Fight for the High Ground* must rank as one of the most important. While works that cover the armored thrust into Baghdad and the euphoria following the toppling of Saddam's regime make for an exhilarating read, Major Pryer has undertaken a more challenging task. In documenting the sad trail of flawed interrogation policies and misconduct that were a boon to al-Qaeda recruiters and pro-Saddam insurgents, and which wrought damage to our country's image and cause for which we still pay, Pryer has homed in on one of the most painful but necessary chapters in the Iraq drama. His remarkable account, subtitled *The U.S. Army and Interrogation during Operation Iraqi Freedom I, May 2003-April 2004,* is like a dose of strong medicine—not pleasant to contemplate, but essential in order to heal.

Major Pryer addresses how the interrogation folly of the Bush Administration played out in the field, and he does so in clear, frank terms that can be understood by any reader. Here you will find an account of the various command levels responsible for interrogation operations in Iraq, and a useful primer on how these operations should be conducted in accordance with international law, domestic law, and Army doctrine. Shortcomings that led to some of the abuses are also highlighted by Major Pryer. There is also an illuminating chapter on actions taken by the Bush Administration to emphasize the concept of "unlawful combatants," and how the Administration set about redefining "torture," producing controversial memos and lawyerly pronouncements that propelled operating forces down the path of abuse. Pryer cites examples of great leadership, as well as examples of those who failed to meet the high standards of leadership so essential to an Army like ours—not to mention to our nation.

In this connection, the 1st Armored Division merits a special mention. Pryer provides an eye-witness account of how, during the summer of 2003, with Saddam Hussein still at large, and evidence that an insurgency was taking hold, frustrated officials in Baghdad championed a "take off the gloves" approach to interrogations. In August 2003, LTG Sanchez's Combined Joint Task Force 7 (CJTF-7) headquarters in Baghdad sent an infamous email to all units that participated in interrogation operations, now known as "the gloves are coming off" communication. The email's author informed subordinate units that it was time to ratchet up the pressure on detainees. Some units welcomed the unleashing, and sent in proposed lists of not-so-pretty coercive measures that might be added to the list of permissible techniques.

The 1st Armored Division, charged with the onerous mission of securing the city of Baghdad, reacted differently. The Commander of the Division's 501st Military Intelligence Battalion, Lieutenant Colonel Laurence Mixon, and his operations officer, Major Nathan Hoepner, saw the dangers in such a policy. Both knew that if the chain of command suggested that prisoners might be treated harshly, it would create a slippery slope fraught with the danger of abusive conduct by soldiers. Hoepner told CJTF-7 and his fellow-intelligence warriors that it was time to "take a deep breath and remember who we are," reminding all hands of the U.S. Army's core values and its long tradition of staying "on the high ground." In taking this position, Hoepner and Mixon were supported by Division Commander, MG Martin Dempsey, who, to his everlasting credit, told his troops, "As you've heard me say before, we must remember who we are. Our example is what will cause us to prevail in this environment, not our weapons. I really believe that. We need to show the Iraqi people what 'right' looks like."

This firm position taken by 1st AD leaders had an effect. While there were a number of incidents of mistreatment of detainees and amateurish attempts to interrogate them in the division's brigades, only five substantiated incidents of interrogation abuse could be laid at the feet of the division, and none of these were carried out by authorized, school-trained interrogators. Pryer points out that the division benefited by the presence of a small cadre of seasoned warrant officers in interrogation elements, valuable assets who could and did keep interrogators focused on professional conduct. In an observation that evokes the Army's experience in Vietnam, Pryer points out that most of the abuse and improper, amateurish interrogation attempts involved overly-aggressive non-intelligence personnel, often right after detainees had been taken into custody. In the end, 1st AD interrogators handled themselves with distinction in an adrenalin-charged environment in which weak leadership could have resulted in an epidemic of abuse. Incidents of detainee and interrogation abuse by non-intelligence personnel declined after MG Dempsey took command of the division.

Reflecting on incidents of misconduct at the small-unit level in the 1st AD, Major Pryer expressed surprise at the number of such, since MG Dempsey was "saying and doing all the right things in this regard." Pryer concludes that, "all it takes is a single point-of-failure in a chain-of- command for bad stuff to start to happen in that command."

Pryer's account is valuable because it is informed and authentic. He was in Iraq when the interrogation debacle occurred, a young, principled captain serving as Major Hoepner's Assistant Operations Officer. By contrast, many writings and pronouncements on the interrogation scandal have come from pundits and critics among the ranks of attorneys, journalists, politicians, and college professors, few (if any) of whom were there, and even fewer who possess professional knowledge of the interrogation discipline.

In the end, Major Pryer's contribution is valuable not only for the reasons described above, but because his account reminds us of something that most people purport to know, but many tend to forget. Enlightened, ethical leaders forge good organizations, which do smart things and positively contribute to mission accomplishment—witness the 1st Armored Division and its organic Military Intelligence Battalion. Conversely, where wise, ethical leadership is lacking, bad things can and will happen, particularly when the leadership failings begin at the White House and at the Department of Defense, and filter down to operating forces, be they a Military Intelligence or Military Police unit at Abu Ghraib, or a Joint Special Operations Task Force on the hunt for Saddam Hussein and his weapons of mass destruction.

                                            Colonel Stuart A. Herrington
                                            United States Army, Retired
                                            August 2009

Prologue: Through the looking glass

"What in the world is this place?" I thought, as I witnessed a small crowd of nude U.S. soldiers being hosed down with icy water and berated by angry men (supposed "interrogators"). These "interrogators" had driven the soldiers outside and against the wall of a gray, two story building, and, like dolphins herding mackerel, were forcing the young men into an ever-tightening, vulnerable bunch. When embarrassed laughter escaped one soldier, his captors seemed to grow enraged, turning the hose's spray on him and quickly shutting him up. In the cool hours of the early morning, the soldiers were shivering and, no doubt, feeling humiliated.

How could this be happening to U.S. soldiers on U.S. soil? As I watched, I felt as if I had, like Alice, stepped into a cruel, bizarre world in which the normal laws of reality do not apply.

It was the summer of 1994, and I was a junior enlisted psychological operations soldier playing the role of guard at a Survival, Evasion, Resistance, and Escape (SERE) course on Camp Mackall, North Carolina. Camp Mackall, a small Special Forces reservation, is located just a few miles southwest of Fort Bragg. I had arrived just the previous day at the camp, which was only a few minutes' drive from my new home in the hamlet of Raeford and a day's drive away from Mount Vernon, Missouri, the small town in which I had been raised. But even if home had been on the other side of the world, on a different planet even, I would have felt no further from it, immersed as I was in the very strange world of SERE training.

Before arriving at Camp Mackall, I had held few expectations about the course. I had known that SERE schools trained military service members on how to survive capture with honor, and I had understood that the soldiers trained were those soldiers whose jobs placed them at high risk of enemy capture (primarily special operations soldiers and pilots). I had also heard stories from a friend of the unappetizing things that hunger had forced him to eat during the "survival" phase of this training. (He had described finding a turtle after he had been in the woods without food for four days, telling me that he and the trainees with him had pounced on the poor turtle like a pack of predators, torn it to pieces, and ate it. I doubt he exaggerated much.)

Nonetheless, I had known very little about what took place during the interrogation phase of the course. That was soon to change. As a "prison guard," I assisted in the harsh treatment of trainees outside the interrogation room. This rough treatment is euphemistically referred to today as "enhanced" interrogation techniques. In addition to the "forced nudity" technique describe above, I observed three of the remaining four SERE interrogation techniques mentioned in a 2008 Senate Armed Service Committee inquiry. (This inquiry identified SERE interrogation techniques as including forced nudity, sleep deprivation, use of loud music and flashing lights, the placing of hoods over subjects' heads, and slapping the face and body of subjects.)

I have several vivid memories from my short time as a role player at SERE school. Two memories from the course stand out the most, though, perhaps because they are so easily and firmly juxtaposed in my mind. The first memory is the image of a Special Forces soldier I saw the day I arrived at the facility. While riding on a bus with other "guards" from other units on Fort Bragg, I looked out the window and saw this soldier stand up in the brush. We were close to the complex of buildings that would serve as the interrogation compound, and this soldier was a SERE trainee. He was tall, lean, good-looking, holding his rifle at port arms, and sporting a faded, camouflaged cap that I knew was shaped "ranger style" (u-shaped brim, the crown of the cap heavily creased at the edges). He seemed to exude absolute confidence and competence as he relayed hand signals to other soldiers behind him in the woods. As I watched him, he quickly grew in my imagination from a flesh-and-blood human being into something greater– the perfect example, the archetype, of the American Soldier. At that moment, even though he was probably not much older than me, I could not help but find myself wishing that I might someday grow up and be as strong and capable as this noncommissioned officer clearly was.

The second memory is of this same soldier, later in the week. In the middle of the night, after several days of harsh interrogations, I saw him again, alone, sitting in a fetal position, sobbing quietly inside a small, cramped box. In this distraught state, he no longer seemed larger than life. Indeed, he seemed as small and fragile as a child. I remember feeling surprised that this seemingly invulnerable soldier could be thus broken. I did not think any less of him for it, but it did inspire in me a kind of awe (fear really) of the tactics that had been used to break him.

One year after this experience, I graduated from Officer Candidate School, having earned my commission as a military intelligence officer after three years of enlisted service (the hard way as they say). In the years that have since passed, I have crossed paths with enhanced interrogation techniques on only a handful of occasions. Yet, each encounter has proven unforgettable.

My next encounter with SERE (or enhanced) interrogation tactics took place in Iraq in August 2003. At the time, I was the assistant operations officer for the 501st Military Intelligence Battalion, 1st Armored Division, Baghdad, and this encounter involved an email discussion as to whether certain enhanced interrogation techniques should be used in Iraq. The specifics of this discussion are described in greater detail in Chapter 1. As I read emails in which officers advocated that, in the face of mounting casualties, we should take "the gloves off" when interrogating prisoners, I grew at turns surprised, excited, and upset. What upset me was that I recognized many of the harsh interrogation tactics suggested by leaders of other units as SERE techniques, and these tactics, I believed, replicated methods used by an enemy unbound by the Geneva Conventions. Since the U.S. is bound by these conventions, I thought, we could not possibly use such techniques on our real-world enemies. When my then supervisor, Major Nathan Hoepner, argued clearly, forcefully, and (I thought) convincingly in an email that U.S. interrogators needed to avoid such techniques and stay on the moral high ground, I relaxed. I somewhat naively considered the matter closed.

A month later, however, the highest military command in Iraq published an interrogation policy that formally promulgated several SERE interrogation techniques. When this occurred, I could hardly believe it. Although the harshest techniques recommended by junior leaders in two units had been left out of this policy, some of the remaining techniques struck me as illegal, counter-productive, and un-American. I was hardly alone in feeling this way. Other leaders I knew expressed similar feelings of dismay. In fact, neither before nor after this memorandum was published did I personally meet a military intelligence leader in Iraq who was a vocal advocate for the use of such techniques. On the contrary, these leaders were generally outspoken with regard to the need for interrogators to adhere to doctrinal interrogation standards. Since those I knew rejected the use of such tactics, I told myself that other leaders across Iraq were probably doing the same.

In retrospect, I believe that I dimly understood that there might be interrogation facilities somewhere in Iraq where leaders allowed interrogators to use the harsh techniques described in this policy memorandum. Still, I hoped that the use of such techniques, in those few facilities where such techniques might be allowed, would be heavily controlled. Tragically, that was not the case.

All of us can remember moments when we received especially shocking news. My first such moment was as a little boy when my dad and I heard on the radio, while parked outside a Venture department store in Springfield, Missouri, the news that Elvis had died. (My dad was a huge Elvis fan.) Yet another such moment, and far more distressing for me personally, was the first time I saw the now infamous photos from Abu Ghraib prison. It was also, though I did not recognize it then, my last encounter with SERE interrogation techniques– not with the application of these techniques, but with the sadistic aftermath of these methods when left unchecked and employed by a particularly twisted group of individuals.

Although I was then involved with interrogation operations in Iraq, like most Americans, I viewed the Abu Ghraib photos for the first time on television. A few weeks earlier, my battalion commander, Lieutenant Colonel Laurence Mixon, had mentioned an investigation into allegations of serious detainee abuse at the prison. But I did not begin to comprehend what had happened at the prison until I saw the actual photos.

When I first saw these photos, I was sitting at night in a dining facility at the Baghdad International Airport. This facility, situated on the south side of the airport, was only 30 kilometers east of Abu Ghraib prison. It was also only a few hundred meters from three other important interrogation facilities– my division's former interrogation facility, the responsibility of which had been assumed by the 1st Cavalry Division; Camp Cropper, where Saddam Hussein and other "high-value targets" were interned; and Camp Nama, run by the special operations task force then hunting high-value targets in Iraq. At this point, I was a company commander, having moved my military intelligence company just a few weeks previously from downtown Baghdad to the airport in anticipation of our imminent return home. (Heartbreakingly, our deployment had been extended three months instead.)

The images of detainee abuse I saw on television that night shocked me. Sickened, I looked around me at other soldiers in the dining facility, and I noted that many of them also looked unwell. One soldier grew defensive, saying aloud, "At least we don't cut peoples' heads off." When he said this, I understood the feeling that had generated this comment. Nonetheless, I dismissed this feeling. The images I was seeing, were absolutely unacceptable and shameful. In fact, I became so disgusted and distraught that I quickly left the facility, food unfinished.

Beneath a clouded night sky, I walked unhappily to my tent, passed through the divider separating my sleeping area from our company's lightly manned command post, turned off the light in my sleeping quarters, and lay down on my cot. In a near-darkness illuminated only by a small seam of light emanating from above the divider, I wrestled with the implications of what I had just seen. I thought of the detainees my division had delivered to Abu Ghraib, many of whom– despite the best efforts of many military intelligence soldiers to screen good guys from bad guys– had no doubt been innocent of any wrongdoing. How many of our former detainees– proud Baghdad fathers, brothers, or sons– had been forced onto those naked human pyramids? I thought also of the effect of these photos on our war effort, and as I contemplated this effect, my previously unbound optimism regarding a U.S. "victory" in Iraq became tempered by pessimism: my army could actually lose this war, I realized. Most distressingly, I wondered how U.S. soldiers– a group of which I proudly counted (and still proudly count) myself a member– could do such things to helpless prisoners.

Once again, it seemed, I had suddenly found myself unexpectedly on the other side of a looking glass, in another world that was far, far from home.

During the years that followed, I have often thought about those photos. Perhaps surprisingly considering my knowledge of SERE techniques and interrogation policy in Iraq, I wondered if there were a link between these techniques and the Abu Ghraib abuses. After all, in the interrogation policy memoranda I had read, there had been no mention of it being permissible for interrogators to forcibly strip and stack detainees in human pyramids (or, for that matter, allowable for soldiers to commit any of the serious crimes committed at Abu Ghraib). Plus, I had difficulty reconciling the actions of the leaders and interrogators I personally knew in Iraq with the actions of the soldiers in those photos. Yet, it always seemed possible that there were a connection between the crimes at Abu Ghraib and the interrogation techniques I had witnessed as a junior enlisted soldier at a SERE course on Camp Mackall.

I have had other questions. In a balanced, fair, and apolitical inquiry, to what degree would the investigator conclude that the chain-of-command of Abu Ghraib soldiers had directed, encouraged, or facilitated the crimes that happened there? During my deployment, where and with what frequency were enhanced interrogation techniques used? Why exactly were these abusive techniques used? Most importantly, what have we done as a nation and an Army since Abu Ghraib to ensure such crimes never recur?

Such questions eventually drove me to seek answers. The answers I found, warts and all, are in this book.

> Major Douglas A. Pryer
> U.S. Army, 14th Signal Regiment (UK)
> Haverfordwest, Wales
> August 28, 2009

CHAPTER 1
A terribly hot summer

> We have taken casualties in every war we have ever fought– that is part of the very nature of war. We also inflict casualties, generally many more than we take. That in no way justifies letting go of our standards. We have NEVER considered our enemies justified in doing such things [torture] to us. Casualties are part of war– if you cannot take casualties then you cannot engage in war. Period. BOTTOM LINE: We are American soldiers, heirs of a long tradition of staying on the high ground. We need to stay there.[1]
> —Major Nathan J. Hoepner
> 501st Military Intelligence Operations Officer

> One day in the spring of 2004, Maj. Gen. James Mattis was walking out of a mess hall in al Asad, in western Iraq, when he saw a knot of his troops intently hunched over a television, watching a cable news show. . . . "What's going on?" Mattis asked. It was, he learned, the revelations about Abu Ghraib, along with sickening photos of cruelty and humiliation. A nineteen-year old lance corporal glanced up from the television and told the general, "Some assholes have just lost the war for us."[2]
> —Thomas E. Ricks

It was the end of what had been a terribly hot summer, and the hopes of coalition forces for quickly establishing stability in Iraq seemed to have slipped out of reach.[3] In July 2003, the number of attacks against coalition forces had been twice the number of attacks in June.[4] Worse, these attacks had increased in both lethality and strategic effect: dangerous roadside bombs had become the weapon of choice for anti-coalition attackers, and vehicle bombs– to include the vehicle bomb that killed 11 people on August 7 and closed the Jordanian Embassy– were exploding at an almost daily rate. Compounding the frustration for coalition forces was the difficulty these forces had in determining just who it was that was attacking them. This difficulty included not only identifying who these attackers were as individuals, but it included even categorizing who these attackers were as a general group. Were these attackers predominantly "regime dead-enders," as Secretary of Defense Donald Rumsfeld would later famously put it in a November 25 press briefing?[5] Or, were they mostly Islamic mujahedeen or "foreign terrorists" as President Bush would later label these attackers in an October 28 news briefing?[6] Or, were they largely part of a bona fide, home-grown insurgency growing from genuine feelings of disenfranchisement within the Sunni community, as would later prove to be the case?

For U.S. soldiers who had deployed to Iraq as part of Operation Iraqi Freedom I (OIF I), the first rotation of U.S. troops to replace the initial U.S. invasion force, it was truly a dismaying time. Rather than getting easier and less dangerous, their deployment was getting harder and more dangerous, and any hope many soldiers may have had of returning home by Christmas was, along with the hope of quickly establishing stability in Iraq, rapidly disappearing.

It was in this tense, hot climate that a military intelligence captain working for the Human Intelligence (HUMINT) section of the Combined Joint Task Force 7 (CJTF-7) wrote an e-mail to division-level intelligence officers throughout Iraq. In this August 14 e-mail, this CJTF-7 captain stated that, because "casualties are mounting," the "gloves are coming off regarding these detainees."[7] He then went on to ask recipients for a "wish list" of interrogation techniques they believed might make their interrogators more effective.[8]

When this email was written, three of CJTF-7's major subordinate commands were responsible for portions of what was called "the Sunni Triangle," the most dangerous area in Iraq: the 3d Armored Cavalry Regiment (3ACR) had responsibility for Al Anbar Province, which was a Sunni stronghold, the primary entry point for Islamic mujahedeen into Iraq, and the future site of two epic battles for Fallujah in 2004; the 4th Infantry Division (4ID) had responsibility for several hotbeds of insurgent activity, including Saddam Hussein's hometown of Tikrit; and the 1st Armored Division (1AD) had responsibility for Baghdad, by far the most important, populated, and hazardous city in Iraq. *(See Figure 1, next page)*

Although the intelligence officers of these three units may have equally felt the pressure to create actionable intelligence, the "gloves are coming off" e-mail from the CJTF-7 captain evoked philosophically antithetical reactions from human intelligence leaders within these three units. The responses of the 3ACR and 4ID officers represented one type of reaction. Chief Warrant Officer 3 Lewis Welshofer, Jr., the senior HUMINT officer for the 3ACR, emailed all previous recipients[9] that he had spent several months in Afghanistan interrogating the Taliban and al Qaeda and that he agreed that "the gloves need to come off."[10] According to Welshofer, who would later be convicted of negligent homicide after a detainee died during interrogation,[11] CJTF-7 should adopt "a baseline interrogation technique that at a minimum allows for physical contact resembling that used by SERE [Survival, Evasion, Resistance, and Escape] instructors," to include "open-handed facial slaps from a distance of no more than about two feet and back-handed blows to the midsection from a distance of about 18 inches."[12] He also added that other techniques should include "close confinement quarters, sleep deprivation, white noise, and a litnany [sic] of harsher fear-up approaches . . . fear of dogs and snakes appear to work nicely."[13] A 4ID non-commissioned officer replied in a similar vein, submitting a "wish list" of interrogation techniques that included "Stimulus Deprivation," "Pressure Point Manipulation," "Close-Fist Strikes," "Muscle Fatigue Inducement," and "Low Voltage Electrocution."[14]

An officer from the 1AD, however, spoke very differently in his reply to all. Major Nathan Hoepner, operations officer for the 501st Military Intelligence (MI) Battalion, wrote that they needed to "take a deep breath and remember who we are." In his email, he argued that increasing casualties did not warrant their letting go of their standards and values as Americans soldiers, and he reminded all recipients of the U.S. Army's long tradition of staying "on the high ground."[15] Then, a few hours after emailing his reply, during an evening humvee ride at the Baghdad airport from his command post to his living area, Major Hoepner expressed concern to his battle captain that the willingness of a few soldiers to do all the wrong things for all the right reasons might lead such soldiers (or those they led) to commit criminal abuses of detainees– some of whom might even be entirely innocent of any wrongdoing.[16]

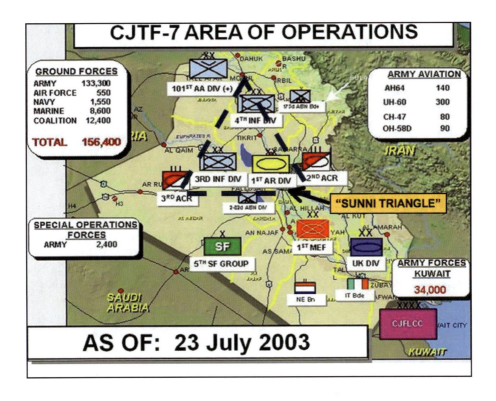

Figure 1) Combined Joint Task Force 7 Area of Operations
Source: General John Keane Press Briefing, July 23, 2003, http://www.defenselink.mil/dodcmsshare/briefingslide/69/030723-D-6570X-001.pdf (May 4, 2009).

Yet, even this perceptive Army major could not have imagined the photos of detainee abuse that would be splashed across newspapers and magazines seven months later. These photos, taken by military police soldiers assigned to the Abu Ghraib Prison west of Baghdad, would be shockingly cruel, lurid, and unforgettable. There would be photos of nude Iraqi males piled on top of one another into human pyramids, of a hooded and wired prisoner standing on a box, of a smiling female Army specialist pointing at the genitalia of nude Iraqi males, and of other equally shameful subject matter. Although most of the soldiers who were present during the crimes in these infamous photographs were military police guards, such investigators as Lieutenant General Anthony Jones and Major General George Fay later concluded that interrogators had encouraged guards to abuse detainees as part of their interrogation approaches.[17]

Before the Abu Ghraib photos were first aired for the American public by *60 Minutes II* on April 28, 2004,[18] few Americans had suspected that any American soldier, let alone a group of American soldiers, was capable of perpetrating such crimes. After April 28, 2004, however, the world would understand differently.

The resulting scandal is today as much a part of America's historical vernacular as "My Lai" and "Watergate." Commonly referred to as simply "Abu Ghraib," this scandal has proven an invaluable recruitment and propaganda tool for America's enemies across the world, to include Iraqi insurgents. "What brought me [to Iraq], for example, is what I have seen on Al-Jazirah and Al-Arabiya of people in Abu Ghurayb torturing naked people," said one Tunisian fighter captured in Hit, Iraq.[19] Said yet another foreign fighter captured and interrogated in Iraq: "They used to show events [on television] in Abu Ghurayb, the oppression, abuse of women, and fornication, so I acted in the heat of the moment and decided . . . to seek martyrdom in Iraq."[20] Matthew Alexander, an Air Force major who led the interrogation team that successfully hunted down Musab al-Zarqawi, said, "I learned in Iraq that the number one reason foreign fighters flocked there to fight were the abuses carried out at Abu Ghraib and Guantanamo."[21]

The scandal also contributed to a significant loss of American political will to continue the fight in Iraq. "We now spend ninety percent of our time talking about the Abu Ghraib stuff, and one percent talking about the valor of the troops," said Bing West, probably the most prominent of the chroniclers of the U.S. Marines during OIF.[22] A CNN poll taken one month after the scandal broke stated that the support of Americans for the war in Iraq had dropped below 50 percent for the first time, with 27 percent of the Americans polled saying that the scandal had made them "less supportive" of the war.[23] In turn, loss of support for the war among Americans contributed to President Bush's rapidly-diminishing popularity, helped the Democratic Party to eventually take control of the U.S. Congress in January 2007, and inspired the party to then try unsuccessfully to force President Bush to order U.S. troops home. In short, the Abu Ghraib scandal threatened to contribute to the defeat of the U.S. in Iraq via the only means the U.S. has ever lost a war– through the loss of political will at home rather than through insurmountable defeat on the battlefield.

Also disturbingly, the Abu Ghraib scandal will no doubt define OIF I in the minds of future generations, just as the My Lai Massacre has unfairly defined the Vietnam War for many members of the war's subsequent generations. With the exception of the role that alleged stockpiles of weapons of mass destruction played in the political decision of the U.S. government to invade Iraq, no other subject has engendered even half as many books, editorials, and documentaries about Iraq as the Abu Ghraib scandal. Many of these books, including some masquerading as fair, scholarly appraisals, have such sensational titles as *Torture and Truth: America, Abu Ghraib, and the War on Terror*, *Abu Ghraib: The Politics of Torture*, and *The Torture Papers: The Road to Abu Ghraib*. A common theme in such books is that unfortunate U.S. soldiers during OIF I carried out the will of their political and military masters by systematically torturing detainees throughout Iraq.

However, should the actions of a group of officers, soldiers, and contract civilians at Abu Ghraib be considered representative of the actions of U.S. military service members during OIF I? All U.S. government-sponsored investigations have concluded thus far that the actions of this group at Abu Ghraib were not representative of the actions of the vast majority of U.S. military service members and contractors in Iraq at the time.[24] On February 10, 2004, the Army's Acting Secretary of the Army, R. L. Brownlee, directed Lieutenant General Paul Mikolashek, the Army's Inspector General, to investigate detainee operations across the Army. The resulting Inspector General task force concluded in a report on July 21, 2004 (referred to as the "Mikolashek Report" throughout this book), that "the overwhelming majority of our leaders and Soldiers understand the requirement to treat detainees humanely and are doing so."[25] James R. Schlesinger, former U.S. Secretary of Defense and Central Intelligence Agency (CIA) director, headed a five-member independent panel which published a report on August 24, 2004 (hereafter referred to as the "Schlesinger Report"), and which concluded that the "vast majority of detainees in Guantanamo, Afghanistan and Iraq were treated appropriately, and the great bulk of detention operations were conducted in compliance with U.S. policy and directives."[26] On March 10, 2005, the U.S. Department of Defense (DoD) presented the unclassified portion of the report of Vice Admiral Albert T. Church, III, the Navy Inspector General, who had investigated detainee operations across the U.S. military. This report (hereafter referred to as the "Church Report") assessed that "the vast majority of detainees held by the U.S. in the Global War on Terror have been treated humanely, and that the overwhelming majority of U.S. personnel have served honorably."[27] Even Major General Antonio Taguba's initial investigation from January to March 2004 into a deeply troubled unit, the 800th Military Police (MP) Brigade, concluded that investigators had "observed many individual Soldiers and some subordinate units under the 800th MP Brigade that overcame significant obstacles, persevered in extremely poor conditions, and upheld the Army values."[28]

When judging if the Abu Ghraib scandal is representative of how detention and interrogation operations were conducted during OIF I, future historians will examine these reports and conclude that either the investigators were lying in order to cover up the crimes committed by the political and military leaders of OIF I, or that these investigators were telling the truth and what military intelligence soldiers and military policemen did to detainees at Abu Ghraib prison in October 2003 was an especially horrific "exception to the rule" of how detainees were treated during OIF I. As will be demonstrated in this book, the latter is closer to the truth; however, other only slightly less horrific exceptions existed as well.

To understand how interrogation abuse could occur during OIF I, one must understand the hidden "war within the war" that started soon after al Qaeda terrorists destroyed the World Trade Center in New York City on September 11, 2001, thus launching the "Global War on Terrorism" (GWOT). Fearing an even worse attack on

U.S. soil, America's political leaders became engaged in a fierce clandestine debate as to just how harsh interrogation methods should be if, by the use of brutal tactics, American lives might be saved. Soon after, this same argument echoed in the secluded offices of a small U.S. detention facility at Guantanamo Bay, Cuba, as well as among military leaders in the mountains of Afghanistan. Then, as described in the email exchange above, mounting U.S. casualties added fuel to the same secret debate in Iraq.

Unfortunately, contrary to generations of law enforcement experience saying otherwise, some of the leaders engaged in this argument came to believe that brutal interrogation techniques are effective methods for extracting reliable intelligence from non-compliant subjects. Since many of these same leaders also believed that the "ends justify the means," in order "to save lives," some of them began covertly pushing U.S. interrogators toward the use of these brutal techniques– techniques that many Americans would have called "torture" if described to them.

In its purest form, the rationale that these leaders adopted is referred to as the "ticking time bomb scenario." In a 2001 interview, the French General Paul Aussaresses, who was a senior French intelligence officer during the French-Algerian War (the outcome of which should have prevented reasonable persons from wanting to repeat this war's losing tactics), expressed this rationale as follows:

> *Imagine for an instant that you are opposed to the concept of torture and you arrest someone who is clearly implicated in the preparation of a terrorist attack. The suspect refuses to talk. You do not insist. A particularly murderous attack is launched. What will you say to the parents of the victims, to the parents of an infant, for example, mutilated by the bomb to justify the fact that you did not utilize all means to make the suspect talk?*[29]

The "intelligence at any cost" mindset of this school of thought, or camp, has had a much longer (and more potent) life in U.S. military history than is commonly taught or understood in America. For example, during the Philippine-American War, the 1902 Senate Committee on the Philippines documented the distressingly frequent use by U.S. troops of the "water cure," a harsher, sometimes fatal version of what we today know as "water boarding."[30] Seemingly far from home and the watchful eyes of the press, deployed American intelligence officers in the Philippines rationalized that the need to quickly end the war and stop further bloodshed justified the use of this torture technique.

Opposing the "ends justify the means" camp in this clandestine battle of the GWOT were leaders who believed that U.S. soldiers do not torture because of the high ideals to which all Americans should subscribe, ideals that make America "America." To not subscribe to these ideals, these leaders argued, is to forget who we are as Americans. When Major Hoepner argued that American soldiers, despite the inherently violent nature of their profession, are nonetheless governed by high moral standards, he was speaking from the vantage point of this camp.

This lofty, idealistic philosophy is the dominant tradition in American history. Indeed, it is as old as America's first enduring colony. In a 1630 sermon, John Winthrop told Puritan colonists (who were soon to disembark from the Arbella and found the Massachusetts Bay Colony) that they should "do justly" and "love mercy" and that their new colony should be "as a city upon a hill" for the rest of the world to watch and emulate.[31] Similarly, during the Revolutionary War, leaders of the Continental Army and Congress judged that it was not enough to win the war; they had "to win in a way that was consistent with the values of their society and the principles of their cause."[32] General George Washington applied this ideal to the treatment of British and Hessian prisoners, adopting an uncommon policy of humanity. During the more than two centuries that have passed since the Revolutionary War, the U.S. Army's treatment of its enemies has been largely consistent with this tradition of humanity, with the Philippine-American War and various Indian wars representing racially motivated exceptions to this rule.[33]

In this book, we chart the course of the clandestine "war within the war" fought between these two camps during the first two years of the Global War on Terrorism, from Washington, D.C., to the fields of Iraq. In Iraq, we examinethe extent and root causes of interrogation abuse. As we shall see, various investigators into cases of abuse may have been right about the limited scope of this abuse, but they were wrong about this abuse's primary cause: this root cause was not over-crowded detention facilities, untrained guards, immature interrogators, or any of the plethora of other reasons these investigators have cited as the causes of abuse for a particular case. The fundamental reason why interrogation abuse in Iraq occurred was a failure in leadership. The answer is that simple.

To see why this is so, we analyze a slice of each level of command, much as a geologist describes the geological history of a region through the careful study of a slice of the earth's strata in that region. Chapter 2 examines interrogation operations within the "strata" of international law, U.S. national law, and U.S. Army doctrine, describing how the "Law of War" and national law influenced the regulations and doctrine that governed U.S. Army interrogation operations during OIF I. This chapter also outlines shortfalls in doctrine that later inspectors and investigators considered contributing causes of detainee abuse. Chapter 3 analyzes the influence of the Bush Administration on interrogation policies and how the concept of "unlawful combatants" and the administration's re-definition of "torture" set the stage for interrogation abuse. Chapter 4 discusses interrogation operations within CJTF-7, the headquarters that was responsible for military operations in Iraq for almost all of OIF I. Chapter 5 explores the extent of the systemic use of enhanced interrogation techniques at the brigade and battalion levels during OIF I. Chapters 6 and 7 shine a much-needed spotlight on how the vast majority of school-trained interrogators actually behaved during OIF I, examining how the interrogators of CJTF-7's largest division and brigades avoided interrogation abuse. Chapter 8 summarizes what the U.S. Army has done to correct the conditions that led to interrogation abuse during OIF I– and indicates where work still needs to be done. Finally, Chapter 9 puts the interrogation abuse that occurred during OIF I in its proper perspective.

Hopefully, this book– as well as the interviews conducted and archived for this book– will prove essential source documents for any researcher seeking a balanced perspective of interrogation operations during OIF I. This balanced perspective is sorely needed: to date, the voices of those leaders and interrogators who stayed on the moral high ground during OIF I have gone largely unheard. Their story, and the good battle they fought, needs to be known.

CHAPTER 2

"It's just not right"

> *Army professionalism is moral because the capability to wield tools of destruction in a brutal environment carries with it a moral responsibility. Our professional moral imperative derives from ancient ethical and religious standards. The Law of Land Warfare, the Uniform Code of Military Justice, and the Code of Conduct give structure to the moral imperative. The moral and ethical tenets of the Constitution, the Declaration of Independence, and Army values characterize the Army's professional ideals. As the environment of conflict becomes more complex, this moral dimension of Army professionalism takes on greater importance.[1]*
>
> —Army Field Manual 1, The Army

> *Our doctrine is not right. It's just not right. I mean, there are so many things that are out there that aren't right in the way that we operate for this war. This is a doctrinal problem of understanding where you bring, what do the MPs do, what do the military intelligence guys do, how do they come together in the right way. And this doctrinal issue has got to be fixed if we're ever going to get our intelligence right to fight this war and defeat this enemy.[2]*
>
> —General John Abizaid

On May 19, 2004, the courts martial of a U.S. Army staff sergeant and specialist began at the CJTF-7 Headquarters, Camp Victory, Baghdad.[3] These two courts martial would be the first trials of the "Abu Ghraib Nine"– seven military policemen and two military intelligence soldiers who were court martialed for the detainee abuses they had committed at the Abu Ghraib Prison. Ultimately, eight of the "Abu Ghraib Nine" would be sentenced to prison. A recurring theme of the testimony of soldiers during these courts martial, to include the courts martial of the Army staff sergeant and specialist mentioned above, would be that military policemen had often abused detainees at the order (or at least with the tacit approval) of military intelligence interrogators. According to numerous testimonies, interrogators had expected military policemen at Abu Ghraib Prison to abuse detainees so that these detainees would be "softened up" for interrogations.

Also on May 19, 2004, and halfway across the world, General Abizaid, Lieutenant General Sanchez, Major General Geoffrey Miller (Deputy Commander for Detainee Operations, Multinational Force-Iraq), and Colonel Marc Warren (CJTF-7 Judge Advocate General) testified about the abuses at Abu Ghraib Prison before a much different audience– the U.S. Senate Armed Services Committee.[4] During this hearing, General Abizaid testified that the causes of the Abu Ghraib abuses had not been simply criminal misconduct but a "breakdown in procedures."[5] General Abizaid also impassionedly referred to a "doctrinal issue" that had left military intelligence soldiers and military policemen unclear about their respective roles in interrogation operations.⁶

Regarding this same doctrinal issue, Senator Ted Kennedy would direct the toughest question of the hearing to Major General Miller. Specifically, Senator Kennedy asked Major General Miller whether, if Miller had indeed recommended to Lieutenant General Sanchez prior to the Abu Ghraib abuses that "the guard force be actively engaged in setting the conditions for the successful exploitation of the internees," then did Miller accept responsibility for the abuses committed by military policemen trying to set these conditions?⁷ Miller's answer to Senator Kennedy's question was that he had never recommended to Lieutenant General Sanchez that military police soldiers "actively participate" in the interrogation process.⁸ But rather, Major General Miller said, he had recommended that military police soldiers set the conditions for interrogations by employing "passive intelligence gathering."⁹ This meant, he said, that guards should "observe the detainees, to see how their behavior was, to see who they would speak with and then to report that to the interrogators."¹⁰

As evidenced by these testimonies delivered on the same date by soldiers of vastly different ranks and responsibility in two very different settings, U.S. Army interrogation doctrine during OIF I was, if not grossly deficient, at the very least unclear. The purpose of this chapter is to lay bare these ambiguities.

Detainees, the Law of War, and U.S. national law

International law has long been the foundation of the U.S. Army's interrogation-related doctrine. During OIF I, this international law consisted primarily of the four conventions which were adopted in Geneva, Switzerland, on August 12, 1949, and which were ratified by the U.S. Congress on August 2, 1955.¹¹ Of these four conventions, Conventions I, III and IV potentially pertained to interrogation operations during OIF I. Convention I, containing nine parts and 64 articles, covers the treatment of wounded soldiers on the battlefield; Convention III, divided into six parts and 143 articles, discusses the treatment of Enemy Prisoners of War; and Convention IV, split into four parts and 159 articles, deals with the protection of civilians in time of war.¹² All of these conventions give extensive rights to certain categories of detainees. The War Crimes Act of 1996, legislation in effect during OIF I, made "grave breaches" of any articles of the Geneva Conventions a crime.¹³

Much legal controversy during the Global War on Terrorism has revolved around the applicability of the Geneva Conventions to a type of detainee that the Bush Administration came to label as an "unlawful combatant." As eventually defined by the Military Commissions Act of 2006, an "unlawful combatant" is "a person who has engaged in hostilities or who has purposefully and materially supported hostilities against the United States or its co-belligerents who is not a lawful enemy combatant (including a person who is part of the Taliban, al Qaeda, or associated forces)."¹⁴ This legislation then defines a "lawful enemy combatant" as "a member of the regular forces of a State party engaged in hostiles against the United States"; "a member of a militia, volunteer corps, or organized resistance movement belonging to a State party engaged in such hostilities, which are under responsible command, wear a fixed distinctive sign recognizable at a distance, carry their arms openly, and abide by the law of war"; or "a member of a regular armed force who professes allegiance to a government engaged in such hostilities, but not recognized by the United States."¹⁵

This definition of "unlawful combatant" derives from a precise reading of the "unencumbered" verbiage of the Geneva Conventions (that is, reading the conventions without referencing the body of interpretative jurisprudence that has been established in international courts since the U.S. ratified the treaty in 1955.) According to such a reading, Convention III applies only to Enemy Prisoners of War, who are essentially members of a hostile country's armed services, and Convention IV does not necessarily provide protection to those combatants who do not belong to an enemy state's armed forces but still attack the United States or its citizens.

Most relevantly to this book, even in a theater where all detainees were to be accorded either Convention III or Convention IV protections as a matter of command policy (as in Iraq), Article 5 of Convention IV provided a potential loophole for giving such protection to certain command-selected insurgents. This article states that, if "an individual protected person is definitely suspected of or engaged in activities hostile to the security of the State, such individual person shall not be entitled to claim such rights and privileges under the present Convention as would, if exercised in the favour of such individual person, be prejudicial to the security of such State."[16] Most notoriously, the U.S. detention facility at Abu Ghraib would take advantage of this seeming loophole. When, at the height of abuse at the prison, the Red Cross complained in writing about the treatment of prisoners there, Brigadier General Janis Karpinski, the 800th MP Brigade commander, attempted to justify this rough treatment by invoking this Article 5 in her formal reply to the complaint.[17]

The U.S. Supreme Court has upheld the Bush Administration's stance that the Geneva Conventions do not apply to "unlawful combatants" with one significant exception: in its landmark June 29, 2006, decision in the case of *Hamdan vs. Rumsfeld*, the U.S. Supreme Court ruled that Common Article 3 of all four Geneva Conventions applies to all detainees held on the territory of a signatory to the Geneva Conventions.[18] The general protections provided by Common Article 3 include protection from "violence to life and person," "taking of hostages," "outrages upon personal dignity," and "the passing of sentences and the carrying out of executions without previous judgment pronounced by a regularly constituted court."[19] Common Article 3 also stipulates that these detainees, when wounded and sick, "shall be collected and cared for."[20]

The United Nations' "Convention against Torture and other Cruel, Inhuman, or Degrading Treatment or Punishment," ratified by the U.S. on October 21, 1994, gave additional protection to all U.S. detainees.[21] Specifically, this "1994 Torture Convention" prohibited the infliction of torture and any "other acts of cruel, inhuman or degrading treatment or punishment."[22] When ratifying this treaty, however, the U.S. government did so with the understanding (or "reservation") that there was nothing in this convention that required additional action beyond national law (such as the 8th Amendment's prohibition against members of the U.S. government inflicting "cruel and unusual punishment").[23] Thus, what made this treaty important was its implementing U.S. legislation, U.S. Code, Title 18, Chapter 113C. Passed in October 1994 by the U.S. Congress, this new law prohibited U.S. citizens and other persons within U.S. jurisdiction from committing any act "specifically intended to inflict severe physical or mental pain or suffering (other than pain or suffering incidental to lawful sanctions) upon another person within his custody or physical control."[24] It also defined "severe mental pain or suffering" as "prolonged mental harm" caused by the "intentional infliction or threatened infliction of severe physical pain or suffering," the administration of "mind-altering substances," the "threat of imminent death," or the threat that another person will be imminently "subjected to death, severe physical pain or suffering, or . . . mind-altering substances."[25]

To summarize, it was not clear during OIF I that any article of the Geneva Conventions applied to "unlawful combatants." Even when the administering of full Geneva protections for all detainees was theater policy (as in Iraq), Article 5 of Convention IV seemed to give subordinate leaders an "out" with regard to providing full Geneva protections to non-uniformed insurgents they deemed to be a security risk. However, the "Torture Convention of 1994" and the U.S. law that implemented this treaty protected all U.S. detainees– even "unlawful combatants"– from "severe physical or mental pain or suffering" at the hands of U.S. citizens.

Detainees and military law, regulations, and doctrine

While international law and its implementing U.S. criminal code provided only limited protection for "unlawful combatants," the Uniform Code of Military Justice gave extensive protection to all detainees in U.S. military custody. U.S. Code, Title 10, Chapter 47 (that is, the Uniform Code of Military Justice) was signed into law on August 10, 1956. This law provides several punitive articles that could be applied to U.S. military service members if these service members were to mistreat detainees, including Article 78 (accessory after the fact), Article 80 (inchoate offense of attempt), Article 81 (conspiracy), Article 82 (solicitation), Article 93 (cruelty and maltreatment), Article 118 (murder), Article 119 (manslaughter), Article 124 (maiming), Article 127 (extortion), Article 128 (assault), and Article 134 (communicating a threat and negligent homicide).[26] (It would be violations of articles of the Uniform Code of Military Justice that would ultimately send most members of the "Abu Ghraib Nine" to prison.)

In addition to protections provided by the Uniform Code of Military Justice, "unlawful combatants" were potentially protected by the directives and regulations of the DoD and its proponent for detainee operations, the U.S. Army. Prior to OIF I, both the DoD and the U.S. Army had published directives and regulations giving full Geneva protections to any U.S. military detainee. DoD Directive 5100.77, published on December 9, 1998, stated that "the Heads of the DoD Components" must ensure "that the members of their DoD Components comply with the law of war during all armed conflicts, however such conflicts are characterized, and with the principles and spirit of the law of war during all other operations."[27] Additionally, Army Regulation 190-8, *Enemy Prisoners of War, Retained Personnel, Civilian Internees and Other Detainees* (October 1, 1997), stated that all "persons taken into custody by U.S. forces will be provided with the protection of the GPW [Geneva Conventions Relative to the Treatment of Prisoners of War] until some other legal status is determined by competent authority."

U.S. Army military intelligence doctrine during OIF I extended full Geneva protections to all Army detainees. Field Manual 34-52, *Intelligence Interrogation* (September 1992), provided this doctrine for OIF I. The preface to this manual stated that Army interrogations were to be conducted within the constraints established by the Geneva Conventions.[28] The section titled "Prohibition Against Use of Force" in Chapter 1 gave four reasons why interrogators needed to apply the law of war in all cases: first, acts of violence, intimidation, torture, threats, insults, and inhumane treatment were illegal; secondly, the "use of torture and other illegal methods was a poor technique that yields unreliable results"; thirdly, the use of such techniques would undermine domestic and international support for the war effort; and fourthly, the use of such techniques would place U.S. personnel who are captured at greater risk of similar abuse from their captors.[29] This section went on to list examples of illegal physical torture, to include "electric shock," "infliction of pain through chemicals or bondage, forcing an individual to stand or kneel for prolonged periods, food deprivation, any form of beating," "mock executions," and "abnormal sleep deprivation."[30] Also listed were unlawful examples of coercion, such as threatening a subject with abuse or intentionally depriving them of medical assistance if they were to withhold information.[31] Fatefully, however, this doctrine described itself in its opening paragraph as providing "doctrinal guidance, techniques, and procedures" and not as delivering new military law or regulation.[32] Thus, military lawyers and interrogators could (and did) interpret this manual's specific prohibitions as interpretations of the law rather than law itself.

U.S. Army military police doctrine during OIF I also extended full Geneva protections to any Army detainee. Field Manual 3-19.40, *Internment/Resettlement Operations*, August 1, 2001, defined all military detainees with reference to Army Regulation 190-8 and specific articles of the Geneva Conventions. According to this field manual, an Enemy of Prisoner of War, who is defined as a detainee meeting the criteria set forth in Article 4 of Geneva Convention III, must receive the extended protections of this convention; a Civilian Internee, who is defined as a detainee who is a security risk (specifically written to include insurgents), must be treated in accordance with all of the provisions of Convention IV; a Retained Person, who is defined as medical personnel, chaplains, and members of duly recognized voluntary aid organizations, must receive the same rights as Enemy Prisoners of War; and an Other Detainee, who is a detainee classified as neither an Enemy Prisoner of War nor a Civilian Internee, must be treated as an Enemy Prisoner of War until "a legal status is ascertained by competent authority."[33] Also, this field manual made it clear that working dogs could only be used for security purposes (and not for coercing intelligence from detainees).[34] Unfortunately, though, this doctrine also described itself as a set of guidelines (or "principles") rather than as military law or regulation.[35]

Interrogation approaches and U.S. Army doctrine

Field Manual 34-52, *Intelligence Interrogation*, September 1992, outlined 17 interrogation approaches that could be used by U.S. military interrogators. *(See Table 1)* Of these 17 approaches, the field manual states that the "Direct" approach is "the most effective": it is "always the first to be attempted," and it was shown to be "90 percent effective as an approach during World War II and 95 percent effective during Operations Urgent Fury, Just Cause, and Desert Storm."

Conversely, the "Fear Up" approaches are identified as having "the greatest potential to violate the law of war" and as working on only a limited number of detainees, that is, detainees who are young, inexperienced, and "exhibit a greater than normal amount of fear or nervousness." Of the three "Fear Up" approaches, the "Fear-Up (Harsh)" approach is singled out as "usually a dead end," and interrogators are cautioned to use this approach only as a final "trump card."

Importantly, this field manual did not direct interrogators to use only those interrogation approaches described in the manual (though if it had, this directive could have been ignored, since the manual was mere doctrine, not law). Moreover,

	U.S. Army Doctrinal Interrogation Approaches during OIF I	
1	Direct	"The interrogator asks questions directly related to information sought, making no effort to conceal the interrogation's purposes."
2	Incentive	". . . based on the application of inferred discomfort upon an EPW or detainee . . . must not amount to a denial of basic human needs"
3	Emotional Love	"This approach usually involves some incentive such as communication with the source's family."
4	Emotional Hate	"The emotional hate approach focuses on any genuine hate, or possibly a desire for revenge, the source may feel."
5	Fear-Up (Harsh)	"In this approach, the interrogator behaves in an overpowering manner with a loud and threatening voice."
6	Fear-Up (Mild)	"In most cases, a loud voice is not necessary . . . fear is increased by helping the source realize the unpleasant consequences the facts may cause..."
7	Fear-Down	"This technique is nothing more than calming the source" and "works best if the source's fear is unjustified."
8	Pride and Ego-Up	"The source is constantly flattered into providing certain information in order to gain credit."
9	Pride and Ego-Down	". . . based on attacking the source's sense of personal worth."
10	Futility	". . . the interrogator convinces the source that resistance to questioning is futile."
11	We Know All	"the interrogator convinces the source that resistance is useless as everything is already known."
12	File and Dossier	A substantial-looking file and dossier is created. Goal is to convince source that "everything is known . . ."
13	Establish Your Identity	"The interrogator insists the source . . . [is] an infamous individual. . . . In an effort to clear himself . . . the source . . . may provide . . . information."
14	Repetition	"the interrogator listens carefully to a source's answer to a question, and then repeats the question and answer several times."
15	Rapid Fire	the interrogator uses rapid fire questions that confuse the source, "the interrogator then confronts the source with the inconsistencies"
16	Silent	". . . the interrogator says nothing to the source, but looks him squarely in the eye . . . [until] the interrogator is ready to break silence"
17	Change of Scene	"The idea . . . is to get the source away from the atmosphere of an interrogation room" so that they are more comfortable.

Table 1) U.S. Army Doctrinal Interrogation Approaches during OIF I
Source: Headquarters, Department of the Army, Field Manual 34-52, *Intelligence Interrogation* (Washington, DC: Government Printing Office, 1992), 3-10 to 3-20.

it did not specify what techniques interrogators could use when employing a specific interrogation approach. Interrogators were reminded throughout the manual to conduct interrogations in accordance with the Law of War, and Figure 1-4 of the manual lists the articles of the Geneva Conventions that are most pertinent to interrogations. Nonetheless, it is not always apparent how the Law of War applies to all of the potential techniques used to implement a given approach. For example, strip searches were sanctioned by military police doctrine, but could interrogators use the technique of "Forced Nudity" as part of a "Pride and Ego-Down" approach? The Geneva Conventions expressly prohibited the employment of "prolonged standing" and "punishment drills" as detainee control measures, but did this apply to making a detainee assume other stress positions or doing light, non-injurious exercise?[36] Could an interrogator lawfully alter a detainee's sleep cycle as part of a Rapid Fire approach?[37] Could military working dogs be used to apply a Fear Up Harsh approach? Unit policy writers and interrogators, it seems, often had to apply their own judgment as to the legality of specific techniques and plans.[38]

Leaving the legality of specific techniques and plans to the judgment of staff officers and interrogators would contribute to interrogation abuse during OIF I. This stands to reason: if the top military and civilian lawyers in the country could debate for years over the legality of certain interrogation techniques (a debate discussed further in Chapter 3), how could tactical-level personnel be expected to know if specific techniques and plans lawfully supported doctrinal interrogation approaches?

Tony Lagouranis, a former Army interrogator, describes his heavy reliance on the "Fear Up Harsh" interrogation approach in *Fear Up Harsh: An Army Interrogator's Dark Journey through Iraq*.[39] When implementing this approach in 2004, Lagouranis' techniques included inducing hypothermia and employing military working dogs. As described in his book, he had picked up these techniques from the "Interrogation Rules of Engagement" provided for him at Abu Ghraib and the Strike Brigade Holding Area in Mosul. Hearsay and the poor examples set by other, more senior and experienced interrogators further reinforced that these techniques were legally permissible. Although emotionally conflicted at using techniques that seemed to run counter to the Law of War, he felt he could use such techniques because they seemed to be acceptable in theater and because he had never seen where such techniques were clearly and specifically prohibited by law.

Colonel John Custer (now Major General Custer) was probably the first GWOT investigator to refer to this significant doctrinal shortfall. After his August 14 to September 4, 2002, investigation of interrogation operations at Guantanamo Bay, Colonel Custer pointed out that some interrogators might adopt an overly conservative interpretation of the interrogation approaches of Field Manual 34-52, resulting in their hands being tied to the degree that they could not effectively employ these approaches, whereas other interrogators might feel unconstrained in their reading of this field manual.[40] Thus, Colonel Custer said, U.S. Southern Command should develop a metric clearly delineating what techniques were permissible for their interrogators.[41]

From the vantage point of Abu Ghraib, it is apparent that not only U.S. Southern Command but all of U.S. DoD should have followed Colonel Custer's advice. Clearly, an unambiguous "metric" of acceptable interrogation techniques could have prevented much interrogation abuse during OIF I. Or, as expressed by the Schlesinger Report, "We cannot be sure how the number and severity of abuses would have been curtailed had there been early and consistent [interrogation] guidance from higher levels."[42]

Ambiguities and inconsistencies

Official government inspectors and investigators have identified other shortfalls in U.S. doctrine that contributed to the abuse of detainees during interrogations. One of the recurring findings of these inspectors and investigators was the same finding impassionedly expressed by General Abizaid in his senate testimony, specifically, the failure of military intelligence and military police doctrine to consistently describe exactly how guards at detention facilities should support interrogation operations. On this subject, Lieutenant General Jones wrote the following:

> MP personnel and MI personnel operated under different and often incompatible rules for treatment of detainees. The military police referenced DoD-wide regulatory and procedural guidance that clashed with the theater interrogation and counterresistance policies that the military intelligence interrogators followed. Further, it appeared that neither group knew or understood the limits imposed by the other's regulatory or procedural guidance concerning the treatment of detainees, resulting in predictable tension and confusion. This confusion contributed to abusive interrogation practices at Abu Ghraib.[43]

The most striking doctrinal inconsistency, as noted in the Mikolashek Report, was that while military police doctrine gave guards a passive role when supporting interrogations (guards could only pass observations on to interrogators regarding detainee behavior), military intelligence doctrine implied an active role for guards in the screening process, to include interrogators telling guards "what types of behavior on their part will facilitate the screenings."[44]

Perhaps surprisingly to those unversed in interrogation operations, a majority of the major reports on DoD interrogation operations during the early years of the GWOT favored military police guards actively setting the conditions for interrogations. First, Colonel Stuart Herrington, a retired Army military intelligence officer who visited the U.S. strategic internment facility at the naval base at Guantanamo Bay, Cuba, on March 16-21, 2002, and who had previously gained extensive interrogation experience in Vietnam, Panama, and Operation Desert Storm, argued strongly in favor of military police guards setting conditions for interrogations.[45] In his trip report, Herrington noted, "one day, we might instruct the guards to be particularly warm and cheerful toward a given detainee . . . on another day, with a different detainee, a cold, firm demeanor by the guards might be more suitable."[46] Other inspectors of interrogation operations in various theaters, such as Colonel John Custer, Major General Geoffrey Miller, Schlesinger's Independent Panel, and Vice Admiral Church's Navy Inspector General team have concurred with Herrington's assessment. For example, the Church Report stated that, "When conducted under controlled conditions, with specific guidance and rigorous command oversight, as at Gitmo, this is an effective model that greatly enhances intelligence collection and does not lead to detainee abuse."

Major General Antonio Taguba and Major General Donald Ryder disagreed, asserting that guards should have no role outside the interrogation room in actively setting the conditions for future interrogations. Ryder, who inspected detention operations in Iraq from October 13 to November 6, 2003, and who was the Army's Provost Marshal General during OIF I, stated in his inspection report that the active setting of conditions for interrogations by guards runs "counter to the smooth operation of a detention facility, [which is] attempting to maintain its population in a compliant and docile state."[47] The Mikolashek Report and the Fay/Jones Report were neutral in this matter, essentially arguing that it matters less whether guards actively or passively set conditions for interrogators than that U.S. Army doctrine is consistent.

Of still greater import, U.S. Army intelligence doctrine during OIF I was not designed for counterinsurgency operations on an irregular, non-contiguous battlefield.[48] This issue was discussed in *On Point II, Transition to the New Campaign: The United States Army in Operation Iraqi Freedom, May 2003 - January 2005*, which is as close to an official history of OIF I and OIF II as the Army is likely to produce for at least a decade. *On Point II* described a "paradigm shift" that occurred during OIF I as intelligence became a bottom-up-driven process rather than a top-down-driven process.[49] This book noted that intelligence shifted from being supplied primarily by division-level and higher units to being supplied primarily by brigades, battalions, and companies.[50] This shift took place largely due to the inability of CJTF-7 and higher echelons to provide adequate intelligence to tactical units.[51]

The Schlesinger Report made similar observations, saying that doctrine needs to be changed to reflect the fact that the vast majority of intelligence collection was taking place in "line combat units."[52] This report stated that "current doctrine assumes a linear battlefield" where detainees can be speedily transferred to the rear for the timely gathering of intelligence by corps-level interrogators.[53] However, the modern battlefield is more likely to be a non-contiguous battle space where there are "no safe areas behind 'friendly lines'."[54] On such battlefields, it is usually impossible or at least very risky to expedite the movement of detainees to the rear. In Iraq, this report noted, detainees were routinely held up to 72 hours in line units even though doctrine states that combat units should hold onto detainees for 12-24 hours only.[55] At the Army corps level, the problem was even worse, with detainees being held at corps holding areas for 30 to 45 days before being sent to an Iraqi-run prison or to coalition forces' theater internment facility.[56]

Another issue was the inadequate support that U.S. Army doctrine provided to the ethical decision-making of its leaders. Alone among the various investigators into OIF I detainee abuse, the Schlesinger Report spoke to this inadequacy. Laying the groundwork for its judgment here, the Schlesinger Report said:

> *For the U.S., most cases for permitting harsh treatment of detainees on moral grounds begins with variants of the "ticking time bomb" scenario. . . . Such cases raise a perplexing moral problem: Is it permissible to employ inhumane treatment when it is believed to be the only way to prevent loss of lives? In periods of emergency, and especially in combat, there will always be a temptation to override legal and moral norms for morally good ends. Many in Operations Enduring Freedom and Iraqi Freedom were not well prepared by their experience, education, and training to resolve such ethical problems.*[57]

The panel concluded that "major service programs, such as the Army's 'core values' . . . are grounded in organizational efficacy rather than the moral good" and that these values "do not address humane treatment of the enemy and noncombatants, leaving military leaders and educators an incomplete tool box with which to deal with 'real-world' ethical problems."[58]

Why was the Schlesinger Panel unimpressed with the U.S. Army's basic tool for ethical decision-making, the "Army Values" paradigm? It was probably because the six "values" of this paradigm ("Loyalty, Duty, Respect, Selfless Service, Honor,

Integrity, and Personal Courage") are broad ideals, not definitive guidelines or a practical methodology for solving specific ethical problems. In fact, these values can actually be used to support an interrogator's use of "the ticking time bomb" rational. One can argue, for example, that Abu Ghraib interrogators displayed their "loyalty" to their Army, unit, and other troops by using harsh techniques to save the lives of these troops; they did their "duty" by working hard and displaying initiative; they treated detainees with the "respect" they deserved (that is, was with no respect, since these detainees were suspected terrorists and criminals); they exercised "selfless service" by doing hard, dirty work for good ends; they showcased "honor" by living up to the other Army values; they demonstrated "integrity" by using only those harsh techniques which they believed to be approved for use; and they exhibited "personal courage" by deliberately agitating dangerous detainees. Thus, what seems patently obvious to most Americans– that, say, leaving an untried suspect naked, alone, and shivering in a brightly lit, air-conditioned cell for days at a time is behavior that is inconsistent with our nation's core values– is easily lost when leaders apply the U.S. Army's basic tool for ethical decision-making.

This is not to say that this tool actually condones harsh interrogation techniques. After all, this same tool could also be used to argue that certain interrogators at Abu Ghraib were disloyal to the U.S. Constitution when they punished detainees without "due process of law;" that they failed in their duty to enforce the prohibition of Common Article 3 of the Geneva Convention's against committing "outrages upon personal dignity, in particular humiliating and degrading treatment" of captives; and that they violated their integrity by thus breaking the law. However, this argument can truly only be made in the light of later U.S. Supreme Court decisions. During OIF I, the legal limits of interrogation techniques were hotly debated by the U.S.'s most senior civilian and military lawyers and were not at all clear to politicians, military leaders, or interrogators. Thus, what the Army needs is a different tool, or at least a sharper tool, to more usefully guide ethical decision-making when laws are ambiguous (as they often are).

Various inspectors and investigators noted other doctrinal shortfalls related to interrogations during OIF I, to include the following deficiencies:

1. A lack of clear command responsibility at detention facilities. (What commander should have command responsibility of a detention facility?)
2. A lack of clear staff responsibility for detainee operations. (What deputy commander or staff section has overall responsibility for detainee operations within a specific unit?)
3. A lack of doctrine concerning the handling and training of contract personnel, especially contract interrogators and interpreters. (How are contract personnel counseled and disciplined? What training do contract personnel receive prior to deploying and upon arriving in theater?)
4. A lack of competent interpreters and a lack of mature, experienced interrogators capable of establishing an advantageous relationship with older, savvy detainees. (Are military intelligence forces sufficiently augmented with capable interpreters and older, experienced contract

interrogators?)
5. A lack of doctrine concerning the handling of interrogations by non-military agencies, particularly the Central Intelligence Agency (CIA), in Army facilities. (What are DoD procedures for handling detainees from other governmental agencies?)
6. A lack of doctrine concerning interrogator access to the medical records of detainees. (Should interrogators be allowed access to these records? If so, how much access?)
7. A lack of doctrine defining the role of behavioral science personnel in support of interrogation activities. (What tasks should and should not be performed by behavioral science personnel?)

Conclusions

During OIF I, it was not clear among interrogators or their leaders whether "unlawful combatants" (a category that described the vast majority of detainees in Iraq) were entitled to the protections of any article of the Geneva Conventions. Even when it was command policy for all detainees to receive full Geneva protections (as was the case in Iraq), Article 5 of Convention IV seemed to provide for legal exceptions to this policy. However, the "Torture Convention of 1994" and its implementing law in the U.S. protected all U.S. detainees in Iraq from "severe physical or mental pain." Furthermore, the Uniform Code of Military Justice protected all U.S. military detainees from grosser forms of mistreatment. What is more, DoD and Army directives ordered U.S. service members to extend full Geneva protections to all U.S. military detainees without exception: if these directives had been enforced, there is little doubt but that interrogation abuse during OIF I would have been greatly curtailed.

Yet, these directives were not consistently enforced. Why was this the case? As described above, part of the answer lays in the ambiguities and inconsistencies of U.S. Army doctrine at the time. Most fatefully, leaders and interrogators were often left to their own judgment as to whether or not specific interrogation techniques and plans were legal, and the descriptions in Army field manuals of illegal techniques did not themselves possess the authority of law or regulation. Other significant doctrinal problems included a lack of consistency in the role of guards outside of the interrogation room, unrealistic expectations regarding what tactical units were resourced to do on an irregular battlefield, and a sadly inadequate tool called the "Army Values" for assisting Army leaders in making ethical decisions.

However, as we shall see in the next chapter, the greater part of the answer as to why directives concerning the humane treatment of detainees were sometimes ignored lies within the interrogation-related policies of the Bush Administration.

CHAPTER 3

The city upon the hill

For we must consider that we shall be as a city upon a hill. The eyes of all people are upon us. So that if we shall deal falsely with our God in this work we have undertaken . . . we shall be made a story and a by-word throughout the world. . . . We shall shame the faces of many of God's worthy servants, and cause their prayers to be turned into curses upon us til we be consumed out of the good land whither we are a-going.[1]
—John Winthrop

Well, we started to connect the dots, in order to protect the American people. And, yes, I'm aware our national security team met on this issue [of enhanced interrogation techniques]. And I approved. I don't know what's new about that; I'm not so sure what's so startling about that.[2]
—President George W. Bush

The naval base at Guantanamo Bay, Cuba, is not only the oldest overseas U.S. naval base, but it also is the only U.S. military base located in a country with which the U.S. does not share diplomatic relations. Since 2002, this naval base has been the site of the U.S. government's only strategic internment facility. During OIF I, this strategic internment facility (often shortened as "Gitmo") consisted of three camps located on a series of low, rolling hills overlooking the eastern side of Guantanamo Bay.

Almost since its inception, this detention facility has served as a lightning rod for international controversy. One of the most hotly debated issues regarding the facility was whether the Bush Administration was legally correct when it suspended Geneva Convention protections for detainees at this facility. (As noted in Chapter 2, the U.S. Supreme Court decided in June 2006 that, as a minimum, all detainees at this facility were entitled to the general protections offered by Common Article 3 of the Geneva Conventions.) Other much-debated issues were whether the Bush Administration and the U.S. Congress made constitutionally lawful decisions when they suspended the rights of detainees at this facility to the due process of law as described in the Fifth Amendment of the U.S. Constitution and to the right of habeas corpus appeals as expressed in Article One of the Constitution. (Although the *Detainee Treatment Act of 2005* and the *Military Commissions Act of 2006* denied due process and habeas corpus appeals to Gitmo detainees, a June 12, 2008, Supreme Court decision subsequently ruled that these denials were unconstitutional.)[3] The most hotly debated legal question concerning Gitmo, however, was whether the Bush Administration sanctioned "torture" during the interrogations of certain detainees at the facility, interrogations that included the use of such coercive techniques as "Waterboarding," "Isolation," and "Forced Nudity" to break the will of detainees.

The net result of this controversy has been the empowerment of our nation's jihadist enemies at the expense of the U.S. government's standing as a moral leader in the world. Speaking to this, Vice Admiral Alberto Mora, the U.S. Navy General Counsel, testified to the Senate Armed Services Committee in June 2008 that "there are serving U.S. flag-rank officers who maintain that the first and second identifiable causes of U.S. combat deaths in Iraq– as judged by their effectiveness in recruiting insurgent fighters into combat– are, respectively the symbols of Abu Ghraib and Guantanamo."[4]

The twin scandals of Gitmo and Abu Ghraib are intimately entwined with interrogations. This chapter explores how these scandals could have occurred when the laws, directives, and doctrine outlined in Chapter 2 should have prevented such scandals.

The Bush Administration and interrogation policy

Within the U.S. government, two individuals have the authority to suspend or override DoD directives, Army regulations, and Army doctrine. These two individuals are the President and the Secretary of Defense. Both the President and the Secretary of Defense began asserting their authority in this regard soon after the fall of the Taliban government in Afghanistan.

In December 2001, the DoD General Counsel requested information regarding the interrogation of detainees from the Joint Personnel Recovery Agency,[5] the component of U.S. Joint Forces Command with oversight of SERE training for U.S. military personnel. SERE training is designed to prepare U.S. military personnel to survive capture by nations that do not adhere to the Geneva Conventions. This training subjects U.S. military personnel to interrogation techniques largely gleaned from the Korean War, where the Chinese Communist Army had used illegal interrogation techniques to extract false confessions for these confessions' propaganda value.[6] At the time of the September 11 attacks, interrogation techniques used within the U.S. military's SERE schools included forced nudity, sleep deprivation, use of extreme temperatures, use of prolonged and uncomfortable "stress positions," use of loud music and flashing lights, putting hoods over subjects' heads, and slapping the face and body.[7] Until recently, "interrogators" at the U.S. Navy SERE School even employed "waterboarding," the controversial interrogation technique that simulates drowning.[8]

The SERE schools' "interrogators," who are not usually real world U.S. military interrogators but rather actors playing the role of hostile enemy interrogators, are legally able to employ such interrogation techniques against U.S. service members because of the "safeguards" that accompany these techniques.[9] The most important of these safeguards is the fact that a U.S. service member attending a SERE school can at any point choose to stop the training (and thus fail the school). Through this safeguard and others, U.S. service members attending SERE school are given some measure of control over their environment.[10] Of course, subjects of real world hostile interrogations do not enjoy similar control.

It is unclear from unclassified sources exactly why the DoD General Counsel's request to the Joint Personnel Recovery Agency was made. By 2002, there may have been dissatisfaction with the specific intelligence that was being produced via conventional, rapport-building "soft" interrogation techniques. For example, one of the behavioral science consultants at Gitmo later testified that his chain-of-command had become frustrated over the inability of interrogators to establish a link between al Qaeda and Iraq.[11] Supporting this psychologist's assertion, David Becker, the Chief of the Interrogation Control Element at Gitmo, told the Senate Armed Services Committee that the office of the Deputy Secretary of Defense, Paul Wolfowitz, had called Major General Michael Dunlavey, the commander of Joint Task Force 170 at Gitmo, on multiple occasions to express concern about insufficient intelligence production.[12] Becker also alleged that Wolfowitz had personally told Dunlavey that his interrogators should use more aggressive interrogation techniques to extract this intelligence.[13] Thus, by December 2001, there may have been a perception within the Bush Administration that "soft" interrogation techniques were not producing the desired intelligence, and because of this perception, DoD leaders moved to consult their only source of expertise regarding non-doctrinal techniques, the Joint Personnel Recovery Agency.

Whatever the reason for the request, this request was unusual. After all, SERE schools specialize in training U.S. soldiers on how to resist providing intelligence when tortured, not in training interrogators how to extract reliable intelligence.[14] One would think that the Joint Personnel Recovery Agency would have been the last place that DoD leaders consulted for reliable interrogation practices, since the Federal Bureau of Investigation (FBI) and various law enforcement agencies had accumulated millions of man-hours of experience extracting information from real-world, non-compliant suspects. Unfortunately, though, the experience of these agencies had led them to depend on rapport-building techniques that were falling out of favor with certain members of the Bush Administration.

Ali Soufan, a former FBI agent who took part in the initial interrogations of Abu Zubaydah (an al Qaeda leader captured in Afghanistan) claims today that the FBI's "soft" techniques were indeed effective when he applied them to Abu Zubaydah. Soufan cites his extracting from Abu Zubaydah the identity of Khalid Sheikh Mohammed as the mastermind of the September 2001 terrorist attacks on U.S. soil as an example of this effectiveness.[15] Regrettably, he says, he was pulled off the case too soon because of his resistance to the plan of the CIA to use harsh interrogation methods on the captured al Qaeda leader. A *Newsweek* writer describes what happened when Soufan then went to train interrogators in early 2002 at Gitmo:

> *He [Soufan] gave a powerful talk, preaching the virtues of the FBI's traditional rapport-building techniques. Not only were such methods the most effective, Soufan explained that day, they were critical to maintaining America's image in the Middle East. 'The whole world is watching what we do here,' Soufan said. 'We're going to win or lose this war depending on how we do this.' As he made these comments, about half the interrogators in the room– those from the FBI and other law-enforcement agencies– were 'nodding their heads' in agreement,' recalls [Robert] McFadden [a U.S. Naval Criminal Investigator]. But the other half– CIA and military officers– sat there 'with blank stares. It's like they were thinking, 'This is bull crap.' Their attitude was, 'You guys are cops; we don't have time for this.'*[16]

Despite the strangeness of the DoD General Counsel's request, this initial contact with the Joint Personnel Recovery Agency would develop into a two-year relationship between this agency and certain interrogation units abroad.[17]

Rumsfeld set the stage for this relationship in a January 19, 2002, memo to the Chairman of the Joint Chiefs of Staff. In this memo, Rumsfeld stated that, although

Geneva protections did not technically apply to unlawful combatants such as al Qaeda and Taliban, U.S. detainees belonging to these organizations should be treated humanely "and, to the extent appropriate and consistent with military necessity, in a manner consistent with the principles of the Geneva Conventions of 1949."[18] What was important in Rumsfeld's memo was not that members of al Qaeda and the Taliban should, if captured, be treated in accordance with Geneva Conventions: existing DoD directives, regulations, and doctrine already required that. Rather, what Rumsfeld was saying that was truly significant was, one, the Geneva Conventions did not technically apply to members of al Qaeda and the Taliban, and two, the U.S. Armed Forces did not have to apply the Geneva Conventions to members of al Qaeda and the Taliban in cases of "military necessity."[19]

Rumsfeld's stand here would be supported by President Bush. In a February 7, 2002, memo to his national security advisors, Bush borrowed Rumsfeld's language, stating that he expected U.S. Armed Forces to "continue to treat detainees humanely and, to the extent appropriate and consistent with military necessity, in a manner consistent with the principles of Geneva."[20] Also noteworthy in Bush's memo were his assertions that, because of the transnational nature of al Qaeda, none of its members were entitled to Geneva protections since "al Qaeda is not a High Contracting Party to Geneva,"[21] and that, because members of the Taliban are "unlawful combatants," they did "not qualify as prisoners of war under Article 4 of the Third Geneva Convention, nor did they qualify for the general protections offered in common Article 3 of the Geneva Conventions."[22] Thus, essentially, President Bush was directing the application of Fourth Geneva Convention protections to members of these two organizations, except in cases of "military necessity." In cases of "military necessity," it would seem, almost any treatment of al Qaeda and Taliban detainees might be permissible.

In late July 2002, Joint Personnel Recovery Agency provided the DoD General Counsel's office with several documents, including a list of SERE interrogation techniques and extracts from training modules for SERE schools' mock interrogators.[23] A week later, the Department of Justice's Office of Legal Counsel issued a legal opinion that "redefined torture" as prohibited in the 1994 Torture Convention and this convention's implementing U.S. legislation. This opinion stated that pain was only "severe" if it caused lasting physical or psychological pain– pain "equivalent in intensity to the pain accompanying serious physical injury, such as organ failure, impairment of bodily function, or even death."[24] Thus, with President Bush and his Secretary of Defense formally expressing their willingness to suspend the Geneva protections of "unlawful combatants" in cases of "military necessity" and with the infliction of non-enduring pain and suffering now, according to the U.S. Department of Justice, permissible under the 1994 Torture Convention, the stage was set for the U.S. government to employ SERE interrogation techniques against suspected real-world adversaries.

Gitmo adopts SERE interrogation techniques

In mid-September 2002, interrogators and behavioral scientists traveled from Gitmo to attend training conducted by SERE instructors.[25] Soon after this trip, two behavioral scientists began drafting a list of proposed interrogation techniques for Gitmo that would include several SERE techniques.[26] During their drafting process, Jonathan Fredman, Chief Counsel to the CIA's Counterterrorist Center, visited Gitmo, telling leaders that, "It [torture] is basically subject to perception. If the detainee dies you're doing it [the interrogation] wrong."[27]

When finalized, the list of techniques drafted by these two scientists served as the basis of an October 11, 2002, memo sent from Major General Dunlavey to his superior, General James Hill, the commander of U.S. Southern Command. In this memo, Dunlavey explicitly requested approval for techniques that derived from "U.S. military interrogation resistance training" (SERE schools).[28] Hill forwarded this documentation on October 25, 2002, to General Richard Myers, the Chairman of the Joint Chiefs of Staff, for approval.[29]

Upon receipt of Hill's request, Myers asked the various military services to review the request.[30] Soon after, each military service replied to Meyers that they had serious legal reservations regarding the request. The Chief of the Army's International and Operational Law Division, for example, pointed out that the implementation of some of the techniques would probably constitute violations of the U.S. "torture statute" and of the Uniform Code of Military Justice.[31] All services also called for an extensive legal review of the proposal, and Navy Captain Jane Dalton, who was Myers' senior legal counsel, began just such a review.[32] However, due perhaps to pressure from Rumsfeld for a quick decision,[33] the DoD General Counsel, William Haynes II, largely ignored the reservations expressed by Dalton and the various military services.[34] On November 27, 2002, Haynes produced a memo for Rumsfeld's endorsement that had Rumsfeld approving all but three of the requested interrogation techniques.[35] On December 2, 2002, Rumsfeld endorsed the memo, and by doing so, formally authorized the use of enhanced interrogation techniques at Gitmo.[36] Myers then directed Dalton to stop her legal review of the initial request.[37] According to Dalton, Haynes ordered her to stop the review because of concerns that people would see the military services' analysis of the Gitmo request as non-supportive.[38] She also stated that this was the only time she was ever ordered to halt a legal review.[39]

There has been a great deal of speculation that a still-classified Executive Order signed by President Bush further sanctioned Rumsfeld's approval of enhanced interrogation techniques for use at Gitmo and elsewhere. This speculation derives chiefly from one of the redacted documents provided by the FBI to the American Civil Liberties Union. This redacted document is a May 22, 2004, email from the "On Scene Commander" of the FBI in Baghdad to another agent (presumably his boss). In this email, this "On Scene Commander" refers to interrogation techniques authorized by "an Executive Order signed by President Bush," an order allegedly including such techniques as "sleep management," "use of MWDs (military working dogs)," "stress positions," "loud music," and "sensory deprivation."[40] Adding fuel to this speculation was the CIA's admission to a U.S. federal court on January 5, 2007, that a document existed that matched the American Civil Liberty Union's description of a "Directive signed by President Bush that grants CIA the authority to set up detention facilities outside the United States and/or outlining interrogation methods that may be used against Detainees."[41] However, since the Bush Administration consistently denied the existence of this classified executive order, at this point in history, this speculation remains precisely that– speculation.[42]

In part due to growing service concerns, Rumsfeld rescinded his blanket approval of enhanced interrogation techniques on January 15, 2003, stating that he would only approve the use of such techniques on a case-by-case basis.[43] On the same day, Rumsfeld ordered the establishment of a working group to review the legal considerations of

U.S. interrogation operations and to propose legally acceptable techniques.[44] As this working group conducted this legal review, various senior lawyers tried unsuccessfully to have their concerns about harsh interrogation techniques incorporated into the working group's report; however, their attempts were unsuccessful.[45] Their concerns were dismissed in favor of a second legal opinion (years later rescinded) which had just been issued by the U.S. Justice Department and which supported the use of harsh interrogation techniques. According to Haynes, this opinion was to be considered "authoritative" by the working group and was to "supplant the legal analysis being prepared by the Working Group action officers."[46]

The working group adhered to Haynes' guidance, publishing a final report on April 4, 2003, that supported the use of 35 interrogation techniques.[47] The enhanced interrogation techniques that this report recommended for approval included "removal of clothing, prolonged standing, sleep deprivation, dietary manipulation, hooding, increasing anxiety through the use of a detainee's aversions like dogs, and face and stomach slaps."[48] The final report was so contentious among Working Group members that, apparently, the members who had argued most vociferously against its reasoning were never directly informed of its publication.[49]

Despite his securing legal cover for the use of enhanced interrogation techniques, Rumsfeld continued to deny blanket approval for the use of most SERE techniques at Gitmo. On April 16, 2003, Rumsfeld issued a memo approving 24 interrogation techniques for Gitmo, also stating that, for the use of "additional interrogation techniques for a particular detainee, you should provide me, via the Chairman of the Joint Chiefs of Staff, a written request describing the proposed technique, recommended safeguards, and the rationale for applying it with an identified detainee."[50] Rumsfeld also directed that interrogators obtain his specific approval for the use of four of the most potentially controversial techniques in the memorandum, which were the Incentive/Removal of Incentive (such as removal of the Koran), Pride and Ego Down, Mutt and Jeff (or good cop, bad cop), and Isolation techniques.[51] After an April 22, 2003, case of substantiated detainee abuse, Brigadier General Miller, Gitmo Commander, restricted controversial interrogation techniques further, prohibiting interrogators from using the Fear-Up Harsh approach.[52] Nonetheless, Rumsfeld later approved the use of enhanced interrogation techniques on at least one Gitmo detainee.[53]

Enhanced interrogation techniques migrate to Iraq

Rumsfeld's blanket approval for the use of enhanced interrogation techniques at Gitmo on December 2, 2002, influenced the adoption of similar techniques by U.S. forces in Afghanistan.[54] From Afghanistan, these techniques migrated to Iraq.

Soon after being formed, Rumsfeld's working group asked U.S. Central Command for a list of interrogation techniques being used in Afghanistan.[55] In response, Lieutenant Colonel Robert Cotell, the Deputy Staff Judge Advocate for the highest military headquarters in Afghanistan, Combined Joint Task Force 180 (CJTF-180), produced a January 24, 2003, memo describing techniques used by CJTF-180 interrogators and recommending the use of five more techniques.[56] Techniques identified as having been previously used by CJTF-180 interrogators included "the use of female interrogators to create 'discomfort' and gain more information; sleep adjustment, defined as 'four hours of sleep every 24 hours, not necessarily consecutive'; use of individual fears; removal of comfort items; use of safety positions; isolation; deprivation of light and sound in living areas; the use of a hood during interrogation; and mild physical contact."[57] The employment of some (if not all) of these techniques required approval on a case-by-case basis from unknown CJTF-180 military intelligence and legal personnel,[58] and the use of these techniques began at approximately the same time that Rumsfeld approved the use of harsh techniques for Gitmo.[59] Cotell's memo also recommended that the DoD working group approve the use of "deprivation of clothing," "food deprivation," "sensory overload – loud music or temperature regulation," "controlled fear through the use of muzzled, trained, military working dogs," and "use of light and noise deprivation."[60]

Cotell acknowledged in his memo that Rumsfeld had rescinded authority for the use of these enhanced interrogation techniques at Gitmo.[61] Nonetheless, in the absence of any specific higher guidance contradicting the use of these techniques in Afghanistan, CJTF-180 leadership concluded that the use of these techniques was acceptable in Afghanistan.[62] In fact, Lieutenant General Dan McNeill, the CJTF-180 commander, endorsed such harsh techniques as "individual fears [exploiting], black out goggles, deprivation of light and sound, sleep adjustment, threat of transfer to another agency or country, and safety positions."[63]

Enhanced interrogation techniques continued to be used in Afghanistan until May 6, 2004, when General Abizaid directed that all U.S. military forces operating in the U.S. Central Command Area of Responsibility use only doctrinal Field Manual 34-52 techniques. Some of these enhanced techniques (as described in the March 27, 2004, CJTF-180 interrogation standard operating procedures) included the use of "safety positions," "sleep adjustment," "sensory overload," "dietary manipulation," "adjusting temperature or introducing an unpleasant smell," and the use of "blacked out goggles."[64]

Leaders and interrogators, who during their previous deployments to Gitmo or Afghanistan had gained knowledge of the SERE techniques sanctioned in these two other theaters, often employed these techniques in Iraq. For example, Chief Warrant Officer 3 Lewis Welshofer, the 3ACR warrant officer who was later convicted in the interrogation homicide of an Iraqi general, employed harsh interrogation techniques that he claimed had been effective for him in Afghanistan. Captain Carolyn Wood, who later led the first contingent of interrogators at Abu Ghraib, is an even more important example of this occurrence. Wood was in charge of the intelligence section at Bagram Airfield in Afghanistan until January 2003. In this position, she had become familiar with the enhanced interrogation techniques approved for use in that theater. She had also become familiar with the techniques used at Gitmo. She later said that, after asking Gitmo for their interrogation "parameters," she had received a faxed PowerPoint slide from Gitmo that had listed the harsh techniques approved by Rumsfeld for the facility on December 2, 2002.[65] Based on this experience and knowledge, she allowed her interrogators at Abu Ghraib to use the enhanced techniques of "sleep adjustment" and "stress positions" even before Lieutenant General Sanchez temporarily approved the use of these techniques. Said Wood: "Because we had used the techniques in Afghanistan, and I perceived the Iraq experience to be evolving into the same operational environment as Afghanistan, I used my best judgment and concluded they would be effective tools for interrogation operations at AG [Abu Ghraib]."[66]

Special operations units were also a significant conduit for the migration of SERE techniques to Iraq. The Special Mission Unit (SMU) in Afghanistan that was responsible for tracking down high-profile al Qaeda and Taliban targets sent a team to Gitmo from

October 8-10, 2002, to assess interrogation operations.[67] This visit occurred when behavioral scientists at Gitmo were drafting the list of harsh interrogation techniques that Rumsfeld would approve for use at Gitmo on December 2, 2002.[68] This team returned with recommendations that the SMU adopt numerous SERE techniques.

On January 10, 2003, the SMU Task Force Commander approved the unit's first interrogation standard operating procedures.[70] This rulebook included four enhanced techniques, specifically, "isolation, multiple interrogators, stress positions, and sleep deprivation."[71] In February 2003, the SMU added the use of military working dogs as an approved interrogation technique.[72]

With the start of OIF in March 2003, a separate SMU Task Force was established in Iraq. According to unclassified news reports, this Joint Special Operations Command task force included members of "the Army unit Delta Force, Navy's Seal Team 6 and the 75th Ranger Regiment."[73] Also, interrogators from the Defense Intelligence Agency and Army reserve units were temporarily assigned to the task force, and CIA and FBI agents worked closely with the unit.[74] During OIF I, the name of this task

Interrogation Policies in Guantanamo, Afghanistan and Iraq

	Gitmo				Afghanistan				Iraq			
Number of Authorized Techniques	Policy	Date	Notes	Number of Authorized Techniques	Policy	Date	Notes	Number of Authorized Techniques	Policy	Date	Notes
17	FM 34-52 (1992)	Jan 02 - 01 Dec 02		17	FM 34-52 (1992)	27 Oct 01 - 24 Jan 03		17	FM 34-52 (1992)		
33	Secretary of Defense Approved Tiered System	02 Dec 02 - 15 Jan 03	1	33	CJTF 180 Response to Director, Joint Staff	24-Jan-03	1, 3, 6	29	CJTF-7 Signed Policy	14-Sep-03	1
20	FM 34-52 (1992) with 3 Cat I Techniques	16 Jan 03 - 15 Apr 03		32	CJTF 180 Detainee SOP	27-Mar-04	1	19	CJTF-7 Signed Policy	12-Oct-03	4
24	Secretary of Defense Memo	16 Apr 03 - Present	1,2	19	CJTF-A Rev 2 Guidance	Jun-04	4	19	CJTF-7 Signed Policy	13-May-04	4

1 Some techniques specifically delineated in this memo are inherent to techniques contained in FM 34-52, e.g. Yelling as a component of Fear Up
2 Five Approved Techniques require SOUTHCOM approval and SECDEF notification.
3 Figure includes techniques that were not in current use but requested for future use.
4 Figure includes one technique which requires CG approval.
5 Memorandum cited for Afghanistan and Iraq are classified.
6 Figure includes the 17 techniques of FM-34-52, alhtough they are not specified in the Memo.

Appendix D
Source: Naval IG Investigation

Figure 2) Interrogation Policies in Guantanamo, Afghanistan and Iraq
Source: James R. Schlesinger, Harold Brown, Tillie K. Fowler, and General Charles A. Horner, "Final Report of the Independent Panel to Review DoD Detention Operations, August 23, 2004," *United States Department of Defense Detainees Investigations*, http://www.defenselink.mil/news/Aug2004/d20040824finalreport.pdf (accessed November 2, 2008), 111.

force evolved from Task Force (TF) 20 to TF 121 to TF 6-26.[75]

The SMU Task Force in Iraq had an interrogation policy already in place before the start of Operation Iraqi Freedom, a policy that was copied verbatim from the policy of the SMU Task Force in Afghanistan.[76] This policy governed SMU Task Force interrogations in Iraq until it was superseded on July 15, 2003, by a new policy adding the technique of "yelling, loud music, and light control" to the techniques that had been previously approved.[77] According to one of this task force's interrogators, the use of enhanced techniques was approved on a case-by-case basis at Camp Nama, the SMU Task Force's detention facility at the Baghdad Airport:

> *There was an authorization template on a computer, a sheet that you would print out, or actually just type it in. And it was a checklist. And it was all already typed out for you, environmental controls, hot and cold, you know, strobe lights, music, so forth. Working dogs, which, when I was there, weren't being used. But you would just check what you want to use off, and if you planned on using a harsh interrogation you'd just get it signed off.*[78]

While SMU Task Force policy never included "forced nudity," this technique was nonetheless employed at Camp Nama. According to the officer who took command of the SMU Task Force in October 2003, he "discovered that some of the detainees were not allowed clothes" as part of interrogation approaches and that he ended the practice in December 2003 or January 2004.[79] Although the use of the "forced nudity" technique at the facility may have had its roots elsewhere, its use was reinforced by the assistance visit of a three-man JPRA team to the facility from September 5-23, 2003.[80] During their visit, this team demonstrated the enhanced interrogation techniques of stress positions, sleep deprivation, and forced nudity.[81] This JPRA team also reported observing an interrogation in which an SMU Task Force interrogator repeatedly slapped a detainee across the face, apparently a common practice at the facility despite its not yet being approved for use by this unit's commander.[82]

The SMU Task Force in Iraq adopted its most aggressive policy on March 26, 2004, a policy that remained in effect until May 6, 2004, at which time General Abizaid suspended the use of all non-doctrinal techniques in the U.S. Central Command area of responsibility (roughly, the Middle East and the Horn of Africa).[83] This March 26, 2004, SMU policy included 14 harsh interrogation techniques, such as the "use of muzzled dogs, 'safety positions (during interrogations),' sleep adjustment/management, mild physical contact, isolation, sensory overload, sensory deprivation, and dietary manipulation."[84]

Interrogation policy for this SMU Task Force directly influenced the drafting of the first interrogation policy for conventional forces in Iraq. This influence began with Captain Wood, who was the de facto head of interrogations at Abu Ghraib from August to December 2003.[85] Wood stated that she "plagiarized" the interrogation policy of TF 121 (the name of this SMU task force at the time of her plagiarization) to create a draft interrogation policy for her own interrogators at Abu Ghraib.[86] She then submitted this draft policy to her higher headquarters (the 519th MI Battalion, the 205th MI Brigade and CJTF-7 Headquarters) for approval.[87] According to the Church Report, CJTF-7's first interrogation policy (published on September 14, 2003) was heavily influenced by Rumsfeld's April 2003 approval memo for Gitmo and by this draft interrogation policy submitted by Captain Wood.[88]

Conclusions

Interrogation techniques that had been designed to train U.S. military personnel on how to resist and survive interrogations by an enemy unconstrained by the Geneva Conventions made their way, via formal and informal means, from U.S. military SERE schools to Gitmo and Afghanistan, and from these two theaters, to Iraq. While the question of whether certain military leaders, Donald Rumsfeld, and possibly President Bush actually violated U.S. national law with their approval of certain harsh interrogation techniques at our nation's strategic internment facility is much debated, what should not be greatly debated is whether their granting of this approval was unwise. For decades if not centuries to come, the twin symbols of Gitmo and Abu Ghraib and all that these symbols have done to fuel the insurgencies in Iraq and Afghanistan and to incur international condemnation of the U.S., should serve as a cautionary tale for any other senior U.S. leader who might someday consider a similarly unwise course of action.

In a famous sermon delivered in 1630 on board the Arbella just prior to its landing, John Winthrop told the Puritan founders of the Massachusetts Bay Colony that their new community would be a "city upon a hill" watched by the world.[89] This metaphor of a lofty city has been frequently invoked in the modern age by various U.S. politicians and political theorists. In his moving farewell speech to the nation, for example, President Ronald Reagan said:

> *The past few days when I've been at that window upstairs, I've thought a bit of the 'shining city upon a hill'. . . . I've spoken of the shining city all my political life, but I don't know if I ever quite communicated what I saw when I said it. But in my mind it was a tall proud city built on rocks stronger than oceans, wind-swept, God-blessed, and teeming with people of all kinds living in harmony and peace, a city with free ports that hummed with commerce and creativity, and if there had to be city walls, the walls had doors and the doors were open to anyone with the will and the heart to get here. That's how I saw it and see it still.*[90]

Ironically, considering the long life this metaphor has enjoyed in the speeches and essays of this nation's political leaders, the interrogation facilities at both Gitmo and Abu Ghraib were situated atop hills. Truly, though, the moral examples set by these two detention facilities for the world to view did not represent the shining city ("America") envisioned by Winthrop, our Founding Fathers, and our nation's finest leaders.

CHAPTER 4
CJTF-7's long list of not nearly enoughs

As you know, you go to war with the Army you have. They're not the Army you might want or wish to have at a later time.[1]
—Donald Rumsfeld

Right from the start of our involvement [March 2003], it was clear that we lacked anywhere near the amount of either trained interrogators or Arabic linguists required to do our job. In fact, for most of my tour in Iraq, my unit– one of the largest HUMINT units in Iraq– never had more than 8-10 Arabic linguists at any one time. . . . With that small cadre, we were conducting dozens of intelligence gathering missions and interviewing 50-100 Iraqis every day. . . . [Consequently,] there were numerous cases of tactical, non-military intelligence units conducting 'CI' operations on their own without any permission to do so, all within the 205th's area of operation (AO). Many of these rogue intelligence gathering operations led to allegations of abuse and misconduct later on.[2]
—David DeBatto
205th MI Brigade
Counterintelligence Specialist

The invasion of Iraq was launched on March 20, 2003. During its fighting march north from Kuwait, the V Corps Headquarters performed magnificently. The headquarters directed its heavy mechanized forces efficiently, ensuring its forces employed precise and devastating firepower against any enemy force that stood in its way. These enemy forces included the Fedayeen Saddam, an irregular enemy militia who, unexpectedly, supplied a ferocious and tenacious resistance to advancing coalition forces. Their fierce resistance caused Lieutenant General William Wallace, the V Corps Commander, to famously remark that this enemy "was not the one we'd war-gamed against," much to the chagrin of his military and civilian superiors. In the suburbs of Baghdad, V Corps forces took advantage of what would probably have proven to be only a temporarily disorganized defense of the city, launching tank-heavy raids (or "thunder runs") into the heart of the city to seize key political and military infrastructure. With the Iraq military's ability to command and control its units effectively destroyed, organized resistance in the city crumbled, and the much-feared block-by-block battle for the city– with all of this battle's accompanying carnage– never took place. Tikrit, Saddam's home city, and Kirkuk in northern Iraq fell a few days later, and on April 14, 2003, the Pentagon declared the end of major fighting.

In retrospect, it is no wonder the V Corps Headquarters performed so magnificently during the invasion of Iraq, for leading this invasion was very much a role this headquarters had been born to play. After their commissioning, officers in this headquarters, just as other officers across the U.S. Army at the time, had been nourished by a myriad of military schools, maneuver training centers, and training exercises to wage just such a conflict. In fact, less than two months before the invasion, the V Corps Headquarters and its subordinate headquarters had conducted a massive exercise called "Victory Scrimmage" at Grafenwoehr, Germany, that had focused almost exclusively on training commanders and their staffs on how to conduct this invasion.[3] What is more, the V Corps Headquarters directed troops that were task-organized for high-intensity conflicts as well as equipped with some of the best war-fighting equipment on the planet, including M1A1 tanks, M2 Bradley infantry fighting vehicles, and M109A6 Paladin self-propelled howitzers. Even the way the headquarters understood the enemy and its own battlespace was defined by high-tech military intelligence sensors that produced imagery, signals, and radar-derived intelligence– intelligence that efficiently pinpointed such enemy targets as combat equipment, headquarters buildings, communications nodes, lines of communication, and uniformed military personnel.

With the destruction of Saddam's Army, however, the V Corps' ability to impact its operational environment in the manner it wanted to decreased dramatically. Although jubilant at the fall of a much-despised regime (even some Sunnis celebrated Saddam's fall), vast numbers of Iraqis turned against coalition forces as law and order, electricity, garbage disposal, and other essential services failed to quickly materialize. Contributing to lawlessness was the problem of police officers, judges, and other government personnel not returning to their jobs, a problem that resulted in chaos as criminal gangs– many populated by the thousands of criminals Saddam had released just a few months earlier in a mass parole– looted government buildings and terrorized other Iraqis. What is more, V Corps forces were ill-equipped, untrained, and mentally unprepared to deal with the problem. Stories abounded of U.S. soldiers staying on their tanks as looters paraded by them with stolen goods. Senior U.S. officers, raised in the cradle of the Cold War, were sometimes gripped by a sense of ennui and confusion at the situation they found themselves in. "I can remember quite clearly," one general officer reportedly said several months later, "I was on a street corner in Baghdad, smoking a cigar, watching some guys carry a sofa by and it never occurred to me that I was going to be the guy to go get that sofa back."[4]

Then, with two signatures from his pen, Ambassador Paul Bremer added fuel to an already smoldering insurgency. The first Coalition Provisional Authority order that Ambassador Bremer signed, Order No. 1, barred members of the top four ranks of the Baath party from government office and subjected lesser ranks of the party to review. The second Coalition Provisional Authority order, Order No. 2, formally dissolved all Iraqi military and intelligence organizations. With these two signatures, hundreds of thousands of Iraqi men– including any Iraqi with any skill at running a large governmental organization as well as nearly all of Iraq's trained saboteurs and combat specialists– found their professional careers and hopes of a steady paycheck decisively ended. Insurgents took immediate advantage of the anger generated by these Coalition Provisional Authority orders to attract more (and more skillful) insurgents– some of whom were motivated by patriotism to join the insurgency, but some of whom were motivated by simple economics and their need for the money paid by insurgent groups for anti-coalition attacks.[5]

As V Corps maneuver leaders tried to keep a lid on lawlessness and a growing insurgency, these leaders found themselves wishing for fewer Abrams tanks, Bradleys, and Paladins and for more dismounted troops to conduct patrols and to secure key sites; for fewer tactical psychological operations teams and for more public affairs detachments to convince, not regular army units to surrender, but rather the great mass of the Iraqi people that it was in their own best interest to support coalition efforts in their country; and for fewer imagery, signals, and radar intelligence collection platforms and for more HUMINT collectors to talk to Iraqis and help them find their soldiers' non-uniformed assailants. What V Corps leaders wanted, in short, was a greater capacity for conducting counterinsurgency and military stabilization operations.

Unfortunately, however, civilian and military leaders in Washington, D.C., had already chosen to reduce rather than increase this capacity. Lulled by the assumption that the situation in Iraq would soon stabilize, leaders in the Pentagon had decided in May 2003 to inactivate Coalition Force Land Component Command at Camp Doha, Kuwait, as the headquarters governing most coalition operations in Iraq and redesignate the much smaller V Corps headquarters as CJTF-7, the headquarters governing all of the coalition's military operations in Iraq.[6] The V Corps headquarters would remain the core headquarters for CJTF-7 throughout OIF I until III Corps headquarters, as part of the second rotation of units for Operation Iraqi Freedom (OIF II), assumed the role of core headquarters for CJTF-7 on February 1, 2004.[7]

Too few MI soldiers

With the establishment of the V Corps Headquarters as CJTF-7 Headquarters on June 14, 2003, the capacity of coalition forces for conducting counterinsurgency and military stabilization operations instantly declined. This loss of capacity started with a lack of sufficient headquarters personnel. Although U.S. Central Command had allocated sufficient personnel for the new headquarters in a joint manning document, this allocation was "not being filled systemically by the other services (except the Marines) or by coalition partners."[8] In fact, when activated, CJTF-7 Headquarters had "only 495 [personnel], or roughly a third, of the manning requirements."[9] As a result of the failure of the various services to adequately fill the CJTF-7 Headquarters, this headquarters would never come close to reaching its authorized strength. Speaking to the CJTF-7 Headquarters' chronic manpower shortage, CJTF-7 Chief of Operations (CJ3), Major General Thomas Miller, said "that the healthiest that [the CJ3 staff] ever got was probably at about the 50 percent mark, but you never sustained that more than 30 to 40 days because of the turnaround ratio you had amongst the various services."[10] Similarly, Major General Barbara Fast, the CJTF-7 Chief of Intelligence (CJ2), noted that her section never exceeded 50 percent of its required manning.[11]

This chronic shortage of personnel led directly to the loss of several key capabilities within the CJTF-7 headquarters. For example, the CJTF-7 staff was consumed by day-to-day tactical operations, resulting in an inability of the staff to adequately address its long-range as well as its strategic- and operational-level responsibilities. Major General Miller said:

> Quite frankly, the day-to-day fight, the turmoil of transition . . . and all the other unforeseen tasks (Iraqi Civil Defense Corps, Police, Iranian Mujahedin-e Khalq forces, etc.), and then the enormous task of orchestrating a force rotation completely consumed the undermanned staff (CJ3). So as a result of that, I would have to say that the tactical situation and associated current operations tasks received the bulk of our attention, especially within the CJ3.[12]

Just as alarmingly for a headquarters leading a counterinsurgency campaign (regardless of what political leaders in Washington were calling it),[13] the CJ2 section lacked a Joint Intelligence Center for conducting advanced HUMINT analysis.[14] This lack of a robust HUMINT analytical capability originated with the V Corps Headquarters' own organic shortfalls, and inadequate augmentation prevented Fast from sufficiently growing this capability throughout OIF I. Another significant intelligence capability lost with the birth of CJTF-7 was that of a "Red Team," a team of analysts that provides oversight of staff planning and ensures staff plans are the best possible plans.[15]

Not only were there too few intelligence officers working for the CJTF-7 CJ2, but generally, the CJ2's military intelligence officers were less skillful than the military intelligence officers of Coalition Forces Land Component Command at conducting strategic- and operational-level analysis in support of counter-insurgency operations. Lieutenant General Sanchez later said of his intelligence officers that, although very smart and hard-working, they had been trained to "fight a conventional fight."[16] As a result, he said, "we were completely lost in a totally different operational environment and we were really struggling."[17]

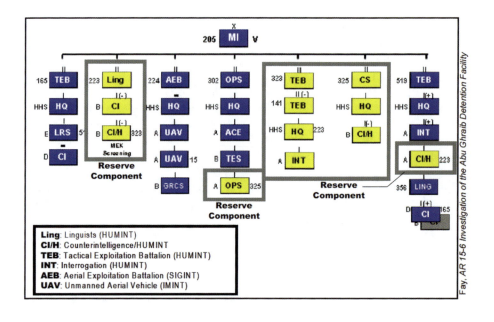

Figure 3) 205th MI Brigade Task Organization, August 2003
Source: Dr. Donald P. Wright and Colonel Timothy R. Reese, *On Point II, Transition to the New Campaign: the United States Army in Operation IRAQI FREEDOM, May 2003, January 2005*, Fort Leavenworth: Combat Studies Institute Press, 2008, 194.

More critically, by the time the CJTF-7 Headquarters was stood up, the Iraq theater had already lost the majority of its strategic- and operational-level intelligence assets. Between January and April 2003, 17 military intelligence battalions supported combat operations in Iraq.[18] By July 2003, however, ten of these 17 military intelligence battalions had redeployed from Iraq. Perhaps most critically, when the 513th MI Brigade returned home to Fort Gordon, Georgia, this brigade took with it this brigade's robust number of strategically-skillful HUMINT operators.[19] Many of the Defense Intelligence Agency's HUMINT teams also redeployed prior to the establishment of CJTF-7, leaving most of the teams it still had in Iraq in support of the quixotic quest of the Iraq Survey Group for weapons of mass destruction.[20] Just as critically, the theater's document exploitation (DOCEX) teams– teams of interpreters and analysts that could have been translating documents and providing analytical support for interrogations across the theater– were similarly tasked to support this quixotic quest. The loss of these military intelligence battalions and theater-level HUMINT and DOCEX teams left CJTF-7 with only the V Corps' own military intelligence Brigade, the 205th, to conduct theater- and operational-level intelligence operations. Although the 205th MI Brigade had been augmented prior to the invasion by three additional military intelligence battalions (that, significantly, included three counterintelligence companies and one interrogation company), it still possessed a sum total of only seven battalions operating in Iraq.[21]

Worse still, these remaining seven battalions were largely irrelevant. Three of the seven military intelligence battalions remaining in Iraq were battalions organic to the 205th MI Brigade and the V Corps. Although these three battalions did have some HUMINT capability, they had been primarily designed for conventional warfare. Major Art LaFlamme, who led a military intelligence company within one of 205th MI Brigade's organic battalions during OIF I, later described how his company used its sophisticated Tactical Exploitation System to provide a great number of enemy targets to coalition maneuver forces during the invasion.[22] His primary mission, as LaFlamme put it, "was finding stuff to kill," and his company was able to use his company's analysts and advanced analytical equipment "to shove intel down their [maneuver units'] throats."[23] But with the defeat of Saddam's Army, LaFlamme said, his mission "dropped to almost freaking nothing."[24]

Albeit hard-working, CJTF-7's small number of HUMINT personnel would prove grossly insufficient to accomplish their required tasks. This reality extended also to division-level operations. The chief of interrogations for the 4ID, for example, later said that, while he had needed 20 to 30 interrogators to accomplish his mission, he had only had six.[25] This shortage of HUMINT personnel throughout Iraq was aggravated even further in January 2004 when the 205th MI Brigade redeployed with its seven battalions, leaving just the two battalions of its replacement brigade, the 504th MI Brigade, to provide theater-level collection and analysis for CJTF-7.

In short, as a result of CJTF-7's lack of capacity for conducting counter-insurgency intelligence operations, CJTF-7's major subordinate commands were unable to rely on significant intelligence support from CJTF-7. Major General Fast has stated that tactical-level units (division-level and lower) generated approximately 95 percent of the intelligence they used to focus their military operations.[26] However, even this low assessment of CJTF-7's contribution to tactical-level intelligence may have been generous. With regard to interrogation support specifically, Major General Raymond Odierno, 4ID Commander, said that "they [CJTF-7 interrogators] were so overwhelmed that they did not, in my mind, provide us with the information we needed."[27] Lieutenant Colonel Mark Crisman, the S2 (Intelligence Officer) for the 3rd Brigade Combat Team (BCT), 1AD, has spoken even more bluntly: "Not once did I, as a BCT S2, receive a single piece of relevant feedback from interrogators at Abu Ghraib, this after personally delivering detainees with all associated target packets, initial interrogation results and associated physical evidence."[28] Colonel Peter Mansoor, commander of the 1st BCT in 1AD, has echoed this sentiment:

> *We also knew that once we transferred a prisoner to Abu Ghraib, no intelligence ever came back to us. Not just any useful intelligence, but no intelligence whatsoever.*[29]

Too few military policemen

Prior to the invasion of Iraq, the planners of Coalition Forces Land Component Command believed that coalition forces would capture between 16,000 and 57,000 Enemy Prisoners of War (EPWs) during the invasion, resulting in the establishment of up to 12 major coalition detention facilities.[30] These vast numbers of EPWs did not materialize, and starting on May 1, 2003, coalition detention facilities began releasing detainees at the rate of 300 EPWs a day.[31] Due to the rapidly shrinking number of EPWs (though these EPWs were being quickly replaced by criminals captured during the initial breakdown of law and order in Iraq) as well as due to the assumption that there would be no insurgency, military leaders in Washington directed the demobilization of reserve military police units which were still in the U.S. and which had been preparing to deploy to Iraq.[32] This decision left three military police brigades operating in Iraq during OIF I: the 18th MP Brigade was attached in direct support to 1AD in Baghdad; the 220th MP Brigade handled various theater-level missions throughout Iraq; and the 800th MP ran theater-level detention operations.[33]

When Brigadier General Janice Karpinski assumed command of the 800th MP Brigade on June 30, 2003,[34] Coalition Forces Land Component Command still controlled her brigade. Her brigade, however, fell under CJTF-7's control when CJTF-7 was activated two weeks later.[35]

For most of OIF I, the 800th MP Brigade had eight battalions in Iraq: starting in July 2003, one battalion with five companies managed the Baghdad Central Confinement Facility at Abu Ghraib; one battalion with two companies ran Camp Ashraf; five companies from two battalions ran Camp Bucca; one battalion with two companies ran Camp Whitford; one battalion with two companies ran the High Value Detainee facility in Camp Cropper; one battalion with two companies ran the Ad Diwaniyah Prison, and one battalion jointly managed several prisons and jails with Iraqi policemen and guards.[36] These Iraqi prisons and jails included the Russafa and Women/Youth detention centers as well as the Irbil and Mosul Interim prisons.[37] Altogether, the 800th MP Brigade was responsible for 11,333 detainees on June 15, 2003, the day after CJTF-7 was established.[38]

By December 1, 2003, four of the 800th MP Brigade's battalions had redeployed home, leaving just four battalions in charge of 11,699 detainees.[39] Also, the Ad Diwaniyah Prison and the Camp Whitford detention facility had been closed, enabling the brigade to more efficiently utilize its remaining military policemen at fewer installations.[40] Nonetheless, this 50 percent reduction in military police battalions marked a dramatic decline in the guard-to-detainee ratio at coalition holding facilities. This ratio only worsened during OIF II, when the 89th and 16th MP brigades of OIF II conducted a transfer of responsibility with the three theater-level military police brigades of OIF I on February 1, 2004.[41]

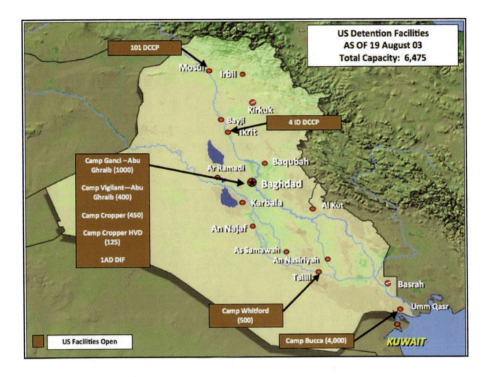

Figure 4) U.S. Detention Facilities as of August 2003
Source: CJTF-7 Staff. "Detention Summit Briefing to LTG Sanchez." Camp Victory, Iraq, August 11, 2003, Slide 31.

The mother of all FRAGOs

Although the CJTF-7 Headquarters published several minor detention-related fragmentary orders in June and July of 2003, the headquarters did not immediately publish a comprehensive directive governing every facet of detainee operations in Iraq. This changed when, on August 24, 2003, CJTF-7 issued Fragmentary Order 749 (Intelligence & Evidence Led Detention Operations Relating to Detainees) to Operations Order 03-036.[42] This order, which served as CJTF-7's base order regarding detainee operations throughout OIF I, was so long that some officers jokingly referred to it as "The Mother of all FRAGOs."[43]

Fragmentary Order 749 began with definitions. First, this order defined two major categories for CJTF-7 detainees, EPWs and Civilian Internees, defining these two categories in accordance with their doctrinal definitions.[44] Undoctrinally, however,

35

CJTF-7 created two additional categorizations within the Civilian Internee category, specifically, "Criminal Detainees" and "Security Internees."[45] These additional sub-categories were created to reflect two different sets of handling procedures, both of which are discussed below. Also, this fragmentary order stated that both Civilian Internees and EPWs could be labeled with up to two additional caveats, "Criminal Investigation Division (CID) Hold" or "MI Hold." A detainee with the additional "CID Hold" caveat could not be released until this caveat had been lifted by a U.S. Army CID agent.[46] Similarly, a detainee with the "MI Hold" caveat could not be released until this caveat had been lifted by a U.S. military intelligence soldier.[47]

According to Fragmentary Order 749, subordinate units had 48 hours to report through operational channels "that a person has been detained."[48] This initial report had to include "the person's name, address, and age; date, time, location, circumstances of capture and if applicable, capture tag number."[49] Subordinate units then had 72 hours (and up to two weeks for security internees) to either release detainees or transport them to the Baghdad Central Confinement Facility at the Abu Ghraib Prison.[50]

CJTF-7 Detainee Classifications	
Category	Description
Civilian Internees (CIs)	A doctrinal term, CJTF-7 applied this category to individuals who had "committed an offense (insurgent or criminal) against the detaining power." According to regulation and this CJTF-7 order, such detainees were entitled to Geneva Convention IV protections
Criminal Detainee	A sub-category of CIs, this is a person detained because "he/she is reasonably suspected of having committed a crime against Iraqi Nationals or Iraqi property on a crime not related to the coalition force mission." Such detainees were to be handed over to the nascent Iraqi legal system for disposition.
Security Internee	A sub-category of CIs, this is primarily suspected insurgents, though it also included individuals suspected of war crimes. This category was further broken down to include High Value Detainees, who were defined as "security internees of significant intelligence or political value."
Enemy Prisoners of War (EPWs)	Another doctrinal term, CJTF-7 applied this category to a "member of armed or uniformed security forces that conform to the requirements of Article 4, Geneva Convention, relating to the treatment of prisoners of war." Such detainees were entitled to Geneva Convention III protections.

Table 2) CJTF-7 Detainee Classifications
Source: Derived from CJTF-7 Headquarters, "FRAGO 749 to CJTF OPORD 03-036 (Annex 17 to Formica Report)," *The Office of the Secretary of Defense and Joint Staff Reading Room*, August 24, 2004, http://www.dod.mil/pubs/foi/detainees/ formica_annexes_1.pdf (accessed January 13, 2009), 40-41.

When transporting detainees to Abu Ghraib, subordinate units were responsible for ensuring all required documentation and evidence accompanied detainees; this documentation included a Coalition Provisional Authority Forces Apprehension Form, two sworn statements "from coalition soldiers/officers or Iraqi nationals that witnessed the crime/incident and apprehension," and an evidence/property custody form for any evidence or personal property accompanying the detainee.[51] At Abu Ghraib, detainees underwent "induction," which was "the process by which a detainee or internee is received in the Coalition Holding Facility"[52] and which involved inputting a detainee's personal data and circumstances of capture into the National Detainee Reporting System,[53] a classified database that military police guard units maintained.[54]

Fragmentary Order 749 also stated that, after induction at Abu Ghraib, the "Detention Review Authority" had 72 hours to determine whether a detainee was a "Criminal Detainee," "Security Internee," or EPW.[55] The Detention Review Authority, consisting of CJTF-7 Judge Advocate General officers (of captain or higher rank), also had the authority to release Iraqis suspected of minor crimes as well as to recommend, in the case of legally insufficient evidence, the release of Iraqis suspected of major crimes.[56] Fragmentary Order 749 defined "serious crime" as any crime considered punishable by more than five years imprisonment under the Iraqi Criminal Act of 1969, and it gives a non-inclusive list of serious crimes. Examples of serious crimes, according to this list, were "murder, rape, armed robbery, kidnapping, abduction, state infrastructure sabotage, car-jacking, assault causing bodily harm, arson, destruction of property or theft with a value in excess of 500 U.S. dollars, or conspiracy or solicitation as an accomplice or attempting to commit one of these offenses."[57]

The Detention Review Authority made recommendation for the release of Criminal Detainees suspected of major crimes to the Release Board, initially consisting of Colonel Marc Warren, the senior legal officer in CJTF-7, and Brigadier General Karpinski, the 800th MP Brigade Commander.[58] The Detention Review Authority also made recommendations for the release of any Security Internees (suspected insurgents) to the Review and Appeal Board, at first comprised of Major General Fast, Colonel Warren, and Colonel Robert Hipwell, the CJTF-7 Provost Marshall.[59] In accordance with Article 78 of Geneva Convention IV, all detainees had the right to appeal their continued internment: in the case of Criminal Detainees, such appeals would be forwarded to the Release Board, and in the case of Security Internees, such appeals would be forwarded to the Review and Appeal Board.[60] If unappealed, the first time either board of senior officers would review a detainee's case was after the detainee had been in detention for six months.[61]

Additionally, Fragmentary Order 749 stated that, when possible, Criminal Detainees were to be turned over to local Iraqi jails. If a local jail were unavailable, a coalition detention facility could intern the detainee, and coalition forces would transport detainees to Iraqi courts as required. Coalition forces were required to honor Iraqi court release orders in cases involving Criminal Detainees. Thus, even if the initial judgment of the Detention Review Board as well as the six-month judgment of the Release Board deemed sufficient evidence existed to keep a specific Criminal Detainee interned, an Iraqi judge could overrule these coalition decision-makers and direct the detainee's release. This was not, however, the case for alleged insurgents (that is, Security Internees). Once the Detention Review Authority deemed the initial evidence sufficient to keep a Security Internee interned, then this detainee stayed interned for at least six months (unless they successfully appealed their internment decision). This requirement for a periodic review every six months was required by Army Regulation 190-8, which in turn derived from Article 78, Geneva Convention IV. The exception to this six-month rule occurred when, as coalition holding facilities grew increasingly overcrowded, mass paroles of both Criminal Detainees and Security Internees took place. But even during such paroles, a Security Internee who was under "MI Hold" or who had "participated in attacks resulting in death or injury of a U.S.,

Coalition, or Fellow Iraqi member" was ineligible for parole.[62]

The theater-wide detention procedures that CJTF-7 put in place in August 2003 were comprehensive and fully commensurate with the Law of War. Plus, these procedures made sense– at least in theory.

Most significantly, the creation of a 72-hour suspense for the Detention Review Authority to conduct detainee status reviews, which was not a requirement by law or doctrine, seemed to promise to reduce overcrowding at coalition detention facilities and to help mitigate the unintended long-term detention of innocents– the so-called "50 meters detainees" swept up in coalition raids for being in the wrong place at the wrong time. Also, prior to this order's directing this board to consist of CJTF-7 senior officers, junior legal officers had often single-handedly made the decisions to release suspected insurgents. The release of suspected insurgents upon the order of a single junior legal officer had frequently caused great consternation among CJTF-7's subordinate maneuver units, who, due to the rate they were starting to lose their soldiers to enemy action, were inclined to adopt a "better safe than sorry" perspective with regard to the long-term detention of alleged insurgents. "In the summer of 2003 we all thought we were going home by Christmas," said Lieutenant Colonel Russell Godsil, the intelligence officer for the 1st BCT, 1AD, during OIF I, "So there was no consideration for the long-term consequences of locking up the wrong guys: commanders just wanted all the 'possible' bad guys out of their neighborhoods until they left."[63]

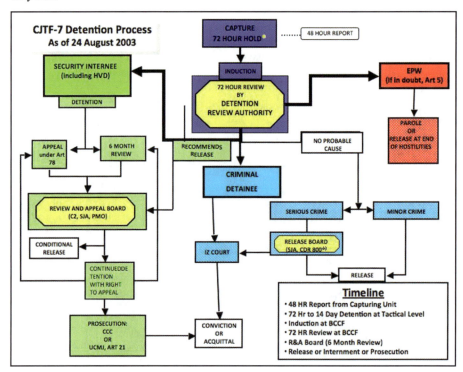

Figure 5) CJTF-7 Detention Process
Source: CJTF-7 Staff, "Detention Summit Briefing to LTG Sanchez," Camp Victory, Iraq, Slide 8.

The use of a board of senior CJTF-7 officers to make such decisions should have, in theory anyway, reduced the feeling among subordinate units that releases were being conducted without due consideration of the opinions and evidence collected by these units to support detainees' continued detention. In practice, however, the process was unwieldy and impractical since the designated senior officers had other duties to which they had to attend, and they could not review detainee packets all day every day, as their new duty required. By early November 2004, however, senior officers were permitted to delegate their responsibility for sitting on these boards to subordinate leaders, and Criminal Detainee and Security Internee boards were consolidated into one board in order to promote efficiency.

Nonetheless, despite CJTF-7's development of comprehensive procedures for handling detainees, serious problems remained in its detention system. The problem (as always) was resources: CJTF-7 simply could not sufficiently resource the detention procedures outlined in Fragmentary Order 749. Significantly, giving subordinate units just 72 hours to build evidence packets and transport criminal detainees to a coalition holding facility was not always practical, considering the dangerous environments through which units maneuvered.

In short, due to no shortage of effort on the part of CJTF-7's leaders but rather due to a lack of resources, CJTF-7 was often unable to accomplish everything its leaders clearly knew they needed to accomplish with regard to detention procedures.

Too few lawyers

Perhaps most troubling, there were not enough military lawyers to meet the suspense of conducting a 72-hour review of a detainee's status once a detainee had been inducted into a coalition detention facility. One CJTF-7 lawyer later referred to a "backlog of 8,000 files" that had accrued during the summer of 2003, and he said that Colonel Warren had been forced to bring in as many lawyers as "he could get his hands on" to reduce this backlog of detainee files.[64] Since it would have taken several weeks if not months for such a backlog to accrue, it can be inferred from this lawyer's statement that, at least through the first half of OIF I, there may have been thousands of detainees held in coalition detention facilities without probable cause for far longer than the 72 hours directed by Fragmentary Order 749. Fortunately, a full-time detainee review board existed by February 2004, and according to Lieutenant General Sanchez' testimony, this board was reviewing 100 detainee packets a day (presumably sufficient to reduce and prevent any backlog).[65] Yet, the detention of Iraqis on little probable cause for weeks or even months for much of OIF I no doubt created much bitterness among wrongfully-detained Iraqis and their families. Such bitterness could have done nothing but aid the insurgency.

CJTF-7's austere interrogation facilities

On March 22, 2003, "Task Force EPW" of the 3rd Infantry Division established a Division EPW Collection Point on Assault Point Barrow at the Talil Air Base in south-central Iraq.[66] Two days later, Task Force EPW handed off control of the Division Collection Point at the air base to the 709th MP Battalion and headed north behind 3rd Infantry Division combat forces.[67] This collection point on Talil Air Base eventually became the Camp Whitford detention facility, the first enduring U.S. detention facility in Iraq. Meanwhile 300 kilometers to the south, U.S. forces assumed responsibility on April 9, 2003, of Camp Freddy, which British forces had established near the Kuwait border and the Iraqi port city of Umm Qasar.[68] Three days later, interrogators from the 1st Marine Expeditionary Force and the 323rd MI Battalion began conducting interrogation operations at this formerly British facility,[69] now re-named Camp Bucca by U.S. forces. Throughout the invasion, Camp Whitford served as a trans-shipment point, the place maneuver units dropped off prisoners for transport by the 800th MP Brigade to Camp Bucca, the theater internment facility, in the south.[70]

During the invasion, Task Force EPW established additional temporary division collection points, first at Life Support Area Bushmaster near An Najaf on April 8, 2003, and then at Camp Dogwood, which was located just an hour south of Baghdad near Iskandaria.[71] On May 1, 2003, the division's detention and interrogation operations moved north again, this time settling within the sprawling confines of the Baghdad International Airport.[72] Within this airport's walls, the 205th MI Brigade's 519th MI Battalion and 223rd MI (Linguist) Battalion and the 513th MI Brigade's 202nd MI Battalion set up the second enduring corps-level interrogation facility to be established in Iraq, Camp Cropper.[73]

When established on June 14, 2003, CJTF-7 assumed responsibility for interrogation operations at four theater-level detention facilities—Camps Cropper, Whitford, Bucca, and Ashraf.[74] Camp Ashraf was located near Baquba, about 100 kilometers west of the Iranian border and 60 kilometers northeast of Baghdad, and it was an Enemy Prisoner of War facility that held about 3,800 members of the Iranian insurgent group, the Mujahedin el-Khalq.[75]

On July 3, 2003, Ambassador Bremer approved the use of Abu Ghraib Prison as a coalition holding facility.[76] Bremer's decision was controversial because of the prison's notoriety: under the oversight of Saddam's Special Security Organization, tens of thousands of political prisoners had been tortured and executed there, and Bremer was sensitive to the Iraqi perception that Saddam's tyrannical Iraqi regime had simply been replaced by a tyrannical U.S. regime– a perception already aided by the coalition tactic of appropriating Saddam's palaces for use by military headquarters units. When making the decision to re-open Abu Ghraib, Bremer did so under the belief that the facility would be closed as soon as an Iraqi government could be formed and a new prison constructed.[77]

With the approval to use Abu Ghraib secured, Lieutenant General Sanchez chose to consolidate interrogation operations by October 1, 2003, at Abu Ghraib, now re-named the Baghdad Central Confinement Facility, and re-designate this facility as the Theater Internment Facility. A component of Sanchez' decision to centrally consolidate interrogation operations was his decision to also close the main Camp Cropper detention facility, resulting in the transfer of interrogators from this facility to the Abu Ghraib detention facility in mid-September 2003. This closure left only the High Value Detainee detention facility still operational at the Camp Cropper site. (This special detention facility is discussed below.) Additionally, Camp Whitford was closed and U.S. interrogation operations at Camp Bucca ceased. By the time British forces resumed responsibility for a few months of Camp Bucca on September 25, 2003, U.S. interrogators had already moved from Camp Bucca and Camp Whitford to the Abu Ghraib detention facility.[78]

CJTF-7 conducted large-scale interrogation operations at three facilities, Camp Bucca, Camp Cropper, and Abu Ghraib.

Camp Bucca

When CJTF-7 inherited Camp Bucca, the detention facility was CJTF-7's least-crowded facility. Although Camp Bucca had a capacity for 4000 detainees, only 2539 detainees were being held at this facility on August 19, 2003.[79] During Major General Taguba's investigation into Abu Ghraib abuses from January to March 2004, however, he found that Camp Bucca had become overcrowded.[80] This temporary overcrowding was remedied by OIF II, thanks in part to a new facility at the camp that could hold 500 more detainees than the old facility.[81]

During an inspection in the spring of 2004, the Army Inspector General inspection team found internal security problems at the camp, to include blind spots for guards along the perimeter, inadequate communications systems, and poorly constructed concertina barriers.[82] The team also pointed out detainee life-support issues at the camp, to include inadequate laundry services and the location of a water source near a sewage point.[83]

On May 12, 2003, a serious incident of detainee abuse involving multiple detainees and multiple military policemen occurred at Camp Bucca.[84] The abuse involved the battering of several detainees by military policemen, to include one detainee having his nose broken.[85] An Army criminal investigation followed, and this investigation's final report substantiated Cruelty and Maltreatment of Detainees and other violations of the Uniform Code of Military Justice against 10 military policemen for the incident.[86] Despite this serious incident of abuse, the Red Cross would report in February 2004 that interrogators at Camp Bucca were not abusing detainees to the degree that their counterparts at Camp Cropper and (especially) Abu Ghraib were abusing detainees. Significantly, this Red Cross report contained no allegations that suggested that Camp Bucca interrogators were using enhanced interrogation techniques: according to the report, although interrogators at Camp Bucca would curse and verbally threaten their subjects, "none of those interviewed by the ICRC [International Committee of the Red Cross] in Um Qasr and Camp Bucca spoke of physical ill-treatment during interrogation."[87]

Nonetheless, one case of substantiated interrogation abuse occurred at Camp Bucca. A counterintelligence specialist (not an interrogator) was questioning three detainees when one of the detainees tried to strike his questioner.[88] The soldier responded by punching the detainee in the left eye with a closed fist.[89] This instance of violence, however, had nothing to do with enhanced interrogation techniques but rather was due to the inexperience of the questioner.

Throughout OIF I, military policemen at Camp Bucca had the ability to induct new detainees into the coalition detention system. However, Abu Ghraib Prison assumed primary responsibility for this function after CJTF-7 consolidated its detention operations at Abu Ghraib Prison on October 1, 2003. Subsequently, even if a criminal or insurgent were captured just outside Camp Bucca's gates, the camp's soldiers had to make the two-day roundtrip to take the detainee to Abu Ghraib for initial induction and interrogation.[90] With regard to the release of detainees, Camp Bucca released detainees during OIF I by dropping them off at a nearby Iraqi bus station with sufficient cash to purchase a ticket home.[91] This release procedure did not change until Major General Geoffrey Miller became Deputy Commander for Detainee Operations of Multi-National Force-Iraq, at which time he required Camp Bucca to transport all detainees to Abu Ghraib for release.[92]

Camp Cropper

By the time CJTF-7 assumed control of Camp Cropper, this camp contained two segregated facilities, the main Camp Cropper camp and a Special Confinement Facility.[93] This Special Confinement Facility was reserved for High Value Detainees.[94] High Value Detainees were primarily senior political members of Saddam's regime; for example, any captured Iraqi from the "deck of 55"– the 55 most wanted fugitives as pictured on a deck of playing cards issued to coalition forces– were held in this special facility.[95]

CJTF-7's major subordinate commands were responsible for transporting detainees to Camp Cropper. Once at Camp Cropper, military policemen from the 115th MP Battalion would induct all new detainees. After detention and possibly interrogation, the camp's soldiers would either transport detainees to Camp Bucca (Iraq's "theater internment facility" for the first half of OIF I) or release them. When releasing detainees, soldiers transported detainees in a coalition-owned passenger bus (nicknamed the "freedom bus") to a release point near their point of capture.[96]

Although the main camp at Camp Cropper had been built to hold no more than 450 detainees,[97] it held approximately 1200 detainees by July 2003.[98] Dramatic overcrowding greatly contributed to the significant life support issues that Camp Cropper struggled with during the first few months of its existence. According to the Red Cross, Camp Cropper's problems at this time included inadequate showers, latrines, waste removal, bedding, food, and water stations for detainees.[99] It should be noted, though, that coalition forces themselves lacked adequate life support at this time in Iraq. The days of air-conditioned tents, giant buffet-style dining facilities, a large post exchange, and even restaurants had not yet arrived for coalition forces at the airport (though these days would arrive impressively fast). Just as living conditions were to dramatically improve for coalition soldiers at the airport as the summer progressed, living conditions were to also greatly improve for detainees at Camp Cropper. The Red Cross reported on August 3, 2003, that Camp Cropper had shown significant improvement with regard to all life support issues, and detainees were even being afforded such Geneva rights as elected representation at regular meetings with camp authorities.[100]

More troubling than poor living conditions, however, was the Red Cross's forwarding in early July 2003 of a list of 50 cases alleging detainee abuse by interrogators at Camp Cropper.[101] The Red Cross alleged that Camp Cropper interrogators were communicating threats to subjects (to include threatening to intern subjects indefinitely, to arrest family members, or to transfer subjects to Gitmo); hooding subjects; employing "stress positions (kneeling, squatting, standing with arms raised above head) for three or four hours;" "taking aim at individuals with rifles;" striking sources "with rifle butts, slaps, punches;" and forcing subjects to endure "prolonged exposure to the sun" and "isolation in dark cells."[102] The use of "isolation" in the High Value Detainee facility was allegedly especially severe, with detainees kept "in cells devoid of sunlight for nearly 23 hours a day."[103] Adding credibility to the Red Cross's allegations are the facts that, one, this abuse is generally consistent with what we know today about enhanced interrogation techniques, and two, at least three interrogators at Camp Cropper had previous experience in Afghanistan, where the use of some of these techniques had been formally promulgated as interrogation policy.[104]

Additionally, the Red Cross alleged that some detainees had been beaten at a nearby location before being taken to Camp Cropper.[105] This is consistent with an allegation later made by a member of the Iraqi Survey Group that special operations soldiers at a location close to Camp Cropper (almost certainly Camp Nama) were beating detainees before transporting them to Camp Cropper or after checking detainees out of the facility.[106] When Colonel (Retired) Stu Herrington inspected Camp Cropper in December 2003, he forwarded a similar allegation to CJTF-7 leadership. This allegation is also consistent with testimonies collected in the Senate Armed Services Committee's report "Inquiry into the Treatment of Detainees in U.S. Custody" as well as various open-source reports regarding physical abuse at Camp Nama.[107]

More than half a year after the Red Cross's allegations of abuse at Camp Cropper, Lieutenant Colonel Natalie Lee investigated the allegation that special operations soldiers had beaten detainees interned at Camp Cropper. Lee concluded that she could find insufficient evidence to substantiate this allegation.[108] According to the Church Report, however, Lieutenant Colonel Lee's report was "extremely brief and cursory, and there were obvious gaps in the investigation methodology."[109] Most importantly, the Church Report noted, she did not locate or interview certain key personnel.[110] (Due to the long passage of time between her investigation and the alleged incidents, these key personnel had already left Iraq.)[111] The Church Report concluded that this "passage of time is unexplained, and represents a lost opportunity to address potential detainee abuse in Iraq early on."[112]

Due to the large number of allegations of abuse at Camp Cropper during its first 3-4 months of existence, the February 2004 Red Cross report put the camp on its short list of the "main places of internment" where alleged detainee abuse had taken place during the previous year.[113] In this report, though, it was noted that soon after forwarding the initial 50 cases of alleged abuse to coalition forces, these alleged practices by Camp Cropper interrogators "declined significantly and even stopped."[114] Conversely, the same Red Cross report stated that its earlier allegations concerning abuse at Abu Ghraib had not only not stopped but had actually been adopted as part of the facility's "standard operating procedures"– an allegation later substantiated by investigators.[115]

Abu Ghraib

After the Abu Ghraib Prison re-opened, CJTF-7's major subordinate units were responsible for taking captured Iraqis to this facility for induction and internment. The Abu Ghraib prison consisted of three separate facilities– the hard site (or main prison building), Camp Vigilant, and Camp Ganci.[116] Although the hard site was a Coalition Provisional Authority-supervised, Iraqi-run detention site for criminals, the 205th MI Brigade Headquarters successfully coordinated with the Coalition Provisional Authority for interrogators to use cells in the Tier 1 section of the hard site.[117] These 40 Tier I cells, which was where the most infamous Abu Ghraib abuses would occur, were employed to hold detainees for immediate interrogation.[118] The advantage of using these cells to house subjects for interrogation was that these detainees could be segregated so that they could not brief each other regarding interrogations.[119]

Camp Ganci was built to hold up to 4,000 criminal detainees, but by March 2004, this eight-compound camp held 5,000 detainees.[120] Camp Vigilant, the long-term holding pen for suspected insurgents (or "Security Internees"), was built to hold no more than 400 detainees.[121] Yet, its population grew to nearly 1,000 detainees by March 2004.[122] In fact, both the hard site and Camp Vigilant were overcrowded as early as November 2003.[123] Compounding the overcrowding issue was the extremely poor guard-to-detainee ratio: for instance, there were only 90 military policemen in charge of 7,000 detainees at the facility in October 2003.[124] Investigators would also note that the 320th MP Battalion, which had transferred from Camp Bucca (where several members had participated in the cases of detainee abuse described above), was running Abu Ghraib.

The Abu Ghraib detention facility suffered from frequent mortar attacks, sometimes with deadly results. These attacks included a mortar attack on August 16, 2003, that killed five detainees and injured 67 other detainees;[125] a mortar attack on September 20, 2003, that killed two U.S. soldiers and injured 11 other soldiers (including the commander of the Joint Interrogation Center);[126] and a mortar attack on April 20, 2004, that left 22 detainees dead and more than 100 injured.[127] In their February 2004 report, the Red Cross pointed out that placing the detainees in this facility at such grave risk constituted a violation of Article 83 of the Fourth Geneva Convention, which states that detainees cannot be interned in areas "particularly exposed to the dangers of war."[128] The Army Inspector General team that visited Abu Ghraib in the spring of 2004 also pointed out significant life support issues at the facility, to include a "deteriorating infrastructure" and "poor food quality and food distribution, lack of laundry capability, and inadequate personal hygiene facilities."[129]

On August 4, 2003, 14 interrogators from Company A, 519th MI Battalion, (including Captain Wood and one warrant officer) arrived at the facility to begin conducting interrogations.[130] Previously, this unit had returned home at the end of January 2003 from Bagram Air Base in Afghanistan, where they had been introduced to SERE techniques.[131] In fact, Army CID was still investigating two of these 14 interrogators for alleged abuse in Afghanistan that had resulted in the deaths of two detainees.[132] (This investigation would ultimately substantiate the charges against these two interrogators. Unsurprisingly, these same two interrogators would sexually assault a female detainee on October 7, 2003, at the Abu Ghraib detention facility.) As discussed in Chapter 3, soon after arrival, Wood's interrogators began using the harsh interrogation techniques of "sleep adjustment" and "stress positions" at Abu Ghraib.

The Red Cross visited Abu Ghraib on October 9-12 and 21-23, 2003, just when the worst, most criminal abuses at the facility had begun.[133] In a subsequent November report, the Red Cross's inspectors gave to coalition forces a long list of abusive interrogation practices at the facility– a report that Lieutenant General Sanchez later testified he had personally reviewed.[134]

Although the Abu Ghraib scandal would mainly involve soldiers of the 372nd MP Company, a reserve unit based out of Maryland that had just arrived in country before the most infamous photographed abuses,[135] two military intelligence soldiers would also be imprisoned for their role in detainee abuse at the facility. One of the Army investigators into the Abu Ghraib scandal, Major General Fay, would find 16 cases of detainee abuse that had been allegedly committed by military policemen at the instigation of interrogators.[136] Fay would find an additional 11 cases of alleged abuse in which military intelligence soldiers had been directly involved.[137] It should be noted here, however, that Fay also classified as abuse the enhanced techniques of "Use of Military Working Dogs," "Forced Nudity," and "Isolation"– techniques believed to be authorized by the interrogators who used them.

"Short-lived and poorly drafted" interrogation policies [138]

During the first few months of OIF I, U.S. Central Command, Coalition Forces Land Component Command, and CJTF-7 did not publish any policy governing interrogation approaches in Iraq.[139] During this time period, the only document that maneuver divisions in Iraq could turn to for interrogation guidance was Field Manual 34-52, *Intelligence Interrogation* (September 1992).

One of the recommendations of Major General Miller's Gitmo team, which inspected CJTF-7's interrogation operations from August 31 to September 9, 2003, was that CJTF-7 establish written guidance "specifically addressing interrogation policies and authorities" for dissemination to units.[140] The Miller Report stated that the CJTF-7 staff had already begun to work on such a policy at the time of the report's writing.[141] Part of the staffing process for this policy probably included the initial request for a "wish list" of interrogation techniques– a request which was emailed out by a CJTF-7 J2X captain on August 14, 2003, and which was discussed in Chapter 1.

Within a week of the departure of Major General Miller's Gitmo team, Lieutenant General Sanchez signed CJTF-7's first interrogation policy. In this September

---

INTERROGATION RULES OF ENGAGEMENT

Approved approaches for All detainees:
- Direct
- Incentive
- Incentive Removal
- Emotional Love / Hate
- Fear Up Harsh
- Fear Up Mild
- Reduced Fear
- Pride & Ego Up
- Futility
- We Know All
- Establish Your Identity
- Repetition
- File & Dossier
- Rapid Fire
- Silence

Require CG's Approval:
- Change of scenery down
- Dietary Manip (monitored by med)
- Environmental Manipulation
- Sleep Adjustment (reverse sched)
- Isolation for longer than 30 days
- Presence of Mil Working Dogs
- Sleep Management (72 hrs max)
- Sensory Deprivation (72 hrs max)
- Stress Positions (no longer than 45 min)

Safeguards:
- Techniques must be annotated in questioning strategy
- Approaches must always be humane and lawful
- Detainees will NEVER be touched in a malicious or unwanted manner
- Wounded or medically burdened detainees must be medically cleared prior to interrogation
- The Geneva Conventions apply within CJTF-7

EVERYONE IS RESPONSIBLE FOR ENSURING COMPLIANCE TO THE IROE. VIOLATIONS MUST BE REPORTED IMMEDIATELY TO THE OIC.

The use of the techniques are subjects to the general safeguards as provided as well as specific guidelines implemented by the 205th MI Cdr, FM 34-52, and the Commanding General, CJTF-7

Figure 6) Interrogation Approaches Posted at Abu Ghraib, Oct-Dec 2003
Source: Captain Carolyn Wood, "Interrogation Rules of Engagement," *American Civil Liberties Union: Torture FOIA*, October-December 2003, http://www.aclu.org/projects/foiasearch/pdf/DODDOA003220.pdf (accessed April 30, 2009), 3.

14, 2003, policy memorandum, several enhanced interrogation techniques were formally authorized for use in CJTF-7.[142] These SERE techniques included "Dietary Manipulation," "Environmental Manipulation," "Sleep Adjustment," "Isolation," "Sleep Management," "Presence of Military Working Dog," "Yelling, Loud Music, and Light Control," "Deception," and "Stress Positions."[143] In addition, this list included an approach from the rescinded 1987 version of Field Manual 34-52. This approach was the "Mutt and Jeff" (or "good cop/bad cop") approach, and the CJTF-7 September policy memo warned that this technique should be used with caution since some countries might consider the use of this technique as "inconsistent" with Article 13 of the Third Geneva Convention.[144]

Six of the interrogation approaches and techniques listed in this September memo required commanding general approval for use on "enemy prisoners of war," though interrogators could still employ such harsh interrogation techniques as "Sleep Adjustment," "Dietary Manipulation," "Environmental Manipulation," "Sleep Management," and "Yelling, Loud Music, and Light Control" on their own.[145] However, the applicability of this restriction on the vast majority of detainees (suspected insurgents) was unclear because these detainees had been classified by Fragmentary Order 749 and other CJTF-7 orders as "Security Internees" rather than Enemy Prisoners of War.

Also, the Fay/Jones Report noted that CJTF-7 Headquarters was using the outdated, 1987 version of Field Manual 34-52 until at least June 9, 2004.[146] The use of this rescinded field manual caused the headquarters to wrongly incorporate the "Mutt and Jeff" technique in this interrogation policy memorandum. In fact, the number of such ambiguities and errors in this memorandum seem to suggest that this policy had been very hastily reviewed by the relevant staff sections of the CJTF-7 Headquarters– if reviewed at all.

Unlike at Gitmo, Rumsfeld's approval was never sought for the use of harsh techniques in Iraq: "As in Afghanistan," the Church Report stated, "interrogation policy in Iraq was developed and promulgated by the senior command in the theater."[147] Both Lieutenant General Sanchez and his superior officer, General Abizaid, testified before the Senate Armed Services Committee that they believed they had the authority to approve these techniques, despite the fact that such techniques ran counter to DoD directives and guidance. In fact, Lieutenant General Sanchez believed that, by specifying the harsh interrogation techniques that could be used, he was actually reducing the chance of abuse by "imposing standards and approval and oversight mechanisms."[148]

After approving the September memorandum, Lieutenant General Sanchez forwarded the memorandum to U.S. Central Command for review. Upon reviewing the memorandum, U.S. Central Command's lawyers deemed some of the memorandum's interrogation techniques to be "unacceptably aggressive."[149] It is unclear from unclassified sources why this was the case since these lawyers were probably familiar with similar techniques then being employed in Afghanistan. The reason for this determination probably had something to do with the fact that national policy had only exempted members of al Qaeda and the Taliban from Geneva protections in the event of "military necessity," and this exemption was commonly perceived at this time as not applying to detainees in Iraq. (Abu Musab Zarqawi had not yet affiliated his growing terrorist organization in Iraq with al Qaeda.) So, another interrogation policy was staffed at CJTF-7 and approved by Sanchez on October 12, 2003.[150]

Since the October policy no longer listed the enhanced interrogation techniques contained in the September memo, this policy seemed to be executing U.S. Central Command's intent of eliminating these "aggressive" techniques. However, since such techniques could still be submitted with "recommended safeguards" and a "legal review" to Sanchez for approval, the October memo actually allowed the continued use of such techniques under the same conditions these techniques had previously been used (that is, with Sanchez' approval).[151] As illustrated in Figure 6, this is certainly how Abu Ghraib interrogators understood the October memo.[152] What is more, because of newly added, ambiguous phrasing in this memo, some interrogators (again, most clearly those at Abu Ghraib) treated the October memo as if it were more permissive than the September memo, giving them the latitude at their level to employ certain SERE techniques.

One of the reasons for this permissive interpretation of the October memo was a sentence in this memo from the outdated, 1987 version of Field Manual 34-52. This new sentence stated that interrogators needed to control "all aspects of the interrogation, to include the lighting, heating and configuration of the interrogation room, as well as the food, clothing and shelter given to the security internee."[153] It is easy to see how interrogators may have thought such earlier CJTF-7 interrogation techniques as "Environmental Manipulation," "Dietary Manipulation," and "Light Control"[154] had simply migrated to this sentence of the October memo.[155] Furthermore, some interrogators at Abu Ghraib misinterpreted the October memo's injunction that interrogators must control even a detainee's clothing as a license to now use, without higher approval, the "Forced Nudity" technique they had become acquainted with during their previous deployments to either Afghanistan or Gitmo.[156] The fact that the October memo kept "Removal of Incentive" as a technique, which some interrogators mistook to potentially include the removal of clothing, reinforced this perception.[157]

Nearly as tragic was how interrogators misinterpreted the October memorandum with regard to the use of military working dogs.[158] The September memorandum had offered the "presence of military working dogs" as a technique that, with Lieutenant General Sanchez' approval, could be used to exploit the "Arab fear of dogs while maintaining security during interrogations." The October memorandum no longer listed the use of dogs as an interrogation technique, but it stated that, "should military working dogs be present during interrogations, they will be muzzled and under control of a handler at all times to ensure safety."[159] Colonel Warren later stated that the intent of the October memorandum had been to convey that military working dogs could be used as a means to control detainees (that is, as a thinly veiled threat against detainee misbehavior) and not as an interrogation technique.[160] However, due to the ambiguity of the phrasing in the October memorandum, almost as soon as military working dogs arrived at Abu Ghraib on November 20, 2003, interrogators began using these dogs as part of "Fear Up (Harsh)" interrogation approaches with the approval of Colonel Thomas Pappas, commander of the 205th MI Brigade.[161]

Many of CJTF-7's subordinate units did not immediately get the word that CJTF-7's September interrogation policy had been rescinded. One of these units was Combined Joint Special Operations Task Force-Arabian Peninsula (CJSOTF-AP), a task force that, according to news reports, included the Army's 5th and 10th Special Forces Groups.[162] After investigating allegations of interrogation abuse within CJSOTF-AP, Brigadier Richard Formica noted that this unit produced an interrogation policy on February 27, 2004, that referenced CJTF-7's September interrogation policy.[163]

Apparently, CJTSOTF-AP did not find out about CJTF-7's October 12, 2003, interrogation policy until May 29, 2004.[164] The problem here was in how CJTF-7 disseminated its October policy: the policy was simply posted on CJTF-7's classified website, and no one bothered to call units to ensure they were aware of the change to a less aggressive policy.[165]

Although CJTF-7 directed that its interrogators receive training on the non-doctrinal interrogation approaches outlined in its interrogation policy memoranda, it did not direct who would conduct this training– and who would train these unit trainers on the new techniques. Since this was the first time most interrogators in Iraq had seen these techniques, expecting they would know how to implement these techniques was (at best) an unrealistic expectation.

In short, thanks to incomplete and inconsistent Army doctrine; vague, ambiguous, and poorly promulgated CJTF-7 policy memoranda, and a lack of effective training on new interrogation techniques, various inspectors found a wide variety of interrogation techniques being employed by different units across Iraq during OIF I. The consequence of this variety was, in some cases, interrogation abuse. Speaking to this controversial issue, the Mikolashek Report noted, "The potential for abuse increases when interrogations are conducted in an emotionally-charged environment by untrained personnel who are unfamiliar with the approved interrogation approach techniques."[166]

Conclusions

Iraq was a tough environment for coalition units during OIF I. Many of the difficulties these units faced, however, could not have been prevented by U.S. civilian and military leaders during 2003. Most notably, since the U.S. military's leaders in the 1980s and 1990s had done a poor job of predicting the Clausewitzian "nature" of its next fight (hardly a singular occurrence in our nation's history), the U.S. Army was simply not built to wage large-scale counterinsurgency operations in 2003. The Army's kinetic mindset in 2003– the personality it had assumed during the previous decades of equipping, training, and doctrine– all but assured that, during that first terribly hot summer of OIF I, the feelings of triumph, even of invincibility experienced by coalition forces would quickly dissipate and be replaced by feelings of confusion, uneasiness, and desperation. It also guaranteed that the V Corps headquarters and many of its subordinate units would find themselves floundering as part of a force of occupation.

Still, the hard-working leaders and soldiers of CJTF-7 would probably have found a way to secure the Iraqi population if only CJTF-7 had been adequately resourced. As opposed to the character of the U.S. Army in 2003, the woefully inadequate resourcing of CJTF-7 did derive from poor decisions made by senior U.S. political and military leaders during 2003. It is hard to even understand today how CJTF-7 could have been so inadequately resourced. When the critics of the Bush Administration (and of Donald Rumsfeld and Paul Wolfowitz in particular) chalk up CJTF-7's lack of resources to poor assumptions and personal hubris, history may very well conclude that these critics are right.

Thanks to poor decisions made in Washington, the list of "not nearly enoughs" with regard to CJTF-7 was extensive: CJTF-7 did not have nearly enough ground troops to secure key sites in Iraq; the CJTF-7 headquarters did not have nearly enough personnel to function effectively; there were not nearly enough construction engineers to build adequate coalition detention facilities while simultaneously rebuilding Iraq's infrastructure; there were not nearly enough guards who had been trained in detention operations to prevent untrained detention personnel from unwittingly abusing detainees; there were not nearly enough military lawyers to ensure that, when innocent Iraqis were swept up with guilty Iraqis, these innocent Iraqis' cases could be promptly reviewed and these innocents released; and, most relevantly to this paper, there were not nearly enough HUMINT and DOCEX personnel supporting tactical missions in Iraq. Largely as a result of this shortage of key intelligence personnel, CJTF-7 often seemed a "black hole" when it came to providing intelligence to subordinate units. This black hole of intelligence at the CJTF-7 level left units like 1AD often seeing little sense to the requirement to rapidly expedite detainees and associated evidence to coalition holding facilities.

Although CJTF-7 cannot be blamed for its lack of resources, the headquarters can be blamed for at least a few bad decisions. Perhaps most unforgivably, based on his staff's recommendations, Lieutenant General Sanchez approved two interrogation policy memoranda that were at best, poorly considered and poorly written.[167] At the theater level, these memoranda set the stage for the systemic use of enhanced interrogation techniques at Abu Ghraib and various special operations facilities (and probably briefly at Camp Cropper as well). At the hands of a twisted few at Abu Ghraib, the systemic use of enhanced interrogation techniques devolved into the sadistic, sexualized violence that shamed a nation.

Unfortunately, the interrogation-related abuse at Abu Ghraib was not the only such abuse that occurred during OIF 1. In the next chapter, we explore the extent that enhanced interrogation techniques seeped down to the tactical level (division-sized units and lower) in Iraq.

CHAPTER 5

Tragic blunders

> *Everyone has evil in them. Everyone! Some have much more than others, but it doesn't hide the fact that we have all had evil thoughts against someone or some group for one reason or another in our lifetimes. The key is that the majority of us are strong enough both morally and ethically to know that when evil does taunt us with a decision, that it is our emotions that are out of sync and that our moral logic will win over in order to prevent us from making a decision in favor of evil. What happened at Abu Ghraib happened because there was a small group of soldiers there with weak moral logic who had enough evil in them to desire to carry out the acts that they did without feeling any remorse or understanding of consequences– even if they were supposedly told to do it.*[1]
>
> — Kenneth Kilbourne
> Chief Warrant Officer 3, Interrogator

> *The insurgents were doing much worse things to our troops and to Iraqis— not just torturing, but killing. Why couldn't this fact help me accept my own cruelty, which paled in comparison? It seemed to work for other people. Unfortunately, I learned, I believed in the highest moral principles embodied in the international ban on torture. I believed them, but I didn't live up to them. In the end, I did what I did because I wanted to. That has been very hard to accept.*[2]
>
> —Tony Lagouranis, Interrogator

Contrary to what the weight of media coverage conveys, the abuse of detainees by school-trained interrogators did not occur within the overwhelming majority of U.S. detention facilities in Iraq during Operation Iraqi Freedom I (OIF I). The Church Report, which took the Naval Inspector General's team 10 months to complete and which was based on more than 800 interviews and unfettered access to Department of Defense documentary evidence, concluded that there had been 16 substantiated cases of interrogation abuse in Iraq before September 30, 2004.[3] This list of documented interrogation abuses is not complete—there were still open cases from OIF I when the Church Report compiled this report—but it provides some indication where and under what circumstances this abuse occurred. Of the 16 cases listed by the Church Report, only six cases involved school-trained interrogators.[4] The other 10 cases involved harsh, unauthorized questioning by non-interrogators.[5] Nearly all of these latter cases seem to have been isolated incidents that occurred when immature, poorly trained soldiers let their emotions get the better of them.

There were, however, three tactical units that had detention facilities in which the use of enhanced interrogation techniques was apparently systemic. Additionally, there was a fourth unit in which interrogation-related abuse was perpetrated by a senior leader who should have known better. The interrogation abuse that occurred within these four units was not just wrong, inhumane, and un-American, the consequences of this abuse received a great deal of adverse international publicity—publicity that further reinforced the strategic defeat of Abu Ghraib. Additionally, these tragic blunders have added to the false impression of rampant interrogation abuse throughout Iraq, a perception that, unfortunately, will echo in history.

In this chapter, we review what took place at these units before considering the proper context of the unfortunate abuse that did occur.

Enhanced interrogations in Al Anbar

Few if any U.S. Army units are more legendary than the 3d Armored Cavalry Regiment (3ACR), currently stationed at Fort Carson, Colorado. This storied regiment has played a role in nearly every major U.S. conflict since the Mexican War. During the Gulf War, the 3ACR demonstrated its prowess in conventional warfare, with the regiment's tanks, infantry fighting vehicles, and Apache helicopters leaving a wake of destruction through three Iraqi divisions. Also, after OIF I, it evolved into a fine counterinsurgent force: as part of OIF III in 2005, Colonel H.R. McMaster masterfully led the regiment during the Battle of Tal Afar, an operation which is generally accepted to be a textbook example of the successful application of tactical counterinsurgent principles and which was one of the few bright spots during a very bad year for coalition forces in Iraq.

During OIF I, however, the 3ACR displayed more of the kinetic, conventional mindset it had shown to such awesome effect during the Gulf War than the effective counterinsurgent outlook it later demonstrated under McMaster's mentorship. Exacerbating its conventional mindset during OIF I was the fact that, as CJTF-7's smallest major subordinate command, it was drastically under-resourced for its mission of exercising military control of Al Anbar Province (a Sunni stronghold and the heart of the insurgency during the first years of Operation Iraqi Freedom). Since the 3ACR's leaders rightly considered themselves to be an "economy of force" operation, due to their limited experience as counterinsurgents, some mistook this to mean that they needed to be extremely aggressive in applying their limited resources.[6] This reasoning extended to interrogation operations, resulting in this unit being one of only three conventional, tactical-level units that aggressively applied enhanced interrogation techniques between May 2003 and April 2004 in Iraq.

In a February 2004 report, the Red Cross summarized its major findings concerning the treatment of detainees from March to November 2003 in 14 U.S. facilities in Iraq.[7] This report listed two facilities at the CJTF-7 level (Abu Ghraib and Camp Cropper) that it assessed as "main places of internment where mistreatment allegedly took place."[8] At the division or brigade level, it assessed three facilities as being centers of alleged detainee abuse: one (and perhaps two) of these three facilities belonged to the 3ACR. The Red Cross described the facility that clearly belonged to the 3ACR as located in "a former train station in Al-Khaim, near the Syrian border, turned into a military base."[9] This description matches descriptions in court testimony of "Forward Operating Base Tiger," operated by the 1st Squadron of the 3ACR.[10] The Red Cross also described a center of detainee abuse as the "Al-Baghdadi, Heat Base and Habbania Camp in Ramadi governorate"[11] While units of the 3ACR operated in the Al Habbaniyah area during the timeframe (July-August 2003) of the Red Cross's allegations of abuse at this facility, the U.S. Army's cursory criminal investigation into this allegation failed to even uncover whether a conventional Army or Special Forces unit had committed this alleged abuse.[12] The Red Cross report was disturbing, though, with 25 detainees alleging at Abu Ghraib that, during their previous internments at Al Habbaniyah, they had undergone such mistreatment as painful stress positions, forced nudity, beatings, dog attacks, and sleep deprivation—all allegations consistent with the use of enhanced interrogation techniques.[13]

There is no question, though, that the 3ACR operated the detention facility on Forward Operating Base (FOB) Tiger. In 2005 and again in 2006, Human Rights Watch interviewed a military police sergeant who had served as a guard at the facility from May 2003 to September 2003.[14] This guard's testimony corroborated the Red Cross's 2004 allegations of abuse at this facility. According to this military policeman, he routinely witnessed interrogation abuse at the facility. This sergeant alleged that guards were regularly ordered to subject detainees to sleep deprivation, dangerously high temperatures, hunger and thirst, and, while facing a wall, prolonged standing (up to 24 hours).[15] He also alleged that he witnessed interrogators beating detainees, threatening them with loaded weapons, and subjecting them to bright strobe lights and loud music.[16] According to this sergeant, both Army (including Special Forces soldiers) and CIA interrogators conducted these abusive interrogations.[17]

Since this guard was describing enhanced interrogation techniques that were common to those facilities that employed such techniques, it seems unlikely that he fabricated these allegations. Moreover, the described techniques are consistent with specific techniques (such as "wall standing") described in recently declassified CIA memoranda.[18]

Unfortunately, the use of enhanced interrogation techniques was not limited to the squadron detention facility at FOB Tiger; these techniques were also employed at FOB Rifles (the 3ACR Regimental Holding Area at Al Asad Air Field) as well as at a temporary detention facility that the regiment established east of Al Qaim for an operation called "Operation Rifles Blitz."[19] Like the FOB Tiger facility, this temporary facility was also located at a train station.[20] The nickname of this facility was "Blacksmith Hotel."[21] The senior interrogator in charge of interrogation operations at these two regimental facilities was Chief Warrant Officer Lewis Welshofer.

As described in Chapter One, Welshofer's response to the request for a "wish list" of interrogation techniques was that CJTF-7 should adopt "a baseline interrogation technique that at a minimum allows for physical contact resembling that used by SERE instructors."[22] He went on to recommend "open-handed facial slaps" as a technique as well as "close confinement quarters, sleep deprivation, white noise, and a litany [sic] of harsher fear-up approaches . . . fear of dogs and snakes appear to work nicely."[23] When CJTF-7 published a permissive interrogation policy on September 14, 2003, that seemed to permit some SERE techniques, Welshofer apparently felt he had permission to use all of the techniques he had previously learned as a SERE instructor. Welshofer applied one of these techniques, "close confinement quarters," in a particularly brutal manner, often wrapping detainees in a sleeping bag to induce feelings of claustrophobia.

This "interrogation technique" would have tragic results. On November 26, 2003, Welshofer interrogated Iraqi Major General Abed Mowhoush at "Blacksmith Hotel."[24] At the end of this interrogation, Welshofer placed Mowhoush in a sleeping bag. Then, Welshofer wrapped the bag tightly with electrical cord, sat on him, and covered his mouth with his hand.[25] Within minutes, the 56-year-old general was dead. Mowhoush's death certificate later listed his cause of death as "asphyxia due to smothering and chest compression," and a December 2, 2003, autopsy stated that Mowhoush had, prior to his death, received numerous "contusions and abrasions" along with six fractured ribs."[26] The fractured ribs were apparently due to a group of Iraqis (who allegedly worked for the CIA) severely beating Mowhoush during an interrogation two days before Mowhoush's death.[27]

This was not the only interrogation-related death in the 3ACR. Five weeks after the conclusion of Operation Rifles Blitz, 47-year-old Lieutenant Colonel Abdul Jameel died during an interrogation at FOB Rifles on Al Asad Airfield. Noteworthy, Welshofer was in Qatar on rest and relaxation leave when this incident occurred, illustrating that his presence was not necessary for the use of brutal tactics at the facility.[28] According to a *Denver Post* article allegedly based on leaked military documents, before dying, Jameel had been kept in an isolation cell with his arms chained to a pipe in the ceiling.[29] When released from these chains, he reportedly lunged at a Special Forces soldier, causing three Special Forces soldiers to allegedly punch and kick him "for approximately one to two minutes."[30] This article states that Jameel later escaped and was recaptured.[31] Upon recapture, his hands were allegedly tied to the top of his cell door, and at some point, he was gagged.[32] Five minutes later, a soldier noticed he was dead.[33/34] Another article in the *New York Times* is more specific about Jameel's gagging, alleging that a "senior Army legal official acknowledged that the Iraqi colonel had at one point been lifted to his feet by a baton held to his throat, and that that action had caused a throat injury that contributed to his death."[35]

The coroner who performed Jameel's autopsy identified the cause of death as "homicide," describing Jameel's body as showing signs of "multiple blunt force injuries" and a "history of asphyxia."[36] An Army criminal investigation was also completed. This investigation recommended charging 11 soldiers from both the 5th Special Forces Group and the 3ACR with crimes related to Jameel's homicide.[37] Two of these soldiers, this report recommended, should be charged with Negligent Homicide and nine others charged with crimes ranging from Assault to False Official Statement.[38] Inexplicably (considering the investigating agent's recommendations and subsequent news reports), the commanders of these soldiers decided to ignore these recommendations altogether, determining that the detainee had died as "a result of a series of lawful applications of force in response to repeated aggression and misconduct by the detainee."[39]

As a result of the Army criminal investigation into Mowhoush's death, Welshofer's commanding general issued Welshofer a letter of reprimand. In his letter of rebuttal to this reprimand, the unrepentant warrant officer repeated a claim he had made in the email to the CJTF-7 captain, namely, that Army doctrine– patterned as it is on the Law of War– is insufficient for dealing with unlawful combatants.[40] Welshofer also referred to Jameel, saying that, before Jameel's death, Jameel had led soldiers to the location of a large explosives cache.[41] Welshofer used this example to justify his own harsh treatment of Mowhoush, saying that this cache had contained "thousands of potential IEDs [Improvised Explosive Devices]" and that the "bottom line is that what interrogators do is a dirty job but saves lives."[42] Despite his specious reasoning here (after all, just because Jameel knew where IED caches were does not mean that Mowhoush did), Welshofer was still charged with negligent homicide, and in January 2006, he was court martialed at Fort Carson, Colorado.

Welshofer's court martial was a media sensation. During his court martial, it was revealed that he had previously served as a SERE instructor in Hawaii.[43] Welshofer also claimed that the only CJTF-7 interrogation policy he had seen in Iraq had been the September 2003 policy (the policy that had explicitly authorized certain enhanced interrogation techniques). A warrant officer who had observed parts of Mowhoush's interrogation testified to a technique used by Welshofer on Mowhoush the day prior to Mowhoush's death that was essentially "waterboarding."[44] According to this warrant officer, Welshofer also hit Mowhoush repeatedly on his elbow with a stick.[45] Welshofer's use of a stick to strike Mowhoush, this warrant officer alleged, "was not that extreme when you consider other things that were happening at the facility."[46] Also, the company commander of these two warrant officers testified that she had authorized the "close quarters" or "sleeping bag" technique and that she had seen Welshofer slap detainees.[47] Disappointingly, despite damning evidence that Welshofer had implemented SERE techniques which had not been approved for use by U.S. soldiers and which had clearly contributed to Mowhoush's death, Welshofer received a sentence extremely controversial for its lightness—a letter of reprimand, restriction to his house and place of worship for two months, and a fine of $6,000.[48]

Just as disappointingly, in a related Article 32 hearing into Mowhoush's death, the 3ACR commander admitted to having known that his interrogators were employing the "sleep deprivation" technique and making detainees stand for hours "just to fatigue them."[49] During this hearing, lawyers also described how this commander had made the case to his supervisor, the 82nd Airborne Division Commander, that the punishment for the soldiers allegedly involved in Mowhoush's death should be either eliminated or reduced.[50] Apparently, this commander thought administrative letters of reprimand were too severe of a punishment for soldiers charged with homicide. In his testimony, this commander excused his soldiers' crimes, citing their lack of training and his belief that Mowhoush's death had been "accidental."[51] (One wonders if this commander believed his soldiers' abusive treatment of Mowhoush to also be unintentional.) In light of this commander's perspective, it becomes perhaps less inexplicable why punishment was non-existent in the case of Lieutenant Colonel Jameel's homicide.

In summary, the 3ACR systematically used enhanced interrogation techniques in at least three interrogation facilities belonging to two units. The use of these techniques contributed to the negligent homicides of two detainees, and, no doubt, to the creation of scores of embittered insurgents from the ranks of the interrogated. The decision to use such methods derived from the core ethical position (the "ends justify the means") adopted by more than one key leader in the 3ACR. Additionally, Welshofer's previous experience as a SERE instructor seemingly colored his vision as to acceptable interrogation techniques, and his supervisors lacked the experience (not to mention the good moral sense) to understand that the enhanced techniques promulgated by Welshofer were illegal, un-American, and violated numerous directives and policies.

Moreover, when leadership uncovered serious cases of interrogation abuse, it did not put a quick end to this abuse with the exacting of swift justice. In fact, justice in the two cases of homicide described above seems to have been largely non-existent. It is thus unsurprising that this abuse allegedly continued in these facilities. One sergeant testified, for example, that after Mowhoush's death, Welshofer "got a hold" of another sleeping bag to use to interrogate detainees.[52]

Ultimately, the media controversy resulting from Welshofer's court martial, though not a strategic defeat of the magnitude of Abu Ghraib, added to the anti-U.S. battle cry of jihadists and reinforced the U.S. military's loss of moral standing among Americans.

Macabre dances at two "discos" in Mosul

Perhaps because the detention facility of the 2nd Brigade Combat Team (2BCT), 101st Airborne Division, did not become an enduring facility until November 13, 2003,[53] this facility was not listed as an alleged center of detainee abuse in the February 2004 report of the Red Cross. Nonetheless, it is clear from testimonies and documentary evidence that, for several months at the end of OIF I, this facility resembled a SERE school far more than it resembled a typical U.S. Army interrogation facility.

The name for this 2BCT facility was the "Strike" Brigade Holding Area—an ironically appropriate name due to the apparent penchant of its guards and interrogators for striking detainees with water bottles. According to Tony Lagouranis, co-author of *Fear Up Harsh* and a former interrogator at the facility, soldiers and local Iraqis nicknamed the Strike Brigade Holding Area "the disco" because of the loud music and bright lights that often emanated from it. Also, on the same Mosul airfield, a Navy SEAL (Sea, Air, Land) special warfare team not only employed enhanced interrogation techniques in the team's make-shift interrogation room inside a military shipping container, but also may have used these techniques in an even more brutal manner than they are applied at U.S. military SERE courses. According to at least one Army investigator, this SEAL team's interrogation room was also nicknamed "the disco."

Less than one month after the Strike Brigade Holding Area was established as an enduring facility (that is, a facility that could hold detainees for a few days rather than a few hours), two incidents occurred at this facility that generated serious criminal investigations. These investigations, in turn, would describe the systemic use of enhanced interrogation techniques there.

The first incident occurred on the morning of December 9, 2003, when a detainee named Abu Malik Kenami died at the facility.[54] At the time, U.S. forces had no means of conducting an autopsy in Iraq, so the body was turned over to a local Iraqi mortician.[55] Since there was no autopsy done and the circumstances of Kenami's death as described by U.S. soldiers did not seem to indicate a single murderous act, neither the investigating officer from the 101st Airborne Division nor the CID agent who investigated Kenami's death concluded that U.S. forces had killed Kenami.[56] Indeed, the Army investigating officer concluded that Kenami had probably died from a heart attack (a strangely incongruous conclusion considering that the U.S. doctor who did Kenami's post-mortem exam stated that the most likely causes of death was either an infectious disease or hypothermia).[57] Despite the inability of the Army investigating officer or CID agent to find sufficient evidence to justify a conclusion of homicide in Kenami's death, they did uncover harsh treatment that most Americans would consider abuse.

Two days after Kenami's death, a teenaged detainee had his jaw broken during an interrogation at this facility. The detainee alleged that his jaw broke when he was struck by an interrogator; the U.S. soldiers who were present stated that the teenager's jaw broke when he collapsed from exhaustion during forced physical training. This case would later make the Church Report's list of six confirmed cases of detainee abuse committed by a school-trained interrogator during OIF I.[58]

The investigations into these two incidents revealed systemic interrogation-related abuse at the facility. Harsh tactics employed at the facility included the following practices:

1. Detainees slept on the floor under a blanket in a crowded, unheated general population cell. Both the doctor at the facility and the company commander stated that they had requested space heaters to warm the facility.[59] The company commander alleged that the response of a senior staff officer in the brigade to his request for space heaters had been, "Fuck 'em, they can freeze."[60] This senior staff officer's response, if true, is especially ugly in the wake of the suggestion by the doctor who did Kenami's post-mortem exam that Kenami may have died from hypothermia.

2. None of the soldiers serving at this facility were military police guards trained in detention operations. Instead, guards serving at this facility were assigned to the 1st Battalion-502 Infantry; the 1st Battalion, 327th Infantry; and the 2nd Battalion, 44th Air Defense Artillery.[61] Thus, there was no protest from any of these guards or their leaders when guards were asked to perform tasks that ran contrary to existing detention doctrine. According to the posted rules for this guard force, guards were expected to set the conditions for successful interrogations by "providing appropriate mental stress on detainees."[62] Mental stress combined with firm control, this document said, "can greatly weaken a detainee's will."[63] The rules did say that guards could not "inflict bodily harm," apparently meaning that guards were not allowed to strike detainees with enough force to cause lasting physical damage to them.[64] However, guards were told that they could administer "physical labor as corrective training" for a time period that "must not exceed two consecutive hours."[65] Typically, this "physical labor" consisted of "smoke" sessions (a term soldiers become familiar with during their basic training) in which detainees would do knee bends, arm raises, or "flutter kicks."[66] Before Kenami's death, for example, guards repeatedly used knee bends to "smoke" Kenami because he kept talking and lifting his sandbag hood.[67] (In hindsight, Kenami may have been doing this so he could breathe better, since he was apparently ill). Similarly, an interrogator was "smoking" the teenager when the teenager's jaw was broken.

3. The investigation into the teenager's broken jaw concluded "the detainees were being systematically and intentionally mistreated (heavy metal music, bullhorn, hit with water bottles, forced to perform repetitive physical exercises until they could not stand, having cold water thrown on them, deprived of sleep, and roughly grabbed off the floor when they could no longer stand.)"[68] Additionally, some detainees (such as this particular teenager) had the letters "IED" written on their sandbag hoods, which the guards believed was intended to make the guards angry and which the investigating officer said "had exactly this effect."[69] (See Figure 7 for this investigating officer's "Synopsis of Witness Statements" regarding the facility's systemic use of enhanced interrogation techniques.)[70]

> ▅▅▅▅ 1/502: We "always harassed the hell out of the detainees." They always told us to "smoke the detainees, but to not physically harm them."
>
> I saw the Chief throw them down, put his knee in his neck and back and grind them into the floor. He would use a bull-horn and yell at them in Arabic and play heavy metal music extremely loud, they got so scared they would urinate on themselves. He was very aggressive and rough with the detainees
>
> We were told to only feed them crackers & water (may have been because of late hour)
>
> ▅▅▅▅ 1/502: They were setting it up to make the infantry guys angry by writing IED on the sand bags over their heads.
>
> ▅▅▅▅ of Guard Detail) 3/327: We would force them to stay awake, by banging on metal doors, playing loud music, screaming at them all night - those were our instructions. We were told to not strike them.
>
> ▅▅▅▅ & ▅▅▅▅ 3/327: Our instructions were to keep them awake, smoke them, yell at them, but to not hurt them.
>
> ▅▅▅▅, 2/44: We "hazed" the detainees – we had a lot fall and hurt themselves
>
> ▅▅▅▅ 1/502; ▅▅▅▅ had IED on the sandbag over his head, the guards were all over him, screaming at him things like "you like to use IED's motherfucker), and smoking him extra. They were smoking him really hard when I heard him cry in pain (he could have been hit or fell).
>
> ▅▅▅▅ 3/327: A lot of detainees had IED written on their bags. I was near ▅▅▅▅ when he fell and I helped him up. Interpreters (ICDC) blew cigarette smoke up their sand bag hoods. They also poured water on them to get them up, after the were exhausted from being smoked.
>
> ▅▅▅▅ 3/327: "We were yelling in a bullhorn at the detainees, making them do PT, things like flutter kicks, ups and downs, stuff like that." We knew we were supposed to do these things because MI was already doing this stuff when we got there. He did not say it was part of the SOP. He stated, "we were briefed to keep them awake, do not let them talk, and to not hurt them." I had seen "detainees collapse before because of the intensive physical training."

Figure 7) Synopsis of Witness Statements
Source: 101st Airborne Division Headquarters, "Report of Proceedings by Investigating Board/Board of Officers," American Civil Liberties Union: Torture FOIA, December 20, 2003, http://www.aclu.org/projects/foiasearch/pdf/DODDOA026578.pdf (accessed August 13, 2009), 5-6.

Although these incidents were investigated promptly, it does not appear that anyone was actually punished for the incidents. The investigating officer into the teenager's broken jaw recommended a General Officer's Memorandum of Reprimand for one unidentified soldier, whose name is redacted in the documentation released by the U.S. Army about this incident.[71] Based on another released document– a request to the assistant division commander (ADC) for the 101st Airborne Division that the commander of Company B, 311th MI Battalion, receive no punishment in this case– it is probable that it was this company commander who was recommended for punishment.[72] Handwritten comments on the request for clemency indicate that the ADC agreed with the requestor's reasoning.[73]

The light or non-existing punishment in these two cases was ineffective in deterring future abuse at this facility. As a result, although the officer investigating the teenager's broken jaw reported "all deficiencies at the Strike BHA [Brigade Holding Area] have been corrected," the treatment of detainees at the facility actually grew more harsh.[74]

Tony Lagouranis worked as an interrogator at the Strike Brigade Holding Area during the spring of 2004. According to him, he and other interrogators at this facility routinely employed such techniques as "sleep deprivation, exposure to severe cold, forced exercises and use of painful stress positions, use of guard dogs to intimidate blindfolded detainees, and use of loud music and strobe lights to disorient detainees and keep them awake."[75] In other words, according to this interrogator, the facility actually added a new enhanced interrogation technique after the two December incidents, specifically, the use of military working dogs to inspire fear in certain interrogation subjects.

According to Lagouranis, the warrant officer in charge of interrogations at the facility provided him with an "Interrogation Rules of Engagement" card that sanctioned these harsh techniques.[76] Lagouranis said that he thought these techniques might have come from Afghanistan and were outdated, but he was unsure.[77] Since Lagouranis had arrived at the Strike Brigade Holding Area from Abu Ghraib, a facility that was still using enhanced interrogation techniques when he had worked there, it is disappointing but not surprising that he failed to question whether such techniques were legal and morally acceptable.

In *Fear Up Harsh*, Lagouranis depicts the 311th MI Battalion warrant officer at the facility as the driving force behind the facility's use of enhanced interrogation techniques. If Lagouranis is right, then this warrant officer probably possessed pre-Iraq experience with SERE techniques (much as Welshofer, his peer in the 3ACR, possessed such a background). Afghanistan, the theater from which Lagouranis said he believed the facility's list of interrogation techniques came, is a likely candidate for this previous experience: Kayla Williams, an Arabic linguist who authored the Iraq memoir, *Love My Rifle More than You*, has alleged that, at the Strike Brigade Holding Area, she had been directed to belittle the manhood of nude detainees—a harsh version of the technique uniquely approved by CJTF-180 policy for use in Afghanistan labeled "the use of female interrogators to create 'discomfort' and gain more information."[78] She has also alleged that she witnessed interrogators "smack" a prisoner across the face, reminiscent of the technique of "mild physical contact" approved for use in Afghanistan.[79] Interestingly, she has written that after the Abu Ghraib scandal, she talked to the warrant officer in charge of this facility, and he told her that he believed those "at the highest levels" had made it permissible for them to disregard the Geneva Conventions.[80]

It is all but certain that these two published authors, Lagouranis and Williams, are talking about the same warrant officer, since there is no evidence of any other warrant officers from the 311th MI Company running interrogation operations for the 2nd Brigade (though it is possible that they are talking about two different warrant officers in the same direct-support MI company). More certainly, documentary evidence attests that the company commander in charge of the interrogators at the Strike Brigade Holding Area had attended a U.S. Army SERE school, reinforcing the strong linkage between the use of enhanced interrogation techniques in Iraq and the previous experience of junior leaders with these techniques either at SERE schools or in other theaters.[81]

Lagouranis's allegations regarding the continued use of enhanced interrogation techniques at the facility after December 2003 are corroborated by other testimony. Two Iraqis alleged to a British lawyer that they had been abused in early 2004 at a U.S. facility at the Mosul airport called "the disco."[82] According to one of these Iraqis, he had been handcuffed, hooded, left standing for hours, kicked hard in the stomach, beaten continuously with a stick, and awakened with cold water.[83] The other detainee alleged that he had been "forced into painful stress positions and doused with cold water."[84] It is unclear from this testimony, however, which of the airfield's "discos" held these two prisoners.

Another detainee alleged to a U.S. Army criminal investigator that, while being held at the Mosul airfield in a facility he called "the disco," his jumpsuit was filled with ice; he was held down and punched on his head; he was hit with "smooth rocks"; he was punched again, resulting in two broken molars; water was poured in his nose and mouth (that is, he was waterboarded); and he was forced to stand in front of an air conditioner in wet clothes.[85] He also alleged that someone rubbed his face in urine on the floor.[86] In *Fear Up Harsh*, Lagouranis admits that he had interrogated this detainee and that, during the interrogation, he had employed the enhanced interrogation techniques of bright lights, loud noise stress positions, sleep deprivation, and use of military working dogs.[87] However, Lagouranis disputed the urine charge, saying:

> Another disturbing thing about this interview was the inclusion of Jafar Ali Abdul Naser. He'd claimed a series of abuses by the SEALs and by me, but he'd evidently padded out his complaint. Special Agent Porter read from his sworn statement that an interrogator had pissed on the floor of the discotheque, and then we forced Jafar's face into it. This was a lie. He did wet his pants when we got the dogs to act up, and we taunted him about that, but we never got so physical with him or pushed his face in the puddle he left on the ground. We certainly didn't piss on the floor ourselves. I explained to Special Agent Porter exactly what we had done, which was bad enough in itself. Porter said that that investigation was going to be conducted in the near future. I expected to hear from him again about it, but I never did.[88]

The Army agent who investigated this detainee's allegations concluded that the detainee's medical screening report at Abu Ghraib, which indicated "bruising around his right eye and face and a broken right molar," was too ambiguous to support the detainee's story.[89]

Throughout this investigation, this agent referred to the military shipping container used by the Navy Seal Team for interrogations as "the disco," seemingly unaware that the Strike Brigade Holding Area was also called "the disco." Speaking to this agent's apparent confusion, Lagouranis states in *Fear Up Harsh* that he may have confused this agent by talking about his own unit's discotheque.[90] Although Lagouranis later alleged that he had told this agent about his use of enhanced interrogation techniques on this subject, there is no mention in the agent's report of Lagouranis's purported confession. This report concludes that "if the alleged offenses occurred they were perpetrated by members of the U.S. Navy or Marine Corps."[91]

Yet another detainee being held at Abu Ghraib in June 2004 alleged that, two months previously, he had been tortured during interrogations on the airfield. According to the CID agent who investigated the incident, members of a Navy SEAL team (NSWRON-7) captured and interrogated this detainee.[92] This time, the allegations of abuse exclusively involved interrogations in the SEAL team's interrogation facility (the airfield's second discotheque).[93] The SEAL team, this detainee alleged, hit him repeatedly on the neck when capturing him. Then, according to this detainee, this team took him to their "disco," and over the course of eight days, kept him naked while they poured cold water over him, hit him on his head, harassed him with loud noise, deprived him of sleep, and fed him almost no food.[94] He stated that when he was transferred to another facility on the camp (the Strike Brigade Holding Area), he physically collapsed and was taken to a field hospital.[95] He also alleged that, after he returned to this brigade holding area, the SEAL team picked him up and again tortured him during interrogations, to include burning him with a hot lamp.[96]

Physical evidence seemed to corroborate at least some of this detainee's allegations. The soldier at the Strike Brigade Holding Area who initially screened this detainee stated that he had seen suspicious bruising on this detainee's chest as well as recent scabs on his knees and feet.[97] Two weeks later, a second medical screening was conducted at the holding area after the SEAL team re-interrogated this detainee. The report from this medical screening indicated "2nd degree burns and singed tissue on his body," which, since he had not left U.S. custody, would seem to strongly corroborate this detainee's allegation of being burned by the SEAL team.[98] To explain these injuries, members of this SEAL team stated that any scratches and bruises on the detainee occurred when he had been thrown to the ground hard during capture.[99] One of the members also somewhat dubiously claimed that this detainee sometimes threw himself on rocks, and another team member stated that any scratches on this detainee's back were also self-inflicted upon a concrete wall.[100] Ultimately, the investigating agent concluded that further investigating the charges "would be of little or no value" and that "there was insufficient evidence to prove or disprove the allegations of Aggravated Assault, Cruelty and Maltreatment and Conspiracy."[101]

Unfortunately, probably the worst case of interrogation abuse at the Mosul airfield has not yet been described. This case occurred at the SEAL team's "disco" on April 5, 2004, when an Iraqi detainee named Fashad Mohammad died after what must have been an especially brutal interrogation.[102] It is unclear from the declassified documents that have been released regarding this case whether this detainee was in SEAL custody the entire time or temporarily transferred into Army custody.[103] What is clear is that he underwent extremely harsh interrogations. The Medical Examiner's report included the following statement:

> *This approximately 27 year-old male civilian, presumed Iraqi national, died in U.S. custody approximately 72 hours after being apprehended. By report, physical force was required during his initial apprehension during a raid. During his confinement, he was hooded, sleep deprived, and subjected to hot and cold environmental conditions, including the use of cold water on his body and hood.*[104]

The Medical Examiner also referred to "multiple minor injuries," various "abrasions and contusions" and "black eyes."[105] Despite these injuries, however, the Medical Examiner concluded that this detainee's manner of death was "undetermined," though "hypothermia may have contributed to his death."[106] According to news reports in late 2004, three Navy SEALs were recommended for courts-martial as a result of this detainee's death.[107] Inexplicably, though, it does not appear that these courts-martial ever occurred.[108]

The pattern of alleged misbehavior in the above-described cases is consistent with techniques implemented at U.S. military SERE schools. Interrogators at the Strike Brigade Holding Area apparently employed enhanced techniques which had been briefly approved for use in Iraq and which were still in use in Afghanistan, whereas the SEAL team may have drawn from a wider range of SERE techniques, including the alleged use of such physically brutal techniques as "water dousing," "facial and abdominal slaps," and "waterboarding."[109]

Just as Welshofer's court martial received much adverse publicity, these two "discotheques" in Mosul have received much negative attention. Not only did such powerhouse newspapers as the *New York Times* and *Washington Post* publish articles with allegations of detainee abuse at these two interrogation facilities, but also one young interrogator published a well-read book about the abuses there. Human Rights Watch has also published at least two reports dealing with interrogation abuse at these two facilities in Mosul.[110]

Although any abuse is inherently tragic, what makes it even more tragic in this case is that there are few indicators that the interrogation techniques employed at these two facilities did what they were designed to do, namely, extract reliable intelligence from detainees unwilling to provide it. When interviewed, Lagouranis said that the harsher methods did not work for him.[111] The only times he received good intelligence from interrogations, he says, is when he combined guile (such as promising rewards he was unable to give) with soft approaches.[112] Lagouranis said:

> But here's what's interesting. These techniques were propagated throughout the Cold War, picked up again after 9/11, used by CIA, filtered down to army interrogators at Guantanamo, filtered again through Abu Ghraib, and used, apparently, around the country by special forces. Probably someone in this chain was a real professional, and if torture works – which is debatable – maybe they had the training to make sure it worked. But at our end of the chain, we had no idea what we were doing. We were just a bunch of frustrated enlisted men picking approved techniques off a menu. We weren't grounded in the history or theory, we were just trying shit out to see if it worked, venting our frustration, and acting like badasses when, in the dark art of torture, we were really just a bunch of rank amateurs.[113]

Troubles in Tikrit

In their February 2004 summary of alleged U.S. detainee abuse in Iraq from March to November 2003, the Red Cross identified the "Tikrit holding area (former Saddam Hussein Islamic School)" as an alleged center of detainee abuse.[114] While the 4th Infantry Division (4ID) was headquartered at this time in Tikrit, it is unclear from this description if this alleged abuse occurred in the 4ID's detention facility on FOB Iron Horse. Also, since this allegation was never investigated, it is unclear exactly what abuse was allegedly committed by whom: as in the case of the "Al-Baghdadi, Heat Base and Habbania Camp," it is just as possible that the alleged abuse occurred– if it occurred at all– at the hands of Special Forces.

Still, the 4ID detention facility at FOB Iron Horse certainly had its troubles. Most significantly, investigators found soldiers at fault in two detainee deaths at the facility. On September 11, 2003, a military policeman shot and killed a detainee for allegedly placing his hands too close to the concertina wire of his isolation area.[115] Major Frank Rangel, Jr., the executive officer for the military intelligence battalion attached to the division, investigated the charge.[116] "I thought the suspect might have committed negligent homicide," Rangel would later say.[117] Instead, the specialist was charged with "manslaughter" and dishonorably discharged in lieu of a court martial.[118] Also, on February 8, 2004, another detainee died due to medical inattention.[119]

More important to this study is the 4ID detention facility which had a case of substantiated interrogation abuse that was a direct result of the decision of HUMINT leaders to take "the gloves off." This case of interrogation abuse began on August 17, 2003, when the non-commissioned officer-in-charge of the 4ID's Interrogation Control Element submitted the requested "wish list" of interrogation techniques.[120] As described in Chapter One, this staff sergeant's "wish list" included "Stimulus Deprivation," "Pressure Point Manipulation," "Close-Fist Strikes," "Muscle Fatigue Inducement," and "Low Voltage Electrocution."[121] He saved this request on his desktop, where it was read by a new interrogator.[122] Soon after, this staff sergeant spoke to his new interrogator about these techniques.[123] They later disagreed in sworn statements about the nature of this discussion: the junior interrogator alleged that the staff sergeant had given him permission to use these techniques (even asking him if he "could handle" implementing such harsh techniques); on the other hand, his supervisor stated that they had discussed the techniques in general and that he had never given this interrogator specific permission to use them.[124]

With the arrival of a detainee at the facility who had been accused of killing three Americans, the stage was set for abusive interrogations. The new interrogator was physically imposing (standing six foot, six inches tall). So, "to extract time-sensitive intelligence information that could save lives," his staff sergeant supervisor assigned him to interrogate this detainee while approving a "Fear Up (Harsh)" approach.[125] During the first abusive interrogation on September 23, 2003, the new interrogator forced the detainee to assume various stress positions, yelled at him, threatened him, and struck him 10-30 times on his feet, buttocks, and possibly his lower back with a police baton.[126] Six days later, a different interrogator with the same interpreter forced the detainee to circle a table on his knees until his knees were bloody.[127] Ironically, just two days before the first harsh interrogation, the 4ID Commander had published policy that prohibited "assaults, insults, public curiosity, bodily injury, and reprisals of any kind."[128] The junior interrogator said he would have reconsidered his techniques if he had seen this policy.[129]

The officer who investigated the incidents recommended a letter of reprimand for the staff sergeant supervisor and a field grade Article 15 for both interrogators.[130] The eventual letter of reprimand admonished the staff sergeant for his failure "to set the proper leadership climate" and for his "inadvertently" leading at least one interrogator to believe he "condoned certain practices that were outside the established regulations."[131] In his rebuttal, however, the junior leader boldly and eloquently alleged it was not he who had failed to set the proper leadership climate for his subordinates but rather the problem was "the command climate of the division as a whole."[132] In support of his claim, he referred to an illegal practice where certain 4ID units would seize the family members of targeted individuals in an effort to coerce these individuals into turning themselves in.[133] This staff sergeant also quoted an unidentified "senior leader" as saying that detainees "are terrorists and will be treated as such."[134]

Although it may not be especially likely that Lieutenant Colonel Allen West was the 4ID "senior leader" that made this remark, he is still worth mentioning in this context. West, a battalion commander within the 4ID's 2nd Brigade, was relieved from command for an incident that occurred one month before the abusive interrogations on FOB Iron Horse. To coerce intelligence from an unwilling detainee, West had watched five of his soldiers beat a detainee on the head and body, then he had taken the detainee outside, placed the detainee's head inside the clearing barrel, and fired one round into the clearing barrel.[135] As a result of this incident, not only media pundits but also U.S. senators hotly debated the morality of West's actions. Ultimately, in the midst of a rancorous public debate that sent mixed signals to troops in the field about what was ethically appropriate behavior, West was allowed to retire rather than face a court martial.

In short, although the interrogation element at FOB Iron Horse flirted with the use of harsh interrogation techniques, the actual use of these techniques was never systemic at FOB Iron Horse as it was at various 3ACR facilities or the Strike Brigade Holding Area. In fact, when such techniques were implemented during two abusive interrogations, a 4ID command policy coupled with swift, decisive punishment seems to have eradicated any confusion these interrogators had regarding acceptable interrogation methods. Thus, in the 4ID the media controversy evolving from abusive interrogation techniques and an intelligence-at-any-cost mindset did not involve interrogators at FOB Iron Horse: this particular media circus rightfully engulfed Lieutenant Colonel West.

Conclusions

All interrogation facilities in Iraq during OIF I faced the same essential "tactical problem."–How do we interrogate effectively, when casualties are mounting, higher interrogation policy is permissive, manning is dramatically inadequate, and our interrogators are young and inexperienced? Unfortunately, the leaders at a few OIF I interrogation facilities believed that solving these problems and saving lives required their interrogators to employ brutal interrogation methods. Such facilities unerringly developed cases of serious detainee abuse.

Thanks to the *Freedom of Information Act* and the more than 100,000 documents that the U.S. government has released pertaining to detention operations during the Global War on Terrorism, we can chart with some confidence the extent of the systemic use of enhanced interrogation techniques at OIF I detention facilities. As described in Chapter 3 and this chapter, the use of these techniques was systemic at Camp Nama and other Special Forces facilities. Additionally, as explained in Chapter 4, these techniques were regularly employed at Abu Ghraib and, perhaps briefly, at Camp Cropper as well. In this chapter, we saw that enhanced interrogation techniques were routinely employed within at least three 3ACR facilities in Al Anbar Province as well as within the Strike Brigade Holding Area in Mosul. Although employed on one detainee and considered for systemic use at the 4th Infantry Division's facility in Tikrit, prompt and decisive disciplinary action prevented the regular use of these techniques at this facility.

Enhanced interrogation techniques were also employed at a fourth tactical-level interrogation facility in Iraq during the latter part of the time period covered by this book—a fact not highlighted in this chapter due to the fact that the unit employing these techniques was actually an OIF II unit. This unit was the 2nd Brigade, 25th Infantry Division, which from January 2004 to February 2005 operated "Camp Honesty" on a forward operating base near Kirkuk.[136] This was the only brigade from the 25th Infantry Division to deploy to Iraq for OIF II. According to the U.S. Senate Armed Services Committee's "Inquiry into the Treatment of Detainees in U.S. Custody," interrogation plans at this facility were "based off of U.S. SERE Training Doctrine." This report stated that detainees at the facility were placed in dark rooms, subjected to loud noise, and touched with "string simulating sensors."[137] It is unclear what "string simulating sensors" are in this report, but if these sensors were some form of electric shock, then few would disagree with the judgment that interrogators at this facility tortured their subjects.

The common denominator of the use of enhanced interrogation techniques at these facilities was, most significantly, an amoral "ends justify the means" mindset. After all, leaders at these facilities were forced neither by higher directive nor by battlefield circumstances to implement harsh interrogation tactics. They each chose to employ these tactics due to their acceptance of the "ticking time bomb" rationale: if they did not employ these tactics, they reasoned, U.S. soldiers and innocent Iraqis would die. Yet another seemingly necessary condition of interrogation abuse was the presence of an influential junior leader who had attended or instructed at SERE schools or who had previously deployed to Gitmo or Afghanistan. Additionally, a contributing cause to the continuation of interrogation abuse at these facilities occurred when the chain-of-command of interrogators at these facilities failed to take decisive disciplinary action even after investigators had identified the abuse.

Sadly, there is little evidence indicating that these facilities collected reliable intelligence by using these methods, and in those few instances where these tactics seem to have worked, the strategic damage done by their use far outweighed any short-term tactical gains. However, in most facilities where these techniques were employed, there were not even shortsighted tactical advantages; there were only the inevitable and disastrous strategic repercussions.

One must keep in mind, though, that the systematically abusive interrogations occurring in the Strike Brigade Holding Area and at Camp Honesty were hardly representative of interrogation operations occurring within their parent units (the 101st Airborne Division and the 2nd Brigade, 25th Infantry Division), let alone other tactical units during OIF I. In early 2004, the 101st Airborne Division and the 2nd Brigade, 1st Infantry Division, had between them at least five enduring and a score of temporary detainee holding areas. There is no evidence that any of their other holding areas employed enhanced interrogation tactics, nor is it likely that such evidence will ever arise. For example, it is a matter of historical record that the commander of the 101st Airborne Division, Major General David Petraeus, clearly understood and communicated to his soldiers the importance of treating the local civilian population with dignity and respect. Two years later, as the commander of Multi-National Force-Iraq, he would say:

> *What sets us apart from our enemies in this fight . . . is how we behave. In everything we do, we must observe the standards and values that dictate that we treat noncombatants and detainees with dignity and respect. While we are warriors, we are also all human beings.*[138]

Based on his command policies during OIF I, there is no doubt that, if Petraeus had known precisely what was going on at the holding area of his 2nd Brigade, he would have stopped the use of enhanced interrogation techniques there. By all accounts, Petraeus is an enlightened, compassionate, and thoroughly engaged general officer who simply did not realize what was continuing to happen at one of his division's many detention facilities. The situation is a cautionary tale concerning the difficulty of providing ethical oversight of a unit's far-flung outposts on today's non-contiguous battlefields. Thus, the real moral of the story of Mosul's two "discos" is that the U.S. Army needs to ensure that its schools and training programs are providing junior leaders with the ethical foundation and tools necessary to operate in accordance with our nation's values before it sends these leaders to remote, isolated outposts far from home.

Despite tragic blunders at a few detention facilities, the overwhelming majority of U.S. military units ensured their school-trained interrogators stayed on the moral high ground during OIF I. Most notably, since "good news is no news" (as U.S. military service members too frequently are heard to say today, often with a sigh), the success in this regard of the largest unit in Iraq during OIF I has not yet been told, in books or the news media.

This huge unit was Task Force 1st Armored Division.

CHAPTER 6

Old Ironsides

> *As you've heard me say before, we must remember who we are. Our example is what will cause us to prevail in this environment, not our weapons. I really believe that. We need to show the Iraqi people what "right" looks like. They must see the difference between us and the former regime. . . . Please reinforce this with your troopers. They will hear this debate. Try to help them not to be confused by it.*[1]
>
> —Major General Martin Dempsey
> Commander, 1st Armored Division

> *Whether or not mock executions, naked pyramids, beatings, and other forms of abuse succeed in extracting information, such behavior often slides down a slippery slope to more severe forms of mistreatment, perhaps leading eventually to injury and death. Prisoner abuse degrades the abuser as well as the abused; as Americans we should stay on a higher moral plane. . . . We had to remain constantly vigilant in this regard, lest we lose our soul in the name of mission accomplishment.*[2]
>
> —Colonel Peter Mansoor,
> Commander
> 1st Brigade Combat Team, 1AD

Prior to its deployment to Iraq, the bulk of the 1st Armored Division ("Old Ironsides")[3] was situated amidst the hilly vineyards, broad rivers, and solitary castles of Germany's wine country. The headquarters for the division was located on Wiesbaden Army Airfield, about one mile from the Rhine River and an hour's drive west of Frankfurt. The division's 1st Brigade, an armored brigade, was stationed a 45 minute drive north of Wiesbaden in the town of Friedberg; its 2nd Brigade, a mechanized infantry brigade, was located about an hour and a half west of Wiesbaden and an hour east of the French border in the town of Baumholder; and its 4th Brigade, an aviation brigade, was stationed in Hanau (just a few minutes from Friedberg).[4] The division's 3rd Brigade, another armored brigade, was across the Atlantic in Fort Riley, Kansas.

The road to stability operations

For the last half of 2002, the leaders and soldiers of the 1AD planned and trained as if they would take part in the invasion of Iraq. In fact, the division was part of the V Corps' invasion plan for Iraq until February 7, 2003, just two months before the 1AD began deploying from Germany to Kuwait.[5] This late change-of-mission from an invasion force to a stabilizing force did not affect all of the division since a substantial portion of the 3rd Brigade began deploying to Iraq on February 20, 2003 and still took part in the invasion.[6] But it did mean that the bulk of the division's units (including nearly all of the division's units in Germany) had focused their training on the wrong type of operations– offensive conventional operations rather than stability operations.

The 501st MI Battalion, stationed across the Rhine River from the 1AD Headquarters amidst the orchards of Wackernheim, was 1AD's organic intelligence battalion. This battalion would be responsible for all of the division HUMINT support during OIF I. Like the rest of the 1AD, the 501st MI Battalion spent 2002 and the first part of 2003 training for the wrong fight. With regard to interrogation operations, the battalion thought much of its time in Iraq would be spent screening (that is, quickly processing, separating, and sending to V Corps) large numbers of Enemy Prisoners of War.[7] The battalion did not cross-train all of its counterintelligence soldiers as interrogators since the assumption was that there would be no counter-insurgency fight and, after the initial mass screenings of EPWs were complete, there would be sufficient interrogators on-hand to accomplish any residual interrogation mission.[8] The battalion's training in Germany and Kuwait included extensive Law of War and Rules of Engagement training, convoy reaction drills, convoy live fire training, first aid training, and training on tasks specific to conventional operations.[9]

The 1AD assembled in Baghdad from May 16-23, 2003,[10] and on May 29, 2003, the division with attachments assumed military responsibility for Baghdad as "TF Baghdad."[11] Once it assumed this responsibility, the division did not relinquish this authority until its transition of authority with the 1st Cavalry Division, its OIF II

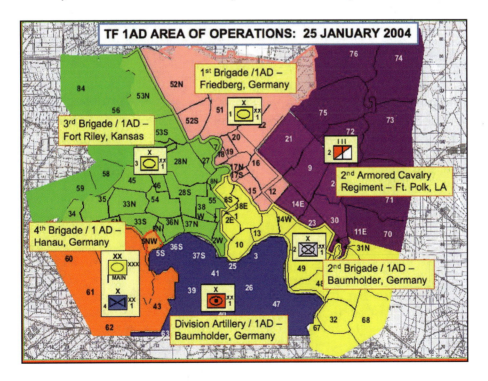

Figure 8) TF 1AD Area of Operations
Source: Headquarters, Task Force 1st Armored Division. *Briefing: TF 1AD Says Thanks to the United States*. Baghdad, July 2004, Slide 6.

replacement, on April 15, 2004.[12]

Throughout OIF I, the 1AD exercised military control of Baghdad with six maneuver brigades. In addition to the division's four organic brigades, the 2nd Light Cavalry Regiment was attached to the 1AD throughout OIF 1.[13] This humvee-mounted regiment was responsible for eastern Baghdad (to include the large, overcrowded slum of Sadr City).[14] Initially, the 2nd Brigade of the 82nd Airborne Division was also attached to the division. This airborne brigade was responsible for southern Baghdad until it was relieved in place by the 1AD's Division Artillery on January 23, 2004.[15] Also, it is worth noting here that the division's 3rd Brigade relinquished control of northwestern Baghdad relatively early (February 12, 2004) to the 2nd Brigade of the 1st Cavalry Division.[16]

Major General Sanchez commanded the 1AD when it deployed to Iraq. On June 15, 2003, Sanchez (now as a Lieutenant General) assumed command of CJTF-7, leaving command of the division to its Assistant Deputy Commander-Maneuver, Major General Fred Robinson.[17] On July 17, 2003, Major General Martin Dempsey assumed command of the 1AD, a responsibility he would have for the next two years. Soon after assuming command, General Dempsey ordered that the division task force be called "Task Force 1st Armored Division" (TF 1AD) rather than Task Force Baghdad.[18]

During OIF I, TF 1AD was not only the largest division-based task force in Iraq, it was the largest division-based task force in U.S. Army history.[19] In addition to the 2nd Light Cavalry Regiment and the 2nd Brigade of the 82nd Airborne Division, other large units attached to TF 1AD at various times included the 18th and 89th military police brigades, the 493rd Engineer Group, seven engineer battalions, the 55th Personnel Service Battalion, the 8th Finance Battalion, the 350th and 354th Civil Affairs Battalions, the 415th and 345th Psychological Operations Battalions, and the 16th Corps Support Group.[20] At its largest, TF 1AD included more than 39,000 soldiers– slightly more than twice the number of soldiers in an ordinary division and one-fourth of CJTF-7's total strength.[21]

Seizing the high ground

Considering the scale and timeframe of its operations in Iraq, it is significant that TF 1AD did not have a single substantiated case of school-trained interrogators abusing detainees. In fact, from declassified written records and verbal testimonies, it appears that the division never even received an allegation of abuse concerning school-trained interrogators– at least not an allegation that anyone deemed serious enough to formally investigate.[22] It also appears that, while one brigade did request an enhanced interrogation technique on one occasion, the use of this technique was disapproved (probably by division-level military intelligence personnel) and the division's school-trained interrogators never actually employed an enhanced interrogation technique.[23] Also, according to various verbal testimonies,[24] all TF 1AD detention facilities passed numerous Red Cross inspections with no major deficiencies and no allegations of detainee abuse. Corroborating this testimony is the fact that, while the February 2004 Red Cross report listed five detention facilities in Iraq with serious detainee abuse problems and several other facilities with less serious abuse problems, this report did not mention any TF 1AD facility in this report.[25] Additionally, a 2006 Human Rights Watch report on interrogation abuse during OIF I was similarly mute regarding TF

1AD's interrogation operations.[26]

The only questionable practice some TF 1AD interrogators and detention personnel employed was the use of stress positions and exercise to control unruly detainees.[27] Although military police doctrine at the time prohibited "physical activity or body positions designed to place undue stress on a prisoner,"[28] it is unclear that the type of light physical activity and body positions employed by some units in the division to regain control of unruly detainees constituted "undue" stress. Military intelligence doctrine, DoD directives, Army regulations, and U.S. national law did not specifically address the practice. With regard to international law, Article 31 of the 4th Geneva Convention did prohibit physical coercion for the purpose of obtaining information, but it did not prohibit physical coercion for the purpose of regaining control of a detainee or modifying his bad behavior.[29] More to the point, Article 100 of the 4th Geneva Convention prohibited detention personnel from making detainees perform physical exertion that was dangerous to their health or involved "physical victimization."[30] In addition, it specifically prohibited "prolonged standing" and "punishment drill."[31] However, whether these prohibitions were applicable to stress positions (other than prolonged standing) that were temporary and only mildly discomforting and whether this prohibition applied to such forms of light exercise as jumping jacks was open to interpretation. Despite the lack of legal and doctrinal clarity on the issue, it appears that only a minority of TF 1AD's holding areas used stress positions and exercise to control detainees, and of these, most (if not all) did so only briefly.

In all other areas, the 1AD's school-trained HUMINT interrogators clearly seized "the moral high ground," particularly with regard to their refraining from the use of enhanced interrogation techniques. This fact begs the key question: how did 1AD's interrogators steer clear of the controversy that eventually surrounded CJTF-7's approval and use of harsh interrogation techniques?

The answer starts with TF 1AD's command climate. Throughout his command, Major General Dempsey made it clear that he expected Iraqis to be treated with dignity and respect. In fact, just four days after Dempsey took command, the TF 1AD Headquarters published Fragmentary Order 383A [General Order - Civilian or Detainee Maltreatment] to Operations Order 03-215 (Iron Stability), a general order that criminalized an extensive list of potentially abusive behaviors of Iraqis by 1AD soldiers.[32] This general order applied to all TF 1AD soldiers (including interrogators), and it specifically stated that detainees undergoing "questioning" or "interrogation" would not be maltreated.[33] Dempsey's general order went on to define "maltreatment" as "an act or actionable omission, which results in physical pain or mental anguish to a person without justifiable cause."[34] This order also specifically forbade specific types of maltreatment, to include some of the behavior exhibited by "actor interrogators" at SERE schools. For example, Dempsey specifically prohibited such maltreatment as the "hitting" of detainees, "using abusive language" on detainees, and "causing mental oppression" of detainees.[35]

Additionally, Dempsey frequently reinforced this general order with multiple verbal and written orders to his subordinates.[36] Consequently, the commanders of TF 1AD's maneuver brigades– who probably did not need to be persuaded of the importance of treating detainees well– made the humane treatment of Iraqi detainees one of their priorities.

Nonetheless, despite a command climate that clearly and consistently reinforced the message that detainees should be treated humanely, there were still instances of substantiated detainee abuse in TF 1AD. Most of these abuses took place at the point of capture, when emotions ran high and soldiers failed to rapidly adjust from fighting enemy combatants to treating these same enemy combatants humanely. However, a few cases of substantiated abuse did take place at TF 1AD holding areas, and what is more, a few of these cases involved abusive interrogations. The TF 1AD soldiers, though, who abused detainees during interrogations, were non-HUMINT soldiers conducting interrogations that they had never been authorized to conduct. Thus, what is truly distinctive about TF 1AD with regard to detainee abuse is that there is no record of the use of an enhanced interrogation technique by school-trained TF 1AD interrogators or of school-trained interrogators being formally accused of detainee abuse.

So, how did TF 1AD's school-trained interrogators manage to "stay on the moral high ground?" We must dig deeper.

Out front!

The 501st MI Battalion was TF 1AD's direct support military intelligence battalion. The motto of the battalion, which was inactivated in 2007, was "Out Front!" Certainly, the battalion's leadership intended their unit to "lead from the front" ethically. For example, in the first sentence of his command philosophy, Lieutenant Colonel Laurence Mixon, who commanded the battalion for most of OIF I, matter of factly asserted that the battalion was a "values-based organization." Then, in the very next sentence, he borrowed from the shining "city upon the hill" metaphor by presenting key moral principles as "guideposts, lighting our way ahead."

The unit's battalion commander during the unit's preparation to deploy and initial deployment was Lieutenant Colonel Kenneth Devan. Major Elizabeth Rogers was the unit's operations officer during the same time period. Six weeks after the unit arrived in Baghdad, Devan became the division's senior intelligence officer, the 1AD G2, and Mixon assumed command of the 501st MI Battalion.[37] One week later, Rogers became the 1AD Deputy G2, and Major Nathan Hoepner moved from the TF 1AD G2 section to become the 501st MI Battalion operations officer.

Both Mixon and Hoepner played pivotal roles in ensuring the 501st MI Battalion's interrogators did not abuse detainees. Their strong ethical stands were especially critical during late summer and early fall of 2003 when SERE-interrogation techniques were officially promulgated in CJTF-7's interrogation policy memoranda. Hoepner's response to a CJTF-7 captain who had said that the CJTF-7's Deputy CJ2 had decided that the "gloves are coming off regarding these detainees" is recorded on page one of this book. Yet, Mixon was just as insistent that his soldiers stay on the moral high ground, and since he was the commander, he exercised more influence than his operations officer in this regard. Captain Nicole Lauenstein, who served as the battalion's HUMINT Operations Cell Chief and then as a platoon leader in the battalion, said:

> I think it [the 501st MI Battalion] was very successful [at staying on the moral high ground], mostly because our Battalion Commander, LTC [Lieutenant Colonel] Mixon, expected the highest moral standards from all of his officers and Soldiers. You were allowed to make mistakes, but moral violations were not acceptable. Also, we had very experienced HUMINT Warrant Officers

at the company level where the HUMINT operations were being conducted, guiding less-experienced Soldiers and advising OMTs. I think the combination of both of these elements led to our success. . . . I think if we had had less experienced warrant officers at the company level, 501st MI Battalion could have succumbed to the mistakes of other units.[38]

Captain Lauenstein's point about the importance of first-line supervisors (warrant officers) in preventing detainee abuse is an extremely important point. For all or most of OIF I, Chief Warrant Officer 2 Kenneth Kilbourne, Chief Warrant Officer 3 Joel Giefer, and Warrant Officer 1 John Groseclose were the senior Operational Management Team (OMT) chiefs for the HUMINT sections of Alpha Company, Bravo Company, and Charlie Company respectively. All three officers were uniformly consistent in insisting that their intelligence personnel operate within the moral parameters outlined by Army doctrine, national law, and the Geneva Conventions. They also served as a sounding board and support group for each other when, as occasionally happened, they were compelled to tell a military leader senior to them that neither they nor their soldiers could perform a certain mission in a certain way.

An MI community takes charge

One week after CJTF-7 published what would be its baseline mission order governing detention operations for the rest of OIF I, TF 1AD published TF 1AD Fragmentary Order 539A. Major Hoepner and Luis Guzman, a G2 planner and contract employee, wrote this August 30, 2003, Fragmentary Order.[39] Among many other directives, this Fragmentary Order tasked subordinate units to input detainee data into an All Source Analysis System-Light (ASAS-L) database.[40] (The ASAS-L was a Panasonic toughbook computer with common software that was owned by intelligence shops throughout TF 1AD.)

Unwritten but implicit in this directive was the fact that TF 1AD's military intelligence community, the owners of the ASAS-L, had become the managers of TF 1AD's detainee population. This assumption of a doctrinally military police mission by military intelligence units and sections was due to necessity: while each detention facility had an associated military intelligence unit or section, military police units were too busy recruiting, training, and supporting Baghdad's new police force to support (let alone manage) all of the division's detention facilities.

Fragmentary Order 539A directed TF 1AD's subordinate units to either release or move detainees to a higher detention facility (either Abu Ghraib or, in the case of "division targets," the TF 1AD's Division Interrogation Facility) within 72 hours of apprehension.[41] It also directed TF 1AD's Division Interrogation Facility (DIF) to hold detainees for only 96 hours.[42] Major General Dempsey reserved for himself the authority to have a detainee transferred to the DIF or, once at the DIF, released or transferred to Abu Ghraib.

Dempsey's decision-making process with regard to DIF operations worked as follows: Hoepner briefed Dempsey each morning on the status of "Detainees of Intelligence Interest" (suspected insurgents, or whom CJTF-7 called "Security Internees").[43] This brief included highlights from Summary Interrogation Reports as well as recommended dispositions for specific detainees.[44] If a Security Internee were being held at a brigade or regimental holding area, the 501st MI Battalion S3 section

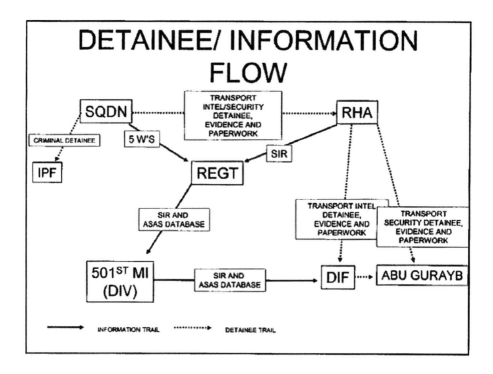

Figure 9) 1AD Detainee/Information Flow
American Civil Liberties Union: Torture FOIA

would pass on Dempsey's disposition guidance (that is, whether to take the detainee to Abu Ghraib or to the DIF) to the appropriate brigade or regimental S2 section.[45] Also, before recommending the release or transfer of a detainee from the DIF, the 501st MI Battalion Tactical Operations Center would build a "disposition packet" for this detainee.[46] This packet would then be staffed through the responsible brigade or regimental commander, the TF 1AD G2, the 501st MI Battalion Commander, and the TF 1AD Staff Judge Advocate, who would each recommend either releasing the detainee, transferring the detainee to Abu Ghraib, or transferring the detainee to Abu Ghraib as an "Intel Hold."[47] Dempsey would then make the final decision on a detainee's disposition based on his subordinate leaders' recommendations.[48]

The TF 1AD Division Interrogation Facility

The TF 1AD DIF was established at the Baghdad International Airport during the same time period (late July 2003) that the Abu Ghraib detention facility was activated and for the same reason– to support the large influx of detainees expected as a result of Operation Victory Bounty.[49] The 501st MI Battalion was neither designed nor trained to run a detention facility. Nonetheless, it would perform this task admirably.

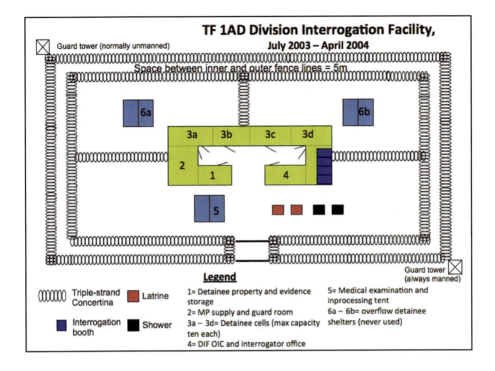

Figure 10) TF 1AD Division Interrogation Facility
Source. Major Douglas A. Pryer, "Interview with LTC Nathan Hoepner," *Operational Leadership Experiences in the Global War on Terrorism*, February 2, 2009, http://cgsc.cdmhost.com/cdm4/item_viewer.php?CISOROOT=/p4013coll13&CISOPTR=1441&CISOBOX=1&REC=6 (accessed March 5, 2009), 7.

TF 1AD engineers did most of the initial construction of the DIF. The headquarters company of 501st MI Battalion locally contracted any work that the division's engineers could not complete.[50] Altogether, construction of the facility took one to two months to complete.[51] When finished, the facility had portable latrines, a portable shower, hand washing and shaving facilities.[52] It also had an inner and outer fence comprised of concertina wire, two guard towers, four cells each able to hold up to 10 detainees, and four interrogation booths.[53]

The headquarters company of 501st MI Battalion provided logistical support to the facility. This support included a water truck, toiletries, towels, meals-ready-to-eat, and eventually, uniforms.[54] Medical support initially came from the 47th Forward Support Battalion of TF 1AD's 2nd Brigade, but this mission eventually transitioned to a medical company that happened to be stationed across the street from the facility.[55]

A military police platoon from the 18th MP Brigade, which was "operationally controlled" by TF 1AD, initially guarded the DIF.[56] Eventually, this platoon was replaced by a platoon from 1AD's organic 501st MP Company, which had a strength of 18 military policemen.[57] Although 501st MI Battalion operationally controlled these two military police platoons, the rating chains for the leaders of these two platoons remained within their respective military police companies. Furthermore, the company leadership of these platoons would visit their soldiers at the DIF on an almost daily basis, thus helping to maintain separation between the facility's military police guards and interrogators.[58] "MPs had no role in the interrogation process," Hoepner said.[59]

During TF 1AD's 15 month-long deployment, its DIF would incur not a single allegation of serious detainee abuse.[60] Declassified documents and interviews indicate that there were only three instances of abuse at the facility, and all three of these instances were fairly minor: there were two cases of guards counseled for yelling at detainees and one instance of a contract interrogator who was fired for yelling at and threatening a detainee.[61]

In addition to the absence of serious detainee abuse, there were none of the indicators of abuse at the TF 1AD DIF that were occurring at a few other detention facilities in Iraq. There was not, for example, a single riot, detainee shooting, detainee death, or escape attempt at the facility.[62] The fact that there were no serious allegations of abuse or even indicators of abuse held true even after TF 1AD was extended into OIF II for an additional three months and DIF operations moved to a new compound.[63] Also, the facility passed all Red Cross inspections with no significant deficiencies or allegations of detainee abuse noted.[64] Thus, it is perhaps no wonder then that, when Colonel Stuart Herrington (a retired counterintelligence officer and one of America's foremost experts on interrogation operations) inspected CJTF-7 interrogation operations in December 2003, he singled out TF 1AD's detention facility as "organized, clean, well-run, and impressive."[65]

MI Shortfalls

The 501st MI Battalion had been organized for high-intensity mechanized warfare, not counterinsurgency operations in a city of seven million people. The fact that TF 1AD lacked sufficient numbers of military intelligence soldiers was obvious at the DIF, which faced serious manning shortages in all military intelligence-related areas–interrogation, interpretation, and analysis.

The number of interrogators at the DIF never exceeded six, and this number was only reached briefly. The facility's first team of interrogators was four junior interrogators provided by CJTF-7.[66] When this team of reservists redeployed home, the battalion was forced to reassign junior interrogators from its direct-support companies to the DIF, hardly a popular move with the brigades to which these highly valued soldiers had been attached.[67] At this point, there was still no experienced warrant officer to guide the facility's interrogators. Early in 2004, the battalion received six experienced contract civilian interrogators for the holding area (which became five contract interrogators when one of them was fired), though the facility still lacked an experienced warrant officer and would not have a warrant officer until it moved to another compound in April 2004.[68]

The DIF had four contract linguists who served as both interpreters for interrogations and translators for the "document exploitation cell."[69] Additionally, there was no analytical support at the holding area until the 501st MI Battalion was able to assign two intelligence analysts (one military and one civilian analyst) to the facility midway through the deployment.[70] The net result of the facility's manning shortfalls was that the facility did not operate as effectively as it could have operated.

Yet, a shortfall in the quantity and experience of military intelligence personnel was not confined to the DIF. The problem was endemic to interrogation operations across TF 1AD. Incredibly, the 501st MI Battalion– the unit responsible for providing HUMINT support to a division with responsibility for securing a city with five million Iraqis– was authorized a sum total of just nine interrogators. These nine interrogators consisted of three sections of three interrogators– one chief warrant officer 2, one E-5 sergeant, and one E-4 specialist. Each section was assigned to a military intelligence company in direct support of a brigade. In addition to 501st MI Battalion's nine interrogators, the maneuver brigades attached to the division were each authorized three interrogators as well. Also, for much of OIF I, the division received four to six interrogators from CJTF-7 to support the DIF. Thus, if TF 1AD's interrogation sections had been at full strength, the division would have had a total of 19-21 interrogators.

Unfortunately, TF 1AD's interrogation sections were never at full strength. For example, although Company B, 501st MI Battalion was authorized an interrogation section with one warrant officer 2, one E-5, and one E-4, it actually had on-hand only two E-4 interrogators. Other interrogation sections periodically faced similar shortages. Thus, in reality, the division had approximately 15-18 school-trained interrogators at any one time. This number, of course, was not nearly sufficient to support counterinsurgency interrogations in a huge and violent city, support that included conducting tens of thousands of screenings of Iraqi applicants for positions in the nascent Iraqi security forces.

Considering this dramatic shortage of interrogators, it is no wonder that counterintelligence specialists were sometimes tasked by their warrant officer supervisors to conduct interrogations. Although not prohibited by Army regulations, this practice was frowned upon by Army doctrine because 97B counterintelligence specialists– although skillful at detecting deception and screening individuals– had never been school-trained to conduct tactical interrogations. The division's school-trained interrogators were unhappy with this situation, but they realized they sometimes had no choice but to ask counterintelligence specialists to interrogate. CW3 Groseclose said:

> *There was a couple times we did that [used counterintelligence specialists as interrogators] because we didn't have anyone else available. . . . I didn't like to use my CI folks for interrogations because they had a hard time doing it. If a detainee was cooperative, they were very good at giving the detainee follow-up questions to get the information we were looking for. On the other hand, if a detainee was uncooperative and they needed to use approaches, they didn't have the training, and they just didn't do very well at it.*[71]

This practice was even more prevalent in military intelligence units (such as Company B of the 501st MI Battalion) that did not have all three of their assigned interrogators.

There was not just a shortage of interrogators in TF 1AD. This shortage existed across all of Iraq. Thus, it is unsurprising that the majority of interrogation abuse that occurred during OIF I was not committed by school-trained interrogators. Such abuse normally took place either at the "point of capture" or in temporary battalion holding facilities. In such cases, angry and frustrated troops resorted to interrogating Iraqis themselves in an attempt to immediately acquire desperately needed intelligence.

As noted in Chapter 5, the Church Report identified 16 substantiated cases of interrogation abuse in Iraq before September 30, 2004.[72] Although none of these cases involved TF 1AD's school-trained interrogators, half of the ten cases of abuse involving non-interrogators belonged to TF 1AD. These five substantiated cases were described in the Church Report:

> On June 21, 2003, a Quick Reaction Force assigned to 4th Battalion, 1st Field Artillery [3rd Brigade] responded to reports of sniper fire from the Iraq Museum of Military History in Baghdad. An Iraqi civilian was taken into custody as a suspect. . . . A private first class approached the detainee . . . struck the detainee in the face, making his nose bleed. . . . Later, a staff sergeant allegedly pointed his M-16 at the detainee's head and then charged it. . . . It was later determined that the detainee, who was subsequently released, had been hired by the U.S. Army to guard the museum.[73]
>
> On August 31, 2003, a specialist from the 1st Battalion, 36th Infantry [1st Brigade], threatened two Iraqi detainees during questioning in a building near Baghdad. . . . In separate interrogations, the SPC handed one detainee a bullet and told him that the round would kill him if he did not talk. . . . Within hearing distance of the detainee but out of his field of vision, the SPC simulated charging an empty weapon to lead the detainee to believe the weapon was loaded.[74]
>
> On September 1, 2003, three detainees were seized near a mosque in Baghdad, their hands were zip-cuffed behind their backs, and they were taken to a nearby Ammunition Collection Point (ACP) operated by the 2nd Battalion, 6th Infantry Regiment [2nd Brigade]. They matched the description of individuals who were seen earlier in the vicinity of the ACP perimeter with weapons . . . [a] SFC asked one detainee if he was there to bomb the base or shoot soldiers, and slapped a detainee during questioning for not telling the truth. As instructed by the SFC, three SSGs alternated in kicking, tripping, and shoving the detainees . . . The detainees claimed they were security guards for the local mosque and were eventually released to a cleric from the mosque.[75]
>
> On October 1, 2003, near the perimeter of the Baghdad International Airport (BIAP), soldiers assigned to A Battery, 1st Battalion, 4th Air Defense Artillery [DIVARTY], apprehended nine detainees suspected of trespassing through a hole in BIAP's southern wall and stealing metal pipe. A captain interrogated the zip-tied detainees at gunpoint and fired his pistol approximately six times to deflate the tires of the tractor the detainees had been riding when caught.[76]
>
> On October 14, 2003, at a temporary holding facility in Al Ademiya, a detainee was questioned about his knowledge of plans to attack a U.S. convoy. . . . Two SGTs from the 32nd Military Police Company [519th MP Battalion, 18th MP Brigade] took the detainee to the Al Ademiya police station. . . . [A] SGT held a pistol to the detainee's head and threatened him during questioning.[77]

To prevent interrogation abuse, it is clearly not enough to ensure school-trained interrogators adhere to the high ground. The U.S. Army also needs to ensure that, one, non-interrogators understand that they cannot interrogate prisoners themselves, and that, two, units go to war with enough interrogators to reduce the temptation of other troops to conduct their own interrogations.

The shortage of military intelligence personnel was also keenly felt in the area of interrogator management. During OIF I, for example, the 501st MI Battalion did not have an organic HUMINT Operations Cell. According to current Army doctrine, this cell is "assigned under the J/G2X to track all HUMINT activities."[78] Among other duties, this section "deconflicts HUMINT collection operations, establishes and maintains a consolidated HUMINT source database, manages requirements and taskings for HUMINT collectors, and expedites preparation of intelligence reports and their distribution to consumers at all levels."[79] During OIF I, however, this cell was new doctrine that the 501st MI Battalion's manning authorization document did not reflect. As a result, the 501st MI Battalion was forced to stand up a HUMINT Operations Cell during OIF I that, frequently, was manned by personnel with no HUMINT experience whatsoever. Near the beginning of the deployment, for example, this two-man cell consisted of a first lieutenant and a 96R (ground surveillance radar specialist) master sergeant– neither of whom had any HUMINT knowledge or experience.[80]

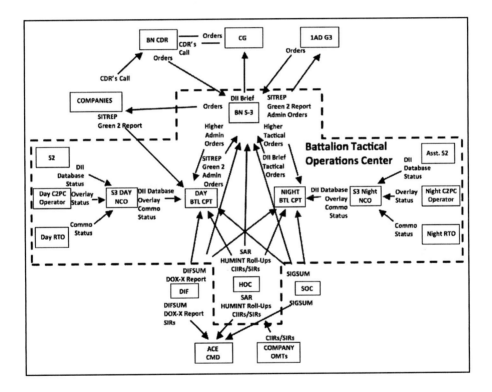

Figure 11) 501st MI Battalion Information Flow
Source: CPT Douglas A. Pryer, "501st MI BTOC SOP," Standard Operating Procedures, Baghdad, November 3, 2003, A-1.

Since the HUMINT Operations Cell was undermanned and inexperienced, the 501st MI Battalion S-3 section (whose members also had little HUMINT experience) assumed many of the tasks that would eventually become this cell's doctrinal tasks. For example, the S3 section tracked and tasked HUMINT assets, distributed the DIF's document exploitation report and interrogation summary, and provided interrogation priorities and lines of questioning to the facility. Thus, for much of the deployment, the cell performed little more than administrative tasks– proofreading Critical Intelligence Information Reports and Summary Interrogation Reports submitted by Company HUMINT sections, rolling up these daily reports into a single report for distribution to intelligence sections across TF 1AD (and adjacent units as needed), compiling the division's source database, and compiling and submitting a daily report of the significant activities of HUMINT teams to CJTF-7. Although the battalion's HUMINT Operation Cell would eventually assume a greater share of its doctrinal tasks, HUMINT assets were probably never managed as effectively as doctrine would envision in the April 2004 version of Field Manual 2.0, *Intelligence*.

Conclusions

TF 1AD's school-trained interrogators adhered to doctrinal interrogation techniques. Although the interrogators and guards of certain TF 1AD units at certain times apparently applied stress positions and light exercises to control unruly detainees, it is doubtful that the division's school-trained interrogators ever used such methods to try to compel prisoners to talk. Consequently, these interrogators incurred zero allegations of serious detainee abuse. Additionally, of great strategic importance, TF 1AD's interrogators stayed out of the news.

Why were 1AD's interrogators more humane and strategically effective than interrogators in certain facilities in other OIF I units? The answer comes down to the quality of the interrogators' ethical leadership. Simply put, there was no leader in the chain-of-command of any 1AD interrogator, from the commanding general to warrant officer supervisors, who prized the acquisition of short-term intelligence at the cost of, as Major General Dempsey put it, our failing to "remember who we are." Thus, one of the key lessons of OIF I is that, on today's decentralized battlefields, all it takes is one single "point of failure" in a chain-of-command to negatively impact the behavior of the soldiers below this command level. Fortunately, in the case of TF 1AD's school-trained interrogators, there were no such weak spots.

Reinforcing the importance of leadership is the fact that those facilities under the influence of leaders who had stated that the "gloves are coming off" of interrogators rapidly descended into sadistic detainee abuse. In contrast, this chapter described how TF 1AD, which shared the same essential tactical problem as these other units, had leaders determined to ensure their interrogators applied only doctrinal interrogation techniques. The resolve of these leaders in this matter empowered professional interrogators to do what they already knew they should do, namely, adhere to the Laws of War in which they had been trained.

Clearly, for interrogation abuse to occur during OIF I, it was not enough for CJTF-7 to publish a vague, permissive interrogation policy. Subordinate leaders still had to decide for themselves to take the "gloves off" and then direct, encourage, or simply permit interrogators to use enhanced interrogation techniques. Thus, in the final analysis, the quality of a unit's ethical decision-making is what truly determines the degree of detainee abuse to which this unit may sink and, in counterinsurgency battles that are more about winning the trust and confidence of the population than about killing the enemy, helps determine this unit's strategic effectiveness.

Of course, those who believe in the efficacy of harsh interrogation techniques will argue that TF 1AD's interrogators were not as successful tactically as they would have been if they had employed such techniques. This is very unlikely to be true. The 501st MI Battalion's HUMINT warrant officers certainly did not accept such an argument. To a man, they believed that they would have been less successful if they had employed harsh techniques, often saying "torture is for amateurs, professionals don't need it."[81] Their judgment is corroborated by expert sources. In *How to Break a Terrorist*, for example, Matthew Alexander (one of the interrogators who led U.S. forces to Musab al Zarqawi), convincingly argues that interrogators who build rapport with sources and then intelligently apply doctrinal approaches are more successful than those who rely on brutal methods.[82]

Now, we make one last stop within TF 1AD, this time to study brigade- and battalion-interrogation operations. Since it was at this level of command that soldiers engaged in constant, direct interaction with Iraqis, this level was unquestionably the most important during OIF I. It was also at this level of command that the many small moral successes of the division's school-trained interrogators were most bittersweet, sadly tempered as these successes were by instances of thoughtless abuse committed by combat soldiers– abuse that, in some cases, was even directed by junior leaders.

CHAPTER 7

> *You can't rely on the THT [Tactical HUMINT Team] to do it all for you. THTs come with varying levels of competency and expertise. If that's the only source of HUMINT you have coming in, you're going to be in a hurt box. At the end of the day, more intelligence means less people dead.*[1]
> —Lieutenant Colonel Larry Wilson,
> Brigade S-2, 2nd Brigade, TF 1AD

> *We were not a "zero-defect" organization, and we were certainly not a "victory at all costs" unit. The commander set the tone that we were in an extremely complex, multi-faceted operation and tactical success alone was not going to win the war. Our conduct and principles were every bit as important as our tactical proficiency and weapons . . . I think we all understood that if we did not hold the moral high ground, we had no chance at all.*[2]
> —Lieutenant Colonel Russell Godsil,
> Brigade S-2, 1st Brigade, TF 1AD

At any one time during OIF I, five maneuver brigades had military responsibility for sections within TF 1AD's area of operations.[3] In this chapter, we examine the strengths and weaknesses of the interrogation operations of three of these brigades, the Ready First Brigade (1st Brigade), the Bulldog Brigade (3rd Brigade), and the Iron Brigade (2nd Brigade).

Of special interest here is our examination of the 2nd Brigade. The 2nd Brigade was not only CJTF-7's largest brigade combat team but also TF 1AD's most innovative brigade with regard to Human Intelligence (HUMINT) operations. Some of these innovations stirred a great deal of controversy during OIF I, at least within the division's intelligence community. Within maneuver channels, however, the reputation of this brigade's intelligence operations was quite high. For example, when Colonel Michael Formica, commander of the 2nd Brigade Combat Team, 1st Cavalry Division, assumed responsibility for northwest Baghdad on February 13, 2004, he dispatched his key leaders to the 2nd Brigade to learn "how to develop targets" and "conduct intelligence operations" because "they were pretty successful at it."[4] If the study of any TF 1AD brigade during OIF I can usefully illustrate what brigade-level intelligence doctrine should look like (or perhaps, what it should not look like), it would be the study of TF 1AD's 2nd Brigade Combat Team (2BCT).

The "Ready First" Brigade

Before moving his unit to Baghdad, Colonel Michael Tucker, the commander of the 1AD's 1st Brigade (nicknamed "Ready First"), had prepared his brigade for a conventional attack into the center of Baghdad, expecting that his unit would bypass elements of the 3rd Infantry Division on objectives along the southern periphery of Baghdad.⁵ When resistance in Baghdad collapsed earlier than expected, his unit instead conducted a relief in place with the 1st Brigade of the 3rd Infantry Division, assuming military responsibility in late May 2003 for two of Baghdad's nine districts, the Adhamiya and Rusafa districts, in central and northeast Baghdad.⁶

The headquarters of the 1st Brigade Combat Team (1BCT) was established at "Martyr's Monument," a memorial Saddam had ordered built to commemorate the more than 100,000 Iraqi lives lost in the war he had started against Iran.⁷ The giant monument, which looked like a hollowed-out, turquoise flower bulb that had been split in half, was chosen for its obvious force protection value: it was surrounded on three sides by an artificial lake, and beneath the towering turquoise edifice was a large cavernous museum with sufficient space for the headquarters' 300 soldiers. With a moat around their headquarters and several feet of reinforced concrete and marble overhead, soldiers inside the monument were nearly invulnerable to car bombs and rocket and mortar fire.⁸

The Ready First brigade had five battalion-size task forces responsible for parts of Baghdad. Task Force 1-37 Armor lived with three companies of the 16th Engineer Battalion on "Baghdad Island," a former pleasure resort which was located on the northern outskirts of Baghdad and which was actually only surrounded by the Tigris River and an artificial lake on three sides.⁹ Task Force 1-37 Armor was responsible for the most northern and eastern districts of Adhamiya, to include the poor, crime-ridden, largely Shiite districts northwest of Sadr City, while the 16th Engineer Battalion operated west of the Tigris River on the northern outskirts of Baghdad.¹⁰ Task Force 1-36 Infantry operated in Rusafa in the southeastern portion of the brigade's sector.¹¹ A Florida National Guard unit, 3rd Battalion, 124th Infantry, operated along the Tigris River in Rusafa in the southwestern part of the brigade's area.¹² Finally, 2nd Battalion, 3rd Field Artillery operated out of "Gunner Palace," one of Uday Hussein's former pleasure palaces, along the Tigris River in the western portion of the brigade's sector.¹³ This field artillery battalion's operating area included the Abu Hanifa Mosque and this mosque's surrounding neighborhoods– an area that, by the fall of 2003, would be a Sunni insurgent stronghold.¹⁴

Initially, the 1BCT had little counterinsurgent work to do. Rather, the unit was focused on countering looting, criminal activity, and restoring such essential services as trash removal and public electricity.¹⁵ Baghdad's citizens, Colonel Tucker found, were at first welcoming and "friendly."¹⁶ Indeed, there are probably no more powerful examples in Iraq of the rapid transition of feeling among Iraqis from exuberance at Saddam's fall to enmity toward their liberators than the examples that took place in areas controlled by 1BCT units. Most notably, Colonel Tucker has described his troops being greeted with flowers as they drove through Sadr City, the crowded Shiite ghetto in eastern Baghdad.¹⁷ A year later, however, these flowers in Sadr City had become rocket-propelled grenades and semi-automatic rifle rounds, as elements of TF 1AD and the 1st Cavalry Division engaged in fierce block-to-block fighting with the *Jaish al-Mahdi*, the militia of the firebrand Shiite cleric, Muqtada al-Sadr.

The reasons for this almost bipolar change in attitude toward U.S. troops were numerous and largely outside the control of the 1BCT. A few have been touched upon in earlier chapters. Perhaps the most compelling explanation for this rapid and extreme change in attitude toward U.S. troops, though, was that local Iraqis expected far more, far sooner from their liberators than units like the 1BCT were able to give them. Most significantly, in a theater that was chronically short of troops, the 1BCT may have suffered the worst shortage of that most basic and critical of counterinsurgent necessities—enough counterinsurgents to adequately secure the population. The Adhamiya and Rusafa districts contained approximately 2.1 million Iraqis, whereas the brigade's strength was 3,500 soldiers.[18] This meant that the brigade had a ratio of fewer than two counterinsurgents for every 1,000 Iraqis in its sector. Although this ratio improved slightly as the brigade slowly trained Iraqi security forces, this ratio never came close to reaching the "minimum troop density required" for effective counterinsurgency operations as codified in current Army doctrine– doctrine that now recommends 20 to 25 counterinsurgents for every 1,000 residents.[19]

Still, the rapid growth of the insurgency within the 1BCT's operating area cannot be attributed to factors outside the brigade alone. During the first few months of OIF I, like nearly every other tactical unit in Iraq (the 101st Airborne Division in northern Iraq being a notable exception to this rule), the Ready First brigade unwittingly contributed to the rise of anti-American sentiment via the use of heavy-handed, culturally insensitive tactics. "We didn't really have an appreciation for what that [the importance of cultural considerations] meant," Colonel Tucker later said.[20] A company commander for Task Force 1-36 Infantry, Major Esli Pitts, has echoed this comment:

> *If I were to go back to Iraq, which is certainly a real possibility, I would take the cultural understanding [which I have now and] which is something I might not have known exactly how to deal with earlier. But I believed in June 2003 that we were doing it wrong, or not doing it right necessarily. We weren't very sensitive to the local culture.*[21]

The 1BCT's initially heavy-handed tactics included kicking in doors, holding families at gunpoint, arresting suspects without legally substantive "probable cause," and putting sandbag hoods on detainees.[22] Colonel Peter Mansoor, who assumed command of the brigade on July 1, 2003, has written that one of his first imperatives was to change how his soldiers were treating the populace. "We were only alienating the Iraqi people through these tactics," he has written. "I emphasized to my commanders that in future searches, unless based on rock-solid intelligence, we would instead knock before entering and would treat all residents with dignity and respect."[23]

<u>Key players</u>

For much of OIF I, the senior intelligence officer for the Ready First brigade was Major Russell Godsil. Prior to his assignment, Godsil had served as a National Guard advisor and recruiting company commander.[24] "Nothing in his background suggested that he would excel in a counterinsurgency environment," Colonel Mansoor later wrote, "But it quickly became clear that Russ had prepared himself well with a program of personal study and development over the years."[25] As the senior intelligence officer, Godsil had overall responsibility for interrogation operations within the brigade.

Company A, 501st MI Battalion, supplied interrogators and other HUMINT operators for the Ready First brigade. Alpha Company had many exceptional soldiers; however, it would suffer one striking moral lapse during the deployment: its company commander was relieved from command in December 2003 for throwing a Christmas party that, for a select few soldiers, included booze and pornography– a violation of the theater's first "General Order" for U.S. troops.²⁶ After this incident, Captain Craig Martin assumed command of this company, leading it for the next year and a half.

Chief Warrant Officer 2 Kenneth Kilbourne, a 351E Human Intelligence Collection Technician, served as the senior interrogator for this company's HUMINT section for the duration of the deployment. Another warrant officer assisted him in these duties until this other officer redeployed six months into OIF I, leaving Kilbourne to manage the section by himself.²⁷ The unit was lucky to have his expertise: he was not only the senior interrogator in all of TF 1AD during OIF I, but since then, he has gone on to serve as the chief developer for the U.S. Army's Joint Interrogation Certification Course as well as to assist in the writing of the Army's most recent interrogation manual—the manual that, by order of the President of the United States, is now the standard for all interrogations conducted by U.S. federal personnel.

Serving as Kilbourne's non-commissioned-officer-in-charge was Sergeant Amanda Meyer. Meyer's expertise was also exceptional: after OIF I, she became a civilian Army employee at Fort Huachuca, where her abilities earned her first the position of HUMINT Collector instructor at Fort Huachuca and then HUMINT Subject Matter Expert on the U.S. Army Intelligence Center's Lessons Learned Team.

During OIF I, Alpha Company had six enlisted HUMINT personnel.²⁸ Of these collectors, four were school-trained interrogators, including one who spoke superb Arabic.²⁹ Although only two of these collectors were interrogators, the section had cross-trained its counterintelligence solders as interrogators before the deployment.³⁰ With additional oversight and on-the-job training, these counterintelligence specialists routinely served as interrogators during the deployment.³¹ Other than the warrant officers, none of the section's soldiers had any real-world operational experience. However, these soldiers were older and more mature than average, a fact that may have helped them develop into capable interrogators more quickly than most.³²

All of the section's collectors served on one of three two-man tactical HUMINT teams. They had a "general support" command relationship with the entire brigade, meaning that the brigade commander rather than subordinate battalion commanders gave direction to these teams.³³ Often, they worked directly with battalions in the screening of newly captured detainees for potential sources of intelligence, though they normally waited to interrogate subjects until these detainees had been transported to the brigade's detention facility on Forward Operating Base (FOB) Provider.³⁴

As was customary throughout Iraq, the section's interrogators not only interrogated, they also participated in Counterintelligence Force Protection Source Operations (CFSO), or what is more commonly known as "running sources." During CFSO, locals are recruited and paid to collect intelligence for their handlers. Today, 35M HUMINT collectors are professionally educated to conduct both interrogations and source operations, but during OIF I, there was a clear distinction between what 97E interrogators and 97B counterintelligence agents were supposed to do. Overburdened HUMINT sections like Alpha Company's section, though, felt forced by circumstances to cross-train and work as a team to accomplish their missions.

Though far from ideal, this practice generally worked since counterintelligence agents carefully mentored interrogators in the art of running sources, and conversely, interrogators closely aided these agents in their planning and conducting of interrogations. Facilitating their ability to train each other was the fact that these soldiers worked on the same small teams and that they had a few interchangeable skills acquired from Fort Huachuca (such as how to detect deception and to adhere successfully to the Law of War). In a few cases, interrogators even learned that they were better at conducting source operations than at interrogating, and vice versa, some counterintelligence agents learned they had a knack for interrogation. "CI and interrogators were interchangeable," said Godsil, "That's the wrong way to do it, but we did not have a choice."[35]

FOB Provider

The Ready First Brigade Holding Area was located about ten minutes west of Martyr's Monument at Forward Operating Base (FOB) Provider.[36] The brigade's supporting logistics unit, the 501st Forward Support Battalion, operated out of this base. The commander of the unit, Lieutenant Colonel Curtis Anderson, was given the responsibility of establishing and running the brigade's detention facility.[37] Thus, since Anderson held command responsibility for detention operations and Captain Martin held command responsibility for the unit's interrogators, there was no unified chain-of-command at this detention facility (which was exactly what doctrine dictated).

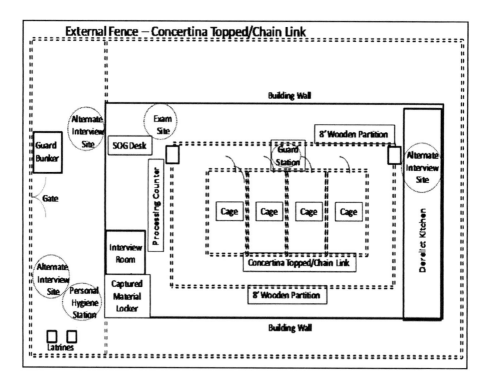

Figure 12) 1BCT, TF 1AD, Detainee Holding Area
Source: "Interview with LTC Russell Godsil," *Operational Leadership Experiences in the Global War on Terrorism*, December 20, 2008, http://cgsc.cdmhost.com/ cdm4/ item_viewer.php?CISOROOT=/p4013coll13&CISOPTR=1443&CISOBOX=1&REC=7 (accessed March 30, 2009), 3.

This command arrangement contained obvious strengths and weaknesses. One strength was that the facility's guards played no role in interrogation operations (that is, in rewarding or punishing subjects outside of the interrogation room).[38] As a result, there was less temptation for guards to "soften up" detainees for interrogations. This strength was also a weakness, though. Since the officer in charge of physical improvements at the facility was responsible for detention operations only, the regular upgrades that occurred at the facility were seldom implemented for the purpose of improving interrogations.

Since the facility was a model facility in terms of detainee security and care, it easily passed numerous Red Cross and TF 1AD inspections.[39] Yet, from an interrogator's point of view, there were several problems with it. For one, it had just one fully enclosed interrogation room– a room in which interrogations were often interrupted as guards transited from the holding area to the evidence room.[40] More importantly still, for the first three months of OIF I, all detainees were held in one general population cell in which they were free to move about and talk about their past or future interrogations to other subjects.[41] Even after the facility was upgraded and detainees were held in four adjoining cages, detainees could easily converse with one another through the chain-link fence.[42] "In the final configuration," Major Godsil said, "after a year of continuous improvement, the cage was a good holding area, but it was never a great site for [intelligence] exploitation."[43]

The 501st Forward Support Battalion used its own mechanics, supply specialists, and medics as guards at the facility.[44] Despite this use of untrained guards, no detainee abuse occurred at the facility. However, potentially lethal violence was employed by one guard who had been inadequately trained in the facility's rules for the use of force. Just prior to Colonel Mansoor's assuming command of the 1BCT, a medic fired a round from her M-16 into the holding cage when an unruly detainee threatened to throw a five-gallon water jug over the holding area's concertina wire at her.[45] The round ricoheted and fragmented with remnants slightly injuring two other prisoners.[46] Although Mansoor understood the medic had been poorly trained for this duty, he felt he had no recourse but to give her non-judicial punishment under Article 15 for such a serious violation of the facility's rules for the use of force.[47] Even more importantly, he took instant action to ensure no such incident recurred. Upon Lieutenant Colonel Anderson's recommendation, he directed that guards inside the facility be armed with batons and taser weapons rather than rifles (which, years later, became standard detention procedure in Iraq).[48] Mansoor also directed that his military police thoroughly train designated soldiers of the 501st Forward Support Battalion on proper detention procedures.[49] Additionally, contract workers replaced the facility's concertina wire "with six-foot chain-link fence topped by barbed wire."[50]

When documents are seized with detainees, effective "document exploitation" (or the extraction of intelligence from documents) becomes a key ingredient of any future interrogation of that detainee (or for that matter, this detainee's criminal prosecution). Unfortunately, the 1BCT received little help from higher in this regard since the theater's documentation exploitation teams were fully committed supporting the Iraq Survey Group in its search for legendary weapons of mass destruction, and TF 1AD, like all U.S. divisions at the time, lacked any organic document exploitation (DOCEX) capability. What resources the brigade could apply to the problem remained inadequate for the duration of OIF I. "We just didn't have the manpower at our level to conduct any type of extensive DOCEX," said Kilbourne.[51]

Interrogation procedures

Each morning, Major Godsil briefed Colonel Mansoor on the location and status of the brigade's detainees. During this brief, Godsil made recommendations to Mansoor as to whether detainees should be released, held for additional interrogation, or sent to the TF 1AD Division Interrogation Facility or the Iraqi police.[52] Additionally, his S2 section provided Kilbourne with "lines of questioning"– items of interest a specific detainee might have information about.[53]

One area, though, in which Godsil never provided direction or input to Kilbourne was in the area of interrogation approaches.[54] That is, in accordance with U.S. Army doctrine, Godsil told Kilbourne what intelligence he was looking for while leaving it to his subject matter experts (his interrogators) to determine how to extract this intelligence. Kilbourne said:

> *The S2 shop ensured that I knew exactly who we did have, and at times, they did instruct me to ensure that certain detainees were interrogated, but that was the extent of their direction. Never was I ordered to conduct any interrogation operations that went against what our initial screening assessment of the detainees established.*[55]

Kilbourne ensured his interrogators used only those approaches described in the Army's interrogation field manual. This was the case even after CJTF-7 published a policy memorandum on September 14, 2003, that told subordinate commands they could employ certain enhanced interrogation techniques. To Kilbourne, the use of these enhanced interrogation techniques was dangerous, and he refused to employ them:

> *Those memos didn't change how we at Ready First conducted ourselves for interrogation purposes because if my soldiers weren't trained to do it, then they weren't going to do it. Interrogation is a skill set just like any other MOS. This memo [the September 14, 2003, CJTF-7 interrogation policy] was idiotic. It was like providing a new, dangerous piece of equipment to a soldier and telling them that they are authorized to use it, but you don't have an instruction manual to give them to show them how to operate it safely and effectively . . . The only one [CJTF-7 interrogation policy memorandum] I remember seeing was the one that authorized stress positions for not more than one hour. This was ignorant enough since it didn't adequately define what a stress position was. Worst part is that interrogators are not trained to use stress positions, so why would we allow "carte blanche" any techniques that interrogators have not been trained to use? This didn't make any sense to me.*[56]

Although Kilbourne's interrogators may have never used stress positions on detainees, they employed the related tactic of forced labor on at least one occasion when an interrogator allowed a guard to order an uncooperative detainee to move boxes of food.[57] However, as was the case with the occasional use of stress positions elsewhere in the division, this event was the result of a detainee's misbehavior and was never part of any interrogation plan.[58] After the incident was recorded in a Summary Interrogation Report, it was reported to Major General Dempsey, the TF 1AD commander. Dempsey immediately ordered the practice stopped, and the brigade complied with this order.⁵⁹

One questionable HUMINT practice deployed throughout the 1BCT seems to have been the "running of sources" by untrained battalion-level personnel. By Department of Defense regulation, tasking informants to collect against specific intelligence requirements could only be conducted by school-trained and certified HUMINT source handlers. However, due to the fact that there were grossly inadequate numbers of these specialists assigned to the brigade, units felt they had little choice but to conduct their own source operations. "All of the BN S2s were running their own sources," said Amanda Meyer. Nonetheless, the brigade's leadership did not encourage this practice. Godsil said:

> I know that there were S2s and Commanders that pushed the limits of what they could do, and I know a couple specific instances where Company Commanders were violating published policies (see the movie "Gunner Palace"), but I fought against these practices constantly. Untrained source handlers produce poor reports, violate OPSEC, and put potentially good sources at risk. We never lost a source that reported to any 1BCT THT[tactical HUMINT team]. When a source was putting himself at risk, we cut him loose; when a reliable and loyal source was losing access, we would provide a reward that could get him out of the country (only a couple times).⁶⁰

Ultimately, the school-trained interrogators of the Ready First brigade incurred no allegations of detainee abuse. When asked why neither she nor any of her section's interrogators ever used harsh interrogation techniques, Sergeant Meyer cited the lack of time available to receive approval for such requests, since they were only allowed to hold detainees for up to 72 hours.⁶¹ But above all other influences, Meyer cited the importance of her warrant officers' mentorship, saying, "Our warrants also taught us to work within the laws and system and emphasized the fact that there was no need for us to utilize these techniques."⁶²

Command climate no doubt had something to do with the 1BCT's success in this regard also. Yet, despite the principled leadership of the brigade and division commanders, occasional interrogation abuse (and other detainee abuse) occurred within 1BCT subordinate units. One important difference between these incidents and more infamous cases such as Abu Ghraib, however, would be the timeliness and manner in which the chain-of-command dealt with them.

A series of unfortunate events

During the summer of 2003, all of the 1BCT's maneuver battalions had temporary holding areas for detainees.⁶³ The purpose of these holding areas was to collect detainees and associated evidence before shipping these people and items to the brigade detention facility. On a dangerous, resource-constrained battlefield, it made sense to thus limit the number of logistics convoys moving across Baghdad.

Initially, Special Forces and military police units unaffiliated with the Ready First brigade were allowed to process their detainees into either the brigade detention facility or battalion holding areas.⁶⁴ This created problems, however, when units disappeared after dropping off detainees with little-to-no evidence to indicate why these detainees had been captured in the first place. To correct this, Godsil drafted a policy in which no 1BCT unit was allowed to accept detainees from units unaffiliated with the brigade without the brigade commander's permission.⁶⁵ Colonel Mansoor signed the policy, thus fixing this problem.⁶⁶ Additionally, Godsil made a point of being present whenever other governmental agencies (such as the CIA) questioned detainees in brigade facilities, thus helping to ensure that these agencies adhered to doctrinal interrogation standards.⁶⁷

Despite such fixes, operating battalion-level holding areas remained problematic. One reason for this was that the brigade had insufficient resources to ensure every holding area met the standards directed by international law for the care and treatment of detainees. For about three weeks during the summer of 2003, for example, Task Force 1-36 Infantry ran a holding area that consisted of a small building with only small slots for light and air and with only sporadic electricity.⁶⁸ As a result, detainees were kept in the dark for most of their stay here– a stay that could last up to three days.⁶⁹ Another reason these areas were problematic was the problem of enforcing the same standards of detainee treatment across a non-contiguous and dangerous battlefield. Although the brigade's leadership was quite clear on the importance of treating detainees with dignity and respect and in accordance with international law, due to the unit's high operational tempo and the hazards of travel, it was impossible for them and their immediate subordinates to practice continuous oversight of every patrol, every operation, and every temporary holding area.

Within the Ready First brigade, two battalions in particular were associated with detainee abuse. One of these battalions was the 2nd Battalion, 3rd Field Artillery, which operated a temporary holding area at Gunner Palace for the duration of OIF I. There were at least two allegations of abuse at this battalion holding area. One case involved the alleged participation of both U.S. soldiers and Iraqi Civil Defense Corps soldiers in the beating of a detainee; yet another allegation involved U.S. Special Forces soldiers employing enhanced interrogation techniques at the facility.⁷⁰ In both of these cases, investigating officers found insufficient evidence to confirm or deny the allegations. Furthermore, a night-shift guard sergeant at FOB Provider provided a sworn statement in December 2003 alleging that he had seen detainees arrive at the brigade facility with bruises and that a "significant number" of these detainees had come from Gunner Palace.⁷¹ Although much of this bruising was no doubt the unavoidable consequences of combat and capture, the fact that there were recurring (albeit unconfirmed) allegations of abuse involving this unit's detention facility could indicate that a systemic problem existed somewhere within this unit– or more likely, within the Special Forces team which operated out of a house adjacent to Gunner Palace and which regularly dropped off detainees there. "The Gunner Palace cage was a pain in the ass," said Godsil. "I never liked it, and I got to talk to CID [Criminal Investigation Division] several times about it."⁷²

More clearly, Task Force 1-36 Infantry had significant problems with regard to detainee abuse. On the day that Colonel Mansoor took command of the 1BCT, the Task Force 1-36 Infantry commander informed Mansoor that a commander's inquiry (an initial informal investigation) indicated that one of his platoons had been beating detainees.⁷³ Mansoor immediately requested a criminal investigation into the allegations of abuse.⁷⁴ This investigation determined that, in the beginning, criminal misbehavior included soldiers extorting a so-called "Robin Hood Tax" from locals to purchase such items as soda, beer, and whiskey.⁷⁵ Then in a slippery moral slope reminiscent of Abu Ghraib, harsher detainee abuse occurred, including an ill-conceived attempt at deterring looters from repeating their crimes by beating them.⁷⁶ Eventually, a few soldiers seem to have beaten some Iraqis just because of the perverse pleasure these soldiers received from doing this. In the end, enough evidence was collected against these soldiers to convict one platoon sergeant (who did jail time) and one soldier of assault.[77] Additionally, the platoon leader was separated from the Army and the platoon's company commander received a written reprimand from Major General Dempsey.[78]

Another incident that occurred in Task Force 1-36 Infantry was an obvious example of interrogation abuse. On August 31, 2003, a junior enlisted military intelligence soldier (a trained analyst and not a trained interrogator) questioned two subjects.[79] During separate questioning of each detainee, the soldier made the two detainees put an M16 bullet in their mouths and told them that if they did not tell him who the insurgents were, the private first class behind them would shoot them.[80] He then took the bullets from the detainees' mouths and directed the even more junior soldier behind them to charge his weapon.[81] Later, this analyst testified that he had received the idea for this interrogation tactic from television and the movies.[82] Additionally, in a junior enlisted version of the higher-level discussions then taking place about harsh interrogation tactics and "interrogation wish lists," he stated he had discussed this tactic with friends as well as another technique involving the placement of sandbags into a body bag and the carrying of this fake body out of the interrogation room to frighten an arriving detainee.[83] Thankfully, this latter tactic was never employed.

Achievements

The 1BCT's commander, staff, and interrogators adhered to doctrinal interrogation standards, not just in terms of interrogation approaches but in terms of the duties and responsibilities of each key player. They were all on the same sheet of music. All came together to form an effective, harmonious team. Additionally, the insistence of leaders that interrogators adhere to the moral high ground ensured that FOB Provider would be no Abu Ghraib or Strike Brigade Holding Area.

Nonetheless, interrogation and detainee abuse did occur within the brigade, some of which was very serious. Such abuse occurred despite clear guidance from leadership regarding the importance of treating detainees with dignity and respect. Thus, the 1BCT in Baghdad serves as the same cautionary tale as the 101st Airborne Division in Mosul: the U.S. Army needs to ensure that its junior leaders, who often deploy to remote outposts in "Indian Country" in which they cannot be adequately supervised, receive before deploying the education and training that they need to be moral leaders on today's decentralized battlefields.

Ultimately, despite tremendous obstacles and several serious missteps, the 1BCT achieved much of which it would later be justifiably proud. Most notably, during the last few months of the deployment, insurgent violence in the area noticeably diminished.[84] This lull in violence could have provided the Coalition Provisional Authority with the opportunity to effect political reconciliation between the various ethnic and insurgent groups in Adhamiya and Russafa.[85] Unfortunately, this opportunity was not seized, and insurgent violence in these two districts rapidly escalated after the Ready First brigade repositioned to Camp Victory as the Corps reserve, and its replacement unit – on orders from CJTF-7 – abandoned the forward operating bases inside central and northeast Baghdad that 1BCT had occupied and defended from June 2003 to April 2004."

Other accomplishments of the 1BCT during OIF I were significant, such as its recruiting, organizing, and training two battalions of the Iraq Civil Defense Corps and thousands of Iraqi security guards and policemen.[86] Also notably, during the 1AD's three-month extension for Operation Iron Saber in the spring and summer of 2004, the Ready First brigade defeated Muqtada al-Sadr's militia, the *Jaish al-Mahdi*, in a critical battle south of Baghdad in the holy city of Karbala. As a result of its Herculean efforts, the brigade would be one of three TF 1AD units awarded the Presidential Unit Citation for collective valor in combat.

The Bulldog Brigade

Prior to OIF I, the home station of the 3rd Brigade, 1AD, was at Fort Riley, Kansas, making this brigade the only maneuver brigade in the division that was not stationed in Europe. In February and early March 2003, the brigade (also called the "Bulldog Brigade") deployed its 2nd Battalion, 70th Armor and 1st Battalion, 41st Infantry battalions to Kuwait.[87] These battalions took part in the initial invasion of Iraq, crossing the berm into Iraq on March 21, 2003.[88] After taking part in battles south and west of Baghdad, these two battalions went to Baghdad and rejoined their parent unit. When the 1AD was stood up as "Task Force Baghdad" on May 29, 2003, the 3rd Brigade Combat Team (3BCT) assumed responsibility in northwest Baghdad for the Mansour District in the southern and north-central portions of its sector and, along the Tigris River in the northeastern part of its sector, the Kadhamiya District.[89] The largely Sunni Mansour district had contained, prior to the invasion, some of the more prosperous shopping areas and affluent neighborhoods in Baghdad, though it also contained an impoverished rural population on the outskirts of western Baghdad.[90] Most famously, the Shiite Kadhamiya district held one of the most holy Shiite shrines in Iraq, the Kadhamiya Mosque, site of the tombs of two of Shiite Islam's 12 Imams.[91]

Where these two districts met represented a major ethnic fault-line in Baghdad, a fault line that, years later, would erupt into terrible scenes of ethnic cleansing and bitter sectarian fighting. During OIF I, however, these districts did not see the same scale of Sunni insurgent and Shiite militia activity that some other parts of Baghdad witnessed. Instead, the main threat to 3BCT soldiers was small but lethal Sunni insurgent cells that targeted U.S. forces, first with such hand-carried weapons as AK-47s and rocket-propelled grenade launchers, then eventually almost exclusively with IEDs. Often these cells consisted of former members of Saddam's intelligence services and Republican Guard, many of whom still lived in upscale neighborhoods in the Mansour district.

Since the Bulldog Brigade consisted largely of armor troops, it needed more infantry soldiers ("boots on the ground") to secure its sector. As a result, the 1AD headquarters attached the 1st Battalion, 325th Infantry, from the 2nd Brigade, 82nd Airborne Division, to the 3BCT.[92] The 3BCT thus had four maneuver battalions it could use to secure areas within its sector, the 1st Battalion, 325th Infantry; the 1st Battalion, 13th Armor; the 2nd Battalion, 70th Armor; and the 4th Battalion, 1st Field Artillery.[93] Despite its infusion of infantry soldiers, the 3BCT still struggled with a severe shortage in the number of counterinsurgents it could place on the streets of Baghdad: even with the addition of 1st Battalion, 325th Infantry, the brigade's total strength was only about 3,500 soldiers.[94] These soldiers had the task of securing and restoring essential services for more than one million Iraqis.[95] This meant that the brigade (at best) had a ratio of less than four counterinsurgents for every 1,000 Iraqis—though better than the 1BCT's ratio, far short of the number of counterinsurgents recommended by current U.S. Army doctrine.

The fact that this brigade's home station was in Kansas gave rise to additional problems with regard to intelligence collection. Specifically, the brigade had not previously trained with the soldiers of its direct support intelligence company, Company C, 501st MI Battalion. This lack of familiarity with the company led to confusion among Bulldog Brigade combat leaders as to how they could best use their Tactical HUMINT Teams. For example, Lieutenant Colonel Mark Crisman, the 3BCT S-2, has stated that he had a tough time convincing Colonel Russell Gold, the brigade commander, of the need to push tactical HUMINT teams off of protected bases and into dangerous areas.[96] Colonel Gold eventually did buy off on the concept, though, even ensuring these teams had personal security escorts when Company C was unable to provide such escorts.[97] This continuous availability of escorts provided the company's HUMINT teams with a mobility and flexibility that the teams of other brigades sometimes envied.

FOB Dakota

For two months, the Bulldog Brigade Holding Area was located in a small caged area on FOB Dakota, the former headquarters of an Iraqi intelligence service, while work was done to clean out and improve another site on the base.[98] At the end of June 2003, detention operations were moved to this other site, a former jail.[99] This new site

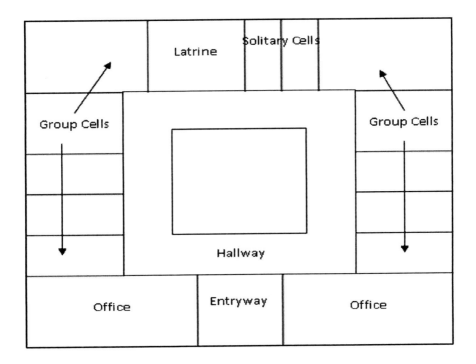

Figure 13) 3BCT, TF 1AD, Detainee Holding Area
Source: MAJ Douglas A. Pryer, "Interview with MAJ Brad Johnson," *Operational Leadership Experiences in the Global War on Terrorism*, http://cgsc.contentdm.oclc.org/ cdm4/ item_viewer.php?CISOROOT=/p4013coll13&CISOPTR=1419&CISOBOX= 1&REC=5 (accessed August 16, 2009), 6.

would prove to be one of the better constructed, more functional brigade holding areas in TF 1AD.

The 1st Battalion, 13th Armor, was responsible for maintaining the brigade detention facility.[100] Initially, this battalion was responsible for providing and managing the guard force as well, which consisted of a platoon from this battalion's engineer company.[101] By August 2003, however, soldiers from a Connecticut National Guard military police company were manning the facility.[102] Thus, in accordance with Army doctrine at the time, military intelligence interrogators and military police soldiers had two separate chains-of-command at the facility. The senior intelligence officer in the brigade, Lieutenant Colonel Crisman, had staff oversight of both intelligence and detention operations at the facility; that is, he provided recommendations regarding operations to Colonel Gold or to the appropriate military intelligence or military police company commander for these commanders to action.[103] He also paid weekly visits to the facility and formally inspected the facility at least once a month.[104]

In terms of detainee care, security, and force protection, the 3BCT holding area was superb. It had thick concrete walls that provided guards and detainees with protection from incoming rocket or mortar rounds. The facility contained one single entry and exit point, and it had bars on the cell windows.[105] Detainees had a courtyard in which they could exercise, and they had access to running water, functioning toilets, and a medical doctor.[106] The 1st Battalion, 13th Armor, even rebuilt the facility's electrical system so that lighting was not a problem at the facility.[107] Certainly, the Red Cross was happy with the facility, noting only minor deficiencies during its inspections.[108]

The facility also supported interrogations better than most brigade-level facilities. Interrogations took place in private rooms in an adjacent building, enabling interrogators to question detainees without interruption. Truly "high value internees" could be segregated from other detainees in one of two "solitary cells," thus ensuring they were not speaking with other detainees. Also, even when these solitary cells were not used, segregation in this facility naturally occurred to a greater degree than was customary during OIF I, since the facility had 10 group cells.

Intelligence operations

The HUMINT section of Charlie Company, 501st MI Battalion, was missing one key person during its support of the Bulldog Brigade—a counterintelligence warrant officer. The shortage of a HUMINT warrant officer was typical: Alpha Company also lacked a second warrant officer for half of OIF I, while Bravo Company lacked a second warrant officer for the duration of the deployment. Fortunately, Charlie Company had an exceptional warrant officer in Chief Warrant Officer 2 John Groseclose. In fact, Groseclose later received the DoD's Top HUMINT Collector of 2003 Award for his performance during OIF I. Moreover, Charlie Company's HUMINT section was somewhat atypical in that it had all of its enlisted HUMINT personnel and that all of these soldiers were extraordinarily capable. Attesting to this is the fact that Charlie Company's HUMINT section, at least for the first six months of OIF I, out-produced other HUMINT sections in the division in terms of the sheer number of HUMINT reports it produced—and often in terms of the quality of these reports as well.[109]

Since Groseclose had a fully manned HUMINT section, he could allow his interrogators to focus more on interrogating and less on running sources. Still, he sometimes had no choice but to direct an interrogator to run a source or a counterintelligence agent to conduct an interrogation. In general, he thought that interrogators did a slightly better job than counterintelligence agents of learning the others' craft. "I think our interrogators probably picked up how to conduct CFSO source operations a little quicker," Groseclose said. "I would say that that was because that was the majority of what we were doing, so we got more practice at it."[110]

Interrogations in the Bulldog Brigade suffered from many of the same ailments that plagued the intelligence operations of most other brigades in the division. For one, the brigade lacked the resources to conduct effective document exploitation to support interrogations.[111] Secondly, until the very end of the 3BCT's deployment, its brigade S2 section and detention facility guards struggled with collecting sworn statements and the other documents needed to support the continued internment of detainees. Thirdly, the brigade S2 section was too overwhelmed to provide consistent analytical support to interrogators.

With regard to interrogation approaches, according to Groseclose, his interrogators employed only doctrinal approaches. This was true even after CJTF-7 published interrogation policy promoting several enhanced interrogation techniques in September 2003. Groseclose said:

> I can't see how any interrogator could go along with it . . . For an interrogator to resort to techniques like that is for that interrogator to admit that they don't know how to interrogate. Personally, I'm offended by it. When you use things like that, when you start pushing people to the point where you are using Fear of Dogs and all these other crazy things that they were doing, yes, the detainee will give you information, but how do you know what the detainee is telling you is the truth? Based on the physical reaction of his response, there is no way of telling whether or not he is telling the truth. You cannot tell based on his posture or on any of the other indicators we use for uncovering deception whether or not they are telling the truth, or whether he is just telling you something just to get you to stop. I really question a lot of the intelligence they were collecting at the time. I know you hear that some detainee at Gitmo was giving great intel, but to be honest with you, I think they should take a really good look at that intel.[112]

Groseclose seems to have largely disagreed with the use of enhanced interrogation techniques due to his perception that such techniques are almost always ineffective. According to Groseclose, he had little use for enhanced interrogation techniques because his teams' doctrinal interrogation techniques "produced results." He was also in agreement with Army doctrine regarding the "Fear Up Harsh" approach, believing this approach was only useful on certain subjects—and then only as a last resort. Because of his utilitarian perspective in this regard, he was apparently the only HUMINT officer in the division to request (on just one occasion and no doubt as "a last resort") the use of an enhanced interrogation technique. This request was denied, almost certainly by the 501st MI Battalion headquarters.

However, as was occasionally allowed in certain other units in the division, his interrogators were apparently permitted to lightly exercise subjects or put them in stress positions if they misbehaved.[113] Groseclose has denied using any stress positions as serious as "having people stand on sandbags for hours," a nod (albeit an exaggerated nod) to a practice of the guards at the 2nd Brigade detention facility.[114] However, he has not denied implementing less harsh techniques to control the misbehavior of detainees. As further evidence of this practice, soon after one of the Charlie Company interrogators was attached to Bravo Company in the summer of 2004, this interrogator immediately tried to control a detainee by making him do push-ups and jumping jacks, causing the Bravo Company, 501st MI Battalion, commander to initiate an inquiry into the incident.[115] The inquiry revealed that this interrogator did not see anything wrong with using exercise to control a detainee. Furthermore, this interrogator alleged that he had previously used this technique in Charlie Company. The strongest evidence of this practice in the unit, though, is that Crisman has bluntly stated that its interrogators employed stress positions for a brief period of time.[116]

In short, it is clear that this company's interrogators at least occasionally employed stress positions and forced exercise to control unruly detainees, though the exact extent of this practice within this company is understandably vague. Fortunately, this method of controlling misbehaving detainees never got out of hand.

Groseclose admits to sometimes receiving pressure during OIF I from combat leaders to try harsher techniques, but thanks to the strength of his personality and to Crisman's support, he says, he was able to weather such requests:

> *Lieutenant Colonel Crisman very much supported us. You know, it doesn't matter which theater you go into, or which rotation that you're on, when you have commanders out there that are losing soldiers, or their soldiers are getting wounded, they're going to pressure you to get more information. They want to know who is doing it; they want to make it stop. So, yes, there were times when we were under pressure to get more information or to do interrogations a certain way that they thought would be more productive. It really is up to interrogators to explain to them why we don't do those things. But, we didn't face undue pressure. The topic did come up on occasion, and I would just sit down with a commander and talk to them, and we'd talk through it. I'd say, first of all, that is not what we're going to do, and this is why we're not going to do it. There are better ways of doing things.*[117]

Nonetheless, one alleged case of detainee abuse occurred at the 3BCT's detention facility. On September 16, 2003, a platoon from 2nd Battalion, 70th Armor, dropped off five detainees at the facility.[118] These detainees were suspected of involvement in an IED attack that had left their platoon leader with "loss of eyesight and the use of one arm," and another soldier's loss of eyesight in one eye.[119] According to the two interrogators who reported the incident, these soldiers pushed one of the hooded detainees off of the back of the truck, screamed at the detainees, and kicked them.[120] The interrogators allege that they were able to stop this abuse, but not before hearing, "They did not kill your LT!" from one of these soldiers.[121]

When the investigating officer later interviewed these soldiers, they only admitted to yelling at these detainees. However, the investigating officer deemed the testimony of the interrogators to be more credible and concluded that the soldiers from Task Force 2-70 had probably determined "the one story to tell" prior to the investigation.[122] The investigating officer also noted, no doubt rightly, that these angry soldiers should never have been put in the situation of transporting detainees they believed responsible for the recent serious injuries (and feared death) of their platoon leader.[123] It is unclear from the documents that the U.S. Army has released regarding this incident what punishment these soldiers received, though the only punishments recommended by the investigating officer were two letters of reprimand.[124]

The conduct of the two school-trained interrogators in this incident—first to stop detainee abuse and then to report it—was exemplary. Regarding the strong female interrogator who took the lead in stopping and reporting this abuse, her platoon leader later said that she even "went so far as to tell the leadership that if she suspected there was mistreatment on their part, she would report them for Geneva Convention violations."[125]

In short, thanks to Groseclose's belief that enhanced interrogation techniques almost never work, a higher headquarters and brigade S2 that supported him, and the willingness of his interrogators to stand up for what they believed was right, Charlie Company's interrogators managed to interrogate with exceptional effectiveness while standing firm on the moral high ground.

Unfortunately, though, as in the case of detainee abuse just described, not all 3BCT soldiers were able to claim as much with regard to their treatment of detainees.

Troubling events in small units

Of the five cases of substantiated interrogation abuse committed by TF 1AD soldiers during OIF I, one of these cases was committed on June 21, 2003, by soldiers of 4th Battalion, 1st Field Artillery, 3BCT. In this incident, a private first class struck an Iraqi mosque guard after asking the guard if the guard had been the individual who had been shooting at his unit.[126] Apparently, this soldier's section leader also tried to get the mosque guard to grab a non-functioning museum weapon so his soldiers would be justified in shooting him.[127]

Yet another disturbing incident, not of interrogation abuse but of detainee abuse at the point of capture, occurred within a platoon of the 1st Battalion, 13th Armor. Like the incident at the 3BCT detention facility described above, this abuse involved a misguided attempt to use fear to prevent looters from looting again.[128] The major difference was the manner in which this fear was inspired: whereas the platoon in the 1BCT had beaten and released looters, this 3BCT platoon employed two mock executions to scare looters before releasing them. In the first incident on June 22, 2003, the platoon leader pointed his pistol at the head of a male teenage looter, then pointed his weapon away from the young looter while firing his weapon.[129] The other incident that day, apparently condoned by this platoon leader, involved a sergeant using his M16 to execute the same scare tactic on another young looter.[130] Thankfully, the platoon leader who performed one of these mock executions (and condoned the other) appears to have been forced out of the Army.[131]

A third incident of detainee abuse may have occurred on October 25, 2003, at the temporary holding facility run by 2nd Battalion, 70th Armor.[132] Like the incident at the 3BCT detention facility described above, this incident involved soldiers dropping off detainees suspected of serious wrongdoing. In this case, six detainees had been "apprehended with a large weapons cache" after "throwing grenades at U.S. soldiers."[133] According to a facility guard, the five soldiers escorting these detainees from a truck to the facility "started to slap the prisoners in the face and sock them in the gut" and "stomped on grey shirted prisoners' bare feet."[134] Interviews and physical examinations of the captured detainees corroborated the guard's testimony.[135] During the investigation, at least two soldiers (including the platoon leader) invoked their rights, refusing to provide testimony.[136] The investigating officer was subsequently able to identify only four of the soldiers involved in the alleged abuse.[137] The battalion commander of these soldiers, during the Article 15 hearing for one of them, concluded that this soldier had "felt threatened by the behavior of the detainee" and had "applied the appropriate amount of force to control the situation."[138] The documentation released by the U.S. Army regarding the incident does not reveal what disciplinary action, if any, was incurred by the other three soldiers identified as participating in this alleged abuse.

Noteworthy here is that the 1st Battalion, 325th Infantry Battalion, which was attached to the 3BCT for most of the deployment, did an admirable job of running a battalion-level holding area that incurred no allegations of detainee abuse.[139] More uniquely, this battalion seems to have been one of the few OIF I maneuver battalions that did not slip into the controversial practice of having battalion S2s conduct source operations, a type of operation that, by U.S. Army doctrine and regulation, only trained HUMINT collectors were supposed to do. Groseclose said:

> I worked a lot with 1-325 Infantry. And those guys did have their informant networks. They would also go out on foot patrols into town, and they would talk to a lot of people while they were on foot patrols. And that would actually work to our benefit, because I would sit down and talk to them and they would point me towards potential sources that I could then pick up. They were actually pretty good about handing off sources.[140]

In other words, the 1st Battalion, 325th Infantry Battalion, operated in accordance with Army doctrine. Its S2 did not task informants to collect specific information, but rather the unit passively collected information from informants and handed-off their best informants to counterintelligence professionals to run as sources.

Nonetheless, other battalion S2s within the brigade—like most battalion S2s across the division—did run sources. Groseclose, along with probably every other HUMINT professional in the division, strongly disagreed with this practice:

> Then there were other S2s within the 3rd Brigade who were running full-blown source operations. There were sources that ended up dying because of the way they were running their operations, or the information was not as accurate as they thought it would turn out to be. So yes, I think that was a problem. There were some S2s out there who went beyond doctrine.[141]

Despite this comment, these S2s felt they had no other choice but to run sources. According to Major Brad Johnson, who was the S2 for Task Force 1st Battalion, 13th Armor, the brigade's HUMINT teams were "stretched thin" and his brigade was receiving "almost no HUMINT support from 1AD."[142] Since they "had to gather information somehow," running sources "was the only way to do it, as SIGINT and IMINT [Signals Intelligence and Imagery Intelligence] were almost useless to us."[143]

Ultimately, the accomplishments of the Bulldog Brigade were varied and significant. In recognition of its achievements, upon redeployment, the 3BCT was awarded the Valorous Unit Award, an award given only to those units who display exceptional gallantry under extremely hazardous conditions.

The Iron Brigade

If Baghdad is the political heart of Iraq, then TF 1AD's 2nd Brigade Combat Team (2BCT) in downtown Baghdad operated within the heart of hearts of Iraq– or at the "tip of the spear" of U.S. stabilization efforts, to use more conventional parlance.

Appropriately symbolizing the key terrain it occupied, the 2BCT's headquarters was located in the Al Faw Palace, a palace that, since it had been Saddam's official residence, could be considered the "White House" of his regime.

Within this "heart of hearts," the 2BCT (nicknamed the "Iron Brigade") was responsible for two of Baghdad's nine districts, the Karada and Karkh districts. The Karada district was on the east side of the Tigris River and extended from the center of Baghdad southeast to the Tuwaitha Nuclear Facility on Baghdad's outskirts. This relatively well-educated, affluent district included Baghdad's main banking district, the University of Baghdad, and most of Baghdad's embassies. On the west side of the Tigris River was the Karkh District, a district that included such notable landmarks as the national Ba'ath Party headquarters, the Iraqi Cultural Museum, the Baghdad Zoo, the Crossed Sabers Monument, and the "Green Zone," the seat of the Coalition Provisional Authority during OIF I. Also, an insurgent stronghold was located in the Karkh District: the violence within this stronghold, encompassing the businesses and high-rise apartments of Haifa Street as well as this notorious street's adjacent neighborhoods, stood in stark contrast to the secure environment established by the 2BCT in the Green Zone.

Five battalions were responsible for geographical sections of the 2BCT's area of responsibility. This included organic units (1st Battalion, 6th Infantry; 2nd Battalion, 6th Infantry; 1st Battalion, 35th Armor; and 4th Battalion, 27th Field Artillery) as well as one attached unit (3rd Squadron, 2nd Light Cavalry Regiment). With these troops, the brigade not only secured the Green Zone and a large amount of critical infrastructure, but most importantly, the 2BCT was responsible for the security of somewhere between 700,000 and one million Iraqis. Since the brigade itself had between 5,000 and 6,000 soldiers, the counterinsurgent-to-population ratio in the brigade's area ranged from five to eight counterinsurgents for every 1,000 Iraqis. Although better than the ratios of the 1st and 3rd brigades, this ratio was still not close to the doctrinal standard.

To accomplish a huge mission with limited troops, Iron Brigade leaders had to come up with creative solutions to their tactical problems. Nowhere was the need for creativity greater than in the field of intelligence.

"HUMINT-centric operations"

The primary architects of the 2BCT's intelligence innovations were Colonel Ralph Baker, the brigade commander, and Major Larry Wilson, the brigade S-2. According to Colonel Baker, soon after he assumed command of the brigade on July 7, 2003, he understood that the brigade had to reform the way it conducted intelligence operations and "transition our conventional BCT intelligence system into a HUMINT-centric system."[144] With the help of Wilson, who arrived in August 2003, Baker began transforming his brigade into an organization that heavily emphasized HUMINT collection and analysis.

Baker published his intelligence section's organizational chart in an article in the March-April, 2007, edition of *Military Review*. (*See Figure 13, page 99*). Although the personnel numbers in this chart are incorrect, the diagram is conceptually accurate.[145] What it accurately describes is how bright, motivated soldiers of various specialties joined soldiers from the brigade's S2 section and direct-support military intelligence company to create a new, HUMINT-focused S2X section. This new section, in turn, was divided into five subordinate sections– Targeting, Enemy Prisoner of War,

Document Exploitation, Passive HUMINT Collection, and Database Functions.

All of these S2X sections played a role in the brigade's interrogation operations: the Targeting, Document Exploitation, and Passive HUMINT sections provided interrogators with reports that helped them develop their interrogation plans; interrogators' reports found their way into detainee packets built by the Enemy Prisoner of War section; and data specialists within the Database Functions section archived data collected through interrogations and screenings. Also, under Major Wilson's guidance, these sections developed and implemented capabilities that may have been unique to the 2BCT among CJTF-7's brigades. These capabilities included:

1. The S2X's Document Exploitation section, which included a dedicated linguist and analyst, seems to have been the only brigade section dedicated exclusively to this task in the division. Augmenting this valuable capability was the brigade's use of FBI software to gather intelligence from captured hard drives.[146]

2. Thanks to its robust manning, the number of soldiers the S2X was able to dedicate to supporting interrogation operations with intelligence analysis was greater than what could be provided by the S2 sections of other brigades.

3. In part due to its location in the Green Zone but also due to its ability to proactively leverage manpower in this regard, the 2BCT's Enemy Prisoner of War section was able to frequently obtain the services of an FBI polygraphist, whose conclusions regarding the truthfulness of detainees could then be passed on to interrogators to enhance interrogation plans.[147]

4. As a result of its having a section dedicated to the processing of detention paperwork, the brigade did not suffer as much as other brigades from deficient evidence packets.

But the S2X capability that Wilson considered most valuable was employed by the Passive HUMINT section, namely, the use of a "cage rat" and other carefully hidden informants to collect intelligence.[148] The "cage rat" was an Iraqi who was planted as a prisoner in the 2BCT detention facility so as to clandestinely collect information from detainees. Wilson considered his "cage rat" to be more effective than a hidden microphone because of this informant's ability to engage detainees in conversation and actively elicit information of value.[149] The brigade also routinely placed an informant masquerading as a prisoner in the trucks used to transport detainees after a raid.[150] In addition, if a detainee strongly suspected of insurgent ties had to be released because of insufficient evidence, the brigade might have an Iraqi taxi driver (who was also an informant) take the detainee home. If the detainee boasted of how he had "fooled the stupid Americans" or provided some other self-incriminating evidence, the brigade could later detain him for further questioning.[151]

In addition to growing his headquarters and its intelligence-collection capabilities, Baker made it a command priority for each of his battalions to develop informant networks. At weekly Reconnaissance and Surveillance meetings, he checked on the number of informants each battalion had gathered and was briefed on the priority intelligence requirements each informant was trying to answer.[152] Eventually, each battalion S2 section developed three to five informants that they considered reliable.[153] Wilson also had three to five informants, as did Captain William Bell, the captain in charge of his S2X section.[154] The brigade's informants included "members of political parties, local government officials, prostitutes, police officers, retired Iraqi generals, prominent businessmen, and expatriates."[155] According to Wilson, informant networks and "EPW collection" (that is, interrogators and hidden informants) had "to operate in concert in order to provide the brigade with the intelligence that it needed."[156]

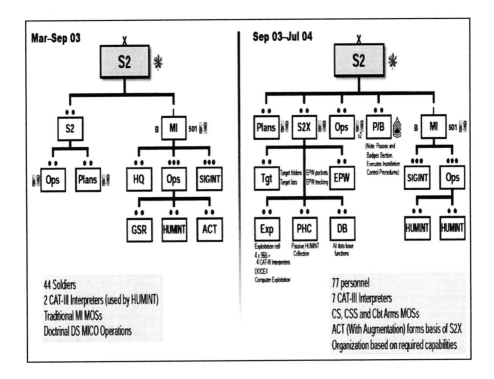

Source: Colonel Ralph O. Baker, "HUMINT-Centric Operations: Developing Actionable Intelligence in the Urban Counterinsurgency Environment," *Military Review* (March-April 2007): 12-21, 14.

During the deployment and still today, Wilson has tried to draw a fine line between the "running of sources" by school-trained HUMINT collectors and what the S2 sections of the Iron Brigade did, which was to "sensitize" informants to the brigade's specific information requirements. Wilson said:

> I think you sensitize them. I don't think you necessarily task them. You sensitize them to what it is that you need and you let them figure out how to do it. You don't say, "I want you to go to this pink house and take a picture." You say, "You know it would be nice if we had a picture of where Ahmed Such and Such lives." Then you let him go out and figure out how to get the picture.[157]

The HUMINT professionals who heard this argument, though, saw no distinguishable difference between this kind of "sensitizing" and running sources. Like the 2BCT's S2s, these professionals did not normally tell a source how to collect against a specific information requirement either. Instead, they leveraged their professional expertise to determine which source with what "placement and access" could collect intelligence on a specific intelligence requirement, then they would provide this requirement to the appropriate source. This providing of intelligence requirements to informants is exactly what 2BCT S2s were doing, only these S2s were working this process without such school-trained skills as the ability to reliably detect deception, prevent compromise of intelligence gaps, and safeguard the source himself.

By aggressively having non-HUMINT personnel conduct source operations, Iron Brigade leadership believed that it achieved operational successes that it would not otherwise have achieved. Most proudly, they pointed to the arrest of an insurgent cell they called the "Muhalla 636 Gang," which they believed responsible for the October 26, 2003, rocket attack on the al Rasheed Hotel. (This rocket attack had killed U.S. Army Lieutenant Colonel Charles Buehring and wounded several others. Uninjured in the attack had been Deputy Secretary of Defense Paul Wolfowitz, also staying in the hotel.)[158] Although interrogators and other professional HUMINT collectors played a role in these captures, the 2BCT's leadership believed that its informant networks deserved most of the credit for the operation.[159]

Many leaders within TF 1AD's military intelligence community, however, had serious reservations regarding both the 2BCT's informant networks and the purported successes of these networks.[160] The concern was not due to the 2BCT's doing something entirely unique: as described in the two sections above, battalion S2s throughout the division commonly ran sources. What was different regarding the way the 2BCT did business was that, while the brigade commanders and S2s of other brigades at best tolerated the practice, Colonel Baker and Major Wilson wholeheartedly embraced it. Indeed, the S2 section of the Iron Brigade was the only brigade-level S2 section in the division that had non-HUMINT soldiers running sources. What is more, Colonel Baker not only tolerated this practice, but he held battalion commanders accountable if they were not sufficiently proactive in acquiring informants.

The division's HUMINT professionals did not like to see S2s running sources, and to see the 2BCT blatantly do so (to the extent even of issuing badges to informants) upset and angered them. Chief Warrant Officer 2 Kilbourne of the 1BCT said:

> What the 2nd Brigade did was highly illegal, directly by policy. However, these policies are classified and cannot be discussed in this forum. Many of these "leaders" that were conducting their own intelligence-gathering operations were reported to higher commands because their ignorance regarding what they were doing were getting people killed. What I heard from reliable members of 2nd Brigade was that the 2nd Brigade's S2X chose not to use his HUMINT assets due to their youth and inexperience and then built a ridiculous 27 member S2X called the "Stryker Service Agency" and gave everyone badges like they were some special three-letter agency. This was a joke and made a mockery of the entire HUMINT skill set. Many others thought that there really wasn't much to HUMINT except talking to people, and they had no clue as to the negative effect they were having on our entire HUMINT collection process by operating so carelessly. The problem was that very few if any of these leaders were punished for what they did, and they should have

> been so that the follow-on education process of what we do and how we do it would be taken much more seriously by those that followed.[161]

According to trained professionals like Kilbourne, running sources is a complex skill requiring years of professional education and hands-on experience to master.[162] In the hands of non-professional handlers, informants might be paid too much, thus adversely impacting source operations across the division. These professionals also argued that informants might be tasked by non-professionals to collect intelligence on requirements for which they did not have placement and access, leading to their being killed by insurgents.[163] Additionally, since the 2BCT's non-professional source handlers had no higher oversight, there was nothing to stop these handlers from using sources known to be unreliable by HUMINT soldiers in other brigades or to interfere with sources in use by other brigades. What is more, they argued, improperly screened (or "vetted") informants were likely to provide misinformation, thus resulting in the brigade's unknowingly actioning poor intelligence, detaining innocent Iraqis, or being used by factions to settle scores. Worst of all, they said, deliberate misinformation might get soldiers ambushed and killed.

A few incidents that allegedly occurred during OIF I may have justified such concerns. To this day, many of TF 1AD's military intelligence leaders and soldiers believe that 2BCT informants died because they were improperly handled.[164] As for such successes as the apprehension of the Muhalla 636 gang, at least one HUMINT operator intimately connected with this operation continues to privately voice his belief that the Iron Brigade's leadership did not capture whom they thought they captured: they captured the wrong bad guys, he says.[165] Although there is no definitive proof to support the largely private and strongly voiced beliefs of many military intelligence professionals with regard to the brigade's extensive informant networks, these leaders and soldiers have earned enough credibility to make their opinions on this subject worth noting.

<u>Camp Striker</u>

The 2BCT had one incident of substantiated interrogation abuse involving, not school-trained interrogators, but combat troops. This incident occurred on September 1, 2003, and it involved soldiers of the 2nd Battalion, 6th Infantry.[166]

According to the three Iraqi guards of a mosque, one of them fired his weapon as the three of them pursued a thief.[167] Soon after, a dismounted U.S. patrol appeared, causing the three guards to immediately lay down their weapons to prevent their being shot.[168] The squad promptly arrested the three guards and took them to the battalion's holding area.[169] Several hours after their detention, several soldiers re-entered the facility and began kicking and hitting them, asking them whether they were al Qaeda or Fedayeen.[170] The soldiers then took them out of the facility, where they slapped and threw them around some more.[171]

When the allegations of misconduct within this infantry platoon surfaced, the unit promptly investigated the incident, turning over the results of the investigation to Army CID. Less than two weeks after the incident, the criminal investigation was complete.[172] As a result of the investigation, the responsible agent concluded that there was sufficient evidence to believe that five soldiers, including one platoon sergeant, three staff sergeants, and one specialist, had committed crimes ranging from Assault to Obstruction of Justice.[173] At least four of these soldiers were found guilty as charged

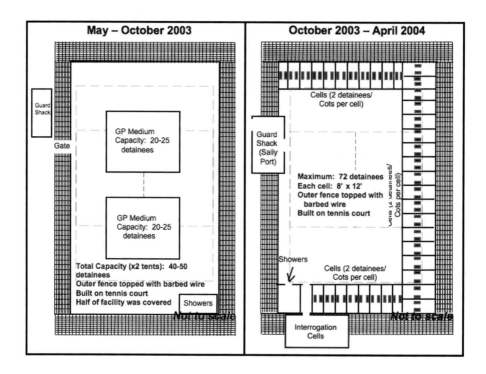

Figure 15) 2BCT, TF 1AD, Detainee Holding Area
Source: Major Douglas A. Pryer, "Interview with LTC Larry Wilson," *Operational Leadership Experiences in the Global War on Terrorism*, January 30, 2009, http://cdm15040.contentdm.oclc.org/cdm4/item_viewer.php?CISOROOT=/p4013coll13&CISOPTR=1471&CISOBOX=1&REC=3 (accessed April 30, 2009), 20.

by either courts martial or Article 15 hearing, resulting in punishments ranging from jail time to loss of rank and pay.[174]

If these guards were indeed not insurgents (as they do not appear to have been), they almost certainly became insurgents after this incident. It should be noted, though, that the battalion's leadership responded commendably to this incident, promptly investigating, reporting, and punishing the offender—swift justice which sent the right message to soldiers throughout the brigade and which did not always occur during OIF I.

There is no record of other substantiated allegations of detainee abuse occurring in the Iron Brigade. This statement holds true, not just for subordinate brigade units, but for the brigade's holding facility as well. According to Major Wilson, Colonel Baker told him "there will be no 15-6's [investigations] in our detention facility."[175] Thus, Wilson says, he was very careful to ensure that the facility followed "both the spirit and the letter of the law for detainees."[176] This indeed was the case, with the facility easily passing inspections by such outside agencies as the Red Cross, U.S. Central Command, the U.S. Army Inspector General, and TF 1AD.[177]

Like a few other facilities in TF 1AD, however, the facility did occasionally employ stress positions to control unruly detainees. According to Wilson, "about the worst thing we ever did was make a guy stand on a sandbag."[178] The use of this questionable tactic was employed only by guards, never by interrogators, though. Even more critically, the brigade's school-trained interrogators never employed harsh interrogation methods on detainees.

The 2BCT's detention facility, called "Camp Striker" after the brigade's radio call sign, was a textbook example of what a brigade holding area should look like. During the first 12 months of the brigade's deployment, this facility was located on a tennis court next to the brigade's headquarters in the Al Faw Palace (leading one to wonder if any of the facility's detainees had played tennis there, on sunnier days for members of Saddam's regime). Initially, the holding area consisted of two tents placed on the tennis court. The tennis court fence was patrolled by guards and topped with barbed wire. Soon after Wilson arrived, however, serious construction began on the site.

By October 2003, the facility had a sally port entrance, interrogation rooms, and 36 cells with two cages each. This upgraded configuration was more secure, kept detainees segregated, and was handier for interrogators since they no longer had to have sources escorted 100 meters to underground interrogation rooms at the palace. Also, the facility was an ideal setting for eavesdropping by the brigade's "cage rat," since this hidden informant could now be placed between the cells of suspected insurgent group members.

The only real drawback to the facility was that, since it did not have either solid walls or ceilings, detainees were not protected from the incoming rocket and mortar rounds that routinely struck within the Green Zone—and occasionally hit within Striker FOB as well. Fortunately, however, none of these rounds ever hit within the 2BCT detention facility.

Three different units served as guards at the facility– platoons from the 38th MP Company; 4th Battalion, 27th Field Artillery; and 2nd Battalion, 6th Infantry.[179] Perhaps surprisingly, Wilson has said that he was the least pleased with the performance of the military police guards, who he says kept having minor administrative issues: "the issue there was that the ability of these troops had nothing to do with their basic skill set; it has to do with basic troop leading procedures when maintaining a standard."[180]

Colonel Baker made it clear to Major Wilson soon after he arrived "that the S2 had staff proponency over all detainee operations," to include "the MPs, the interrogators, the military intelligence company, and the transportation assets we used to move detainees around the battlefield."[181] Although Wilson did not have command authority over interrogators or guards, he nonetheless possessed a strong personality and exercised much more control over the guards than was common for a staff officer, frequently giving them very specific directives. Consequently, Wilson probably could have gotten by with telling guards to "soften up" detainees for interrogations if he had so chosen. Much to his credit, though, he did not choose to do this.

"Colonel Baker and I had a discussion early on that," said Wilson, "if a guy wasn't going to talk to us, it wasn't going to do us any good to try to beat information out of him. "At the end of the day, if a guy wasn't going to talk to us, our only recourse was just to process him for Abu Ghraib."

Unknown at the time, this decision to protect uncooperative detainees by simply shipping them to Abu Ghraib would be, in retrospect, an ironic one.

Accomplishments

Although the largest brigade combat team in Iraq during OIF I, the Iron Brigade was still dramatically under-resourced for its huge mission. Most critically, the brigade's S2 section and direct-support military intelligence company were inadequately manned and ineffectively structured to provide the brigade with all of the intelligence capabilities that the brigade needed. So, the brigade's leadership employed non-standard intelligence personnel and methods to solve this tactical problem– sometimes improvising brilliantly. Examples of methods that worked include the creation of a standing document exploitation section; this DOCEX section's use of FBI computer-exploitation software to support intelligence collection; the employment of bright military intelligence soldiers who had not been formally trained as analysts to serve as analysts; the creation of a section dedicated to the handling of detainees' evidence packets; and the brigade's use of an FBI polygraphist to support interrogations and provide additional evidence for detainee packets.

The results of the brigade's extensive use of informants, however, were mixed. Having seven military intelligence officers (the brigade S2, brigade S2X, and five battalion S2s) essentially "run sources" may have provided the brigade with more intelligence than it would have been able to otherwise obtain. However, it was an extremely dangerous practice, and, if the brigade's HUMINT professionals were correct, the quality of the intelligence gleaned in this fashion was much worse than the Iron Brigade's leadership realized. Additionally, this leadership may not have understood that HUMINT soldiers were neither screening the informants being run by S2s nor being given the opportunity to assume responsibility for especially valuable informants.[182]

The aggressive placing of the lives of civilian informants in the hands of untrained handlers struck many HUMINT professionals as amoral and unworthy of our nation's tradition of staying on the moral high ground. Before agreeing with this judgment, though, one must consider that the informants themselves were willing participants: these informants knowingly risked their lives for ends they themselves believed worth obtaining. Thus, while one can perhaps reasonably argue that relegating informants to non-professional handlers was improper, it was certainly not amoral considering the informants' freedom of choice in the matter. More troubling is the idea that this practice was amoral because of the inferior quality of the intelligence it produced. This perspective argues that poor intelligence may lead to the detention of innocents or even worse, the injuries or even deaths of local civilians and soldiers. According to this view, contrary to Wilson's philosophy, more intelligence does not necessarily mean fewer people dead if this intelligence is poor intelligence.[183]

Still, though this argument will no doubt continue, the writers of *On Point II* probably got it right when they judged that, due to the drastic shortage of tactical HUMINT personnel, "tactical commanders had little choice" but to sanction this practice.[184] The consequences of this limited choice were sometimes grave, though, and the U.S. Army must ensure that tactical commanders are given more resources– and better choices– in the future.

Regardless of the controversy surrounding its informant operations (source operations really), the 2BCT accomplished much of which it would later be rightly proud. These accomplishments included establishing and securing the Green Zone; recruiting and training a 960-man battalion of the Iraqi Civil Defense Corps; recruiting, screening, training, clothing, arming, and paying 2035 Facility Protection Services personnel; recruiting and screening 1,858 candidates for the Iraqi police; coordinating, securing, and paying for the renovation and reconstruction of 1,002 projects worth $13.5 million; and standing up 18 Neighborhood Advisory Councils and two democratically selected District Advisory Councils.[185] Finally, the 2BCT built a superb brigade detention facility that effectively supported interrogation operations. This structure was not only extremely well-designed, but it also remained free of interrogation abuse. It is thus no wonder that Major Hoepner, who as operations officer for the 501st MI Battalion regularly inspected the division's interrogation facilities, has stated:

> I would say the 2BCT probably ran the best interrogation operation in the division, including the DIF [Division Interrogation Facility]. I frankly wish I had been that creative.[186]

Thus, with regard to the conduct of its school-trained interrogators, the Iron Brigade clearly stood with the rest of TF 1AD on the moral high ground.

In recognition of the collective valor its soldiers had displayed during this deployment, the Iron Brigade was awarded the Presidential Unit Citation, America's highest unit award.

Conclusions

At the brigade and battalion levels, interrogators often worked as hard running sources as they did conducting interrogations. In many cases, due to the higher pay-off frequently accompanying source reporting, interrogators actually spent more time meeting with sources than interrogating.

Across Iraq and probably to a man, tactical-level interrogators and other HUMINT professionals were upset at the degree to which non-HUMINT professionals engaged in the complex task of running sources, charging these non-professionals with "tainting the source pool" and producing "inferior" intelligence. These professionals were correct that this practice often had these results and should have been an unacceptable risk. However, units who employed this means of intelligence collection also had a point when they said that, due to the paucity of professional HUMINT assets, they really had no choice in the matter: they could either run sources themselves or operate in a near-vacuum of local intelligence—an even more unacceptable option. True to form, the 2BCT pursued this form of potential intelligence more aggressively than other brigades, a fact that created more than a little anger and resentment among the division's HUMINT professionals.

The question of whether the Iron Brigade (and all other OIF I brigades to some degree) should have permitted this practice is still hotly debated today in certain circles. Happily, though, the question of whether this practice should be pursued today has been both idealistically and pragmatically answered: the answer is not just "no" as a matter of DoD policy, but it is a pragmatic "no" thanks to the large number of HUMINT collectors now assigned to brigades. In other words, additional collectors at the brigade-level have made this discussion moot, since maneuver units are no longer confronted with the need to run their own sources.

Perhaps ironically considering this controversy, the S2 section of the Iron Brigade has in other respects served as a template for today's brigade S2 sections. Current S2 sections have grown greatly in size and are now typically structured to reproduce the capabilities this brigade possessed almost uniquely during OIF I (such as the capability of a standing DOCEX section and the benefit this capability lends to successful interrogations). Certainly, Baker and Wilson deserve kudos for their ground-breaking and innovative work here.

Another controversial practice amongst TF 1AD's subordinate units was the use of light stress positions and exercise by some interrogators and guards to impose discipline on unruly detainees. One justification for this tactic was that such practice paralleled basic discipline that Army non-commissioned officers used on their own soldiers, beginning with basic training. It therefore fulfilled, this argument went, the spirit of reciprocity (that is, "the Golden Rule") that underpins the Geneva Conventions.[187] Nonetheless, although the interrogators and guards who may have employed this tactic did not know it, a strict reading of Article 100 of the Fourth Geneva Convention indicates that this tactic was probably technically illegal. Fortunately, this practice never got out of hand and degenerated into obvious detainee abuse. Leadership had much to do with this: on perhaps the only occasion when Major General Dempsey heard of this tactic, he quickly and decisively ordered its cessation.

The five instances of interrogation abuse that did occur within the TF 1AD occurred at the battalion (or lower) command level. In all of these instances, unauthorized interrogations took place that were forbidden by command policies. More commonly, the detainee abuse that occurred in the TF 1AD was not interrogation-related but rather occurred at the small-unit level as frustrated and angry troops practiced vigilante justice on captured Iraqis—some of whom were not guilty of wrongdoing, but rather guilty only of being at the wrong place at the wrong time.

This fact brings us to an important point. In today's wars, the U.S. Army is even more decentralized than it was during the days of the Frontier Army in America's "Wild West." In Baghdad during OIF I, each brigade had scores of fixed sites where soldiers lived and operated. Some of these sites were as large as battalion-size FOBs. Other sites were buildings that a platoon or perhaps just a section guarded. Generally, a leader had to travel through "Indian Country" (a phrase sometimes used by soldiers to refer to hostile neighborhoods or areas) to visit their troops in small units at various sites, thus limiting the ability of these leaders to directly supervise these troops. In such circumstances, even the best of military leaders could not hope to prevent misbehavior at all of his far-flung outposts. To some degree, he had to rely on the education, training, and moral character of his soldiers. Usually during OIF I, subordinate leaders rose to the challenge, meeting or exceeding their leaders' expectations. Too frequently, though, this was sadly not the case.

Clearly, to minimize crimes that too often today have adverse strategic effects, the U.S. Army needs to take seriously the ethical education it provides its leaders.

CHAPTER 8

> *In accordance with the Detainee Treatment Act of 2005, the only interrogation approaches and techniques that are authorized for use against any detainee, regardless of status or characterization, are those authorized and listed in this Field Manual.*[1]
> —Field Manual 2-22-3
> Human Intelligence Collector
> Operations (September 2006)

> *So much of what the divisions are doing is just so much eye wash. Shifting assets between modular BCTs is extremely difficult and nearly impossible concerning the organic systems/personnel that the BCT brings into theater. In the end, the CG [Commanding General] is left with an extremely biased and lopsided view of the battlefield since his view comes through the lens of the BCT collection effort.*"[2]
> —Lieutenant Colonel Russell Godsil,
> 1AD Deputy G2

During World War II, U.S. forces were defeated soundly by Field Marshall Erwin Rommel's Afrika Corps at the Battle of Kasserine Pass. After this defeat, American forces reorganized and fought differently, greatly contributing to the surrender of Germany's forces in North Africa just three months later. Shortly before his death, Rommel reflected on the North African campaign, writing "what was astonishing was the speed with which the Americans adapted themselves to modern warfare."[3] Indeed, there has probably been no army in the history of warfare that has proven more adaptable in war than the U.S. Army, which has led some to argue that it has never truly been defeated (though none can reasonably argue, thanks to the Vietnam War and numerous "small wars" like Lebanon and Somalia, that America has never lost a war).

At no time in history has the U.S. Army's adaptability been more on display than during the Global War on Terrorism. In just a few short years, the U.S. Army's conventional forces have transformed from a kinetic organization capable only of destroying enemy armies to an effective counterinsurgent organization capable of building nations and winning "the long war." This rapid adaptation has applied to interrogation operations as well. Since the nightmare of Abu Ghraib, the U.S. Army has improved greatly in almost all aspects of interrogation operations.

As we shall see in this chapter, though, these great changes have not been nearly great enough.

Publishing new doctrine

U.S. Army doctrine published post-OIF I more clearly promotes adherence to the Law of War than doctrine published before OIF I. Other doctrinal deficiencies uncovered during the course of this paper have largely been corrected as well. The next sections summarize how current doctrine addresses (and in a few cases, does not address) the major doctrinal deficiencies of OIF I.

Interrogation approaches

Many SERE and other abusive interrogation techniques are explicitly prohibited in military intelligence doctrine today, to include "damaging or destroying an individual's religious articles," "forcing the detainee to be naked," "placing hoods or sacks over the head of a detainee," "applying beatings, electric shock, burns, or other pain," "waterboarding," "using military working dogs," "inducing hypothermia or heat injury," "conducting mock executions," and "depriving the detainee of necessary food, water, or medical care."[4] However, since "pain" is left undefined (a critical shortcoming in light of the Bush Administration's so-called "torture memos"), it is unclear whether such SERE techniques as the use of mild "stress positions," "bright lights and loud noise," "environmental manipulation," "close-quarters confinement," and "sleep deprivation" are prohibited for use on all detainees. Failing to explicitly prohibit every SERE technique might prove a serious oversight if it were not for the *Detainee Treatment Act of 2005*, which made it illegal for any military interrogator to use approaches or techniques other than those included in Field Manual 2-22.3, *Human Intelligence Collector Operations*. Nonetheless, doctrine should be updated so as to help prevent potential misunderstanding.

POINT OF CAPTURE THROUGH EVACUATION

MP Functions	HUMINT Functions
• Maneuver and Mobility Support Operations • Area Security • Internment and Resettlement Operations • Law and Order Operations • Police Intelligence Operations • Ensure detainee abuse is avoided and reported	• Screen and question detainees at TCPs and checkpoints • Question contacts, local civilians, refugees, and EPWs • Conduct liaison with military and civilian agencies • Report information obtained • Ensure detainee abuse is avoided and reported • Support DOCEX

DETENTION FACILITY

MP Functions	HUMINT Functions
• Detain and guard EPWs, civilian internees, and other detainees • Conduct reception and processing • Coordinate Classes I, II, and VIII supplies • Coordinate NGOs, PVOs, and interagency visits • Ensure detainee abuse is avoided and reported • Transport detainees within the detention facility to interrogation area • Maintain security during interrogation operations	• Debrief guards • Screen detainees and EPWs for PIR and IR • Provide linguist support when possible • Observe detainees under MP control • Ensure detainee abuse is avoided and reported • Conduct interrogations • Report information obtained • Cross-cue other intelligence disciplines (as needed) • Support DOCEX

Figure 16) MI versus MP Responsibilities
Source: Department of the Army, Field Manual 2-22.3, *Human Intelligence Collector Operations* (Washington, DC: U.S. Department of the Army, September 2006), 5-18.

MI versus MP responsibilities

Any ambiguity with regard to whether guards can actively set conditions for screenings or interrogations has been removed. According to current military intelligence doctrine, "MPs will not take any actions to set conditions for interrogations (for example, 'softening up' a detainee)."[5] Military intelligence doctrine states that guards may, however, provide incentives to detainees at the behest of interrogators if these incentives are "approved by the facility commander," do "not affect the baseline standards of humane treatment," and do "not violate detainee custody and control or facility security."[6] Military police doctrine precisely mirrors military intelligence doctrine here, stating that guards "never set conditions for future interrogation operations"[7] and that guards may provide incentives to detainees under the same three conditions outlined by military intelligence doctrine.[8] Figure 15, taken from the current interrogations manual, further delineates military intelligence and military police responsibilities– a delineation that is mirrored by a nearly identical table in current military police doctrine, Field Manual 3-19.40, *Internment/Resettlement Operations*.[9]

Staff proponency

With regard to staff proponency for detainee operations, the Secretary of the Army has designated the Provost Marshal General as having "the executive role for detainee operations and long-term confinement of U.S. military prisoners."[10] Also, military intelligence doctrine now lays out clearly which military intelligence element has what staff responsibility with regard to all HUMINT operations. There remains at least one significant issue within this framework: doctrine states that the "MI Commander/ OMT" is responsible for mission execution at the division level;[11] yet, divisions lost their organic military intelligence battalions during the Army's transition to modular brigades. Due to this loss, it is unlikely that a division will receive a military intelligence headquarters with the ability to perform this doctrinal responsibility during a deployment.

Chain of command

Command and control at detention facilities has been clarified. Military police doctrine states that, "All HUMINT units are under the TACON of the facility commander for the humane treatment, evacuation, and custody and control (reception, processing, administration, internment, and safety) of detainees; protection measures; and the operation of the internment facility."[12] It also states, "The MI unit commander is responsible for the conduct of interrogation operations, to include prioritizing effort and controlling the technical aspects of interrogation or other intelligence operations."[13] Military police doctrine does not direct that military police officers serve as facility commanders, presumably since the senior commander with soldiers at a facility may not be a military policeman. Military police doctrine is clearer, however, with regard to who the overall Commander of Detainee Operations should be for a specific theater: this commander should be "the senior military police commander" in theater.[14]

Tactical interrogation timeline

Since tactical-level units routinely operate on non-contiguous battlefields and must generate the majority of their own intelligence, doctrine no longer dictates the length of time a detainee must spend at tactical command levels. The matter is now rightly left to "command policy guidance."[15]

Contract interrogator management

Field Manual 2-22.3, *Human Intelligence Collector Operations*, now dedicates an entire appendix to the management of contract interrogators. This appendix covers the responsibilities of commanders and unit contracting officer representatives with regard to contract interrogators. It also states that contract interrogators "must successfully complete a training program approved by the United States Army Intelligence Center and Fort Huachuca, or the Defense HUMINT Management Office, which will serve as validation to perform MI interrogations."[16]

Other governmental agencies

Army doctrine now restricts CIA (and other non-DoD) agents from using abusive interrogation techniques in Army facilities. Field Manual 2-22.3, *Human Intelligence Collector Operations*, states that non-DoD agencies may only use Army detention facilities upon approval of the appropriate Joint Task Force commander, theater commander, or "appropriate higher level official."[17] Once approval is obtained, the non-DoD interrogator may only use Army-sanctioned approaches and techniques and must sign a statement agreeing to abide by Army rules.[18] Also, non-DoD interrogations must be observed by DoD personnel.[19]

Medical records

Military intelligence regulation and doctrine still does not say whether interrogators should be granted access to the medical records of detainees. This is clearly a matter that needs to be corrected. Army doctrine does state, however, that "HUMINT collectors may interrogate a wounded or injured detainee provided that they obtain permission from a competent medical authority."[20] Also, in accordance with the Geneva Conventions, an interrogator is not authorized to "give the impression that any type of medical treatment is conditional on the detainee's cooperation in answering questions."[21]

Polygraphists

Military intelligence doctrine now explicitly states that polygraphists may support interrogations. There is still a lack, however, of both polygraphists and machines to support interrogations. The Army fielded 94 portable lie detectors called the Preliminary Credibility Assessment Screening System to troops in Afghanistan in April 2008.[22] Troops are authorized to use the machines after receiving a one-week training course.[23] While declassified data is currently unavailable regarding the usefulness of these particular machines in the field, this technology–if proven accurate by soldiers in combat– represents a step in the right direction.

Behavioral scientists

Some doctrinal guidance is now provided for the employment of behavioral science consultants. For example, behavioral science consultants are "authorized to make psychological assessments of the character, personality, social interactions, and other behavioral characteristics of interrogation subjects and advise HUMINT collectors of their assessments, as needed."[24] Unfortunately, although doctrine now provides some guidance regarding how behavioural scientists may support interrogations, no change in force structure has occured that would actually place these specialists in support of tactical interrogators.

Ethical toolkit

Unfortunately, the Army possesses the same "ethical toolkit" to assist leaders that it possessed during OIF I. This toolkit largely consists of the "Army Values" paradigm, which remains an unclear methodology for helping leaders solve complex, real-world ethical problems. For example, doctrine still defines the Army value of "respect" as to "treat someone as they should be treated."[25] Clearly, such a definition merely encourages the approach that, if a detainee were to be considered a "terrorist," this detainee should be treated as the captor thinks terrorists should be treated (that is, perhaps, treated very badly).

An unnecessary, crippling handicap

Army doctrine now contains one unnecessary and crippling over-reaction to the strategic damage done to the United States by the use of enhanced interrogation techniques during the early years of the GWOT. According to Appendix M of FM 2-22.3, interrogators may not keep subjects separated from other detainees without the approval of a General Officer. However, the separation described in this appendix is not the enhanced interrogation technique of "Isolation," which involves sensory deprivation, but rather it is the manner of housing a detainee that is almost always a precondition for the successful interrogation of that detainee. Unless separated from a detention facility's general population, potential sources will always be briefed on how to resist their upcoming interrogations by other detainees. Also, sources are far less inclined to cooperate with interrogators when they know that other detainees will be watching should they meet regularly with interrogators. Thus, since potentially cooperative subjects often become firmly non-cooperative during the time it takes an interrogator to obtain General Officer approval to separate them from the general detainee population, the requirement to obtain this approval needs to be rescinded while maintaining the new doctrinal assurances that separated subjects will be housed humanely and will not suffer from sensory deprivation.

Growing the interrogation force

Since OIF I, the Army's interrogation force structure has grown dramatically. At the end of Fiscal Year 2005, the Army had 2,500 HUMINT soldiers. This number is projected to grow to 6,000 by Fiscal Year 2011.[26] Although significant in itself, this increase in the number of HUMINT soldiers does not reflect the real growth in capability, since most of these HUMINT soldiers belong to the new 35M "HUMINT Collector" military occupational specialty. Soldiers with this occupational specialty are trained both on how to interrogate and how to conduct source operations– tasks split previously between the 97B counterintelligence and 97E interrogation specialties. Thus, on paper, the addition of 3,000 35M HUMINT collectors is equivalent to the addition of 3,000 of what used to be 97E interrogators and 3,000 97B counterintelligence agents. The question here is one of quality. Speaking to this, CW3 Kilbourne said:

> I would say that HUMINT Collectors of today are ill-equipped to perform the jobs of a HUMINTer successfully. Most of them are too young and immature to be taken seriously by our potential source pool, and they literally do not have the personal skills to interact appropriately or understand what rapport really is.

Still, the vastly greater numbers of interrogators is a step in the right direction, and over time, these interrogators should gain the maturity and experience they need to be effective.

Combat brigades have been the main beneficiaries of the Army's dramatic growth in HUMINT capability, though theater internment facilities have also benefitted. Unfortunately, despite the overall growth in HUMINT capability, the ability of divisions to manage HUMINT operations has declined. Below is a summary of major changes in interrogation-related force structure.

Tactical HUMINT support

Direct support military intelligence battalions are no longer organic to divisions. Instead, the headquarters units of these battalions have been inactivated, and the companies of these battalions have been task-organized with both HUMINT and SIGINT assets and assigned to the new "special troops battalions" of combat brigades. The military intelligence companies now organic to combat brigades have a much greater HUMINT capability than the capability possessed by the direct-support military intelligence companies of OIF I. As opposed to just four counterintelligence soldiers and three interrogators per military intelligence company, each company now have three four-man HUMINT collection teams as well as a four-man OMT team.[27] Since

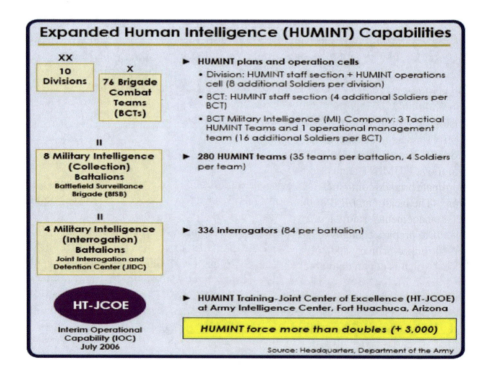

Figure 17) Increased MI Capability
Source: Association of the United States Army, "Torchbearer National Security Report," AUSA, July 2007, http://www3.ausa.org/webpub/DeptILW.nsf/byid/JRAY-75LT2E/$File/TB-Intel.pdf?OpenElement (accessed April 24, 2009), 5.

all of these 16 personnel can either run sources or interrogate, each combat brigade is assigned more than four times the number of personnel who can lawfully run sources and more than five times the number of personnel who can lawfully interrogate than combat brigades had during OIF I. In fact, one combat brigade now has as many (or nearly as many) school-trained interrogators as all of TF 1AD had during OIF I. What is more, each combat brigade now has its own four-man S2X section providing much-needed HUMINT expertise in brigade S2 sections.

HUMINT Operational Cells

The HOC and HUMINT Analytical Cell of inactivated military intelligence battalions have been reassigned to the headquarters of divisions. With this reassignment, divisions have lost some ability to effectively manage their HUMINT assets. For example, since the HOC now works for a staff officer (the Division G2) rather than a commander (the military intelligence Battalion Commander), the HOC cannot directly task the HUMINT soldiers of subordinate brigades. Thus, it is often a struggle for the G2 and HOC to know what brigades are doing with regard to HUMINT operations. As recently stated by Lieutenant Colonel Godsil, the deputy G2 for the 1AD: "The loss of the direct support MI battalions takes the discussion of interrogation operations out of the command channel and puts it into the murky staff channels with the G2, PMO [Provost Marshal Officer] and IG [Inspector General] trying to figure out who is who [in the detention facilities of subordinate brigades]."[28] Similarly, a Division G2 lacks the ability to provide effective command and control of the HUMINT teams which are attached to a division and which may be performing a "general support" role for that division.[29]

Division-level task organization

In addition to being unable to adequately track brigade HUMINT operations, a Division G2 now lacks the command authority to effectively task-organize subordinate HUMINT assets in support of the "division fight." If one brigade has a more violent sector or fewer organic HUMINT assets than another brigade, it is very difficult for the G2 to move HUMINT teams from one brigade to another brigade: almost invariably, subordinate brigade commanders fight the loss of valuable (and now organic) HUMINT teams. "The lack of an MI Battalion is disastrous in terms of MI task organization and asset management," said Lieutenant Colonel Godsil. "Without the MI Commander and staff to prepare changes to task organization, the G2 (a staff wiener and probably the most junior primary staff officer) is stuck arguing against a BCT Commander in contact, which is not an equitable argument."[30]

Joint Interrogation and Debriefing Center battalions

Through 2005, the Army possessed only one battalion (the 202nd MI Battalion) that was designed to operate as a Joint Interrogation and Debriefing Center (JIDC).[31] Due to this uniqueness, the soldiers of 202nd MI Battalion spent 28 of the first 36 months of OIF deployed to Iraq.[32] Since then, the Army activated its first formally designated JIDC battalion in January 2006.[33] A total of four JIDC battalions (two active-duty and two reserve battalions) are projected to be activated. Once this occurs, the Army will possess the ability to surge more interrogators to support theater-level interrogation operations or, in the absence of such a surge, the ability to ensure JIDC soldiers deploy no more than other American soldiers.

Battlefield Surveillance Brigades

The Army has created a modular brigade in support of corps and/or division operations called the Battlefield Surveillance Brigade (BFSB). Each BFSB has a comparable HUMINT capability to that possessed by the 205th MI brigade, the brigade that supported CJTF-7 during OIF I. Whereas the 205th MI Brigade organically had two interrogation companies with 15 five-man interrogation teams each (a total of 150 interrogators), a BFSB has 35 four-man HUMINT teams (a total of 140 interrogators).[34] What is most significant here is not the capabilities of the BFSBs but the number of them: eight new military intelligence battalions have been created to support the three active-duty BFSBs and the seven new national guard BFSBs.[35] Thus, if the U.S. Army were to engage in interrogation operations again on the scale these operations occurred during OIF I, two to three supporting BFSBs and a JIDC battalion would not only possess a greater interrogation capability than possessed by the augmented 205th MI Brigade during OIF I, but this capability would be easily sustainable through subsequent troop rotations.

Legal support

The analysis of recent corps- and division-level unit manning documents (or MTOEs) shows that there has been no increase in the number of lawyers assigned to these units since OIF I. Hopefully, if the U.S. were to conduct again an invasion such as the invasion of Iraq, Army leadership has learned that it would need to attach a large number of lawyers to the initial invasion and stabilization force, thus ensuring a more expeditious release of wrongly detained innocents. In turn, a quick release of innocents would help reduce the number of insurgents created by wrongful detention as well as, by reducing overcrowding in detention facilities, create the conditions for interrogators to operate more effectively.

Interrogator experience

Although military interrogators today generally have less experience than their counterparts possessed during OIF I, the number of civilian contract interrogators (who are normally older and more experienced) has dramatically increased in Iraq. At the end of OIF I, there were a total of 19 contract interrogators in Iraq.[36] Since then, the L-3 Corporation has signed a contract with the Army that requires the company to provide 306 interrogators, screeners, and intelligence analysts on 22 bases in Iraq.[37] It is unclear from unclassified sources how many of these employees are assigned as interrogators, but if at least one-third of these employees are interrogators (as seems likely), then there are at least five times as many contract interrogators on the ground in Iraq today as there were during OIF I. "Contract (L-3) interrogation teams did most of the heavy lifting in terms of the conduct of interrogation," stated Lieutenant Colonel Godsil in reference to the 1AD's October 2007 to December 2008 deployment to Iraq. "Most of the HCTs [HUMINT Collection Teams] were away from the detainee holding areas and focused on source operations."[38]

Warrant Officers

Experienced and competent warrant officers played a critical role in ensuring interrogators performed their tasks in accordance with legal and doctrinal constraints during OIF I. Unfortunately, since it is much easier to "grow" new interrogators than it is to grow their warrant officer supervisors, the warrant officer supervisor-to-interrogator ratio is decidedly less favorable than it was during OIF I. For example, while Company A, 501st MI Battalion, was authorized both a counterintelligence warrant officer and an interrogation warrant officer for its seven-man HUMINT section during OIF I, this military intelligence company (now part of the Special Troops Battalion, 1st Brigade, 1AD) is only authorized one warrant officer for its entire 16-man HUMINT section. Referring to the 1AD's recent deployment, Lieutenant Colonel Godsil said, "A lesson learned here is that MSO [military source operations] is a leadership intensive operation and more collectors does not necessarily mean more of better collection . . . Junior troops are stuck as HCT [HUMINT Collection Team] leaders, answering directly to a Rifle Battalion Commander, and the technical art of MSO suffers."[39]

The Army is even having difficulty filling the reduced number of interrogation warrant officer slots it has. As of April 27, 2009, U.S. Recruiting Command identifies the interrogation warrant officer specialty (351M) and counterintelligence warrant officer specialty (351L) as two of nine specialties facing an "application shortage."[40] To fill this shortage, U.S. Recruiting Command is offering the "expanded warrant officer opportunity" of opening the two HUMINT warrant officer specialties to any enlisted soldier with the requisite rank and test scores.[41] This is a highly questionable "fix" and does not bode well for the short-term future of HUMINT operations. As stated by CW3 Kenneth Kilbourne:

> . . . DA [Department of the Army] opened up the HUMINT Warrant Officer MOS to any and all to join who could at least pass a DLAB [Defense Language Attitude Battery test]. Currently, most WO1/CW2 351Ms in the Army have been HUMINT Collectors for only a few years. How do you manage important operations such as HUMINT that still accounts for over 70% of all information collection from the battlefield if you don't even know the job yourself? We can only hope that there isn't a big blow-back from this.[42]

Ultimately, the Army may not be able to address this problem adequately until today's surge of new 35M HUMINT collectors has gained enough rank and experience to become warrant officers.

Improving professional education and training

The Army has improved professional education and training in all interrogation-related areas except one– ethical leadership. The points below summarize the key directions the Army has travelled with regard to interrogation-related training since OIF I.

<u>HUMINT Training Joint Center of Excellence</u>
The Army partnered with the Defense Intelligence Agency to establish the HUMINT Training Joint Center of Excellence at Fort Huachuca in April 2007.[43] Three of this center's five courses are directly related to interrogation operations. The ten-week Joint Interrogations Certification Course ensures contract interrogators are trained to Army interrogation standards before they deploy;[44] the five-week Defense Strategic

Debriefer Course, open to officers, warrant officers, and non-commissioned officers in the counterintelligence and interrogation disciplines, teaches "techniques and methodologies for conducting strategic debriefings;"[45] and the six-week Joint Analyst-Interrogator Collaboration Course, open only to warrant officers, trains "collectors and analysts to perform duties in a GWOT environment with advanced collector and analytical skills."[46]

Although a significant improvement over the training that was available to interrogators and their leaders before OIF I, this center's influence is not as great as it should be due to the fact that this training is unit- rather than Army-directed training (the exception being the Joint Interrogation Certification Course, which is required training for all contract interrogators). Thus, the influence of this training extends only to those units whose leadership, deployment schedule, and funds allow for this training. "Once you finish AIT," said CW3 John Groseclose, the DoD's HUMINT Collector of the Year for 2003. "The only additional training you can get as far as interrogations go is an interrogations course over at Huachuca. But, this course is difficult to get into because you have to pay for it, and there aren't a lot of units willing to foot the bill."[47]

Pre-Deployment Training

The Army has initiated several pre-deployment training programs that have the potential (when utilized) to greatly enhance the effectiveness of interrogators. These programs include Project Foundry, Cultural Awareness Training, and Language Training. Project Foundry provides advanced skills training for military intelligence soldiers about to deploy. There are nine permanent sites where this training occurs. However, units may also coordinate through the G3 section of the U.S. Army Intelligence and Security Command for mobile training teams to deploy to the unit's home station.[48] The Army's new Culture Center, which opened on February 1, 2006, at Fort Huachuca, offers mobile training teams and a curriculum of up to 200 hours of regionally specific training in support of the GWOT.[49] The Army's expanded language program now includes the Army's extensive promulgation of the "Rosetta Stone" commercial language software, expanded support from mobile training teams to units, and the creation of eleven Defense Language Institute Foreign Language Center training support detachments to support enduring language training at unit home stations.[50]

Ethics education and training

The Schlesinger Report recommended a "review of military ethics education" and said that a "professional ethics program" was needed to equip military leaders "with a sharper moral compass for guidance in situations often riven with conflicting moral obligations."[51] Unfortunately, the Army has neither completed a review of military ethics education, nor implemented a professional ethics program.

Ethical training in U.S. Army units today looks much as it did during OIF I. In general, this training consists of uncertified instructors giving a non-standard "Army Values" brief once a year. Commonly, this brief includes a review of the doctrinal definitions that pertain to each Army Value as well as examples of leaders who exemplified (or did not exemplify) these values. Seldom does such training employ practical exercises to help troops reason through complex moral problems for themselves, and seldom does someone conduct this training who has received the professional education necessary to usefully guide troops toward ethical solutions.

Furthermore, school curriculum that makes a serious attempt at improving the ethical decision-making skills of U.S. Army leaders is rare. Nearly all U.S. Army officers, for example, attend Command and General Staff College, but the school provides few blocks of instruction related to improving ethical decision-making. This lack of attention is not the fault of any one college department, for all departments have subject matter in which they can introduce ethical vignettes. Instead, it is symptomatic of a lack of emphasis that still exists across the U.S. Army.

Conclusions

The U.S. Army has a tradition of rapid, successful innovation in the wake of defeat on the battlefield. In the five years since the Abu Ghraib scandal, this army has lived up to this tradition by making dramatic improvements in its ability to conduct interrogation operations effectively and humanely. However, problems still remain. Matters still of great concern include the reliance of U.S. Army doctrine on an "incomplete tool box" for helping leaders solve real-world ethical dilemmas; the loss of a military intelligence battalion headquarters at the division level; a shortage of experienced warrant officers who can wisely guide the 35M HUMINT Collectors now being mass-produced; and a ridiculous, counterproductive requirement for interrogators to obtain General Officer approval to keep potential sources in individual cells separated from the general detainee population—a separation that is actually almost always a precondition for their then being successfully interrogated.

Most critically, however, the U.S. Army has failed to systematically review military ethics education and to implement a professional ethics program. The potential ramifications of the Army's continued failure to take seriously the importance of ethical education is frightening. Indeed, if the U.S. Army continues to inadequately address this problem, the most urgent question facing America on today's frequently chaotic, decentralized battlefields is not, "Will the U.S. Army ever contribute again to a strategic defeat like My Lai or Abu Ghraib?" The only real question is, "Where and when will America's next great strategic defeat occur?"

CHAPTER 9

A tale of two cities

> *And so, to all the other peoples and governments who are watching today, from the grandest capitals to the small village where my father was born, know that America is a friend of each nation, and every man, woman and child who seeks a future of peace and dignity. And we are ready to lead once more.*[1]
> —President Barrack Obama
> Inaugural Address

> *My experiences have landed me in the middle of another war– one even more important than the Iraq conflict. The war after the war is a fight about who we are as Americans. Murderers like Zarqawi can kill us, but they can't force us to change who we are. We can only do that to ourselves.*[2]
> —Matthew Alexander
> Interrogator

In *A Tale of Two Cities*, Charles Dickens contrasted the horrors of Paris during the French Revolution with ordinary life in law-bound London. When drawing this contrast, Dickens chose the guillotine to symbolize the horrors of revolutionary Paris– horrors he describes as unleashed upon the aristocracy by the irrational fears and thirst for vengeance of the peasantry.

During OIF I, there were also two "cities," or schools of thought, on the use of harsh interrogation methods. One of these cities was dark and subterranean, lying concealed as it were beneath the classification caveats of "TOP SECRET" or "SECRET NOFORN."[3] Those who dwelt in this city believed that the "ends justify the means," that is, if the end were noble enough, then they were obliged to extend the limits of what was legally permissible in order to achieve this end. Like the peasantry of Dickens' Paris, this city's dwellers were motivated by feelings of vengeance and fear– vengeance in the wake of deadly terrorist attacks and fears that, if they did not respond ruthlessly, even worse attacks might occur again. However, unlike the single image (the guillotine) that symbolized the citizenry of Dickens' Paris, it was two U.S. interrogation facilities, Abu Ghraib and Gitmo, which came to symbolize the denizens of this clandestine "city."

During OIF I, the citizens of this "city" occupied the highest levels of command. At the national level, President Bush was aware of his senior security advisors meeting on the issue of enhanced interrogation techniques, and he approved of this discussion.[4] Rumsfeld sanctioned enhanced interrogation techniques for Gitmo that derived from the U.S. military's SERE schools– schools that, in training U.S. service members how to resist torture, had adopted the methods of the Chinese Communist Army of the Korean War for eliciting false confessions from prisoners. Also, although not in the chain-of-command of military interrogators, CIA operatives influenced military interrogators, and these operatives interrogated in accordance with a January 28, 2003, memo which had been signed by George Tenet and which had approved the use of enhanced interrogation techniques for up to 30 days on subjects.[5]

At the theater level, enhanced techniques were approved for use in Afghanistan. These techniques then migrated to Iraq, where Lieutenant General Sanchez authorized the use of similar techniques on September 14, 2003. After October 12, 2003, Sanchez' policy was that only he could approve such techniques. However, due to a poorly written and promulgated policy memo, Sanchez' updated policy did not stop the blanket use of such techniques at a few facilities governed by CJTF-7. In fact, at some facilities, the use of these techniques would not stop until May of 2004.

Investigators have described the systemic use of enhanced interrogation techniques at Abu Ghraib, the Strike Brigade Holding Area, Camp Honesty, various special operations facilities, and a minimum of three 3ACR facilities. SERE techniques were also allegedly used for a brief time at Camp Cropper, though the investigation into these charges occurred too late to potentially substantiate these allegations. Additionally, interrogators at Forward Operating Base Iron Horse employed abusive enhanced interrogation techniques on at least one detainee. Fortunately, a new command policy letter and decisive punishment seem to have prevented the use of enhanced techniques from becoming systemic at this facility.

Almost invariably, the use of enhanced techniques during OIF I led to more serious detainee abuse and strategic damage to the United States. This damage included the energizing of the Iraqi insurgency and the loss of popular support for the war at home—a loss of popular support that nearly led to America's premature withdrawal from Iraq. What is more, this damage has been like a hydra that has continually grown new heads, as the adverse publicity surrounding the recent declassification of the CIA's harsh interrogation techniques from 2003 to 2005 has shown.

Yet, as terrible as these military and political effects have been, these effects do not represent the most pernicious effects of this damage. Troublingly, the Abu Ghraib and Gitmo scandals as well as other similar media controversies (such as those surrounding Lieutenant Colonel Allen West and Chief Warrant Officer 3 Lewis Welshofer) have tarnished the professional image of the U.S. soldier in the eyes of Americans. Mere months before this tarnishing, *Time Magazine* had named "The American Soldier" its "Man of the Year" for 2003. Now, it may be decades before U.S. soldiers again enjoy such uncritical support and lofty tribute at home.

More troubling still, the extent of the psychological effects of interrogation abuse– on the abuser, on the abused, and on affected family members– will negatively impact the lives of many Americans and Iraqis for decades to come. Although no psychologist, Lieutenant Colonel Hoepner has probably expressed as eloquently as anyone the amorality of this predicament, saying, "I'm not sure any society has a right to turn a person into that kind of monster, even for a little while, not knowing how much of the monster will remain with them for the rest of their lives."[6]

It is frightening to think that, as extensive as this damage has been, this damage could have been far greater. The reason it was not worse was that the ends-justify-the-means mentality of one school of thought never represented the vantage point of most school-trained interrogators in Iraq. Instead, most of these interrogators resided morally within the "city upon the hill," a city that had been first envisioned by John Winthrop in 1630 and then, more than a century later, given a firm foundation by America's Founding Fathers.

As described in this book, thanks to strong ethical leadership, the school-trained interrogators of TF 1AD were truly citizens of this higher "city." Furthermore, TF 1AD's interrogators were far from alone in this regard. Although the 101st Airborne Division had a brigade holding area where enhanced interrogation techniques were employed, there are no indicators that these techniques were used at the score or so of other holding areas operated by this division. Similar conclusions can also be drawn regarding the vast majority of detention facilities operated by CJTF-7's other major subordinate commands. There are also no indicators that such theater-level camps as Camp Ashraf, Camp Whitford, or Camp Bucca systemically applied enhanced interrogation techniques. Thus, the numerous investigations which were initiated n the wake of the Abu Ghraib scandal and which concluded that the vast majority of U.S. soldiers had not abused detainees were undoubtedly correct.

It is nonetheless profoundly disappointing that, if interrogation abuses were not commonplace during OIF I, they were at least far more common than they should have been. Encouragingly, the U.S. Army has come a long way with regard to interrogation doctrine, force structure, and training since Abu Ghraib. The extent of the changes the U.S. Army has undergone in a very short time are truly impressive and a tribute to its perhaps singular capability among the world's armies for rapid adaptation. However, the U.S. Army must continue to improve doctrine. The new and unnecessary requirement for interrogators to obtain General Officer approval to house subjects in cells that are separate from the general detainee population is especially troubling, since such separation is almost always a necessary precondition for a successful interrogation. Also, the quality of the U.S. Army's HUMINT soldiers, particularly its HUMINT warrant officers, needs to continue to improve. Additionally, the lack of a military intelligence battalion commander and headquarters at the division-level presents new challenges that must be overcome.

Key Conclusion

In closing, we return to the beginning. At the start of this book, an email exchange was recounted in which four U.S. Army leaders, faced with mounting U.S. casualties, took antithetical stands on the use of harsh interrogation techniques. The decision of three of these leaders to take the gloves off during interrogations led to the use of enhanced interrogation methods in the facilities these leaders influenced. The employment of these techniques, in turn, led to worse forms of detainee abuse. Conversely, one of the many military intelligence units that did not abuse detainees was a unit whose leader spoke of the need for U.S. soldiers to stay on the moral high ground.

This brings us back to the most critical point of this history. Since the Abu Ghraib tragedy, a myriad of investigators have amassed an extremely lengthy list of reasons for detainee abuse. These reasons have ranged from a shortage of a certain resource to confusion over some item of doctrine or policy to soldiers being improperly trained for performing a specific task. Certainly, these various issues are important and need to be corrected. Consequently, during the course of this book, we have uncovered and discussed many of these issues, as well as the U.S. Army's subsequent corrective actions.

However, the U.S. Army is in real danger of missing the proverbial forest for the trees, for most essentially, what was at the heart of any instance of interrogation abuse during OIF I was a leader (or leaders) making poor ethical decisions. In other words, leaders with flawed ethical decision-making skills were the sine qua non (or root) cause of interrogation abuse in Iraq. This weakness was exacerbated on a decentralized battlefield that had many small units operating on remote outposts. Above all else, America needed its Army leaders on these outposts to display sound ethical decision-making ability, but due to their poor skills in this regard, these leaders too frequently let America down.

Unfortunately, there are few signs to indicate that the U.S. Army has progressed in this area. Indeed, if anything, today's situation is worse. Not only is the professional education of leaders on the subject of ethics still lacking, but leaders are stretched increasingly thin by high operational tempo, multiple taskings, and limited resources—circumstances that effectively condition them to seek shortcuts for the sake of mission accomplishment. If uncorrected, high operational tempo coupled with poor ethical training will once again fertilize the darkest embryo of the human soul, and one of history's greatest armies will give birth to yet another Abu Ghraib or My Lai. When this occurs, we Army leaders will have only ourselves to blame.

This is not hyperbole. Just one troubling example of the resilience of the "ends justify the means" mindset, despite the obvious strategic defeat this outlook inflicted upon America, has been offered by Amanda Meyer. A few years after deploying to Iraq as an interrogator for Company A, 501st MI Battalion, Meyer served as an instructor at the military intelligence interrogation school at Fort Huachuca, Arizona. One day, she attended an "Army Values" class that was full of instructors from across the base. She relates what then happened:

> *I don't remember the purpose of the conversation, but Lieutenant Colonel West came up. [West was the 4th Infantry Division battalion commander that, in order to extract intelligence, allowed his soldiers to beat a detainee before firing his weapon near this detainee's head.] There were about five of us 35M interrogation instructors and the rest of the noncommissioned officers were other MOSs [military occupational specialties] from around Ft Huachuca. When Lieutenant Colonel West's actions were opened up for discussion amongst the noncommissioned officers, the 35M instructors were the only ones to speak out against his actions. Everyone else that spoke up justified his actions as necessary in his situation. I was highly disturbed by the conversation.*[7]

Thus, above all else, the U.S. Army needs to turn its attention to getting ethical training and professional education right. At stake is not just the prevention of such future strategic defeats as Abu Ghraib, which is important enough, but the U.S. Army's permanently solving what has become an existential crisis. This crisis arose when the denizens of a subterranean "city" grew far more influential than they should have grown. Although this city will always have its residents, this city is not where American soldiers belong.

American soldiers belong in the city upon the hill.

Acknowledgements

First, I would like to thank Dr. Jonathan House and Lieutenant Colonel Nathan Hoepner for their remarkable diligence and mentorship while helping me to produce this history. I am also grateful for the insightful comments of others who reviewed the transcript at various points, especially Colonel (Retired) Pete Mansoor, Chairman of Military History, Ohio State University; John McCool, Operational Leadership Experiences Team Chief; Lieutenant Colonel Jeffery Lippert, Chief of Detention, Judicial, and Legal Policy, Multi-National Force-Iraq; and Flight Lieutenant Justin Salmon, 14th Signal Regiment (UK) Intelligence Officer.

Secondly, I would like to thank the former 1st Armored Division and 501st Military Intelligence Battalion leaders who consented to interviews in support of this project, including Lieutenant Colonel Hoepner, Lieutenant Colonel Russell Godsil, Lieutenant Colonel (Retired) Elizabeth Rogers, Lieutenant Colonel Larry Wilson, Lieutenant Colonel Mark Crisman, Major Craig Martin, Major Brad Johnson, Captain Nicole Lauenstein, Captain Scott Linker, Chief Warrant Officer 5 (Retired) Robert Ferguson, Chief Warrant Officer 3 Kenneth Kilbourne, Chief Warrant Officer 3 John Groseclose, and Ms. Amanda Meyer. I have truly enjoyed crossing paths with all these great leaders again.

Thirdly, I would like to thank my wife, Bhabinder, for her enduring love and support. This nine-month project has been akin to an extremely difficult pregnancy, not just because of the occasionally-sickening revelations I endured during the course of my research but because of the pains of knowing I was not spending nearly as much time with my wife and children as I (and they) would have liked. But my wife has has been patient during the many long weekday nights and weekends of this book's gestation, and I am grateful to her for that. Still, any year spent at home is a good year in today's Army, and I feel blessed to have seen so much of my lovely wife lately (even if it too often were from across the room and over the top of my laptop's screen).

Lastly, I would like to express my heartfelt admiration for the Human Intelligence leaders and soldiers of Operation Iraqi Freedom I, the vast majority of whom fought hard to keep themselves and others on the moral high ground. It is painful today to imagine how much worse things would have been without their good deeds.

I dedicate this project to them.

Notes

CHAPTER 1: A TERRIBLY HOT SUMMER

1. 4th Infantry Division Headquarters, "Exhibit A (Email correspondences)." *American Civil Liberties Union: Torture FOIA*, October 6, 2003, http://www.aclu.org/torturefoia/released/041905/6570_6668.pdf (accessed February 20, 2009), 53. Although Major Hoepner's name is redacted in this email exchange, I knew the writer– who was my boss for five months– during OIF I.

2. Thomas E. Ricks, *Fiasco: The American Military Adventure in Iraq* (New York: The Penguin Press, 2006), 290. Fiasco is a flawed masterpiece. Ricks deliberately emphasizes the negative in U.S. efforts in Iraq, deemphasizes the positive, and almost melodramatically presents U.S. civilian and military leaders as either heroes or villains in the "fiasco" he says resulted from the U.S.-led invasion of Iraq. Still, as a source of dramatic, negative anecdotes and as a compendium of harsh criticisms (some certainly valid) of the U.S.'s political and military leadership before, during, and immediately after the invasion of Iraq, it is probably unmatched by any other secondary source published-to-date. Also, this controversial book's ability to get the U.S. Army to take a good, hard look at the direction it had been travelling and to steer a course correction has been unrivalled by any other book yet published during the Global War on Terrorism. Thus, more than any other war critic, Ricks deserves the U.S. Army's thanks for the helpful (albeit painful) enema he gave it with *Fiasco*.

3. According to Kenneth Estes in "U.S. Army Soldier," the command-supported but privately published campaign narrative of 1AD in Iraq from 2003 to 2004, the end in Baghdad of 91 straight days of temperatures over 100 degrees Fahrenheit occurred on September 6, 2003 (page 6).

4. Anthony H. Cordesman, "Iraq's Evolving Insurgency: the Nature of Attacks and Patterns and Cycles in the Conflict," *Center for Strategic & International Studies*, http://www.csis.org/media/csis/pubs/060203_iraqicombattrends.pdf (accessed December 4, 2008), 32.

5. Federal Document Clearing House, "Political/Congressional Transcript Wire: Donald H. Rumsfeld Holds Defense Department News Briefing, November 25, 2003;" *AccessMyLibrary*, http://www.accessmylibrary.com/coms2/summary_0286-2787794_ITM (accessed December 5, 2008).

6. Joel Brinkley and Eric Schmitt, "U.S. Officers in Iraq Find Few Signs of Infiltration by Foreign Fighters," *The New York Times*, November 19, 2003, http://query.nytimes.com/gst/fullpage.html?res=950CE1DA163BF93AA25752C1A9659C8B63 (accessed December 5, 2008).

7. 4th Infantry Division AR 15-6 Investigation, 54. Names in this document are redacted. Thomas Ricks provides this captain's name in *Fiasco* as well as the name of the CJTF-7 Deputy J2 who had prompted this captain's email.

8. Ibid.

9. Nicholas Riccardi, *Los Angeles Times: Interrogator Convicted in Iraqi's Death*, January 22, 2006, http://articles.latimes.com/2006/jan/22/nation/na-interrogate22 (accessed February 20, 2009). This article is one of many that provides the name of the warrant officer involved in this email exchange. Due to the scandal resulting from his conviction in the death of an Iraqi detainee (see Chapter 5), Welshofer's notoriety has earned him his own Wikipedia entry.

10. 4th Infantry Division 15-6 Investigation, 53-54.

11 Riccardi, *Los Angeles Times*; Josh White, *Washington Post: Documents Tell of Brutal Improvisation by GIs*, August 3, 2005, http://www.washingtonpost.com/wp-dyn/content/article/2005/08/02/AR2005080201941_pf.html (accessed February 20, 2009).

12 4th Infantry Division 15-6 Investigation, 54.

13 Ibid.

14 Ibid., 59. The name and rank of this 4ID non-commissioned officer is redacted; all that is given is his duty position, which was non-commissioned-officer-in-charge (NCOIC) of the 4ID Interrogation Control Element (ICE). This case is also discussed further in Chapter 5.

15 Ibid.

16 I was this battle captain.

17 Lieutenant General Anthony R. Jones, "AR 15-6 Investigation of the Abu Ghraib Prison and 205th Military Intelligence Brigade," *United States Department of Defense Detainees Investigations*, August 25, 2004, http://www.defenselink.mil/news/Aug2004/d20040825fay.pdf (accessed March 20, 2009), 4. Based on Major General Antonio Taguba's recommendation in his investigation into the 800th MP Brigade and the Abu Ghraib abuses, on March 31, 2004, Lieutenant General Sanchez appointed Major General George Fay to investigate any role members of the 205th MI Brigade had in detainee abuses. On June 16, 2004, the acting Secretary of the Army, R.L. Brownlee, directed General Paul Kern, U.S. Army Materiel Command, to appoint an additional investigating officer that could also investigate the chain of command above the 205th MI Brigade for misconduct. General Kern appointed Lieutenant General Jones to conduct this supplemental investigation on June 26, 2004. (In the U.S. military, an officer cannot find a senior officer guilty of negligence or misconduct. Thus, by appointing Jones to conduct a supplemental investigation, the most senior military leaders of CJTF-7 became potentially subject to a finding of negligence or misconduct– to include Lieutenant General Sanchez himself since Jones outranked Sanchez by date-of-rank.) Jones would find that Sanchez and the CJTF-7 staff held some responsibility for instances of "non-violent and non-sexual abuses" at Abu Ghraib. However, subsequent Army inquiries would absolve Lieutenant General Sanchez, Major General Wojdakowski (the CJTF-7 Deputy Commander) and Major General Barbara Fast (the CJTF-7 senior military intelligence officer) of any wrongdoing. The joint report filed by Jones and Fay is hereafter referred to as the Fay/Jones report.

18 CBS News, *Abuse of Iraqi POWs by GIs Probed*, April 28, 2004, http://www.cbsnews.com/stories/2004/04/27/60II/main614063.shtml (accessed December 5, 2008).

19 Ahmed S. Hashim, *Insurgency and Counter-Insurgency in Iraq* (Ithaca: Cornell University Press, 2006), 144-45.

20 Ibid., 144.

21 Matthew Alexander, "I'm Still Tortured by What I Saw in Iraq," *The Washington Post*, November 30, 2008, http://www.washingtonpost.com/wp-dyn/content/article/2008/11/28/AR2008112802242.html (accessed April 22, 2009).

22 Ricks, 380.

23 Keating Holland, *CNN, Poll: Support for Bush, Iraq War Dropping*, May 22, 2004, http://www.cnn.com/2004/ALLPOLITICS/05/14/bush.kerry/index.html (accessed December 12, 2008).

24 Of the major investigations derived from the abuses at Abu Ghraib, only Major General Taguba's report had been completed prior to the publication of the infamous Abu Ghraib photos by the press on April 30, 2004. Two other investigations, however, had already been initiated– Major General Fay's investigation into the 205th MI Brigade and the Department of the Army's Inspector General inspection of the U.S. Army's detention

operations. Three other major investigations soon followed the media's publication of the Abu Ghraib photos– the investigation of Lieutenant General Jones and Major General Fay into intelligence operations at the CJTF-7 level, the Independent Panel to Review DoD Detention Operations, and the Navy Inspector General's inspection of DoD detention operations. The pages of these reports are among the more than 100,000 declassified and frequently redacted pages which pertain to DoD detention operations during the Global War on Terrorism (GWOT) and which can be found on the American Civil Liberty Union's "Torture FOIA" website, http://www.aclu.org/safefree/ torture/torturefoia.html. Since these reports represent the cumulative efforts of scores of investigators and inspectors and go into far more detail regarding strategic- and operational-level detention and interrogation operations than I am able to delve into within this book, I strongly encourage anyone with a scholar's interest in interrogation operations during the GWOT to consult these sources directly. Also, the U.S. Department of Defense maintains copies of these reports on various websites, copies that have the advantage over documents on the ACLU website of often being saved in word-searchable formats. Probably the most comprehensive site for these reports is on the Office of the Secretary of Defense and Joint Staff Reading Room website, http://www.dod.mil/pubs/ foi/detainees/other_related.html#cid_reports. For those of a less scholarly interest in the subject matter, transcripts of press briefings of various investigators and inspectors (which serve well as succinct summaries of key findings), are found on the defenselink website, http://www.defenselink.mil/news/brieftrans.html. The best unclassified source of information regarding the influence of national policy on harsh interrogation techniques in Iraq is the Senate Armed Services Committee's *Inquiry into the Treatment of Detainees in U.S. Custody* (November 20, 2008). This report was declassified on April 20, 2009, and it is posted on the committee's website at the following url: http://levin.senate.gov/newsroom/supporting/2009/SASC.DetaineeReport.042209.pdf.

25 Department of the Army Inspector General, "Detainee Operations Inspection, July 21, 2004," *United States Department of Defense Detainees Investigations*, http:// www4.army.mil/ocpa/reports/ArmyIGDetaineeAbuse/DAIG%20Detainee%20Operations%20Inspection%20Report.pdf (accessed November 2, 2008), 3. The specific scope of the investigation was the inspection of detainee operations in Iraq, Afghanistan, and the continental U.S.. (The team did not inspect detention operations at Guantanamo Bay, Cuba.) The Inspector General's methodology was as follows: "Two teams conducted inspections of 25 locations in Iraq, Afghanistan, and the Continental United States (CONUS). The CONUS team consisted of seven personnel, including augmentees, and visited seven locations while the OCONUS team consisted of nine personnel, including augmentees, and inspected 16 locations. We interviewed and surveyed over 650 leaders and Soldiers spanning the ranks from Private to Major General. We also reviewed 103 reports of allegations of abuse from Criminal Investigation Division (CID) and 22 unit investigations that cover the period of September 2002 to June 2004" (Mikolashek Report, 25).

26 James R. Schlesinger, Harold Brown, Tillie K. Fowler, and General Charles A. Horner, "Final Report of the Independent Panel to Review DoD Detention Operations, " August 23, 2004, *United States Department of Defense Detainees Investigations*, http://www.defenselink.mil/news/Aug2004/d20040824finalreport.pdf (accessed November 2, 2008), 18. Secretary of Defense Donald Rumsfeld requested the formation of this panel on May 12, 2004 to review DoD Detention Operations. This panel examined detention operations across the DoD, to include in Iraq, Afghanistan, and Guantanamo Bay. As part of its methodology, the panel reviewed all significant investigations into DoD detention operations during the previous two years as well as interviewed any senior DoD political or military leader with significant influence on DoD detention operations, to include Rumsfeld himself.

27 Department of the Navy Inspector General, "Review of Department of Defense Detention Operations and Detainee Interrogation Techniques," *The Office of the Secretary of Defense*

and Joint Staff Reading Room, Detainee Related Documents, March 7, 2005, http://www.dod.mil/pubs/foi/detainees/church_report_1.pdf (accessed February 10, 2009), 21. This investigation, which Rumsfeld initiated two weeks after he chartered Schlesinger's Independent Panel, took nearly ten months to complete and was focused on analyzing any role interrogation policies and specific interrogation techniques may have played in the abuse of detainees by U.S. military interrogators. When appointing Admiral Church to conduct this investigation, Rumsfeld directed that all of DoD allow the Naval Inspector General (IG) Team complete and unfettered access to any available DoD documentary evidence pertaining to detention operations. In addition to surveying vast troves of documentary evidence, according to page one of the Executive Summary, the investigation "included over 800 interviews with personnel serving or having served in Iraq, Afghanistan and Guantanamo Bay, Cuba and senior policy makers in Washington." The Executive Summary for this report is unclassified; the rest of this report is slightly redacted.

28 General Antonio Taguba, "AR 15-6 Investigation of the 800th Military Police Brigade, May 27, 2004," *American Civil Liberties Union: Torture FOIA*, http://www.aclu.org/torturefoia/released/TR3.pdf (accessed December 12, 2008), 60. As of May 5, 2009, this report had not been posted on the DoD defense link website. Instead, an unclassified, word-searchable extract has been published on the Department of the Army's IG website. The entire, redacted version of this report is found on the ACLU website. Unfortunately, this version of the report is not by-word searchable. At the time of this investigation, Major General Taguba was the Deputy Commanding General Support for the Coalition Forces Land Component Command, a command that was headquartered in Kuwait. Taguba's investigation primarily addressed the 800th Military Police Brigade and the role several of this brigade's members played in the most infamous of the abuses at Abu Ghraib. Although Taguba collected some evidence that is relevant to interrogation operations at Abu Ghraib, the investigations conducted by Lieutenant General Anthony Jones and Major General George Fay into the interrogation operations of CJTF-7 and the 205th Military Intelligence Brigade respectively, are much more relevant to this book.

29 Martin Brass, *Torture to Prevent Terrorism?* Interview with a French Master Torturer, 2004, http://www.military.com/NewContent/0,13190,SOF_0704_Torture,00.html (accessed March 20, 2009).

30 Henry Graf, ed., *American Imperialism and the Phillipine insurgection; testimony taken from hearings on affairs in the Phillipine Islands before the Senate Committee on the Phillippines, 1902*, Boston: Little, Brown and Company, 1969.

31 "John Winthrop: 1630," In *Speeches that Changed the World*, edited by Owen Collins, Westminster: John Knox Press, 1999, 65.

32 David Hackett Fisher, *Washington's Crossing* (New York: Oxford University Press, 2004), 375.

33 Numerous historical studies have highlighted the role racism has played in creating exceptions to this rule. See, for example, Wayne E. Lee's essay, "From Gentility to Atrocity: The Continental Army's Way of War," which contrasts the restraint shown by the Continental Army when fighting the British Army with its brutality when fighting the Iroquois in 1779.

CHAPTER 2: "IT'S JUST NOT RIGHT"

1 Department of the Army, Field Manual 1, *The Army* (Washington, DC: U.S. Government Printing Office, 2001), 8.

2 Federal Document Clearing House, Senate Armed Services Committee, "Hearing on Treatment of Iraqi Prisoners, May 19, 2008," *American Civil Liberties Union: Torture FOIA*, http://www.aclu.org/projects/foiasearch/pdf/DODDOA010336.pdf (accessed December 9, 2008), 49.

3   III Corps Headquarters, "Verbatim Record of Trial, Staff Sergeant Ivan Frederick, September 21, 2005," *American Civil Liberties Union: Torture FOIA*, http://www.aclu.org/projects/foiasearch/pdf/DOD041193.pdf (accessed December 12, 2008), 2.; III Corps Headquarters, "Verbatim Record of Trial, Specialist Jeremy Sivits," January 27, 2005, *American Civil Liberties Union: Torture FOIA*, http://www.aclu.org/projects/foiasearch/pdf/DOD002393.pdf (accessed December 12, 2008), 4.

4   Federal Document Clearing House, Senate Armed Services Committee, 1.

5   Ibid., 49.

6   Ibid.

7   Ibid., 25.

8   Ibid.

9   Ibid.

10 Major General Miller's testimony in this regard is incomplete. According to such later investigations as the Church and Schlesinger reports, guards at Gitmo actively set conditions for successful interrogations by giving incentives to detainees (or taking away these incentives) as directed by Gitmo interrogators. However, it should be noted that this condition-setting at Gitmo was only occasionally abusive, and both the Church and Schlesinger reports concluded that this was a humane, effective practice. Indeed, this practice is the same practice condoned by current U.S. Army doctrine. Due to the harsh circumstances surrounding his testimony (which partisan commentators characterized as a "witch hunt"), it is disappointing but unsurprising that Miller was somewhat circumspect in his testimony on this matter.

11 International Committee of the Red Cross, *Geneva Conventions of 12 August 1949*, http://www.icrc.org/ihl.nsf/WebSign?ReadForm&id=375&ps=P (accessed December 12, 2008). This website lists the dates each signatory country ratified the Geneva Conventions of 1949. To access the text of all four conventions, one should go to the Red Cross website in English, http://www.icrc.org/eng. Then, one navigates to the text of the Geneva Conventions through the hyperlink on the left side of the website.

12 International Committee of the Red Cross, *The Geneva Conventions: The Core of International Humanitarian Law*, January 9, 2006, http://www.icrc.org/Web/Eng/siteeng0.nsf/htmlall/genevaconventions (accessed December 9, 2008).

13 United States of America, *Torture, U.S. Code, Title 18, Chapter 113C*, April 30, 1994, http://www.icrc.org/ihl-nat.nsf/ (accessed February 10, 2009). The Red Cross website contains the national laws and military regulations that implement the Geneva Conventions by signatory country. To find these laws, simply navigate from this site to the implementing laws and regulations that are specific to the U.S. government.

14 The Library of Congress, *Military Commissions Act of 2006*, October 7, 2009, http://thomas.loc.gov/cgi-bin/query/F?c109:1:./temp/~c109tSnoDs:e839 (accessed August 20, 2009).

15 Ibid.

16 International Committee of the Red Cross, "Convention (IV) Relative to the Protection of Civilian Persons in Time of War," *International Humanitarian Law– Treaties & Documents*, August 12, 1949, http://www.icrc.org/ihl.nsf/7c4d08d9b287a421 41256739003e636b/6756482d86146898c125641e004aa3c5 (accessed February 10, 2009).

17 Brigadier General Janis Karpinski, "ICRC Visits to Camp Cropper and Abu-Ghrurayb in Oct 03," *Four Corners*, December 24, 2003, http://www.abc.net.au/4corners/content/2004/20040607_command/letter_2.htm (accessed August 24, 2009).

18. Supreme Court of the United States, "Hamdan v. Rumsfeld, Secretary of Defense, Et Al," *Supreme Court of the United States*, June 29, 2006, http://www.supremecourtus.gov/opinions/05pdf/05-184.pdf#search=%22Salim%20Ahmed%20Hamdan%20and%20Supreme%20Court%20decision%22 (accessed February 10, 2009). Specifically, the U.S. Supreme Court opined that "Common Article 3, by contrast, affords some minimal protection, falling short of full protection under the Conventions, to individuals associated with neither a signatory nor even a non-signatory 'Power' who are involved in a conflict 'in the territory of' a signatory" (page 75).

19. International Committee of the Red Cross, "Convention (IV) Relative to the Protection of Civilian Persons in Time of War."

20. Ibid.

21. United Nations, "Convention Against Torture and Other Cruel or Degrading Treatment or Punishment," *Office of the United Nations High Commissioner for Human Rights*, http://untreaty.un.org/english/treatyevent2001/pdf/07e.pdf (accessed December 12, 2008).

22. Ibid.

23. Ibid.

24. United States of America, Torture, U.S. Code, Title 18.

25. Ibid.

26. Department of the Army, Field Manual 34-52, *Intelligence Interrogation* (Washington, DC: U.S. Government Printing Office, 1999), 1-8 - 1-9. This listing of relevant UCMJ articles comes from the interrogation field manual in effect during OIF I. The text of these articles can be found on the Red Cross website as U.S. implementing regulations of the 1949 Geneva Conventions, http://www.icrc.org/ihl-nat.nsf.

27. Department of Defense, Directive Number 5100.77, *DoD Law of War Program* (Washington, DC: U.S. Government Printing Office, 1998), 4.

28. Department of the Army, Field Manual 34-52, *Intelligence Interrogation*, iv-v.

29. Ibid., 1-8.

30. Ibid.

31. Ibid.

32. Ibid., iv.

33. Department of the Army, Field Manual 3-19.40, *Internment/Resettlement Operations* (Washington, DC: U.S. Government Printing Office, 2001), 1-2 - 1-4.

34. Ibid., 117.

35. Ibid., v.

36. On this subject, Field Manual 34-53, *Intelligence Interrogation*, describes "forcing an individual to stand, sit, or kneel in abnormal positions for prolonged periods of time" as illegal, but it does not describe what constitutes "abnormal positions" or "prolonged periods of time" (pg. 1-8).

37. Field Manual 34-53 describes "abnormal sleep deprivation" as illegal, but again, it does not define exactly what "abnormal" is (pg. 1-8).

38. As the Church Report stated, "Nevertheless, to a significant degree this [lack of clear legal guidelines] left implementation of interrogation techniques up to individual interrogators' judgment."

39. Tony Lagouranis and Allen Mikaelian, *Fear Up Harsh: An Army Interrogator's Dark Journey Through Iraq*, New York: Penguin Books Ltd., 2007. Mr. Lagournis and his co-author tend to de-emphasize Mr. Lagournis' personal responsibility for his own actions

and broadly blame senior political and military leaders without clearly delineating exactly how and where the decisions of these senior leaders may have contributed to his personal actions. Yes, ambiguity existed in Army doctrine as well as in CJTF-7 interrogation policies at the time. Nonetheless, Mr. Lagournis must bear the brunt of the responsibility for his willingness to interpret policies in a shameful manner—or to accept questionable "Interrogation Rules of Engagement" without doing the research to determine if these guidelines were valid. Still, his case is hardly an isolated one, and any leader of interrogators who wants to understand why an interrogator would choose to employ techniques in the field that he believed ran counter to the principles that he had been taught at the MI schoolhouse should read this book.

40 Department of the Navy Inspector General, "Review," 109.
41 Ibid.
42 Schlesinger, Brown, Fowler, and Horner, 14-15.
43 Jones, 8-9.
44 Department of the Army Inspector General, "Detainee Operations Inspection," v-vi.
45 Department of the Navy Inspector General, "Review," 49.
46 Ibid., 52.
47 Major General Donald Ryder, "Report on Detention and Corrections Operations in Iraq," *American Civil Liberties Union: Torture FOIA*, November 6, 2003, http://www.aclu.org/torturefoia/released/a19.pdf (accessed February 15, 2009), 27.
48 "Non-contiguous" is a U.S. military term used to describe an irregular battlefield in which there are no front lines.
49 Dr. Donald P. Wright and Colonel Timothy R. Reese, *On Point II, Transition to the New Campaign: the United States Army in Operation IRAQI FREEDOM*, May 2003 - January 2005 (Fort Leavenworth, KS: Combat Studies Institute Press, 2008), 196.
50 Ibid., 196-201.
51 Ibid., 196.
52 Schlesinger, Brown, Fowler, and Horner, 57-58.
53 Ibid., 57.
54 Ibid.
55 Ibid., 58.
56 Ibid.
57 Ibid, 123.
58 Ibid., 125-126.

CHAPTER 3: THE CITY UPON THE HILL

1 "John Winthrop: 1630," In *Speeches that Changed the World*, edited by Owen Collins, 63-65, Westminster: John Knox Press, 1999, 65.
2 ABC News, *Full Transcript of ABCs Martha Raddatz Interview with President Bush*, April 11, 2008, http://abcnews.go.com/Politics/Story?id=4634219&page=4 (accessed April 20, 2009).
3 Supreme Court of the United States, "Boumediene Et Al v. Bush, President of the United States, Et Al," *Supreme Court of the United States*, June 12, 2008, http://www.supremecourtus.gov/opinions/07pdf/06-1195.pdf (accessed February 10, 2009), 3.

4   Vice Admiral Alberto Mora, "Statement of Alberto J. Mora," *U.S. Senate Committee on Armed Services*, June 17, 2008, http://armed-services.senate.gov/statemnt/2008/June/Mora%2006-17-08.pdf (accessed January 17, 2009), 5.

5   U.S. Senate Armed Services Committee, "Inquiry into the Treatment of Detainees in U.S. Custody," *U.S. Senate Armed Services Committee*, November 20, 2008, http://levin.senate.gov/newsroom/supporting/2009/SASC.DetaineeReport.042209.pdf (accessed August 20, 2009), xiii. This report is hereafter referred to as the "U.S. Senate Armed Services Committee Inquiry."

6   Ibid.

7   Ibid.

8   Ibid. Recently declassified CIA memoranda contain many more examples of interrogation techniques which are referred to as employed at SERE schools.

9   Ibid, xiii, xix.

10 Ibid., xix. According to this Senate Armed Services report, safeguards at U.S. SERE schools include students being subjected to "extensive medical and psychological pre-screening"; the imposing of "strict limits on the frequency, duration, and/or intensity of certain techniques"; the presence of psychologists "to intervene should the need arise"; and giving to students "a special phrase they can use to immediately stop the techniques from being used against them."

11 Ibid., 41.

12 Ibid.

13 Ibid., 41-42.

14 Ibid., xiii.

15 Michael Isikoff, "We Could Have Done This the Right Way," *Newsweek*, May 4, 2009: 21.

16 Ibid.

17 U.S. Senate Armed Services Committee, "Inquiry," xiv. The JPRA's influence on the development of interrogation techniques for Gitmo is documented in pages xiii to xv of this report.

18 Donald Rumsfeld, "George Washington University's The National Security Archives," *Counter-Resistance Techniques in the War on Terrorism*, April 16, 2003, http://www.gwu.edu/~nsarchiv/NSAEBB/NSAEBB127/03.04.16.pdf (accessed November 2, 2008), 1.

19 Ibid., 1.

20 President George W. Bush, "Memorandum, Humane Treatment of al Qaeda and Taliban Detainees, 7 February 2002," *George Washington University's The National Security Archive*, http://www.gwu.edu/~nsarchiv/NSAEBB/NSAEBB127/02.02.07.pdf (accessed November 2, 2008), 2.

21 Ibid, 1. This is a hard argument for someone who is not a lawyer to follow. If another international group, say, the International Rugby Association, were to suddenly commence hostilities against the U.S., should not this group's members, when captured by U.S. forces, be granted Geneva protections based on the country of their citizenship rather than their group membership? The Bush Administration's argument here is certainly not the customary interpretation of the Geneva Conventions, in which there is no such thing as "unlawful combatants" and all detainees are guaranteed either the extended protections of Convention III or of Convention IV. Although it may be a hard argument to follow, there is indeed some ambiguity within the Geneva Conventions– ambiguity, it should be noted, that is erased in Protocol 1 of the Geneva Conventions of 1949. Protocol 1 binds all signatories to customary interpretations of the Geneva Conventions (or in other words,

binds signatories to the judicial opinions rendered by international courts). However, while Protocol I has been ratified by 167 countries, it has not been ratified by the United States. In his inaugural address, President Barrack Obama stated that "we are ready to lead once more." Perhaps ratifying Protocols I and II of the Geneva Conventions would send a stronger signal to the world that the U.S. is ready to resume its role as a moral leader than the closure of a facility (Gitmo) that is finally operating effectively and will just need to be reestablished elsewhere.

22 Ibid., 2.
23 U.S. Senate Armed Services Committee, "Inquiry," xiv.
24 Ibid., xv.
25 Ibid., xvi.
26 Ibid., xvii.
27 Ibid., xvii.
28 Ibid., 4.
29 General James T. Hill, "Memorandum for Chairman of the Joint Chiefs of Staff; SUBJECT: Counter-Resistance Techniques," *George Washington University National Security Archive*, October 25, 2002, http://www.gwu.edu/~nsarchiv/NSAEBB/ NSAEBB127/02.10.25.pdf (accessed January 17, 2009), 1.
30 U.S. Senate Armed Services Committee, "Inquiry," xvii.
31 Ibid., xviii.
32 Ibid.
33 Ibid., xix. Mr. Haynes is quoted as saying, "There was a sense by the DoD Leadership that this decision was taking too long." Rumsfeld allegedly prompted his senior advisors, "I need a recommendation."
34 The Schlesinger Report later concluded that, if the "Secretary of Defense had [possessed] a wider range of legal opinions and [allowed] a more robust debate regarding detainee policies and operations," the fluctuations in policy that occurred between December 2, 2002, and April 16, 2003, might well have been avoided" (Schlesinger, 10).
35 Rumsfeld, *Counter-Resistance Techniques in the War on Terrorism*, April 16, 2003, 1.
36 Ibid. These interrogations techniques were tiered, with Category III techniques being the harshest techniques. All interrogation techniques described in the U.S. Senate Armed Services Committee Inquiry as SERE techniques are listed as either Category II or Category III techniques in this Gitmo policy memorandum.
37 U.S. Senate Armed Services Committee, "Inquiry," xviii.
38 Ibid., xxx.
39 Ibid.
40 Redacted, "Email from REDACTED to Briese, M.C. (Div13) (FBI)," *American Civil Liberties Union: Torture FOIA*, May 22, 2004, http://www.aclu.org/torturefoia/ released/ FBI.121504.4940_4941.pdf (accessed January 11, 2009), 1. The cited interrogation techniques are consistent with allegations of the interrogation techniques employed by the secretive Special Mission Unit task force in Iraq. Corroborating this, the FBI agent even mentions this unit by its name at that time ("TF 6-26") in the email.
41 Marilyn Dorn, "Sixth Declaration of Marilyn A. Dorn, Information Review Officer, Central Intelligence Agency," *American Civil Liberties Union*, January 5, 2007, http://www.aclu.org/pdfs/safefree/20070110/cia_dorn_declaration_items_1_29_61.pdf (accessed February 10, 2009), 4.

42   The ostensible reason for this email was that, in the wake of the Abu Ghraib scandal, the FBI "On Scene Commander" wanted guidance from his superiors regarding which U.S. military interrogation techniques, if observed by his FBI agents, should be reported to his higher. President Bush's later admission to ABC News White House Correspondent Martha Raddatz on April 9, 2008, that he knew of and approved of his national security team meeting to discuss such controversial interrogation techniques as sleep deprivation and waterboarding has further intensified speculation that President Bush did indeed sign a still-classified Executive Order approving SERE interrogation techniques. Altogether, the circumstantial evidence gathered from unclassified sources suggests strongly that President Bush signed a still-classified order authorizing SERE interrogation techniques, though this order– if it indeed existed– probably applied only to CIA interrogation operations.

43   Rumsfeld, *Counter-Resistance Techniques in the War on Terrorism*, April 16, 2003, 1.

44   Donald Rumsfeld, "Memorandum for the General Counsel of the Department of Defense, Subject: Detainee Interrogations," *George Washington University's National Security Archives*, January 15, 2003, http://www.gwu.edu/~nsarchiv/NSAEBB/ NSAEBB127/ 03.01.15b.pdf (accessed January 19, 2009), 1.

45   U.S. Senate Armed Services Committee, "Inquiry," xxi.

46   Ibid., 120.

47   Ibid., xxii.

48   Ibid.

49   Ibid., 131.

50   Donald Rumsfeld, "Memorandum for the Commander, U.S. Southern Command," 1.

51   Ibid., 1-4.

52   Department of the Navy Inspector General, "Review," 55. Although often associated with the Fear-Up Harsh approach, SERE techniques can also be used when implementing other doctrinal approaches, such as the Pride (Ego Down) approach

53   U.S. Senate Armed Services Committee, "Inquiry," xxii. It should be noted that the fact that all U.S. detainees (including all unlawful combatants) were entitled to at least the minimum legal protections of U.S. national law held true even where and when Rumsfeld chose to override DoD directives and U.S. Army regulations. Thus, while the interrogation techniques used at Gitmo may have been legally permissible within the letter of international law as agreed upon and ratified by the U.S. government, these techniques when implemented probably constituted, even with the use of substantial safeguards, violations of national law– law that included the 8th Amendment to the Constitution; U.S. Code, title 18, Chapter 113C (prohibition against torture), and the UCMJ. Based on these potential violations of national law, Rumsfeld could conceivably face prosecution for authorizing certain controversial interrogation techniques at Gitmo. Calls for Rumsfeld's prosecution have grown increasingly strident with the December 11, 2008, publication of the Executive Summary of the Senate Armed Services Committee report on the "Treatment of Detainees in U.S. Custody" as well as the April 20, 2009, release of the full report. This summary and report, which are referenced throughout this chapter, faulted Rumsfeld for approving interrogation techniques at Gitmo that conveyed "the message that physical pressures and degradation were appropriate treatment for detainees in U.S. military custody."

54   Ibid., 154. Conversely, the Church Report concluded that harsh interrogation techniques in Afghanistan, though nearly identical to the techniques approved by Rumsfeld at Gitmo, evolved independently from techniques approved for use at Gitmo. However, the subsequent DoD Inspector General Report of 2006 and the Senate Armed Services Committee Report of 2008, both of which referenced the Church Report and other sources, concluded that techniques used in Afghanistan had indeed been influenced by Rumsfeld's

approval of harsh interrogation techniques for Gitmo. Here, I have chosen the conclusions of the two more recent reports over the conclusions of the earlier Church Report.

55 Ibid., 155.
56 Ibid.
57 Ibid. These techniques approved in Afghanistan are essentially the same that the U.S. Senate Armed Services Committee Inquiry attributed to SERE schools.
58 Captain Carolyn Wood, "Sworn Statement of CPT, 519th MI BN; Annex to Fay/Jones/Kern Report," *American Civil Liberties Union: Torture FOIA*, May 21, 2004, http://www.aclu.org/projects/foiasearch/pdf/DOD000598.pdf (accessed January 10, 2009), 5. Although Captain Wood's name is redacted in this sworn statement, the name of the commander of Company A, 519th MI Battalion, during this time period can be found in thousands of unclassified sources. Captain Wood even has a very extensive entry in Wikipedia, courtesy of the Abu Ghraib scandal.
59 Department of the Navy Inspector General, "Review," 6; U.S. Senate Armed Services Committee, "Inquiry" 151.
60 U.S. Senate Armed Services Committee, "Inquiry," xxiii.
61 Ibid., 155.
62 Ibid.
63 Ibid., 157.
64 Ibid., 221-222.
65 Ibid., 155-156.
66 Captain Wood, "Sworn Statement," 5-6. The Taguba Report rightly found 205th MI Brigade leaders at fault for allowing two of Captain Wood's interrogators to continue to interrogate despite an on-going criminal investigation– later substantiated– that these two interrogators had been involved in the physical abuse and deaths of two detainees in Afghanistan.
67 U.S. Senate Armed Services Committee, "Inquiry," 149. The composition of this SMU Task Force in Afghanistan was probably similar to the composition of the SMU Task Force in Iraq, namely, select members of Joint Special Operations Command, U.S. Army Rangers, U.S. Navy Seals, and various intelligence units and agencies.
68 Ibid.
69 Ibid., 150.
70 Ibid., 153.
71 Ibid.
72 Ibid., 156.
73 Eric Schmitt and Carolyn Marshall, *New York Times: In Secret Unit's 'Black Room,' a Grim Portrait of U.S. Abuse*, March 19, 2006, 3. http://www.nytimes.com/2006/03/19/international/middleeast/19abuse.html?_r=2&pagewanted=1 (accessed February 17, 2009), 3.
74 Ibid.
75 ABC News, *The Blotter: Secret U.S. Task Force 145 Secretly Changes Its Name, Again*, June 12, 2006, http://blogs.abcnews.com/theblotter/2006/06/ssecret_us_task_.html (accessed February 17, 2009).
76 U.S. Senate Armed Services Committee, "Inquiry," 149.

77 Ibid., 159-160.

78 Human Rights Watch, "No Blood, No Foul," *Human Rights Watch*, July 2006, http://www.hrw.org/en/reports/2006/07/22/no-blood-no-foul-0 (accessed February 17, 2009), 12. The title of this Human Rights Watch report is a reference to the signs that personnel had allegedly posted at Camp Nama– signs that allegedly condoned the bloodless beatings of detainees.

79 Ibid., 161. The SMU Task Force Legal Advisor contradicted this statement, stating that the TF SMU commander explicitly directed the continuation of the "Forced Nudity" technique in a meeting that took place in December 2003 or January 2004.

80 U.S. Senate Armed Services Committee, "Inquiry," 173, 186-187.

81 Ibid., 182-183.

82 Ibid., 176-178. According to Lieutenant Colonel Steven Kleinman, who headed the JPRA team, he stopped this interrogation and other interrogations which were conducted by SMU Task Force personnel and which he deemed illegal. He also alleged that one SMU Task Force member subsequently threatened him, sharpening a knife and telling him to "sleep lightly" because they did not "coddle terrorists" at the facility (U.S. Senate Armed Services Committee, "Inquiry into the Treatment of Detainees in U.S. Custody," 186). It should be noted that Kleinman's observations regarding physical abuse at Camp Nama are consistent with other allegations that a special operations unit close to Camp Cropper was regularly dropping off detainees at Camp Cropper with signs of physical abuse. These allegations, investigated by Lieutenant Colonel Natalie Lee, are discussed further in Chapter 4. Furthermore, this observation of physical abuse is consistent with testimony concerning Camp Nama that is collected in the Human Rights Watch report, "No Blood, No Foul," http:// www.hrw.org/en/reports/ 2006/07/22/no-blood-no-foul-0 and in such open-source reports as Eric Schmitt's and Carolyn Marshall's article in the *New York Times*, "In Secret Unit's 'Black Room,' a Grim Portrait of U.S. Abuse," http://www.nytimes.com/ 2006/03/19/international/middleeast/19abuse.html?_r= 2&pagewanted=1.

83 Ibid., 222.

84 Ibid.

85 According to the Taguba Report (among other reports), the titular head of interrogation operations at Abu Ghraib, Lieutenant Colonel Steve Jordan, had essentially abdicated his operational responsibilities, focusing on force protection and life support issues rather than interrogations.

86 Captain Wood, "Sworn Statement," 6.

87 Ibid., 6.

88 Department of the Navy Inspector General, "Review," 8.

89 Winthrop, *Speeches that Changed the World*, 63.

90 Ronald Reagan, *Farewell Address to the Nation*, January 11, 1989, http://www.reaganfoundation.org/reagan/speeches/farewell.asp (accessed February 10, 2009).

CHAPTER 4: CJTF-7'S LONG LIST OF NOT NEARLY ENOUGHS

1 William Kristol, *The Defense Secretary We Have*, December 15, 2004, http://www.washingtonpost.com/wp-dyn/articles/A132-2004Dec14.html (accessed August 20, 2009).

2 David DeBatto, "Testimony of Former U.S. Army Counterintelligence Special Agent David DeBatto, previously assigned to 205th Military Intelligence Brigade under Colonel Thomas Pappas in 2003, for the German criminal procedure against DOD Donald Rumsfeld and others," *Republikanischer Anwaltinnen-und Antwalteverein*, http://www.rav.de/download/

Testimony_DeBatto.pdf (accessed January 10, 2009), 2. David DeBatto was a senior enlisted counterintelligence soldier in the 223rd MI Battalion, which was attached to the 205th MI Brigade for OIF I. Mr. DeBatto's testimony was part of a criminal complaint filed by the Center for Constitutional Rights and four Iraqi citizens against Rumsfeld and ten other American political and military leaders. This complaint, filed on November 30, 2004, in the Stuttgart State Supreme Court, alleged violations of Law of War. Citing jurisdiction concerns, this court declared the petition inadmissable on September 13, 2005. When an appeal was then heard by the German Federal Supreme Court, the highest German court upheld the lower court's decision and declined to initiate proceedings. The court's decision here can be read at the following url, http://ccrjustice.org/files/ProsecutorsDecision.pdf.

3. Wright and Reese, 622. I can attest to the purpose and character of this exercise because I participated in this exercise as the S2 staff intelligence officer for 1st Battalion, 35th Armor, 2nd Brigade Combat Team, 1st Armored Division.

4. Ricks, 152.

5. Bruce Hoffman, "Insurgency and Counterinsurgency in Iraq, June 2004," *Rand National Security Research Division*, http://www.rand.org/pubs/occasional_papers/ 2005/RAND_ OP127.pdf (accessed January 10, 2008), 12. Hoffman quotes Major General Raymond Odierno, 4ID Commander, as saying that the bounty paid by insurgents to many anti-coalition attackers rapidly increased during OIF I: "When we first got here," Major General Odierno said, "We believed it was about $100 to conduct an attack against coalition forces, and $500 if you're successful. We now believe it's somewhere between $1,000 and $2,000 if you conduct an attack, and $3,000 to $5,000 if you're successful."

6. Wright and Reese, 160.

7. Ibid., 38.

8. Unidentified CJTF J2 Planner, "Sworn Statement of LTC, G2 planner for V Corps/CJTF-7; Annex to Fay/Jones/Kern Report," *American Civil Liberties Union: Torture FOIA*, July 16, 2004, http://www.aclu.org/projects/foiasearch/pdf/ DOD000766.pdf (accessed January 10, 2009), 6.

9. Jones, 9.

10. Wright and Reese, 159.

11. Ibid., 160.

12. Ibid.

13. As late as November 2005, Donald Rumsfeld was still saying that coalition forces faced "terrorists," not "insurgents," in Iraq. The first senior U.S. political or military leader to publicly state he believed that coalition forces faced an insurgency, or a "classic guerilla-type campaign," was the new U.S. Central Command Commander, General Abizaid, on July 16, 2003.

14. Wright and Reese, 159.

15. Ibid. "Red Teams" have gained widespread acceptance only recently in the Army. A Red Team serves as a kind of "devil's advocate" during the development of any staff plan, ensuring that the plan's assumptions are considered and, if necessary, questioned; that the plans adequately address all facets of an operation; that staff-sections are cross-talking during plan development; and that, in general, the plan is as sound as possible considering a particular planning process's time and personnel constraints.

16. Ibid., 160.

17. Ibid.

18. Ibid., 192.

19 Ibid.

20 Ibid., 193.

21 Colonel Thomas Pappas, "Sworn Statement of Col, HHD, 205th MI Brigade, Annex to Fay/Jones/Kern Report," *American Civil Liberties Union: Torture FOIA*, May 14, 2004. http://www.aclu.org/torturefoia/released/030905/DOD616_653.pdf (accessed January 10, 2009), 11. Although Colonel Pappas' personal information is redacted from this sworn statement, the Commander of the 205th MI Brigade at this time can be ascertained from numerous investigations and websites. According to this statement, Colonel Pappas' 165th, 223rd, 224th, and 325th MI Battalions were headquartered at Camp Anaconda in Balad, Iraq; the 302nd MI Battalion was headquartered at Camp Victory in Baghdad; the 323rd MI Battalion was headquartered at the Baghdad International Airport; the 519th MI Battalion was headquartered near Tikrit at Camp Speicher; and the 1st MI Battalion remained in Wiesbaden, Germany.

22 John H. McCool, "Interview with MAJ Art La Flamme," *Operational Leadership Experiences in the Global War on Terrorism*, September 13, 2006, http://cgsc.cdmhost.com/cgi-bin/showfile.exe?CISOROOT=/p4013coll13&CISOPTR =286&filename=287.pdf#search=%22command%22 (accessed January 10, 2009), 5. The Operational Leadership Experiences Project has built a substantial database of interviews of U.S. Army leaders who participated in combat operations during the GWOT. This collection is especially important in light of the fact that units typically purge their classified hard drives before redeployment, a practice that has left a paucity of primary source materials on military operations in the GWOT. This project's collection of interviews is a great starting point for anyone looking for primary sources regarding the GWOT. I personally have archived 14 interviews for this book on this site. The site is located on the Fort Leavenworth's Digital Library website, http://cgsc.leavenworth.army.mil/carl/ contentdm/home.htm. This site also includes a number of first-rate secondary-source offerings,

23 Ibid., 7, 12. The U.S. Army's Tactical Exploitation System brings together signals-, imagery-, and radar-derived intelligence from national- and operational-level intelligence collection platforms. Thus, during the invasion of Iraq, Major LaFlamme's analysts fused intelligence from multiple sources to create products in support of maneuver forces. Perhaps most proudly for Major LaFlamme, his company provided "intelligence overwatch" for the operators who rescued Private First Class Jessica Lynch.

24 Ibid., 15.

25 Wright and Reese, 206.

26 Ibid., 200.

27 Ibid., 205.

28 Major Douglas A. Pryer, "Interview with LTC Mark Crisman," *Operational Leadership Experiences in the Global War on Terrorism*, January 27, 2009, http://cgsc.cdmhost.com/cdm4/item_viewer.php?CISOROOT=/p4013coll13&CISOPTR=1418&CISOBOX=1&REC=2 (accessed February 13, 2009), 10.

29 Peter R. Mansoor, *Baghdad at Sunrise* (New Haven & London: Yale University Press, 2008), 182.

30 Department of the Navy Inspector General, "Review," 244, 250.

31 Ibid., 243.

32 Ibid., 243, 250.

33 CJTF-7 Headquarters, "FRAGO 176 (Military Police Task Org Change and OIF I to OIF 2 Transition)," *American Civil Liberties Union: Torture FOIA*, February 1, 2004, http://www.aclu.org/torturefoia/released/a29.pdf (accessed January 12, 2009), 3-5.

34 Colonel Ralph Sabatino, "Annex 47, Taguba Report," *The Center for Public Integrity: The Abu Ghraib Supplementary Documents*, February 10, 2004, http://www.publicintegrity.org/assets/pdf/Abu16.pdf (accessed January 12, 2009), 11.

35 Redacted, "Sworn Statement of S-3, 205th MI Bde," 1.

36 800th MP Brigade Headquarters, "Order of Battle Slides (Annex 41 to Taguba Report)," *The Office of the Secretary of Defense and Joint Staff Reading Room*, February 2004, http://www.dod.mil/pubs/foi/detainees/taguba/ANNEX_041_ORDER_OF_BATTLE_SLIDES.pdf (accessed January 12, 2009), Slide 1.

37 CJTF-7 Headquarters, "Detention Summit Briefing to LTG Sanchez," Camp Victory, Iraq, Slide 39. I obtained this briefing along with some detention-related emails of CJTF-7 leaders from Mr. Fred Huff, the current V Corps Historian. The slide deck itself is undated; however, supporting data for the slides was retrieved on August 19, 2003. Thus, this slide deck was probably presented to Lieutenant General Sanchez as a decision brief for CJTF-7 FRAGO 749, which was the baseline FRAGO for CJTF-7 detainee operations for the rest of OIF I and which CJTF-7 published on August 24, 2003. This briefing to Lieutenant General Sanchez had, in turn, probably been based on an earlier slide deck presented at a Detention Summit hosted by Major General Fast, the CJ2, on August 11, 2003. It is indicative of the undoctrinally large role that the military intelligence branch played early-on in detainee operations during OIF I that the CJ2 staff intelligence section rather than the CJTF-7 provost marshal office (that is, the military police) hosted this August 11, 2003, CJTF-7 detention summit. In fact, I possess an August 12, 2003, email from Major General Fast to a subordinate that states that it was not until this summit that the CJTF-7 Headquarters resolved that the provost marshal would be the proponent for future detention operations.

38 800th MP Brigade Headquarters, "Order of Battle Slides," Slide 1.

39 Ibid., Slide 2.

40 Ibid.

41 CJTF-7 Headquarters, "FRAGO 176 (Military Police Task Org Change and OIF I to OIF 2 Transition)," 3.

42 CJTF-7 Headquarters, "FRAGO 749 to CJTF OPORD 03-036 (Annex 17 to Formica Report)," *The Office of the Secretary of Defense and Joint Staff Reading Room*, August 24, 2004, http://www.dod.mil/pubs/foi/detainees/formica_annexes_1.pdf (accessed January 13, 2009), 39.

43 Wright and Reese, 205.

44 CJTF-7 Headquarters, "FRAGO 749," 40-41.

45 Ibid.

46 Ibid, 41.

47 Ibid.

48 Ibid., 43.

49 Ibid.

50 CJTF-7 Headquarters, "Detention Summit Briefing," Slide 8.

51 CJTF-7 Headquarters, "FRAGO 749," 48. This fragmentary order also required that the unit transporting a detainee obtain a detainee's new Individual Serial Number, or ISN, once the detainee was transported to the Abu Ghraib detention facility. The transporting unit was then required to provide to the capturing unit this identification number for the capturing unit's tracking purposes.

52 Ibid., 42.

53 Christopher Ives, "Interview with MAJ Douglas Smith," *Operational Leadership Experiences in the Global War on Terrorism*, November 3, 2005, http://cgsc.cdmhost.com/cdm4/item_viewer.php?CISOROOT=/p4013coll13&CISOPTR=86&CISOBOX=1&REC=19 (accessed January 10, 2009), 6. Major Smith was the operations officer for the military police battalion who ran Camp Bucca during OIF II. In this interview, Major Smith pointed out that, when he arrived at Camp Bucca in early 2004, Camp Bucca still retained the capability to induct detainees. However, all detainees had to be initially transferred and inducted at Abu Ghraib, even if the detainee were captured just outside of Camp Bucca's gates. Similarly, he said, the release of detainees would eventually be centralized through the Abu Ghraib detention facility as well, but this would not happen until after Major General Miller became Deputy Commander for Detainee Operations, Multinational Force-Iraq, in April 2004. Although Camp Bucca no longer initiated the induction process, it would repeat the induction process for all of its detainees, double-checking to ensure detainees' electronic records were accurate and complete.

54 Major General Barbara Fast, "Highlights from Detainee Summit," Email Forwarded to MAJ Douglas A. Pryer from V Corps Historian, Camp Victory, Baghdad, August 12, 2004, 1. Although not mentioned in Fragmentary Order 749, CJTF-7 was also in the process of adopting a supplemental database called the Biometric Automated Tool System (BATS). The advantage of this system for inducting detainees was that it incorporated biometrics. Thanks to the implementation of this database, Iraqis with variant English transliterations of their names could be accurately tracked in and out of coalition detention facilities. According to the Detainee Summit Briefing, other advantages of the BATS included the ability of the BATS database to handle relatively large files, to interface with a HUMINT database called "CHIMS" and, even more significantly, to interface with unclassified databases then being established for use by Iraqi courts.

55 CJTF-7 Headquarters, "FRAGO 749," 43.

56 Ibid.

57 Ibid.

58 CJTF-7 Headquarters, "Detention Summit Brief," Slide 8.

59 Ibid. The names of these leaders are in the notes page of this slide.

60 Ibid.

61 Ibid.

62 Darius Khaghani, "Conditional Release Program (Parole)," *Email Forwarded to MAJ Douglas A. Pryer from V Corps Historian*, Camp Victory, Baghdad, December 29, 2003.

63 Major Douglas A. Pryer, "Interview with LTC Russell Godsil," *Operational Leadership Experiences in the Global War on Terrorism*, December 20, 2008, http://cgsc.cdmhost.com/cdm4/item_viewer.php?CISOROOT=/p4013coll13&CISOPTR=1443&CISOBOX=1&REC=7 (accessed March 8, 2009), 6.

64 Laurence Lessard, "Interview with LTC Paul Perrone," *Operational Leadership Experiences in the Global War on Terrorism*, March 28, 2007, http://cgsc.cdmhost.com/cgi-bin/showfile.exe?CISOROOT=/p4013coll13&CISOPTR=813&filename=814.pdf (accessed January 13, 2009), 8.

65 Federal Document Clearing House, Senate Armed Services Committee, "Hearing on Treatment of Iraqi Prisoners, May 19, 2008," 10.

66 Department of the Navy Inspector General, "Review," 242, 245. According to the Church Report, Task Force EPW was an ad hoc force established due to the unavailability of combat-ready military police units when the invasion commenced. (The planners of Coalition Forces Land Component Command had decided to put military police units in the "tail" of forces flowing into theater.) Task Force EPW consisted of the division's

military police company and numerous medical, legal, and HUMINT assets.

67 Ibid. According to Army doctrine at the time, detention camps or facilities consisted of "collecting points," "holding areas," and "Internment/Resettlement facilities." "Collecting points," normally operated by the military police companies attached to Army divisions, were further classified as forward or central collecting points. Forward collecting points were supposed to hold detainees no more than 12 hours, and central collecting points were allowed to hold detainees up to 24 hours. Holding areas, usually ran by the military police companies attached to Army corps, could hold up to 2,000 detainees. Internment/Resettlement facilities, normally operated by specially trained military police battalions, normally consisted of semi-permanent structures capable of holding up to 4,000 detainees (Church, 38).

68 Sabatino, "Annex 47," 4. On page 14 of their February 2004 Report, the Red Cross lists the date that U.S. forces assumed administrative control of Camp Freddy as April 7, 2009. It is unclear which date is accurate.

69 205th MI Brigade Headquarters, "Annex 40 to Taguba Report, Joint Interrogation & Debriefing Center Briefing," *The Center for Public Integrity: The Abu Ghraib Supplementary Documents*, January 23, 2004, http://www.publicintegrity.org/ assets/ pdf/ Tag29.pdf (accessed January 12, 2004), Slide 4.

70 Department of the Navy Inspector General, "Review," 243.

71 205th MI Brigade Headquarters, "Annex 40," Slide 4.

72 Ibid.

73 Ibid.

74 Colonel Thomas Pappas, "Sworn Statement," 1.

75 Department of the Navy Inspector General, "Review," 249. Prior to the U.S. invasion, the U.S. State Department had classified the Mujahedin el-Khalq, a Saddam-supported insurgent group dedicated to the overthrow of the Islamic Republic of Iran, as a terrorist organization. The Mujahedin el-Khalq was comprised of Iranians, and according to the authors of *On Point II*, the group had risen during Saddam's reign to become an elite force that had joined the Iraqi Army to fight invading coalition forces. Very little information has been declassified about operations at Camp Ashraf, probably due to the politically sensitive fact that these detainees were Iranian citizens. The 530th MP Battalion ran Camp Ashraf, and in the Taguba Report, Major General Taguba lauded this battalion for its administration of this facility.

76 Colonel Robert Hipwell, "800th MP BDE Inaugural Jails/Justice/Jails Meeting with CPA 1000 hrs Thursday," *Email Forwarded to MAJ Douglas A. Pryer from V Corps Historian*, Camp Victory, Baghdad, July 3, 2003, 1.

77 Jones, 10.

78 International Committee of the Red Cross, "Report of the International Committee of the Red Cross," 14.

79 Detainee Summit Briefing, Slide 36.

80 DAIG, "Detainee Operations Inspection," 71.

81 Ibid.

82 Ibid., 70.

83 Ibid.

84 10th Military Police Detachment (CID) Headquarters, "CID Report of Investigation – Final(C) 0031-03-CID519-62147-9J/5C1N/5X1/5Y2D2/5Y2G," *The Center for*

Public Integrity: The Abu Ghraib Supplementary Documents, June 8, 2003, http://www.publicintegrity.org/articles/entry/506/ (accessed January 12, 2009), 1.

85 Major Stacy Garrity, "Interview Conducted by Panel of Officers," *The Center for Public Integrity: Abu Ghraib Supplementary Document*, February 14, 2004, http://www.publicintegrity.org/articles/entry/506/ (accessed January 12, 2009), 5.

86 10th Military Police Detachment (CID) Headquarters, "CID Report of Investigation," 3. The investigative summary lists ten names, six of which have been redacted, and states that there is "probable cause" that these "individuals committed the offenses of Aggravated Assault, Conspiracy, Cruelty and Maltreatment of EPW, Dereliction of Duty and False Swearing when they physically and verbally assaulted EPWs under their charge." The senior-ranking NCO on this list, a female master sergeant, had two previous allegations of detainee abuse unsubstantiated against her. One of the two previous cases had been unsubstantiated because there had been no additional witnesses to the incident. All of these soldiers presumably transferred with their unit to Abu Ghraib when Abu Ghraib opened.

87 International Committee of the Red Cross, "Report of the International Committee of the Red Cross," 14.

88 Department of the Navy Inspector General, "Review," 301-302.

89 Ibid., 302.

90 Ives, "Interview with MAJ Douglas Smith," 6.

91 Ibid.

92 Ibid., 7.

93 John H. McCool, "Interview with LTC Wayne Sylvester," *Operational Leadership Experiences in the Global War on Terrorism*, October 10, 2005, http://cgsc.cdmhost.com/cdm4/item_viewer.php?CISOROOT=/p4013coll13&CISOPTR=65&CISOBOX=1&REC=2 (accessed January 10, 2009), 8.

94 Ibid., 8.

95 Ibid., 10.

96 John H. McCool, "Interview with CPT Amos Nelson," 7. According to CPT Nelson, the bus had been nicknamed "The Freedom Bus" by the first Iraqi prisoners released via this bus. This nickname was reinforced, Captain Nelson says, as Iraqi prisoners at Camp Cropper chanted frequently each day, "Freedom, freedom!"

97 Detainee Summit Briefing, Slide 33. In her sworn statement, Captain Wood actually provides a number of 200 for the maximum capacity for detainees at Camp Cropper. Other estimates of Camp Cropper's detainee capacity range from 200 to 450. I selected the number of 450 because this estimate was the officially accepted estimate at the time, even if it were probably optimistic.

98 Sabatino, "Annex 47," 4.

99 Detainee Summit Briefing, Slide 33.

100 Ibid.

101 International Committee of the Red Cross, "Report of the International Committee of the Red Cross," 15.

102 Ibid.

103 Ibid, 4.

104 Lieutenant Colonel Natalie Lee, "Army Regulation 15-6 Investigation into Alleged Mistreatment of EPWs and HVDs held at JIDC, Camp Cropper," *The Office of the Secretary of Defense and Joint Staff Reading Room*, January 23, 2004, http://www.dod.mil/pubs/foi/detainees/Lee_Report_release_dec07.pdf (accessed May 11, 2009), 24.

105 International Committee of the Red Cross, "Report of the International Committee of the Red Cross, 15.

106 Lee, 14-17.

107 These observations of physical abuse are consistent with testimony concerning Camp Nama that is collected in the Human Rights Watch report, "No Blood, No Foul," http://www.hrw.org/en/reports/ 2006/07/22/no-blood-no-foul-0 and in such open-source reports as Eric Schmitt's and Carolyn Marshall's article in the *New York Times*, "In Secret Unit's 'Black Room,' a Grim Portrait of U.S. Abuse," http://www.nytimes.com/ 2006/03/19/international/middleeast/19abuse.html?_r= 2&pagewanted=1.

108 Department of the Navy Inspector General, "Review," 61.

109 Ibid.

110 Ibid.

111 Ibid.

112 Ibid. Although the main Camp Cropper detention facility closed in September 2003, a new detention facility was eventually built at Camp Cropper. In 2006, the Abu Ghraib site closed and all of its detainees moved to the newly constructed site at Camp Cropper. As of May 2009, all coalition detainees in Iraq are interned at two coalition detention facilities, Camp Cropper and Camp Bucca. Unfortunately, even though Camp Cropper and Camp Bucca have interned far more detainees during Operation Iraqi Freedom than the relatively short-lived facility at Abu Ghraib, the facility at Abu Ghraib is the only corps holding area in Iraq of which the vast majority of Americans have heard.

113 International Committee of the Red Cross, "Report of the International Committee of the Red Cross, 7.

114 Ibid., 16.

115 Ibid., 11.

116 Captain Wood, "Sworn Statement," 8.

117 Ibid.

118 Ibid., 5.

119 Ibid.

120 DAIG, "Detainee Operations Inspection," 23.

121 Detainee Summit Briefing, Slide 35.

122 DAIG, "Detainee Operations Inspection," 23.

123 Captain Wood, "Sworn Statement," 6.

124 Department of the Navy Inspector General, "Review," 80.

125 International Committee of the Red Cross, "Report of the International Committee of the Red Cross," 23.

126 Fay, 38.

127 Armed Forces Press Service, *Insurgents Attack Abu Ghraib Prison, Kill Detainee*, September 21, 2004, http://www.defenselink.mil/news/newsarticle.aspx?id =25250 (accessed January 16, 2009).

128 International Committee of the Red Cross, "Report of the International Committee of the Red Cross," 23.

129 DAIG, "Detainee Operations Inspection," 27.

130 Wright and Reese, 207.

131 Captain Wood, "Sworn Statement," 1, 5.

132 Fay, 119. Also, according to the Church Report, the Army's Criminal Investigative Division eventually substantiated the allegations of homicide in these two cases and recommend charges be filed against 15 soldiers (11 military police and 4 military intelligence soldiers) for the December 4, 2002, case and against 17 soldiers (20 military police and seven military intelligence soldiers) for the December 10, 2002, case (14-15). According to numerous news reports, both cases of detainee deaths at Bagram involved the two detainees being tethered to ceilings and beaten over the course of several days.

133 Ibid., 64.

134 Federal Document Clearing House, "Hearing on Treatment of Iraqi Prisoners," 24. Adding to the credibility of the Red Cross's allegations regarding other detention facilities in Iraq (such as Camp Cropper) is the fact that nearly all of the types of detainee abuse the Red Cross alleged had occurred at Abu Ghraib were actually substantiated later by Army investigators. Within this context, it is unsurprising that the Schlesinger Report faulted CJTF-7 leadership for failing to heed the Red Cross's allegations regarding Abu Ghraib (17).

135 Fay, 40. The 372nd MP Company arrived at Abu Ghraib on October 1, 2003.

136 Ibid., 7.

137 Ibid.

138 Department of the Navy Inspector General, "Review," 82.

139 Ibid., 258.

140 Major General Geoffrey Miller, "Assessment of DoD Counterterrorism Interrogation and Detention Operations in Iraq," *American Civil Liberties Union: Torture FOIA*, September 9, 2003, http://www.aclu.org/torturefoia/released/a20.pdf (accessed January 11, 2009), 2.

141 Ibid.

142 Although not identified as SERE techniques in the policy memorandum, some of the techniques approved on September 14, 2003, for Iraq match the SERE techniques described by the Senate Armed Services Committee in its "Inquiry into the Treatment of Detainees in U.S. Custody."

143 CJTF-7 Headquarters, "Interrogation and Counter-Resistance Policy Memorandum, 14 September 2003," *American Civil Liberties Union: Torture FOIA*, http://www.aclu.org/FilesPDFs/september%20sanchez%20memo.pdf (accessed November 2, 2008), 4-5.

144 Ibid., 4.

145 Ibid., 1.

146 Jones, 16.

147 Department of the Navy Inspector General, "Review," 7.

148 Wright and Reese, 214.

149 Schlesinger, Brown, Fowler, and Horner, "Final Report of the Independent Panel," 12.

150 CJTF-7 Headquarters, "Interrogation and Counter-Resistance Policy Memorandum, October 12, 2003," *American Civil Liberties Union: Torture FOIA*, http://www.aclu.org/FilesPDFs/october%20sanchez%20memo.pdf (accessed December 12, 2008), 1.

151 Ibid., 2.

152 Captain Wood, "Sworn Statement," 3. When CJTF-7's October memorandum was published, Captain Wood said, it was explained to her by someone "from higher" that the September techniques were still permissible, they just needed Commanding General approval. Thus on the slide she posted at Abu Ghraib (Figure 6), she simply moved several interrogation techniques from the September memorandum to a column on the posted slide indicating techniques that needed the approval of the Commanding General to implement.

The result was that the October memorandum applied few (if any) additional restrictions on how her interrogators did business: she simply continued to forward requests to use such SERE techniques as "sleep deprivation" and "use of military working dogs" to her boss, Colonel Pappas, whom she believed had been delegated the authority to approve the use of such techniques by Lieutenant General Sanchez.

153 CJTF-7 Headquarters, "Interrogation and Counter-Resistance Policy Memorandum, October 12, 2003," 1.

154 CJTF-7 Headquarters, "Interrogation and Counter-Resistance Policy Memorandum, September 14, 2003," 4-5.

155 The earlier, outdated 1987 field manual had not intended to sanction the denial of basic necessities of food and clothing to interrogation subjects, for such would have constituted clear violations of the Geneva Conventions. This outdated Army field manual did intend, however, to allow interrogators to use additional food, clothing, and other items– beyond the basic requirements directed by the Geneva Conventions– as incentives. Due perhaps to the potential for misunderstanding here, doctrine-writers had deleted this paragraph from the 1992 field manual.

156 Jones, 10. In addition to the Company A, 519 MI Battalion, personnel who had previously served in Afghanistan, there were six trainers from Gitmo assisting and conducting interrogations at Abu Ghraib from October 4, 2003, to December 2, 2003, a period concurrent with the most significant instances at Abu Ghraib of detainee abuse. (Fay, 59)

157 CJTF-7 Headquarters, "Interrogation and Counter-Resistance Policy Memorandum, October 12, 2003," 3.

158 Colonel Warren, "Sworn Statement," 1. The ambiguity in the October memorandum is so obvious, it is tempting to conclude that the ambiguity in this policy was a deliberate attempt to enable the "aggressive" interrogation techniques of the CENTCOM-rejected September memorandum to find their way into the October policy. To take such an approach– subtly refusing to execute the intent of a higher directive via deliberately ambiguous phrasing– would have certainly been within the capability of the bright CJTF-7 lawyers who drafted the October memorandum, and the motivation for doing so (which can be articulated as "U.S. Central Command is far away and does not understand what our soldiers are dealing with") may have existed. After all, this is the same headquarters that dispatched the "gloves are coming off" email. For those of a conspiratorial mindset, the uniquely ineffective manner in which the October memorandum was disseminated is suspicious as well. However, since Colonel Warren and other CJTF-7 lawyers have provided a satisfactory alternative explanation for this ambiguity and since none of the various investigators into the interrogation operations of CJTF-7 have discussed this possibility, one must assume that the mistakes made by the overburdened lawyers who drafted the October memorandum were honest mistakes. Further supporting this assumption is the fact these CJTF-7 lawyers had possessed no experience with regard to drafting verbiage for interrogation approaches prior to CJTF-7's September and October policy memoranda. In short, it is extremely likely (though by no means certain) that the gross ambiguities in the CJTF-7 October policy memorandum were simply the mistakes of inexperience on the part of CJTF-7's lawyers.

159 CJTF-7 Headquarters, "Interrogation and Counter-Resistance Policy Memorandum, October 12, 2003," 4.

160 Colonel Warren, "Sworn Statement," 1

161 Fay, 10. According to the Fay-Jones Report, the arrival of military working dogs at Abu Ghraib had grown out of a recommendation made by Major General Miller's Gitmo team to CJTF-7.

162 Eric Schmitt, *The New York Times: Pentagon Study Describes Abuse by Units in Iraq*, June 17, 2006, http://www.nytimes.com/2006/06/17/washington/ 17formica. html?ex=1308196800& (accessed February 17, 2009).

163 Brigadier General Richard Formica, "CJTF-7 Interrogation Techniques as of 30 May 04," *The Office of the Secretary of Defense and Joint Staff Reading Room: Formica Report Annexes, Part I*. November 8, 2004, http://www.dod.mil/pubs/foi/detainees/ formica_ annexes_1.pdf (accessed February 2009, 17), 85.

164 Ibid.

165 Ibid.

166 Department of the Army Inspector General, "Detainee Operations Inspection," 35.

167 The Schlesinger Report, echoed in this conclusion by the Church Report, states that "there is no evidence of a policy of abuse promulgated by senior officials or military authorities." Despite these conclusions, whether such CJTF-7 techniques as "Presence of Military Working Dogs," "Sleep Management," and "Stress Positions" were humane, non-abusive, legal, and moral techniques during OIF I– even when properly implemented– remains a subject of much debate. This noted, it should be pointed out that Lieutenant General Sanchez and his team of lawyers almost certainly did not intend for their CJTF-7 interrogation memoranda to be understood in the fashion these memoranda were understood by some interrogators (most dramatically at Abu Ghraib). This misunderstanding was due to ambiguity within the memoranda themselves as well as to CJTF-7's failure to adequately proscribe training for interrogators on new techniques. Thus, the lack of clarity of the commander and staff of CJTF-7 regarding what actions new interrogation techniques actually permitted as well as their failure to adequately provide for training for interrogators on new techniques was their most unfortunate (and ultimately most tragic) failure with regard to interrogation operations.

CHAPTER 5: TRAGIC BLUNDERS

1 Chief Warrant Officer 3 Kenneth Kilbourne, "RE: The Good Fight Continues," *Email to MAJ Douglas A. Pryer*, August 20, 2009.

2 Lagouranis and Mikaelian, 135.

3 Department of the Navy Inspector General, "Review," 294.

4 Ibid., 294-302.

5 Ibid., 294-302.

6 United States of America, "Article 32 Hearing: United Staves v. CW2 Wiliams, SFC Sommer and SPC Loper," *Washington Post*, December 2, 2004, http://www. washingtonpost.com/wp-srv/nation/documents/mowhoush_court_document.pdf (accessed March 21, 2009), 41-42.. In the section cited here, the 3ACR commander testifies that, since the 3ACR was an "economy of force" operation, he and his leaders had had to trust Welshofer when Welshofer told them that enhanced interrogation techniques were acceptable.

7 International Committee of the Red Cross, "Report of the International Committee of the Red Cross," 3, 6.

8 Ibid, 7.

9 Ibid.

10 United States of America, "Article 32 Hearing: United Staves v. CW2 Wiliams, SFC Sommer and SPC Loper," *Washington Post*, December 2, 2004, http://www. washingtonpost.com/wp-srv/nation/documents/mowhoush_court_document.pdf (accessed March 21, 2009), 20, 33.

11 International Committee of the Red Cross, "Report of the International Committee of the Red Cross," 7.
12 United States Army Criminal Investigation Command, " CID Report of Investigation – Final (C)/SSI –0177-04-CID259-80266/5C2B/5Y2E/5X1," *American Civil Liberties Union: Torture FOIA*. August 3, 2004, http://www.aclu.org/ projects/foiasearch/pdf/ DODDOACID004133.pdf (accessed March 22, 2009), 12, 14. Inexcusably, in his search for the detainees and unit in question, the investigating agent did not even interview any soldiers responsible for detention operations at the Al Habbiniyah airfield during the time period of the alleged abuse.
13 Ibid., 20.
14 Human Rights Watch, "No Blood, No Foul," Human Rights Watch, July 2006, http://www.hrw.org/en/reports/2006/07/22/no-blood-no-foul-0 (accessed February 17, 2009), 25-26.
15 Ibid., 26-30.
16 Ibid.
17 Ibid., 26.
18 Steven G. Bradbury, *Memorandum for John A. Rizzo, Senior Deputy General Counsel, Central Intelligence Agency*, May 10, 2005, http://luxmedia.vo.llnwd.net/ o10/clients/aclu/ olc_05102005_bradbury_20pg.pdf (accessed August 21, 2009), 33.
19 The 3ACR operated out of the Al Asad Air Field from September 2003 to March 2004 (United States of America, "Article 32 Hearing," 19). "Operation Rifles Blitz" was a two-week cordon-and-search operation that took place at the end of November 2003 in the Al Qaim area (United States of America, "Article 32 Hearing," 21).
20 United States of America, "Article 32 Hearing," 33.
21 Ibid.
22 4th Infantry Division Headquarters, "AR 15-6 Investigation," 54.
23 Ibid.
24 United States of America, "Article 32 Hearing," 100.
25 Josh White, "Documents Tell of Brutal Improvisation by GIs," *Washington Post*, August 3, 2005, http://www.washingtonpost.com/wp-dyn/content/article/ 2005/08/02/AR2005080201941_pf.html (accessed March 22, 2009).
26 Human Rights Watch, "No Blood, No Foul," 39.
27 Ibid., 38.
28 CW3 Lewis Welshofer, "Memorandum For Commander 82d ABN DIV," *American Torture*, February 11, 2004, http://www.americantorture.com/documents/ iraq/10.pdf (accessed March 20, 2009), 2. Welshofer actually refers here to an "incident involving the death of LTC Jallel." According to Welshofer, this detainee led a Special Forces team to the explosives cache site. Since this detainee has the same rank, a similar name, and was also questioned by Special Forces before he died, it is all but certain that Welshofer is referring here to Lieutenant Colonel Jameel. Further corroborating this connection is the allegation of news reports that Jameel, like the lieutenant colonel that Welshofer refers to, was detained for possessing explosive devises.
29 Mike Moffeit, *Brutal Interrogation in Iraq*, May 19, 2004, http://www.denverpost.com/search/ci_0002157003 (accessed August 24, 2009).
30 Ibid.
31 Ibid.
32 Ibid.

33 Ibid.
34 Ibid.
35 Douglas Jehl, *Pentagon Will Not Try 17 G.I.'s Implicated in Prisoners' Deaths*, March 26, 2005, http://www.nytimes.com/2005/03/26/politics/26abuse.html?_r=1, (accessed August 24, 2009).
36 "Final Autopsy Report," *American Civil Liberties Union: Torture FOIA*, http://www.aclu.org/torturefoia/released/041905/m001_203.pdf (accessed August 22, 2009), 108.
37 United States Army Criminal Investigation Command, "Army Criminal Investigators Outline 27 Confirmed or Suspected Detainee Homicides for Operation Iraqi Freedom, Operation Enduring Freedom," *United States Army Criminal Investigation Command*, http://www.cid.army.mil/ Documents/OIF-OEF%20Homicides.pdf (accessed August 23, 2009) 7.
38 Ibid.
39 Ibid.
40 Welshofer, 2.
41 Ibid.
42 Ibid.
43 Marc Kusnetz, "Torture on Trial – HRF Observes Court Martial of Army Officer Accused in Death of Iraqi Major General," *Human Rights First*, January 13-17, 2006, http://www.humanrightsfirst.org/us_law/etn/trial/welshofer-011706.asp (accessed March 20, 2009). This fact is at the "Welshofer in his own Words" hyperlink.
44 Ibid. At "In Their Own Words" hyperlink; Steven G. Bradbury, *Memorandum for John A. Rizzo, Senior Deputy General Counsel, Central Intelligence Agency*,. May 30, 2005, 15. During Welshofer's court martial, this warrant officer testified under oath, "We basically held him [Mowhoush] down on his back and poured water on his face." The CIA memorandum cited here says that when waterboarded, "the detainee is placed face-up on a gurney with his head inclined downward" and "a cloth is placed over his face on which cold water is then poured for periods of at most 40 seconds." Other than the use of a cloth specified in the SERE-derived CIA technique, there is no discernable difference between the tactic employed here by Welshofer on Mowhoush and the CIA technique known as waterboarding.
45 Kusnetz. At "In Their Own Words" hyperlink.
46 Ibid.
47 Ibid.
48 Ibid. At "Case Closed?" hyperlink.
49 United States of America, "Article 32 Hearing," 36.
50 Ibid., 25. The reason that the 3ACR commander provides for recommending that his supervisor, the 82nd Airborne Division commander, rescind all letters of reprimand pertaining to Mowhoush's homicide was "extenuating circumstances" that are then redacted. Based on news reports, it is almost certain he is referring to Mowhoush's alleged beating at the hands of CIA operators.
51 Ibid., 34, 39-40.
52 Kusnetz. At "In Their Own Words" hyperlink.
53 101st Airborne Division Headquarters, "AR 15-6 Investigation into the Death of Abu Malik Kenami," *American Civil Liberties Union: Torture FOIA*, December 28, 2003, http://www.aclu.org/projects/foiasearch/pdf/DODDOA026695.pdf (accessed August 13, 2009), 42.

54 Ibid., 4-5.
55 Ibid., 6, 12.
56 Ibid., 1; 31st Military Police Detachment (CID) Headquarters, "CID Report of Investigation – Final – 0140-03-CID389-61697–5H9B," *American Civil Liberties Union: Torture FOIA*, January 1, 2004, http://www.aclu.org/projects/foiasearch/pdf/ DODDOACID007319.pdf (accessed August 12, 2009), 1.
57 101st Airborne Division Headquarters, "AR 15-6 Investigation," 15, 51.
58 Department of the Navy Inspector General, "Review," 297.
59 Ibid., 51; 101st Airborne Division Headquarters, "Report of Proceedings by Investigating Board/Board of Officers," *American Civil Liberties Union: Torture FOIA*, December 20, 2009, http://www.aclu.org/projects/foiasearch/pdf/DODDOA026578.pdf (accessed August 13, 2009), 10.
60 Ibid., 11.
61 Human Rights Watch, 41.
62 101st Airborne Division Headquarters, "AR 15-6 Investigation into the Death of Abu Malik Kenami," 55.
63 Ibid., 54.
64 Ibid.
65 Ibid., 55.
66 "Flutter kicks" are a standard U.S. Army exercise designed to strengthen the lower abdominal region. It is also a favorite of many drill sergeants who want to "smoke" a basic training trainee. To execute, the exerciser lies on his back, places his hands beneath his buttocks to support his hips, and, while keeping his legs straight, rapidly alternates moving his legs up and down in a scissor fashion. While facility guards were authorized by unit standard operating procedure to administer "corrective training" for up to two hours, the Army investigator concluded that "smoke sessions" typically lasted only 10-20 minutes.
67 101st Airborne Division Headquarters, "AR 15-6 Investigation into the Death of Abu Malik Kenami," 16.
68 Ibid., 51; 101st Airborne Division Headquarters, "Report of Proceedings by Investigating Board/Board of Officers," 5.
69 Ibid.
70 When reading this synopsis, I always feel as if I am being transported back to 1994 and my short time as an enlisted guard at a SERE school in North Carolina.
71 101st Airborne Division Headquarters, "Report of Proceedings by Investigating Board/ Board of Officers," *American Civil Liberties Union: Torture FOIA*, December 20, 2003, http://www.aclu.org/projects/foiasearch/pdf/DODDOA026578.pdf (accessed August 13, 2009), 5.
72 Ibid., 10-12.
73 Ibid., 10.
74 Ibid., 5.
75 Human Rights Watch, 39.
76 Ibid., 41.
77 Ibid.
78 Kayla Williams, *Love My Rifle More than You: Young and Female in the U.S. Army*, New York: W.W. Norton, 2005, 230; U.S. Senate Armed Services Committee, "Inquiry," 155.

79 Ibid.
80 Kayla Williams, "On Torture," VetVoice, April 22, 2009, http://www.vetvoice.com/userDiary.do?personId=419 (accessed August 22, 2009).
81 101st Airborne Division Headquarters, "Report of Proceedings by Investigating Board/Board of Officers," 17.
82 Human Rights Watch, 48.
83 Ibid.
84 Ibid.
85 United States Criminal Investigation Division, "CID Report of Investigation – Final Referred/SSI – 0233-2004-CID259-80270-5C1C/5Y2E/5X1," *American Civil Liberties Union: Torture FOIA*, May 1, 2005, http://www.aclu.org/projects/foiasearch/ pdf/DOD049418.pdf (accessed August 13, 2009), 2.
86 Ibid.
87 Lagouranis and Mikaelian, 119-120.
88 Ibid., 164.
89 United States Criminal Investigation Division, "CID Report of Investigation – Final Referred/SSI – 0233-2004-CID259-80270-5C1C/5Y2E/5X1," 9.
90 Lagouranis and Mikaelian, 164.
91 United States Criminal Investigation Division, "CID Report of Investigation – Final Referred/SSI – 0233-2004-CID259-80270-5C1C/5Y2E/5X1," 3. Although his name is redacted in the online investigation, the agent's interview with Lagouranis seems to be captured on pages 32 and 33 of this investigation. Strangely, Lagouranis' purported testimony regarding the use of hypothermia and military working dogs at the facility are not mentioned anywhere in this agent's report.
92 United States Criminal Investigation Division, CID Report of Investigation – Final (C)/SSI – 0180-04-CID259-80227-/5C1C/5Y2E/5X1. *American Civil Liberties Union: Torture FOIA*. July 28, 2004. http://www.aclu.org/torturefoia/ released/1248_1288.pdf (accessed August 12, 2009), 5.
93 Ibid., 11.
94 Ibid.
95 Ibid.
96 Ibid.
97 Ibid., 18
98 Ibid., 5.
99 Ibid., 20.
100 Ibid., 20.
101 Ibid., 3, 29.
102 Human Rights Watch, 44.
103 Ibid.
104 Armed Forces Institute of Pathology, "Final Autopsy Report," *American Civil Liberties Union: Torture FOIA*. November 22, 2004. http://www.aclu.org/projects/ foiasearch/pdf/DOD013279.pdf (accessed August 12, 2009), 1.
105 Ibid., 10.
106 Armed Forces Institute of Pathology, 10.

107 Human Rights Watch, 47.
108 Ibid.
109 One of the recently released CIA memoranda states that "water dousing, as done in SERE training, involves complete immersion in water that may be below 40 degrees Fahrenheit." (Bradbury, *Memorandum for John A. Rizzo, Senior Deputy General Counsel, Central Intelligence Agency*, May 30, 2005, 37).
110 These two reports are *No Blood, No Foul* and *By the Numbers: Findings of the Detainee Abuse and Accountability Project*.
111 Tim Shipman, *Sunday Telegraph: I blame myself for our downfall in Iraq*, June 10, 2007, http://www.telegraph.co.uk/news/worldnews/1554137/I-blame-myself-for-our-downfall-in-Iraq.html (accessed August 14, 2009).
112 Ibid.
113 Lagouranis and Mikaelian, 118-119.
114 International Committee of the Red Cross, "Report of the International Committee of the Red Cross," 7.
115 4th Infantry Division Headquarters, "Documents provided by the 4th Infantry Division SJA," *American Civil Liberties Union: Torture FOIA*, May 12, 2004, http://www.aclu.org/projects/foiasearch/pdf/DOD043552.pdf (accessed March 22, 2009), 2. Of note here is that "Isolation" is a SERE technique.
116 Ricks, 282.
117 Ibid.
118 Ibid.
119 Unidentified Investigating Officer, "Memo for Record – Evidence," *American Civil Liberties Union: Torture FOIA*, February 4, 2004, http://www.aclu.org/projects/ foiasearch/pdf/DOD043571.pdf (accessed March 22, 2009), 1.
120 4th Infantry Division Headquarters, "AR 15-6 Investigation," 43.
121 Ibid., 59.
122 Ibid., 74.
123 Ibid., 73-74.
124 Ibid., 26, 73-74.
125 Ibid., 56.
126 Ibid., 5.
127 Ibid., 47, 62.
128 Major General Raymond Odierno, "Treatment of Detainees in the Custody of U.S. Forces," *American Civil Liberties Union: Torture FOIA*, September 21, 2003, http://www.aclu.org/projects/foiasearch/pdf/DOD043596.pdf (accessed March 22, 2009), 1-2.
129 4th Infantry Division Headquarters, "AR 15-6 Investigation," 48.
130 Ibid., 49.
131 Ibid., 24.
132 Ibid., 28.
133 Ibid. This practice violates Common Article 3 of the 1949 Geneva Conventions, an article the U.S. Supreme Court has upheld as applying even to "unlawful combatants." For alleged use of this technique by 4ID units, see Ricks' *Fiasco*, pgs. 236, 256, 260, 283, 357.
134 Ibid.

135 Department of the Navy Inspector General, "Review," 299.

136 U.S. Senate Armed Services Committee, "Inquiry into the Treatment of Detainees in U.S. Custody," 252.

137 Ibid.

138 Ibid., xii.

CHAPTER 6: OLD IRONSIDES

1 Peter R. Mansoor, *Baghdad at Sunrise*, 178.

2 Ibid., 178-179.

3 The 1st Armored Division was activated on July 15, 1940, at Fort Knox, Kentucky. Its commander at the time, Major General Bruce Magruder, nicknamed the division "Old Ironsides" after nickname of the famously resilient and undefeated U.S. warship, the U.S.S. *Constitution*.

4 The 1AD is currently in the process of moving to Fort Bliss, a move that will be complete by Fiscal Year 2012. The headquarters, 1AD, is scheduled to move to Fort Bliss in 2011. The 1st Brigade completed its move to Fort Bliss on October 27, 2008. The 2nd Brigade is still at Baumholder and will be re-flagged as the 170th Infantry Brigade in 2010, whereupon it will stay in Germany (a brigade from the 1st Cavalry Division will be flagged as the 2BCT, 1AD, at that time on Fort Bliss). The 3rd Brigade is still at Fort Riley, but it was re-flagged as the 2nd Brigade, 1st Infantry Division, on March 28, 2008 (a new 3rd Brigade, 1AD, has not yet been established on Fort Bliss). The 4th Brigade, now a heavy combat team instead of an aviation brigade, has been re-designated from the 4th Brigade, 1st Cavalry Division, and has been established on Fort Bliss. The 1AD now has a 5th Brigade that was activated in 2007 on Fort Bliss. The 1AD Engineer Brigade, Division Artillery (DIVARTY), and the 501st MI Battalion have all been inactivated. Also, a combat aviation brigade will be moved from Fort Hood to Fort Bliss, where it will be assigned to the 1AD.

5 Estes, *U.S. Army Soldier Baghdad 2003-04*, 6.

6 Ibid. Two battalions of the 3rd Brigade, the 1st Battalion, 41st Infantry, and the 2nd Battlion,-70th Armor, were attached to the 3rd Infantry Division for the invasion.

7 Major Douglas A. Pryer, "Interview with CW3 John Groseclose," *Operational Leadership Experiences in the Global War on Terrorism*, January 7, 2009, http://cgsc.cdmhost.com/cdm4/item_viewer.php?CISOROOT=/p4013coll13&CISOPTR=1429&CISOBOX=1&REC=1 (accessed March 1, 2009), 6. The assumption that the battalion would be conducting large-scale screening operations was rooted in the battalion's experience a decade earlier during Desert Storm.

8 Ibid; Major Douglas A. Pryer, "Interview with CW3 Kenneth Kilbourne," 5. Chief Warrant Officer 3 Groseclose, who managed HUMINT operations for Company C, 501 MI Battalion, says that he did not cross-train his counterintelligence personnel as interrogators before deployment. On the other hand, CW3 Kilbourne, who managed HUMINT operations for Company A, 501st MI BN, states he did conduct this cross-training. I commanded Company B, 501st MI BN for one year after November 2003, and I do not believe that Company B conducted this pre-deployment cross-training in early 2003. Since these three companies held all of 1AD's HUMINT personnel, approximately one-third of the 1AD's counterintelligence personnel had been cross-trained as interrogators prior to the OIF I deployment.

9 Major Douglas A. Pryer, "Interview with CW3 John Groseclose," 7; and Major Douglas A. Pryer, "Interview with LTC (Ret.) Elizabeth Rogers," *Operational Leadership Experiences in the Global War on Terrorism*, January 11, 2009, http://cgsc.cdmhost.com/cdm4/

item_viewer.php?CISOROOT=/p4013coll13&CISOPTR=1442&CISOBOX=1&REC=4 (accessed March 5, 2009), 3-4.

10. In addition to two of the 3rd Brigade's battalions, the 2nd Brigade of the 82nd Airborne Division, which would be attached to the 1AD for the first half of OIF I, took part in the invasion.

11. Estes, *U.S. Army Soldier Baghdad 2003-04*, 6.

12. Ibid., 7.

13. At the time of its deployment to Iraq, the 2nd Light Cavalry Regiment's home station was Fort Polk, Louisiana. After redeployment, the unit moved to Fort Lewis, Washington, and was transformed into a Stryker Brigade. On June 1, 2006, the unit was re-designated as the 4th Brigade, 2nd Infantry Division.

14. Zone 21 has had several names. When it was built in 1959, it was called "Al Thawra" (or Revolution City). After the Baath Party Coup of 1963, it was officially re-named Saddam City in honor of Saddam Hussein, though many continued to refer to it as al-Thawra. After the coalition invasion of Iraq, the district was unofficially renamed Sadr City by its residents after the assassinated Shiite leader, Mohammad Sadeq al-Sadr. This district, unquestionably the most populated slum in Iraq, has more than one million residents.

15. Estes, *U.S. Army Soldier Baghdad 2003-04*, 7.

16. Ibid. Unlike most of the division, which had a 15-month deployment due to its extension for Operation Iron Saber, most of the 3rd Brigade had only a 12-month deployment, since the brigade both deployed and redeployed early. When the 1AD got the news of its extension, the 3rd Brigade was already home and most of its soldiers on leave.

17. Charlie Coon, "'Stability Operation' Turned into 15-Month Street Fight," *Stars and Stripes*, September 2004: 5-16, 16.

18. Major General Dempsey's star has risen rapidly since taking command of the 1AD. Since OIF I, he has held such notable jobs as acting commander for U.S. Central Command and (his current job) the commanding general of U.S. Training and Doctrine Command.

19. 1st Armored Division Headquarters, *1st Armored Division History*, http://www.1ad.army.mil/History.htm (accessed March 23, 2009).

20. Ibid.

21. Ibid. TF 1AD's nation-building efforts were truly prodigious during OIF I. For example, TF 1AD recruited, equipped, and trained 12,000 policemen, 6,200 Iraqi civil defense corps personnel; 5,500 Facility Protection Services guards (Hensley, 1-2, and Estes, 40). The division also increased Baghdad's fire departments from 10 to 23 fire stations and from 450 to 1250 firemen (Hensley, 2). Additionally, the division discovered caches that included over 55 million rounds of small-arms ammunition and more than one million items of explosives and arms (Estes, 50). What is more, the division supervised an estimated $2 billion in improvements to Baghdad on thousands of community projects, to include improved hospitals, clinics, schools, electrical infrastructure, police stations, and sewage treatment plants (Hensley, 2). Perhaps most importantly, though, the 1AD helped initiate democracy from the "ground up," establishing 88 democratically-elected neighborhood advisory councils that, in turn, elected members to nine district advisory councils in the city (Hensley, 3). As a result of these and other efforts, the division slowly reduced criminal violence during OIF I and, although not successful in preventing insurgent violence, successfully kept a lid on truly significant insurgent violence during OIF I. Such violence would not erupt until OIF II, at which time acts of violence steadily increased, a trend that would continue for three years.

22. Major Douglas A. Pryer, "Interview with LTC Nathan Hoepner," *Operational Leadership Experiences in the Global War on Terrorism*, February 2, 2009, http://cgsc.cdmhost.com/

cdm4/item_viewer.php?CISOROOT=/p4013coll13&CISOPTR=1441&CISOBOX=1 &REC=6 (accessed March 5, 2009), 11; Major Douglas A. Pryer, "Interview with LTC (Ret.) Elizabeth Rogers," 5. These interviews of the 501st MI Battalion S-3 and the 1AD Deputy G2 corroborate the assertion that no 501st MI Battalion school-trained HUMINT interrogator was ever formally investigated for detainee abuse.

23 Major Douglas A. Pryer, "Interview with CW3 John Groseclose," 13. Considering the character of the commander and S-3 of the 501st MI Battalion, it is unlikely that these leaders would have forwarded a request for the use of a SERE interrogation technique to CJTF-7. After all, it was the S-3 for the 501st MI Battalion, Major Hoepner, who refused to submit a "wish list" for harsh interrogation techniques to CJTF-7 and who cautioned other CJTF-7 J2X personnel to stay "on the high ground" (as described in the email exchange at the start of this book).

24 Major Douglas A. Pryer, "Interview with LTC Russell Godsil, 6; Major Douglas A. Pryer, "Interview with LTC Mark Crisman," 5. These two interviews are of the 1st and 3rd Brigade S-2s respectively, both of whom state their inspections with the Red Cross went very well. Lieutenant Colonel Larry Wilson, the 2BCT S2, also confirmed for me that the Red Cross never found a deficiency at the 2BCT's holding area.

25 International Committee of the Red Cross, "Report of the International Committee of the Red Cross," 1-24.

26 Human Rights Watch, "No Blood, No Foul," 1-55.

27 The exact nature and extent of 1AD's use of stress positions on detainees is unclear and will be discussed further in the next chapter.

28 Department of the Army, Field Manual 3-19.40, *Internment/Resettlement Operations*, (2001), 7-27.

29 International Committee of the Red Cross,"Convention (IV) Relative to the Protection of Civilian Persons in Time of War."

30 Ibid.

31 Ibid.

32 1AD Headquarters, "FRAGO 383A [General Order - Civilian or Detainee Maltreatment] to OPORD 03-215 (Iron Stability)," *American Civil Liberties Union: Torture FOIA*, July 21, 2003, http://www.aclu.org/projects/foiasearch/pdf/ DODDOA027333.pdf (accessed March 4, 2009), 58-60. This Fragmentary Order is archived as part of an investigation into allegations of detainee abuse at the temporary holding area of 2nd Battaion, 70th Armor, 3rd Brigade Combat Team.

33 Ibid., 59.

34 Ibid.

35 Ibid.

36 Major Douglas A. Pryer, "Interview with LTC Nathan Hoepner," 11. Also see Dempsey's email to his brigade commander's at the beginning of this chapter.

37 I extracted the timeline cited in this paragraph from my personal emails during this period.

38 Major Douglas A. Pryer, "Interview with Captain Nicole Lauenstein," *Operational Leadership Experiences in the Global War on Terrorism*, March 4, 2009, http://cdm15040. contentdm.oclc.org/cgi-bin/showfile.exe?CISOROOT=/p4013coll13 &CISOPTR=1454& filename=1457.pdf#search=%22Pryer%22 (accessed April 30, 2009), 7.

39 Major Douglas A. Pryer, "Interview with LTC Nathan Hoepner," 15.

40 1st Armored Division Headquarters, "1 AD PAM 1-201 Command Inspection Checklist, September 2003," *American Civil Liberties Union: Torture FOIA*, http:// www.aclu.org/projects/foiasearch/pdf/DOD045364.pdf (accessed December 12, 2008), 3, 12.
41 Ibid., 13.
42 Ibid.
43 CPT Douglas A. Pryer, "501st MI BTOC SOP," Standard Operating Procedures, Baghdad, November 3, 2003, B-a-1. I compiled this SOP for the 501st MI Battalion Tactical Operations Center while serving as the night battle captain for this center. I completed the SOP just a few days before moving to downtown Baghdad to take command of Company B, 501st MI Battalion. Almost certainly, I have the only remaining copy of this document.
44 Ibid., D-c-1.
45 Ibid., B-a-1.
46 Ibid., D-k-1.
47 Ibid., D-k-2.
48 Ibid.
49 Major Douglas A. Pryer, "Interview with LTC Nathan Hoepner," 6; Estes, *U.S. Army Soldier Baghdad 2003-04*, 54.
50 Ibid.
51 Ibid., 8.
52 Ibid.
53 Ibid., 7.
54 Ibid., 8.
55 Ibid.
56 Ibid., 5.
57 Ibid.
58 Ibid., 15.
59 Ibid., 12.
60 Major Douglas A. Pryer, "Interview with LTC Nathan Hoepner," 18.
61 Ibid., 16; 501st MP Platoon Leader, "Collection Point & Internment Facility Interview Questions," *American Civil Liberties Union: Torture FOIA*, March 23, 2004, http://www.aclu.org/projects/foiasearch/pdf/DOD018576.pdf (accessed March 23, 2009), 17.
62 LTC Nathan Hoepner, "Re: Interview!," *Email to MAJ Douglas A. Pryer*, March 25, 2009.
63 Ibid.
64 LTC Nathan Hoepner, "Re: Interview!," *Email to MAJ Douglas A. Pryer*, March 28, 2009.
65 Department of the Navy Inspector General, "Review," 60.
66 Major Douglas A. Pryer, "Interview with LTC Nathan Hoepner," 4.
67 Ibid.
68 Ibid.
69 Ibid.
70 Ibid.
71 Major Douglas A. Pryer, "Interview with CW3 John Groseclose," 5-6.

72   Department of the Navy Inspector General, 294.
73   Ibid., 298. The investigation for this incident is posted at http://www.aclu.org/projects/foiasearch/pdf/DODDOA027333.pdf
74   Ibid., 300. The investigation for this incident is posted at http://www.aclu.org/projects/foiasearch/pdf/DODDOA027333.pdf
75   Ibid. The investigation for this incident is posted at http://www.aclu.org/torturefoia/released/DOA_779_843.pdf
76   Ibid., 300-301.
77   Ibid., 301.
78   Department of the Army, Field Manual 2-22.3, *Human Intelligence Collector Operations* (Washington, DC: U.S. Government Printing Office, 2006), 30.
79   Ibid.
80   Major Douglas A. Pryer, "Interview with Captain Nicole Lauenstein," 4.
81   Major Douglas A. Pryer, "Interview with LTC Nathan Hoepner," 11.
82   Matthew Alexander and John R. Bruning, *How to Break a Terrorist: The U.S. Interrogators Who Used Brains, Not Brutality, To Take Down the Deadliest Man in Iraq* (New York: Free Press, 2008).

CHAPTER 7: THREE BRIGADES

1   Major Douglas A. Pryer, "Interview with LTC Larry Wilson," *Operational Leadership Experiences in the Global War on Terrorism*, January 30, 2009, http://cdm15040.contentdm.oclc.org/cdm4/item_viewer.php?CISOROOT=/p4013coll13&CISOPTR=1471&CISOBOX=1&REC=3 (accessed April 30, 2009), 8

2   Major Douglas A. Pryer, "Interview with LTC Russell Godsil," *Operational Leadership Experiences in the Global War on Terrorism*, December 20, 2008, http://cgsc.cdmhost.com/cdm4/item_viewer.php?CISOROOT=/p4013coll13&CISOPTR=1443&CISOBOX=1&REC=7 (accessed March 8, 2009), 10.

3   A unit's "tactical problem" is a term used by the U.S. Army to summarize the critical issues a deployed tactical unit (that is, a division or smaller unit) must solve to accomplish its mission. A unit's tactical problem is often analyzed using the METT-TC paradigm (Mission, Enemy, Terrain, Troops Available, Time, and Civil Considerations).

4   Matt Matthews, "Interview with COL Michael Formica," *Operational Leadership Experiences in the Global War on Terrorism*, April 21, 2006, http://cgsc.cdmhost.com/cdm4/item_viewer.php?CISOROOT=/p4013coll13&CISOPTR=134&CISOBOX=1&REC=8 (accessed August 15, 2009), 6.

5   Jim Tenpenny, "Interview with BG Michael Tucker," *Operational Leadership Experiences in the Global War on Terrorism*, January 20, 2006, http://cgsc.cdmhost.com/cdm4/item_viewer.php?CISOROOT=/p4013coll13&CISOPTR=511&CISOBOX=1&REC=1 (accessed August 16, 2009), 3.

6   Mansoor, *Baghdad at Sunrise*, xvii.
7   Ibid. 19.
8   Ibid., 20-21.
9   Ibid., 31.
10 Ibid., 41.
11 Ibid., 31, 36.

12 Ibid., 30, 36.
13 Ibid.
14 Ibid.
15 Tenpenny, "Interview with BG Michael Tucker," 4.
16 Ibid.
17 Ibid. Sadr City was not in the 1BCT area of operations. However, 2nd Battalion,-37th Armor, a 1BCT unit attached during OIF I to the 2nd Light Cavalry Regiment, operated in Sadr City.
18 Mansoor, *Baghdad at Sunrise*, xvii, 35.
19 Department of the Army, Field Manual 3-24, *Counterinsurgency* (Washington, DC: U.S. Government Printing Office, 2006), 1-13.
20 Tenpenny, "Interview with BG Michael Tucker," 4.
21 Scott Davis, "Interview with MAJ Esli Pitts," *Operational Leadership Experiences in the Global War on Terrorism*, January 27, 2006, http://cgsc.cdmhost.com/cdm4/item_viewer.php?CISOROOT=/p4013coll13&CISOPTR=249&CISOBOX=1&REC=2 (accessed August 16, 2009), 11.
22 Ibid., 8; Pryer, "Interview with CW3 Kenneth Kilbourne," 9; Pryer, "Interview with LTC Russell Godsil," 9. Kilbourne said "we had a couple battalions who were problematic" with regard to the mass round-ups of detainees, while Godsil refers to this practice "as a huge problem." Pitts, whose company ran a temporary detention facility during the summer of 2003, said that it was standard operating procedure in 1st Battalion, 36th Infantry, for soldiers to transport detainees in sandbag hoods. It is unclear whether all combat units in the 1BCT adopted this practice during this time period, though it seems likely. Colonel Ralph Baker, who took command of TF 1AD's 2BCT on July 7, 2003, believed that the 2BCT was the first TF 1AD combat unit to put an end to this practice (Connors, "Interview with COL Ralph Baker," 18).
23 Mansoor, *Baghdad at Sunrise*, 35.
24 Ibid., 48.
25 Ibid., 48.
26 As noted by Colonel Mansoor, the subsequent company commander, Captain Craig Martin, led the company "with distinction." (Mansoor, *Baghdad at Sunrise*, 261)
27 Pryer, "Interview with CW3 Kenneth Kilbourne," 3.
28 Pryer, "Interview with MAJ Craig Martin," *Operational Leadership Experiences in the Global War on Terrorism*, December 21, 2008, http://cgsc.cdmhost.com/ cdm4/item_viewer.php?CISOROOT=/p4013coll13&CISOPTR=1431&CISOBO=1&REC=9 (accessed April 10, 2009), 2.
29 Ibid., 3.
30 Major Douglas A. Pryer, "Interview with Ms. Amanda Meyer," Operational Leadership Experiences in the Global War on Terrorism, January 5, 2009, http://cgsc. cdmhost.com/cdm4/item_viewer.php?CISOROOT=/p4013coll13&CISOPTR=1395&CISOBOX=1&REC=10 (accessed April 1, 2009), 2.
31 Ibid.
32 Ibid.
33 Pryer, "Interview with LTC Russell Godsil," 2.
34 Pryer, "Interview with CW3 Kenneth Kilbourne, 2.
35 Pryer, "Interview with LTC Russell Godsil," 2.

36 Pryer, "Interview with MAJ Craig Martin, 4.
37 Mansoor, *Baghdad at Sunrise*, 56.
38 Pryer, "Interview with CW3 Kenneth Kilbourne, 2.
39 Mansoor, *Baghdad at Sunrise*, 56.
40 Pryer, "Interview with Ms. Amanda Meyer," 2.
41 Pryer, "Interview with CW3 Kenneth Kilbourne, 3.
42 Ibid.
43 Pryer, "Interview with LTC Russell Godsil," 3.
44 Mansoor, *Baghdad at Sunrise*, 55.
45 Ibid., 56.
46 Ibid.
47 Ibid.
48 Ibid.
49 Ibid.
50 Ibid.
51 Pryer, "Interview with CW3 Kenneth Kilbourne, 6.
52 Pryer, "Interview with LTC Russell Godsil," 2.
53 Ibid.
54 Ibid., 5
55 Pryer, "Interview with CW3 Kenneth Kilbourne, 4.
56 Ibid., 6.
57 Pryer, "Interview with MAJ Craig Martin, 4.
58 Chief Warrant Officer 3 Kenneth Kilbourne, "RE: The Good Fight Continues," *Email to MAJ Douglas A. Pryer*, August 20, 2009. According to Kilbourne, the detainee "was not cooperating in providing even simple administrative data for inprocessing," prompting one of his interrogators to direct the detainee to move meal-ready-to-eat boxes into a storage area.
59 Peter Mansoor, "RE: The Good Fight Continues," *Email to MAJ Douglas A. Pryer*. August 21, 2009.
60 Pryer, "Interview with LTC Russell Godsil," 8.
61 Pryer, "Interview with Ms. Amanda Meyer," 7.
62 Ibid.
63 Pryer, "Interview with CW3 Kenneth Kilbourne," 1-2
64 Pryer, "Interview with LTC Russell Godsil," 10.
65 Ibid.
66 Ibid.
67 Ibid.
68 Scott Davis, "Interview with MAJ Esli Pitts," 8.
69 Ibid.
70 48th Military Police Detachment (CID) Headquarters, "CID Report of Investigation – Final/ SSI – 0396-2004-CID259-80377-5C2/5Y2E". *American Civil Liberties Union: Torture FOIA*. August 11, 2005. http://www.aclu.org/projects/ foiasearch/pdf/DOD044497.pdf

(accessed August 19, 2009); Brigadier General Richard Formica, "Annex 62, Article 15-6 Investigation of CJSOTF-AP and 5th SF Group Detention Operations," *American Civil Liberties Union: Torture FOIA*, http://www.aclu.org/projects/foiasearch/pdf/DOD056779.pdf (accessed August 18, 2009).

71. Brigadier General Richard Formica, "Annex 230, Article 15-6 Investigation of CJSOTF-AP and 5th SF Group Detention Operations," *American Civil Liberties Union: Torture FOIA*, http://www.aclu.org/projects/foiasearch/pdf/DOD057167.pdf, 1.

72. Pryer, "Interview with LTC Russell Godsil," 1.

73. Mansoor, *Baghdad at Sunrise*, 34.

74. Ibid.

75. 323rd Military Police Detachment (CID) Headquarters, "CID Report of Investigation – Final(C)/Supplemental – 0046-03-CID899-63502-5C1D/5C1J/5N2D1/5R/5Y2," *American Civil Liberties Union: Torture FOIA*, October 2, 2003, http://www.aclu.org/projects/foiasearch/pdf/ DODDOACID000403.pdf (accessed August 19, 2009), 20.

76. Ibid., 21.

77. Mansoor, *Baghdad at Sunrise*, 34.

78. Ibid., 34, 181.

79. 323rd Military Police Detachment (CID) Headquarters, "CID Report of Investigation – Initial – 0129-03-CID899-63556-5C2A," *American Civil Liberties Union: Torture FOIA*, September 24, 2003, http://www.aclu.org/projects/foiasearch/pdf/ DODDOACID006782.pdf (accessed August 17, 2009), 14, 23.

80. Ibid., 14.

81. Ibid.

82. Ibid., 13.

83. Ibid., 14.

84. Mansoor, *Baghdad at Sunrise*, 275.

85. Ibid. I concur with Colonel Mansoor's assessment in this regard.

86. Ibid.

87. Laurence Lessard, "Interview with MAJ Shane Celeen." *Operational Leadership Experiences in the Global War on Terrorism*, December 18, 2007, http://cgsc.cdmhost.com/cdm4/item_viewer.php?CISOROOT=/p4013coll13&CISOPTR=1023&CISOBOX=1&REC=1 (accessed August 17, 2009), 5.

88. Ibid.

89. Estes, 6; Matthews, "Interview with COL Michael Formica," 5-6.

90. Matthews, "Interview with COL Michael Formica," 5-6.

91. Ibid.

92. Estes, 28.

93. Wright and Reese. *On Point II*, 631.

94. The 3BCT had a task organization similar to the 1BCT's task organization, so presumably it had approximately the same number of soldiers.

95. This number is an estimate based on the total population of Baghdad (seven million) and published estimates by TF 1AD's other brigades of the civilian population in their areas.

96. Pryer, "Interview with LTC Mark Crisman," 2.

97. Pryer, "Interview with CW3 John Groseclose," 4.

98 Major Douglas A. Pryer, "Interview with MAJ Brad Johnson," *Operational Leadership Experiences in the Global War on Terrorism*, http://cgsc.contentdm. oclc.org/cdm4/item_viewer.php?CISOROOT=/p4013coll13&CISOPTR=1419&CISOBOX=1&REC=5 (accessed August 16, 2009), 1-2.

99 Pryer, "Interview with MAJ Brad Johnson," 2; Pryer, "Interview with CW3 John Groseclose," 2; Pryer, "Interview with LTC Mark Crisman," 3.

100 Pryer, "Interview with LTC Mark Crisman," 2.

101 Ibid.; Pryer, "Interview with MAJ Brad Johnson," 2.

102 Pryer, "Interview with LTC Mark Crisman," 2.

103 Ibid.

104 Ibid.; Pryer, "Interview with MAJ Brad Johnson," 3.

105 Ibid., 2.

106 Ibid.; "Interview with LTC Mark Crisman," 3.

107 "Interview with LTC Mark Crisman," 3.

108 Ibid., 3.

109 This judgment is based on my experience as the Assistant S-3 for the 501st MI Battalion during the first seven months of OIF I. My daily duties in this position included compiling the division's HUMINT reports into a "Tactical HUMINT Team Cross-Boundary Report," and archiving the division's HUMINT reports onto a file server. During these seven months, Charlie Company's HUMINT section not only produced more than twice as many reports as some sections in the division, but their reports were often better written with more interesting intelligence. I was so impressed that I thought this section might be significantly larger than other HUMINT sections in the division, and I had a conversation with my boss, Major Hoepner, to this effect.

110 Pryer, "Interview with CW3 John Groseclose," 4.

111 Ibid., 9.

112 Ibid., 8.

113 An example of such misbehavior would be one detainee talking to another detainee, even after told not to.

114 Pryer, "Interview with CW3 John Groseclose,"10.

115 I was the Bravo Company commander who initiated this informal commander's inquiry. To the best of my knowledge, no record of this inquiry exists since 1AD's classified hard drives were purged upon redeployment. (Due to the desire not to travel with classified hard drives and media, this purging is standard operating procedure within U.S. Army units. Future historians will have a tough time finding original military documents to piece together the history of the Global War on Terrorism.) Ultimately, I verbally directed this interrogator not to force detainees to exercise, even though this tactic was not unheard of in the division and I was not at all certain that it was illegal. Also, my HUMINT section chief, Chief Warrant Officer 3 Joel Giefer, gave this interrogator a written counseling with the same guidance.

116 It should be noted here that, in my interview of Lieutenant Colonel Crisman, he specifically stated that he believed the company's interrogators used stress positions during the brief period in which CJTF-7 approved the use of stress positions as a coercive interrogation technique — that is, if subordinate units had first obtained Lieutenant General Sanchez's approval. However, Crisman was probably mistaken with regard to the reason why Charlie Company's interrogators employed such tactics. The weight of evidence suggests that these interrogators employed stress positions and forced exercise to discipline a

few misbehaving detainees and not to coerce intelligence from these detainees. This evidence is as follows: One, Groseclose states that his interrogators never used enhanced interrogation techniques (Pryer, "Interview with CW3 John Groseclose,"10). Two, using stress positions and forced exercise to control detainees (and not to coerce intelligence from them) was a fairly common technique elsewhere in the division. Three, Lieutenant Colonel Hoepner has stated that when he visited 501st MI Battalion detention facilities, he told interrogators that they could use stress positions to control detainees but not as part of coercive interrogation approaches (Pryer, "Interview with LTC Nathan Hoepner," 12). Four, there is no record of Sanchez ever approving a request from TF 1AD to use an enhanced interrogation technique, nor reason to believe that the 501st MI Battalion headquarters had ever made such a request. Five, the Charlie Company interrogator who made a detainee do push-ups and jumping jacks when assigned to my company said he only did so as a discipline measure. Despite the weight of evidence, though, it remains possible that Crisman is right.

117 Major Douglas A. Pryer, "Interview with CW3 John Groseclose," 13.
118 4th Battalion, 1st Field Artillery, Headquarters, "Informal 15-6 Investigation Findings," *American Civil Liberties Union: Torture FOIA*, November 10, 2003, http://www.aclu.org/torturefoia/released/032505/1581_1680.pdf (accessed August 16, 2009), 39.
119 Ibid.
120 Ibid.
121 Ibid., 43.
122 Ibid., 45.
123 Ibid., 40-41.
124 Ibid., 41
125 Pryer, "Interview with CPT Nicole Lauenstein," 4. The female interrogator mentioned here had apparently departed by the time Charlie Company interrogators allegedly used light exercise and stress positions to control detainees.
126 323rd Military Police Detachment (CID) Headquarters, "CID Report – INITIAL – 0041-03-CID899-63500-5C1B," *American Civil Liberties Union: Torture FOIA*. February 2003, http://www.aclu.org/projects/foiasearch/pdf/ DODDOACID007016.pdf (accessed August 17, 2009), 63.
127 Ibid., 20.
128 10th Military Police Battalion (CID) Headquarters, "CID Report of Investigation – Final 0030-03-CID899-63499-5YIG4/5Q1A/5T4/5R4B/ 5Y2D2/5X5/5S1C," American Civil Liberties Union: Torture FOIA, http://www.aclu.org/projects/foiasearch/pdf/DODDOACID001553.pdf (accessed August 19, 2009), 6-7.
129 Ibid.
130 Ibid.
131 3rd Brigade Combat Team Headquarters, "Recommendation on Resignation for Good of the Service," *American Civil Liberties Union: Torture FOIA*, October 1, 2003, http://www.aclu.org/projects/ foiasearch/pdf/DOD006788.pdf (accessed August 19, 2009.
132 3rd Brigade Combat Team Headquarters, "Report of Proceedings under Article 15, UCMJ," *American Civil Liberties Union: Torture FOIA*, October 21, 2003, http://www.aclu.org/projects/foiasearch/pdf/DODDOA027333.pdf (accessed August 17, 2009), 9. The unit and location of the alleged abuse is identified on page 17.
133 Ibid., 15.
134 Ibid., 17.

135 Ibid., 22-27.

136 Ibid., 18.

137 Ibid., 19.

138 Ibid., 13.

139 Major Douglas A. Pryer, "Interview with CW3 John Groseclose," 2. Here, Groseclose identifies this unit as having a temporary holding area.

140 Ibid., 12.

141 Ibid.

142 Major Douglas A. Pryer, "Interview with MAJ Brad Johnson," 6. By TF 1AD's manning document, there were no HUMINT teams at the division-level. All HUMINT teams belonged to the direct-support military intelligence companies that were attached to brigades. Thus, during OIF I, the only HUMINT capability at the division-level was provided by the various military and civilian interrogation teams that CJTF-7 assigned to the division to support operations at the division's interrogation facility.

143 Ibid.

144 Colonel Ralph O. Baker, "HUMINT-Centric Operations: Developing Actionable Intelligence in the Urban Counterinsurgency Environment," *Military Review* (March-April 2007): 12-21, 13.

145 Since I was the Company B, 501st MI Battalion, commander at this time, I can speak with some authority regarding its manning. By its manning document, this company was authorized 43 soldiers. A Signals Intelligence (SIGINT) platoon from Company D, 501st MI Battalion, was attached to the company throughout the deployment, and it was authorized 18 soldiers. The BDE S2 section was authorized 10 soldiers. Although not at 100 percent manning, these units were close to that level. Thus, the baseline number of military intelligence soldiers assigned or attached to the 2BCT headquarters should be 61 soldiers. Plus, the number of Category II interpreters (who were used by HUMINT operators because of their SECRET security clearances) and the number of Category III interpreters (who were used by SIGINT operators because of their TOP SECRET security clearances) fluctuated only slightly during the course of OIF I. The number of Category II and III interpreters assigned to the Company B headquarters, which was consistently 4-6 interpreters, was also a number that brigades had no control (and very little influence) over. Thus, 65 military intelligence personnel would be a more accurate total baseline number than 44 military intelligence personnel. What may be accurate numbers-wise is that there may indeed have been more than 20 non-military intelligence soldiers added to the Brigade S2 section, though this number still seems high. Additionally, there are two conceptual inaccuracies in this diagram. The first is that the diagram seems to illustrate the military intelligence company's Ground Surveillance Radar (GSR) section as being absorbed by the S2X. This in fact never happened: although only occasionally conducting GSR missions, this section reinforced brigade scouts on occasion while, much more frequently, providing convoy security for HUMINT and other military intelligence company assets. The second conceptual inaccuracy is that the company's Common Ground Sensor section is not depicted. The personnel of this section were either absorbed within the BDE's new S2X section or were tasked to run the Company B headquarters.

146 Baker, 19.

147 Pryer, "Interview with LTC Larry Wilson," 18. The 2BCT had greater access to the polygraphist because the polygraphist, who was a CJTF-7 resource, resided inside the Green Zone. The TF 1AD DIF coordinated with the CJTF-7 J2X for the polygraphist on a few occasions, but the DIF used him less frequently, at least in part because of the drive through hostile terrain from the Green Zone to the Baghdad International Airport where

the DIF was located.

148 Ibid., 12-13.
149 Ibid., 12.
150 Baker, 20-21.
151 Ibid.
152 Ibid., 15.
153 Ibid., 17.
154 Pryer, "Interview with LTC Larry Wilson," 14.
155 Baker," 15.
156 Pryer, "Interview with LTC Larry Wilson," 8.
157 Ibid., 13.
158 Wright and Reese, 201-202.
159 Pete Connors, "Interview with COL Ralph Baker," *Operational Leadership Experiences in the Global War on Terrorism*, November 11, 2005, http://cgsc.cdmhost. com/cgi-bin/showfile.exe?CISOROOT=/p4013coll13&CISOPTR=126&filename= 127.pdf (accessed May 10, 2009), 7-8; Pryer, "Interview with LTC Larry Wilson," 17. See also *On Point II*, pages 201-203, which describes the "Muhalla 636 Operation."
160 "Interview with LTC Nathan Hoepner," 13; Pryer, "Interview with LTC Russell Godsil," 10-11; Major Douglas Pryer, "Interview with MAJ Craig Martin," *Operational Leadership Experiences in the Global War on Terrorism*. December 21, 2008, http://cgsc.cdmhost.com/cdm4/item_viewer.php? CISOROOT= /p4013coll13&CISOPTR =1431&CISOBOX=1&REC=9 (accessed April 10, 2009), 10; Pryer, "Interview with CW3 Kenneth Kilbourne," 10-11; Pryer, "Interview with CW3 John Groseclose," 15-16.
161 Pryer, "Interview with CW3 Kenneth Kilbourne, 8.
162 Pryer, "Interview with LTC Nathan Hoepner," 13.
163 Pryer, "Interview with LTC Nathan Hoepner," 13; Pryer, "Interview with LTC Russell Godsil," 10-11; Pryer, "Interview with MAJ Craig Martin," 10; Pryer, "Interview with CW3 Kenneth Kilbourne," 10-11; and Pryer, "Interview with CW3 John Groseclose," 15-16.
164 Pryer, "Interview with LTC Russell Godsil," 10-11; Pryer, "Interview with MAJ Craig Martin," 10; Pryer, "Interview with CW3 Kenneth Kilbourne," 10-11. I can also attest to the fact (since I was their commander at this time) that all of the HUMINT soldiers in direct support of the 2BCT shared this perception.
165 This former Company B, 501st MI Battalion, HUMINT operator declined to be formally interviewed for this history, wishing to remain anonymous.
166 10th Military Police Detachment (CID) Headquarters, "CID Report of Investigation: Initial/Final - 0117-03-CID899-63549-5Y2C/5Y2D1/5C1J/5Y2E2, *American Civil Liberties Union: Torture FOIA*, http://www.aclu.org/projects/ foiasearch/pdf/ DODDOACID007713.pdf (accessed August 21, 2009), 158.
167 Ibid., 146-148.
168 Ibid.
169 Ibid.
170 Ibid.
171 Ibid.
172 Ibid., 158.

173 Ibid., 145.

174 Ibid., 160-167.

175 Pryer, "Interview with LTC Larry Wilson," 12.

176 Ibid.

177 Ibid., 7. Although unnoted in my online interview with Wilson, he informed me during this meeting that the 2BCT passed all of these inspections with no deficiencies noted. Lieutenant Colonel Hoepner, who inspected the 2BCT's detention facility on more than one occasion, has corroborated this assertion.

178 Ibid., 12.

179 Ibid., 4.

180 Ibid.

181 Ibid.

182 To this day, even though I had a significant role in this brigade's intelligence operations, I am unsure why my HUMINT professionals were never asked to "vet" (or screen) 2BCT informants or to run themselves those informants deemed to be especially valuable. Indeed, my soldiers consistently reported "push back" whenever they inquired about units' informants. Perhaps an unintended consequence of Colonel Baker's decision to praise units with the most robust HUMINT networks was to instill a competition that, at least with regard to encouraging units to hand-off their sources to HUMINT professionals, was not always a healthy competition.

183 Pryer, "Interview with LTC Larry Wilson," 8.

184 Reese and Wright, 192.

185 2nd Brigade Combat Team Headquarters, "2nd BCT Collective Accomplishments, May 12, 2003, through April 14, 2004," Flyer, Baghdad, Iraq, 2004. 2BCT leaders received a copy of this two-page flyer upon the conclusion of OIF I for distribution to their troops. I maintain a copy of this flyer.

186 Lieutenant Colonel Nathan Hoepner, "Re: RE: Part II." *Email to MAJ Douglas A. Pryer*. August 25, 2009.

187 As pointed out, however, by Scott Andrew Ewing in his fine *Military Review* article,. "Discipline, Punishment, and Counterinsurgency," it is technically even illegal for non-commissioned officers to "smoke" junior soldiers.

CHAPTER 8: THE ASCENT FROM ABU GHRAIB

1 Department of the Army, Field Manual 2-22.3, *Human Intelligence Collector Operations* (2006), 5-18.

2 LTC Russell Godsil, "RE: RE: RE: Interview!" *Email to MAJ Douglas A. Pryer*, February 23, 2009.

3 Erin Rommel, *The Rommel Papers*, Edited by B.H. Liddell Hart, New York: Harcourt, Brace, and Jovanovich, 1953, 521.

4 Department of the Army, Field Manual 2-22.3, *Human Intelligence Collector Operations* (2006), 5-21.

5 Ibid., 5-16.

6 Ibid. As an example of a violation of "facility security," the manual states that a guard should not provide a detainee additional food at an interrogator's request if that detainee has been spitting food at guards.

7 Ibid., 4-3.

8. Department of the Army, Field Manual 3-19.40, *Internment/Resettlement Operations* (Fort Leonard Wood: U.S. Government Printing Office, 2007), 4-3, 4-4.
9. Ibid., 4-3.
10. Ibid., 3-3.
11. Ibid., 4-1.
12. Ibid., 2-5.
13. Ibid.
14. Ibid., 2-3.
15. Department of the Army, Field Manual 2-22.3, *Human Intelligence Collector Operations* (2006), 5-24.
16. Ibid., K-5.
17. Ibid., 5-14.
18. Ibid., 5-14, 5-15.
19. Ibid., 5-15.
20. Ibid., 5-27.
21. Ibid.
22. Bill Dedman, "New Anti-Terror Weapon: Hand-held lie detector," MSNBC. April 9, 2008, http://www.msnbc.msn.com/id/23926278 (accessed May 2, 2009).
23. Ibid.
24. Ibid., 7-11.
25. Department of the Army, Field Manual 6-22, *Army Leadership: Competent, Confident, and Agile* (Washington, DC: U.S. Government Printing Office, 2006), 4-5.
26. Association of the United States Army, "Torchbearer National Security Report," AUSA. July 2007, http://www3.ausa.org/webpub/DeptILW.nsf/byid/JRAY-75LT2E/ $File/TB-Intel.pdf?OpenElement (accessed April 2009, 24), 5.
27. Ibid.
28. LTC Russell Godsil, "Re: Re: Douglas MacArthur & Your Points," *Email to MAJ Douglas A. Pryer*, April 20, 2009.
29. LTC Russell Godsil, "Re: Re: Interview!" *Email to MAJ Douglas A. Pryer*, February 19, 2009.
30. Ibid.
31. Lieutenant Colonel Dean Bland, *The Abu Ghraib Scandal: Impact on the Army Profession and the Intelligence Process*, Academic Research Paper, Carlisle Barracks, Carlisle, PA: U.S. Army War College, 2005, 20.
32. Ibid.
33. Lieutenant Colonel Steve Iwicki, "CSA's Focus Area 16: Actionable Intelligence," *Military Intelligence Professional Bulletin*, January-March 2005: 51-53, 53.
34. Association of the United States Army, 5.
35. Command and General Staff College Department of Tactics, *Battlefield Surveillance Brigade*, Fort Leavenworth, Kansas, February 2009,
36. Department of the Army Inspector General, "Detainee Operations Inspection," 87.
37. Amnesty International, "Outsourcing Intelligence in Iraq." *Amnesty International USA*. December 2008, http://www.amnestyusa.org/pmscs/corpwatch 13rpt.pdf (accessed April 25, 2009), 7.

38   Godsil, "Re: Re: Interview!" *Email to MAJ Douglas A. Pryer*, February 19, 2009.
39   Ibid.
40   U.S. Army Recruiting Command, *Warrant Officer Recruiting Information Site*, April 20, 2009, http://www.usarec.army.mil/hq/warrant/index.htm (accessed April 27, 2009).
41   Ibid.
42   Pryer, "Interview with CW3 Kenneth Kilbourne, 10.
43   Association of the United States Army, 6.
44   U.S. Army, *Army Training Requirements and Resources System: Information for Course 241-F4 (CT)*, August 19, 2008, https://atrrs.army.mil/atrrscc/courseInfo. aspx?fy=2008&sch=307&crs=241-F4+(CT)&crstitle=JOINT+INTERROGATION+CERTIFICATION&phase= (accessed April 27, 2009).
45   U.S. Army, *Army Training Requirements and Resources System: Information For Course 3A-SI3Q/3C-ASI9N/241-ASIN*. April 1, 2009. https://atrrs.army.mil/ atrrscc/courseInfo. aspx?fy=2008&sch=307&crs=3A-SI3Q%2F3C-ASI9N%2F241-ASIN&crstitle=DOD+STRATEGIC+DEBRIEFING&phase= (accessed April 27, 2009).
46   U.S. Army, *Army Training Requirements And Resources System: Information For Course 3A-F82/243-F30*, August 21, 2008, https://atrrs.army.mil/atrrscc/ courseInfo.aspx?fy=2008&sch=307&crs=3A-F82%2F243-F30&crstitle =JOINT+ANALYST-INTERROGATOR+COLLABORATION&phase= (accessed April 27, 2009).
47   Major Douglas A. Pryer, "Interview with CW3 John Groceclose," 18.
48   Association of the United States Army, 6.
49   Ibid., 12.
50   Ibid.
51   Schlesinger, Brown, Fowler, and Horner, 126.

CHAPTER 9: A TALE OF TWO CITIES

1   The White House, *President Barack Obma's Inaugural Address*, January 21, 2009, http://www.whitehouse.gov/blog/inaugural-address/ (accessed April 27, 2009).
2   Matthew Alexander, "I'm Still Tortured by What I Saw in Iraq."
3   "NOFORN" is shorthand for "no foreign nationals."
4   ABC News, *Full Transcript of ABCs Martha Raddatz Interview with President Bush*.
5   Steven G. Bradbury, *Memorandum for John A. Rizzo, Senior Deputy General Counsel, Central Intelligence Agency*. May 30, 2005, http://luxmedia.vo.llnwd.net/ o10/clients/aclu/olc_05302005_bradbury.pdf (accessed April 20, 2009), 7. An example of the extensive media coverage of this declassification is Josh Meyer's and Gregg Miller's April 17, 2009, article in the *Los Angeles Times* titled "Memos Reveal Harsh CIA Interrogation Methods."
6   Nathan Hoepner, "Re: Two More New Documents, Old Format," *Email to MAJ Douglas A. Pryer*, April 20, 2009.
7   Amanda Meyer. "Re: Our Interview & Lessons Learned &...Merry Christmas!" *Email to MAJ Douglas A. Pryer*, April 6, 2009.

Sources

Primary Sources

501st MP Platoon Leader. "Collection Point & Internment Facility Interview Questions." *American Civil Liberties Union: Torture FOIA*. March 23, 2004. http://www.aclu.org/projects/foiasearch/pdf/DOD018576.pdf (accessed March 23, 2009).

Headquarters, 800th MP Brigade. "Order of Battle Slides (Annex 41 to Taguba Report)." *The Office of the Secretary of Defense and Joint Staff Reading Room*. February 2004. http://www.dod.mil/pubs/foi/detainees/taguba/ ANNEX_041_ORDER_OF_BATTLE_SLIDES.pdf (accessed January 12, 2009).

ABC News. *Full Transcript of ABC's Martha Raddatz Interview with President Bush*. April 11, 2008. http://abcnews.go.com/Politics/Story?id=4634219&page=4 (accessed April 20, 2009).

Alexander, Matthew. "I'm Still Tortured by What I Saw in Iraq." *The Washington Post*. November 30, 2008. http://www.washingtonpost.com/wp-dyn/content/article/2008/11/28/AR2008112802242.html (accessed April 22, 2009).

Alexander, Matthew, and John R. Bruning. *How to Break a Terrorist: The U.S. Interrogators Who Used Brains, Not Brutality, To Take Down the Deadliest Man in Iraq*. New York: Free Press, 2008.

Armed Forces Institute of Pathology. "Final Autopsy Report." *American Civil Liberties Union: Torture FOIA*. November 22, 2004. http://www.aclu.org/projects/ foiasearch/pdf/DOD013279.pdf (accessed August 12, 2009).

———. "Final Autopsy Report." *American Civil Liberties Union: Torture FOIA*. http://www.aclu.org/torturefoia/released/041905/m001_203.pdf (accessed August 22, 2009).

Baker, Colonel Ralph O. "HUMINT-Centric Operations: Developing Actionable Intelligence in the Urban Counterinsurgency Environment." *Military Review* (March-April 2007): 12-21.

Bradbury, Steven G. *Memorandum for John A. Rizzo, Senior Deputy General Counsel, Central Intelligence Agency*. May 10, 2005. http://luxmedia.vo.llnwd.net/ o10/clients/aclu/olc_05102005_bradbury_20pg.pdf (accessed August 21, 2009).

———. *Memorandum for John A. Rizzo, Senior Deputy General Counsel, Central Intelligence Agency*. May 30, 2005. http://luxmedia.vo.llnwd.net /o10/clients/aclu/olc_05302005_bradbury.pdf (accessed April 20, 2009).

Bush, President George W. "Memorandum, Humane Treatment of al Qaeda and Taliban Detainees, February 7, 2002." *George Washington University's The National Security Archive*. http://www.gwu.edu/~nsarchiv/NSAEBB/NSAEBB127/ 02.02.07.pdf (accessed November 2, 2008).

Connors, Pete. "Interview with COL Ralph Baker." *Operational Leadership Experiences in the Global War on Terrorism.* November 11, 2005. http://cgsc.cdmhost. com/cgi-bin/showfile.exe?CISOROOT=/p4013coll13&CISOPTR= 126&filename=127.pdf (accessed May 10, 2009).

Davis, Scott. "Interview with MAJ Esli Pitts." *Operational Leadership Experiences in the Global War on Terrorism.* January 27, 2006. http://cgsc.cdmhost.com/cdm4/ item_viewer.php?CISOROOT=/p4013coll13&CISOPTR=249&CISOBOX=1&REC=2 (accessed August 16, 2009).

DeBatto, David. "Testimony of Former U.S. Army Counterintelligence Special Agent David DeBatto, previously assigned to 205th Military Intelligence Brigade under Colonel Thomas Pappas in 2003, for the German criminal procedure against DOD Donald Rumsfeld and others." *Republikanischer Anwaltinnen-und Antwalteverein.* http://www.rav.de/download/Testimony_DeBatto.pdf (accessed January 10, 2009).

Department of Defense. Directive Number 5100.77, *DoD Law of War Program.* Washington, DC: U.S. Government Printing Office, 1998.

Department of the Army. Army Regulation 190-8, *Enemy Prisoners of War, Retained Personnel, Civilian Internees and Other Detainees.* Washington, DC: U.S. Government Printing Office, 1997.

———. Field Manual 1, *The Army.* Washington, DC: U.S. Government Printing Office, 2001.

———. Field Manual 2-22.3, *Human Intelligence Collector Operations.* Washington, DC: U.S. Government Printing Office, 2006.

———. Field Manual 3.0, *Operations.* Washington, DC: U.S. Government Printing Office, 2008.

———. Field Manual *3-19.40, Internment/Resettlement Operations.* Fort Leonard Wood: U.S. Government Printing Office, 2007.

———. Field Manual 3-19.40, *Internment/Resettlement Operations.* Washington, DC: U.S. Government Printing Office, 2001.

———. Field Manual 3-24, *Counterinsurgency.* Washington, DC: U.S. Government Printing Office, 2006.

———. Field Manual 34-52, *Intelligence Interrogation.* Washington, DC: U.S. Government Printing Office, 1992.

———. Field Manual 6-22, *Army Leadership: Competent, Confident, and Agile.* Washington, DC: U.S. Government Printing Office, 2006.

Department of the Army Inspector General. "Detainee Operations Inspection, July 21, 2004." *United States Department of Defense Detainees Investigations.* http:// www4.army.mil/ocpa/reports/ArmyIGDetaineeAbuse/DAIG%20Detainee%20 Operations%20Inspection%20Report.pdf (accessed November 2, 2008).

Department of the Navy Inspector General. "Review of Department of Defense Detention Operations and Detainee Interrogation Techniques." *The Office of the Secretary of*

Defense and Joint Staff Reading Room, Detainee Related Documents. March 7, 2005. http://www.dod.mil/pubs/foi/detainees/church_report_1.pdf (accessed February 10, 2009).

Dorn, Marilyn. "Sixth Declaration of Marilyn A. Dorn, Information Review Officer, Central Intelligence Agency." *American Civil Liberties Union.* January 5, 2007. http://www.aclu.org/pdfs/safefree/20070110/cia_dorn_declaration_items_1_29_61.pdf (accessed February 10, 2009).

Dunlavey, Major General Michael E. "Memorandum for Commander, United States Southern Command: Counter-Resistance Strategies." *George Washington University National Security Archive.* October 11, 2002. http://www.gwu.edu/ ~nsarchiv/NSAEBB/NSAEBB127/02.10.11.pdf (accessed January 17, 2009).

Fast, Major General Barbara. "Highlights from Detainee 'Summit'." *Email Forwarded to MAJ Douglas A. Pryer from V Corps Historian.* Camp Victory, Baghdad, August 12, 2004.

―――. "Sworn Statement of Barbara G. Fast, C2 for CJTF-7; Annex to Fay/Jones Report." *American Civil Liberties Union: Torture FOIA.* May 9, 2004. http:// www.aclu.org/torturefoia/search/searchdetail.php?r=814&q= (accessed January 10, 2009).

Fay, Major General George R. "AR 15-6 Investigation of the Abu Ghraib Detention Facility and 205th Military Intelligence Brigade." *United States Department of Defense Detainees Investigations.* August 25, 2004. http://www.defenselink.mil/ news/Aug2004/d20040825fay.pdf (accessed March 20, 2009).

Federal Document Clearing House. "Political/Congressional Transcript Wire: Donald H. Rumsfeld Holds Defense Department News Briefing, November 25, 2003." *AccessMyLibrary.* http://www.accessmylibrary.com/coms2/summary_0286-2787794_ITM (accessed December 5, 2008).

Federal Document Clearing House. "Senated Armed Services Committee Hearing on Treatment of Iraqi Prisoners, May 19, 2008." *American Civil Liberties Union: Torture FOIA.* http://www.aclu.org/projects/foiasearch/pdf/DODDOA010336.pdf (accessed December 9, 2008).

Formica, Brigadier General Richard. "Article 15-6 Investigation of CJSOTF-AP and 5th SF Group Detention Operations." *The Office of the Secretary of Defense and Joint Staff Reading Room.* November 8, 2004. http://www.dod.mil/pubs/foi/detainees/FormicaReportRelease.pdf (accessed February 15, 2009).

―――. "Annex 62, Article 15-6 Investigation of CJSOTF-AP and 5th SF Group Detention Operations." *American Civil Liberties Union: Torture FOIA.* http://www.aclu.org/projects/foiasearch/pdf/DOD056779.pdf (accessed August 18, 2009).

―――. "Annex 230, Article 15-6 Investigation of CJSOTF-AP and 5th SF Group Detention Operations." *American Civil Liberties Union: Torture FOIA.* http://www.aclu.org/projects/foiasearch/pdf/DOD057167.pdf.

―――. "CJTF-7 Interrogation Techniques as of 30 May 04." *The Office of the Secretary of Defense and Joint Staff Reading Room: Formica Report Annexes, Part I.* November

8, 2004. http://www.dod.mil/pubs/foi/detainees/ formica_annexes_1.pdf (accessed February 17, 2009).

Garrity, Major Stacy. "Interview Conducted by Panel of Officers." *The Center for Public Integrity: Abu Ghraib Supplementary Documents*. February 14, 2004. http://www.publicintegrity.org/articles/entry/506/ (accessed January 12, 2009).

Godsil, LTC Russell. "Re: Re: Interview!" *Email to MAJ Douglas A. Pryer,* February 19, 2009.

———. "Re: Re: Douglas MacArthur & Your Points." *Email to MAJ Douglas A. Pryer,* April 20, 2009.

———. "Re: Re: Re: Interview!" *Email to MAJ Douglas A. Pryer,* February 23, 2009.

Headquarters, 101st Airborne Division. "AR 15-6 Investigation into the Death of Abu Malik Kenami." *American Civil Liberties Union: Torture FOIA*. December 28, 2003. http://www.aclu.org/projects/foiasearch/pdf/DODDOA026695.pdf (accessed August 13, 2009).

———. "Report of Proceedings by Investigating Board/Board of Officers." *American Civil Liberties Union: Torture FOIA*. December 20, 2003. http://www.aclu.org/ projects/foiasearch/pdf/DODDOA026578.pdf (accessed August 13, 2009).

Headquarters, 10th Military Police Detachment (CID. "CID Report of Investigation – Final(C) 0031-03-CID519-62147-9J/5C1N/5X1/5Y2D2/5Y2G." *The Center for Public Integrity: The Abu Ghraib Supplementary Documents*. June 8, 2003. http://www.publicintegrity.org/articles/entry/506/ (accessed January 12, 2009).

———. "CID Report of Investigation – Final 0030-03-CID899-63499-5YIG4/5Q1A/5T4/5R4B/5Y2D2/5X5/5S1C." *American Civil Liberties Union: Torture FOIA*. http://www.aclu.org/projects/foiasearch/pdf/ DODDOACID001553.pdf (accessed August 19, 2009).

———. "CID Report of Investigation: Initial/Final – 0117-03-CID899-63549-5Y2C/5Y2D1/5C1J/5Y2E2. *American Civil Liberties Union: Torture FOIA*. http://www.aclu.org/projects/foiasearch/pdf/ DODDOACID007713.pdf (accessed August 21, 2009).

Headquarters, 1st Armored Division. "1 AD PAM 1-201 Command Inspection Checklist, September 2003." *American Civil Liberties Union: Torture FOIA*. http://www.aclu.org/projects/foiasearch/pdf/DOD045364.pdf (accessed December 12, 2008).

Headquarters, 205th MI Brigade. "Annex 40 to Taguba Report, Joint Interrogation & Debriefing Center Briefing." *The Center for Public Integrity: The Abu Ghraib Supplementary Documents*. January 23, 2004. http://www.publicintegrity.org/ assets/ pdf/Tag29.pdf (accessed January 12, 2004).

Headquarters, 2nd Armored Cavalry Regiment. "15-6 Report of Investigation, Maltreatment of Detainees, July-August 2003." *American Civil Liberties Union: Torture FOIA*. http://www.aclu.org/torturefoia/released/032505/1781_1880.pdf (accessed December 12, 2008).

———. "Camp Duke Detainee Facility S.O.P., June 1, 2004." *American Civil Liberties Union: Torture FOIA*. http://www.aclu.org/torturefoia/released/032505/ 780_880.pdf (accessed December 12, 2008).

———. "Guidance on Minimum Standards for Brigade Holding Areas, August 13, 2003." *American Civil Liberties Union: Torture FOIA*. http://www.aclu.org/ torturefoia/released/032505/780_880.pdf (accessed December 12, 2008).

———. "SEP 03 PPT Briefing/Laydown of Division Detention Operations." *American Civil Liberties Union: Torture FOIA*. September 2003. http://www.aclu.org/ projects/foiasearch/pdf/DOD043598.pdf (accessed April 1, 2009).

Headquarters, 2nd Brigade Combat Team. "2nd BCT Collective Accomplishments, May 12, 2003, through April 14, 2004." Flyer, Baghdad, Iraq, 2004.

Headquarters, 3rd Brigade Combat Team. "Report of Proceedings under Article 15, UCMJ." *American Civil Liberties Union: Torture FOIA*. October 21, 2003. http://www.aclu.org/projects/foiasearch/pdf/DODDOA027333.pdf (accessed August 17, 2009).

———. "Recommendation on Resignation for Good of the Service." *American Civil Liberties Union: Torture FOIA*. October 1, 2003. http://www.aclu.org/projects/ foiasearch/pdf/DOD006788.pdf (accessed August 19, 2009).

Headquarters, 31st Military Police Detachment (CID). "CID Report of Investigation – Final – 0140-03-CID389-61697–5H9B." *American Civil Liberties Union: Torture FOIA*. January 1, 2004. http://www.aclu.org/projects/foiasearch/pdf/ DODDOACID007319.pdf (accessed August 12, 2009).

Headquarters, 323rd Military Police Detachment (CID). "CID Report – INITIAL – 0041-03-CID899-63500 5C1B." *American Civil Liberties Union: Torture FOIA*. February 2003. http://ww.aclu.org/projects/foiasearch/pdf/ DODDOACID007016.pdf (accessed August 17, 2009).

———. "CID Report of Investigation – Initial – 0129-03-CID899-63556-5C2A." *American Civil Liberties Union: Torture FOIA*. September 24, 2003. http://www.aclu.org/projects/foiasearch/pdf/DODDOACID006782.pdf (accessed August 17, 2009).

———. "CID Report of Investigation – Final(C)/Supplemental – 0046-03-CID899-63502-5C1D/5C1J/5N2D1/5R/5Y2." *American Civil Liberties Union: Torture FOIA*. October 2, 2003. http://www.aclu.org/projects/foiasearch/pdf/ DODDOACID000403.pdf (accessed August 19, 2009).

Headquarters, 4th Battalion, 1st Field Artillery. "Informal 15-6 Investigation Findings." *American Civil Liberties Union: Torture FOIA*. November 10, 2003. http://www.aclu.org/torturefoia/released/032505/1581_1680.pdf (accessed August 16, 2009).

Headquarters, 4th Infantry Division. "AR 15-6 Investigation." *American Civil Liberties Union: Torture FOIA*. August 24, 2003. http://www.aclu.org/torturefoia/released/041905/6570_6668.pdf (accessed February 20, 2009).

———. "Documents provided by the 4th Infantry Division SJA." *American Civil Liberties Union: Torture FOIA*. May 12, 2004. http://www. aclu.org/projects/foiasearch/pdf/

DOD043552.pdf (accessed March 22, 2009).

———. "Exhibit A (Email Correspondences)." *American Civil Liberties Union: Torture FOIA.* October 6, 2003. http://www. aclu.org/torturefoia/released/ 041905/6570_6668.pdf (accessed March 15, 2009).

Headquarters, 48th Military Police Detachment (CID), "CID Report of Investigation – Final/SSI – 0396-2004-CID259-80377-5C2/5Y2E". *American Civil Liberties Union: Torture FOIA.* August 11, 2005. http://www.aclu.org/projects/ foiasearch/pdf/DOD044497.pdf (accessed August 19, 2009).

Headquarters, III Corps. "Verbatim Record of Trial, Specialist Jeremy Sivits, January 27, 2005." *American Civil Liberties Union: Torture FOIA.* http://www.aclu.org/ projects/foiasearch/pdf/DOD002393.pdf (accessed December 12, 2008).

———. "Verbatim Record of Trial, Staff Sergeant Ivan Frederick, Septempter 21, 2005." *American Civil Liberties Union: Torture FOIA.* http://www.aclu.org/ projects/foiasearch/pdf/DOD041193.pdf (accessed December 12, 2008).

Headquarters, CJTF-7. "Detention Summit Briefing to LTG Sanchez." Camp Victory, Iraq, August 11, 2003.

———.. "FRAGO 176 (Military Police Task Org Change and OIF I to OIF 2 Transition)." *American Civil Liberties Union: Torture FOIA.* February 1, 2004. http://www.aclu.org/torturefoia/released/a29.pdf (accessed January 12, 2009).

———. "FRAGO 749 to CJTF OPORD 03-036 (Annex 17 to Formica Report)." *The Office of the Secretary of Defense and Joint Staff Reading Room.* August 24, 2004. http://www.dod.mil/pubs/foi/detainees/formica_annexes_1.pdf (accessed January 13, 2009).

———. "Interrogation and Counter-Resistance Policy Memorandum, October 12, 2003." *American Civil Liberties Union: Torture FOIA.* http://www.aclu.org/ FilesPDFs/october%20sanchez%20memo.pdf (accessed December 12, 2008).

———. "Interrogation and Counter-Resistance Policy Memorandum, September 14, 2003." *American Civil Liberties Union: Torture FOIA.* http://www.aclu.org/ FilesPDFs/september%20sanchez%20memo.pdf (accessed November 2, 2008).

Headquarters, Task Force 1st Armored Division. *Briefing: TF 1AD Says Thanks to the United States.* Baghdad, July 2004.

———. "FRAGO 383A [General Order - Civilian or Detainee Maltreatment] to OPORD 03-215 (Iron Stability)." *American Civil Liberties Union: Torture FOIA.* July 21, 2003. http://www.aclu.org/ projects/foiasearch/pdf/DODDOA027333.pdf (accessed April 1, 2009).

Hensley, LTC Charles. "Narrative: Task Force 1AD May 2003 to July 2004." 2004.

Hill, General James T. "Memorandum for Chairman of the Joint Chiefs of Staff; SUBJECT: Counter-Resistance Techniques." *George Washington University National Security Archive.* October 25, 2002. http://www.gwu.edu/~nsarchiv/ NSAEBB/NSAEBB127/02.10.25.pdf (accessed January 17, 2009).

Hipwell, Colonel Robert. "800th MP BDE Inaugural Jails/Justice/Jails Meeting with CPA 1000 hrs Thursday." *Email Forwarded to MAJ Douglas A. Pryer from V Corps Historian.* Camp Victory, Baghdad, July 3, 2003.

Hoepner, Lieutenant Colonel Nathan. "Re: Interview!" *Email to MAJ Douglas A. Pryer.* March 25, 2009.

———. "Re: Interview!" *Email to MAJ Douglas A. Pryer.* March 28, 2009.

———. "Re: RE: Part II." *Email to MAJ Douglas A. Pryer.* August 25, 2009.

———. "Re: Stress Positions." *Email to MAJ Douglas A. Pryer.* January 12, 2009.

———. "Re: Two More New Documents, Old Format." *Email to MAJ Douglas A. Pryer.* April 20, 2009.

International Committee of the Red Cross. "Convention (III) Relative to the Treatment of Prisoners of War, 1949." *International Humanitarian Law – Treaties & Documents.* August 12, 1949. http://www.icrc.org/ihl.nsf/7c4d08d9b287a4214125 6739003e636b/ 6fef854a3517b75ac125641e004a9e68 (accessed February 10, 2009).

———. "Convention (IV) Relative to the Protection of Civilian Persons in Time of War." *International Humanitarian Law – Treaties & Documents.* August 12, 1949. http://www.icrc.org/ihl.nsf/7c4d08d9b287a42141256739003e636b/ 6756482d86146898c1 25641e004aa3c5 (accessed February 10, 2009).

———. *Geneva Conventions of 12 August 1949.* http://www.icrc.org/ ihl.nsf/WebSign?ReadForm&id=375&ps=P (accessed December 12, 2008).

———. *International Humanitarian Law National Implementation, Implementing Laws & Regulations - By State.* http://www.icrc.org/ihl-nat.nsf/WebLAW! OpenView&Start=1&Count=300&Expand=165#165 (accessed December 13, 2008).

———. "Report of the International Committee of the Red Cross (ICRC) on the Treatment by the Coalition Forces of Prisoners of War and Other Protected Persons by the Geneva Conventions in Iraq During Arrest, Internment and Interrogation, May 10, 2004." *GlobalSecurity.org: Military.* http://www. globalsecurity.org/military/library/report/2004/icrc_report_iraq_feb2004.htm (accessed January 16, 2009).

———. *The Geneva Conventions: the Core of International Humanitarian Law.* January 9, 2006. http://www.icrc.org/Web/Eng/siteeng0.nsf/htmlall/ genevaconventions (accessed December 9, 2008).

———. "War Crimes, U.S. Code, Title 18, Chapter 118." *International Humanitarian Law National Implementation, Implementing laws & Regulations– By State.* August 21, 1996. http://www.icrc.org/ihl-nat.nsf/6fa4d35e5e302539 4125673e00508143/ 442ba359975b55a 0c1256a460049a7f7!OpenDocument (accessed February 10, 2009).

Ives, Christopher. "Interview with MAJ Douglas Smith." *Operational Leadership Experiences in the Global War on Terrorism.* November 3, 2005. http://cgsc.cdmhost.com/cdm4/item_viewer.php?CISOROOT=/p4013coll13&CISOPTR= 86&CISOBOX=1&REC=19

(accessed January 10, 2009).

Jones, Lieutenant General Anthony R. "AR 15-6 Investigation of the Abu Ghraib Prison and 205th Military Intelligence Brigade." *United States Department of Defense Detainees Investigations.* August 25, 2004. http://www.defenselink.mil/news/ Aug2004/d20040825fay.pdf (accessed March 20, 2009).

Karpinski, Brigadier General Janis. "ICRC Visits to Camp Cropper and Abu-Ghrurayb in Oct 03." *Four Corners.* December 24, 2003. http://www.abc.net.au/4corners/content/2004/20040607_command/letter_2.htm (accessed August 24, 2009).

Khaghani, Darius. "Conditional Release Program (Parole)." *Email Forwarded to MAJ Douglas A. Pryer from V Corps Historian.* Camp Victory, Baghdad, December 29, 2003.

Kilbourne, Chief Warrant Officer 3 Kenneth. *Email to MAJ Douglas A. Pryer, RE: The Good Fight Continues."* August 20, 2009.

Kusnetz, Marc. "Torture on Trial – HRF Observes Court Martial of Army Officer Accused in Death of Iraqi Major General." *Human Rights First.* January 13-17, 2006. http://www.humanrightsfirst.org/us_law/etn/trial/welshofer-011706.asp (accessed March 20, 2009).

Lagouranis, Tony, and Allen Mikaelian. *Fear Up Harsh: An Army Interrogator's Dark Journey Through Iraq.* New York: Penguin Books Ltd., 2007.

Lee, Lieutenant Colonel Natalie. "Army Regulation 15-6 Investigation into Alleged Mistreatment of EPWs and HVDs held at JIDC, Camp Cropper." *The Office of the Secretary of Defense and Joint Staff Reading Room.* January 23, 2004. http:// www.dod.mil/pubs/foi/detainees/Lee_Report_release_dec07.pdf (accessed May 11, 2009).

Lessard, Laurence. "Interview with LTC Paul Perrone." *Operational Leadership Experiences in the Global War on Terrorism.* March 28, 2007. http://cgsc.cdmhost.com/cgi-bin/showfile.exe?CISOROOT=/ p4013coll13&CISOPTR=813&filename=814.pdf (accessed January 13, 2009).

———. "Interview with MAJ Shane Celeen." *Operational Leadership Experiences in the Global War on Terrorism.* December 18, 2007. http://cgsc.cdmhost.com/cdm4/ item_viewer.php?CISOROOT=/p4013coll13&CISOPTR=1023&CISOBOX=1&REC=1 (accessed August 17, 2009).

Mansoor, Peter R. *Baghdad at Sunrise.* New Haven & London: Yale University Press, 2008.

———. "RE: The Good Fight Continues." *Email to MAJ Douglas A. Pryer.* August 21, 2009.

Matthews, Matt. "Interview with COL Michael Formica." *Operational Leadership Experiences in the Global War on Terrorism.* April 21, 2006. http://cgsc.cdmhost.com/cdm4/item_viewer.php?CISOROOT=/p4013coll13&CISOPTR=134&CISOBOX=1&REC=8 (accessed August 15, 2009).

McCool, John H. "Interview with CPT Amos Nelson." *Operational Leadership Experiences in the Global War on Terrorism.* March 2, 2006. http://cgsc.cdmhost.com/cdm4/item_viewer.php?CISOROOT=/p4013coll13&CISOPTR=468&CISOBOX=1&REC=1

(accessed January 10, 2009).

———. "Interview with LTC Wayne Sylvester." *Operational Leadership Experiences in the Global War on Terrorism*. October 10, 2005. http://cgsc.cdmhost.com/ cdm4/item_viewer.php?CISOROOT=/p4013coll13&CISOPTR=65&CISOBOX=1&REC=2 (accessed January 10, 2009), 8.

———. "Interview with MAJ Art La Flamme." *Operational Leadership Experiences in the Global War on Terrorism*. September 13, 2006. http://cgsc.cdmhost.com/cgibin/showfile.exe?CISOROOT=/p4013coll13&CISOPTR=286&filename=287. pdf#search=%22command%22 (accessed January 10, 2009).

Miller, Major General Geoffrey. "Assessment of DoD Counterterrorism Interrogation and Detention Operations in Iraq." *American Civil Liberties Union: Torture FOIA*. September 9, 2003. http://www.aclu.org/torturefoia/released/a20.pdf (accessed January 11, 2009).

Meyer, Amanda. "Re: Our Interview & Lessons Learned &...Merry Christmas!" *Email to MAJ Douglas A. Pryer*. April 6, 2009.

Mora, Vice Admiral Alberto. "Statement of Alberto J. Mora." *U.S. Senate Committee on Armed Services*. June 17, 2008. http://armed-services.senate.gov/statemnt/2008/ June/Mora%2006-17-08.pdf (accessed January 17, 2009).

Odierno, Major General Raymond. "Treatment of Detainees in the Custody of U.S. Forces." *American Civil Liberties Union: Torture FOIA*. September 21, 2003. http://www.aclu.org/projects/foiasearch/pdf/DOD043596.pdf (accessed March 22, 2009).

Pappas, Colonel Thomas. "Sworn Statement of Col, HHD, 205th MI Brigade, Annex to Fay/Jones/Kern Report." *American Civil Liberties Union: Torture FOIA*. May 14, 2004. http://www.aclu.org/torturefoia/released/030905/DOD616_653.pdf (accessed January 10, 2009).

Pryer, Major Douglas A. "501st MI BTOC SOP." Standard Operating Procedures, Baghdad, November 3, 2003.

———. "Interview with Captain Nicole Lauenstein." *Operational Leadership Experiences in the Global War on Terrorism*. March 4, 2009. http://cdm15040. contentdm.oclc.org/cgibin/showfile.exe?CISOROOT=/p4013coll13&CISOPTR=1454&filename=1457. pdf#search=%22Pryer%22 (accessed April 30, 2009).

———. "Interview with CW3 John Groceclose." *Operational Leadership Experiences in the Global War on Terrorism*. January 7, 2009. http://cgsc. cdmhost.com/cgi-bin/showfile.exe?CISOROOT=/ p4013coll13&CISOPTR=1429&filename= 1431. pdf#search=%22Pryer%22 (accessed March 25, 2009).

———. "Interview with CW3 Kenneth Kilbourne." *Operational Leadership Experiences in the Global War on Terrorism*. December 21, 2008. http://cgsc.cdmhost.com/ cdm4/item_viewer.php?CISOROOT=/p4013coll13&CISOPTR=1440&CISOBOX=1&REC=2 (accessed March 31, 2009).

———. "Interview with LTC (Ret.) Elizabeth Rogers." *Operational Leadership Experiences in the Global War on Terrorism.* January 11, 2009. http://cgsc.cdmhost.com/cdm4/item_viewer.php?CISOROOT=/ p4013coll13&CISOPTR=1442&CISOBOX=1&REC=4 (accessed March 5, 2009).

———. "Interview with LTC Larry Wilson." *Operational Leadership Experiences in the Global War on Terrorism.* January 30, 2009. http://cdm15040.contentdm. oclc.org/cdm4/item_viewer.php?CISOROOT=/p4013coll13&CISOPTR=1471&CISOBOX=1&REC=3 (accessed April 30, 2009).

———. "Interview with LTC Mark Crisman." *Operational Leadership Experiences in the Global War on Terrorism.* January 27, 2009. http://cgsc.cdmhost.com/ cdm4/item_viewer.php?CISOROOT=/p4013coll13&CISOPTR=1418&CISOBOX=1&REC=2 (accessed February 13, 2009).

———. "Interview with LTC Nathan Hoepner." *Operational Leadership Experiences in the Global War on Terrorism.* February 2, 2009. http://cgsc.cdmhost.com/cdm4 /item_viewer.php?CISOROOT=/p4013coll13&CISOPTR=1441&CISOBOX=1&REC=6 (accessed April 1, 2009).

———. "Interview with LTC Russell Godsil." *Operational Leadership Experiences in the Global War on Terrorism.* December 20, 2008. http://cgsc.cdmhost.com/ cdm4/item_viewer.php?CISOROOT=/p4013coll13&CISOPTR=1443&CISOBOX=1&REC=7 (accessed March 30, 2009).

———. "Interview with MAJ Brad Johnson." *Operational Leadership Experiences in the Global War on Terrorism.* http://cgsc.contentdm.oclc.org/cdm4/ item_viewer.php?CISOROOT=/p4013coll13&CISOPTR=1419&CISOBOX=1&REC=5 (accessed August 16, 2009).

———. "Interview with MAJ Craig Martin." *Operational Leadership Experiences in the Global War on Terrorism.* December 21, 2008. http://cgsc.cdmhost.com/ cdm4/item_viewer.php?CISOROOT=/p4013coll13&CISOPTR=1431&CISOBO=1&REC=9 (accessed April 10, 2009).

———. "Interview with Ms. Amanda Meyer." *Operational Leadership Experiences in the Global War on Terrorism.* January 5, 2009.http://cgsc.cdmhost.com/cdm4/ item_viewer.php?CISOROOT=/p4013coll13&CISOPTR=1395&CISOBOX=1&REC=10 (accessed April 1, 2009).

Reagan, Ronald. *Farewell Address to the Nation.* January 11, 1989. http://www.reaganfoundation.org/reagan/speeches/farewell.asp (accessed February 10, 2009).

Redacted. "Email from REDACTED to Briese, M.C. (Div13) (FBI)." *American Civil Liberties Union: Torture FOIA.* May 22, 2004. http://www.aclu.org/torturefoia/ released/ FBI.121504.4940_4941.pdf (accessed January 11, 2009).

———. "Sworn Statement of S-3, 205th MI Bde, V Corps; Annex to Fay/Jones/Kern Report." *American Civil Liberties Union: Torture FOIA.* May 24, 2004. http://www.aclu.org/torturefoia/search/searchdetail.php?r=791&q= (accessedJanuary 12, 2009).

Rommel, Field Marshall Erwin. *The Rommel Papers.* Edited by B.H. Liddell Hart. New York: Harcourt, Brace, and Jovanovich, 1953.

Rumsfeld, Donald. "Action Memo, Counter-Resistance Techniques, December 2, 2002." *George Washington University's National Security Archive.* http://www.gwu.edu/~nsarchiv/NSAEBB/NSAEBB127/02.12.02.pdf (accessed December 12, 2008).

— — —. "Memorandum for Chairman of the Joint Chiefs of Staff, Status of Taliban and Al Qaeda, January 19, 2002." *George Washington University's The National Security Archives.* http://www.gwu.edu/~nsarchiv/NSAEBB/NSAEBB127/ 02.01.19.pdf (accessed December 12, 2008).

— — —. "Memorandum for the Commander, U.S. Southern Command, Subject: Counter-Resistance Techniques." *George Washington University's National Security Archives.* April 16, 2003. http://www.gwu.edu/ ~nsarchiv/NSAEBB/ NSAEBB127/03.04.16.pdf (accessed January 17, 2009).

— — —. "Memorandum for the General Counsel of the Department of Defense; Subject: Detainee Interrogations." *George Washington University's National Security Archives.* January 15, 2003. http://www. gwu.edu/~nsarchiv/NSAEBB/ NSAEBB127/03.01.15b.pdf (accessed January 19, 2009).

Ryder, Major General Donald. "Report on Detention and Corrections Operations in Iraq." *American Civil Liberties Union: Torture FOIA.* November 6, 2003. http://www.aclu.org/torturefoia/released/a19.pdf (accessed February 15, 2009).

Sabatino, Colonel Ralph. "Annex 47, Taguba Report." *The Center for Public Integrity: The Abu Ghraib Supplementary Documents.* February 10, 2004. http://www. publicintegrity.org/assets/pdf/Abu16.pdf (accessed January 12, 2009).

Schlesinger, James R., Harold Brown, Tillie K. Fowler, and General Charles A. Horner. "Final Report of the Independent Panel to Review DoD Detention Operations, 23 August 2004." *United States Department of Defense Detainees Investigations.* http://www.defenselink.mil/news/Aug2004/d20040824finalreport.pdf (accessed November 2, 2008).

Supreme Court of the United States. "Boumediene Et Al v. Bush, President of the United States, Et Al." *Supreme Court of the United States.* June 12, 2008. http://www.supremecourtus.gov/opinions/07pdf/06-1195.pdf (accessed February 10, 2009).

— — —. "Hamdan v. Rumsfeld, Secretary of Defense, Et. Al." *Supreme Court of the United States.* June 29, 2006. http://www.supremecourtus. gov/opinions/ 05pdf/05-184.pdf #search=%22Salim%20Ahmed%20Hamdan%20and%20 Supreme%20Court%20decision%22 (accessed February 10, 2009).

Taguba, Major General Antonio. "AR 15-6 Investigation of the 800th Military Police Brigade, May 27, 2004." *American Civil Liberties Union: Torture FOIA.* http://www.aclu.org/torturefoia/released/TR3.pdf (accessed December 12, 2008).

Tenpenny, Jim. "Interview with BG Michael Tucker." *Operational Leadership Experiences in the Global War on Terrorism.* January 20, 2006. http://cgsc.cdmhost.com/cdm4/item_viewer.php?CISOROOT=/p4013coll13&CISOPTR=511&CISOBOX=1&REC=1 (accessed August 16, 2009).

The Library of Congress. *Military Commissions Act of 2006.* October 7, 2009. http://thomas.loc.

gov/cgi-bin/query/F?c109:1:./temp/~c109tSnoDs:e839 (accessed August 20, 2009).

The White House. *President Barack Obama's Inaugural Address*. January 21, 2009. http://www.whitehouse.gov/blog/inaugural-address/ (accessed April 27, 2009).

Unidentified Investigating Officer. "Memo for Record– Evidence." *American Civil Liberties Union: Torture FOIA*. February 4, 2004. http://www.aclu.org/projects/ foiasearch/pdf/ DOD043571.pdf (accessed March 22, 2009).

Unidentified CJTF J2 Planner. "Sworn Statement of LTC, G2 planner for V Corps/CJTF-7; Annex to Fay/Jones/Kern Report." *American Civil Liberties Union: Torture FOIA*. July 16, 2004. http://www.aclu.org/projects/foiasearch/pdf/ DOD000766.pdf (accessed January 10, 2009).

United Nations. "Convention Against Torture and Other Cruel or Degrading Treatment or Punishment." *Office of the United Nations High Commissioner for Human Rights*. http://untreaty.un.org/english/treatyevent2001/pdf/07e.pdf (accessed December 12, 2008).

United States Army Criminal Investigation Command. "Army Criminal Investigators Outline 27 Confirmed or Suspected Detainee Homicides for Operation Iraqi Freedom, Operation Enduring Freedom." *United States Army Criminal Investigation Command*. http://www.cid.army.mil/ Documents/OIF-OEF%20Homicides.pdf (accessed August 23, 2009).

— — —. "CID Report of Investigation – Final (C)/SSI –0177-04-CID259-80266/5C2B/5Y2E/ 5X1. *American Civil Liberties Union: Torture FOIA*. August 3, 2004. http://www.aclu.org/projects/ foiasearch/pdf/DODDOACID004133.pdf (accessed March 22, 2009).

— — —. CID Report of Investigation – Final (C)/SSI – 0180-04-CID259-80227-/5C1C/5Y2E/ 5X1. American Civil Liberties Union: Torture FOIA. July 28, 2004. http://www.aclu.org/torturefoia/released/1248_1288.pdf (accessed August 12, 2009).

— — —. "CID Report of Investigation – Final Referred/SSI – 0233-2004-CID259-80270-5C1C/5Y2E/5X1." *American Civil* Liberties Union: Torture FOIA. May 1, 2005. http://www.aclu.org/projects/foiasearch/pdf/DOD049418.pdf (accessed August 13, 2009).

United States of America, "Article 32 Hearing: United Staves v. CW2 Wiliams, SFC Sommer and SPC Loper," *Washington Post*, December 2, 2004, http://www. washingtonpost.com/wp-srv/nation/documents/mowhoush_court_document.pdf (accessed March 21, 2009), 20, 33.

— — —. *Torture, U.S. Code, Title 18, Chapter 113C*. April 30, 1994. http://www.icrc.org/ihl-nat.nsf/ (accessed January 20, 2009).

U.S. Army. "165th MI Battalion Modified Table of Organization and Equipment." April 18, 2003.

— — —. "519th Modified Table of Organization and Equipment." October 17, 2001.

———. *Army Training Requirements and Resources System: Information for Course 241-F4 (CT)*. August 19, 2008. https://atrrs.army.mil/atrrscc/ courseInfo.aspx?fy =2008&sch=307&crs=241-F4+(CT)&crstitle=JOINT +INTERROGATION+ CERTIFICATION&phase= (accessed April 27, 2009).

———. *Army Training Requirements And Resources System: Information For Course 3A-F82/243-F30*. August 21, 2008. https://atrrs.army.mil/atrrscc/ courseInfo.aspx?fy= 2008&sch=307&crs=3A-F82%2F243-F30&crstitle =JOINT+ANALYST- INT ERROGATOR+COLLABORATION&phase= (accessed April 27, 2009).

———. *Army Training Requirements and Resources System: Information For Course 3A-SI3Q/3C-ASI9N/241-ASIN*. April 1, 2009. https://atrrs.army.mil/ atrrscc/ courseInfo. aspx?fy=2008&sch=307&crs=3A-SI3Q%2F3C-ASI9N%2F241-ASIN&crstitle=DO D+STRATEGIC+DEBRIEFING&phase= (accessed April 27, 2009).

U.S. Army Recruiting Command. *Warrant Officer Recruiting Information Site*. April 20, 2009. http://www.usarec.army.mil/hq/warrant/index.htm (accessed April 27, 2009).

U.S. Government Accountability Office. "299317; B-299317.2; B-299317.3, L-3 Communications Titan Corporation." *GAO*. March 29, 2007. http://www.gao. gov/ decisions/bidpro/299317.htm (accessed April 26, 2009).

U.S. Senate Armed Services Committee. "Inquiry into the Treatment of Detainees in U.S. Custody." *U.S. Senate Armed Services Committee*. November 20, 2008. http://levin. senate.gov/newsroom/supporting/2009/SASC.DetaineeReport.042209.pdf (accessed August 20, 2009).

Warren, Colonel Marc. "Sworn Statement of Col, OSJA, MNF-I (senior Legal Advisor to LTG Sanchez)." *American Civil Liberties Union: Torture FOIA*. June 18, 2004. http://www. aclu.org/torturefoia/search/searchdetail.php?r=811&q= (accessed January 16, 2009).

Welshofer, CW3 Lewis. "MEMORANDUM FOR Commander 82d ABN DIV," *American Torture*, February 11, 2004, http://www.americantorture.com/ documents/ iraq/10.pdf (accessed March 20, 2009).

Williams, Kayla. *Love My Rifle More than You: Young and Female in the U.S. Army*. New York: W.W. Norton, 2005.

———."On Torture." VetVoice. April 22, 2009. http://www.vetvoice.com/ userDiary. do?personId=419 (accessed August 22, 2009).

Winthrop, Roger. "1630 Sermon." In *Speeches that Changed the World*, edited by Owen Collins, 63-65. Westminster: John Knox Press, 1999.

Wood, Captain Carolyn. "Interrogation Rules of Engagement." *American Civil Liberties Union: Torture FOIA*. Oct-Dec 2003. http://www.aclu.org/projects/ foiasearch/pdf/ DODDOA003220.pdf (accessed April 30, 2009).

———. "Sworn Statement of CPT, 519th MI BN; Annex to Fay/Jones/Kern Report." *American Civil Liberties Union: Torture FOIA*. May 21, 2004. http://www. aclu.org/projects/ foiasearch/pdf/DOD000598.pdf (accessed January 10, 2009).

Secondary Sources

1st Armored Division Headquarters. *1st Armored Division History.* http://www.1ad.army.mil/History.htm (accessed March 23, 2009).

ABC News. *The Blotter: Secret U.S. Task Force 145 Secretly Changes Its Name, Again.* June 12, 2006. http://blogs.abcnews.com/theblotter/2006/06/secret_us_task_.html (accessed February 17, 2009).

Amnesty International. "Outsourcing Intelligence in Iraq." *Amnesty International USA.* December 2008. http://www.amnestyusa.org/pmscs/corpwatchl3rpt.pdf (accessed April 25, 2009).

Armed Forces Press Service. *Insurgents Attack Abu Ghraib Prison, Kill Detainee.* September 21, 2004. http://www.defenselink.mil/news/newsarticle.aspx?id =25250 (accessed January 16, 2009).

Association of the United States Army. "Torchbearer National Security Report." *AUSA.* July 2007. http://www3.ausa.org/webpub/DeptILW.nsf/byid/JRAY-75LT2E/$File/TB-Intel.pdf?OpenElement (accessed April 24, 2009).

Bigelow, Bruce V. "Iraq: 136 Titan Corp. Workers Killed Since Iraq War Began." *CorpWatch: The San Diego Union-Tribune.* March 25, 2005. http:// www.corpwatch.org/article.php?id=12000 (accessed April 25, 2009).

Bland, Lieutenant Colonel Dean. *The Abu Ghraib scandal: Impact on the Army Profession and the Intelligence Process.* Academic Research Paper, Carlisle Barracks, Carlisle, PA: U.S. Army War College, 2005.

Brinkley, Joel, and Eric Schmitt. "U.S. Officers in Iraq Found Few Signs of Infiltration by Foreign Fighters." *The New York Times.* November 19, 2003. http://query.nytimes.com/gst/fullpage.html?res=950CE1DA163BF93AA25752C1A9659C8B63 (accessed December 5, 2008).

CBS News. *Abuse of Iraqi POWs by GIs Probed.* April 28, 2004. http://www.cbsnews.com/stories/2004/04/27/60II/main614063.shtml (accessed December 5, 2008).

Command and General Staff College Department of Tactics. *Battlefield Surveillance Brigade.* Fort Leavenworth, Kansas, February 2009.

Coon, Charlie. "'Stability Operation' Turned into 15-Month Street Fight." *Stars and Stripes*, September 2004: 5-16.

Cordesman, Arthony H., and Arleigh A. Burke. "Iraq's Evolving Insurgency: The Nature of Attacks and Patterns and Cycles in the Conflict, February 3, 2006." *Center for Strategic & International Studies.* http://www.csis.org/index.php?option= com_csis_pubs&task=view&id=2696 (accessed December 4, 2008).

Dedman, Bill. "New Anti-Terror Weapon: Hand-held Lie Detector." *MSNBC.* April 9, 2008. http://www.msnbc.msn.com/id/23926278 (accessed May 2, 2009).

Estes, Kenneth W. *U.S. Army Soldier Baghdad 2003-04*. Oxford: Osprey Publishing Ltd., 2007.

Ewing, Scott Andrew. "Discipline, Punishment, and Counterinsurgency." *Military Review* (September-October 2008): 10-20.

Fisher, David Hackett. *Washington's Crossing*. New York: Oxford University Press, 2004.

GlobalSecurity.Org. *Camp Ashraf MEK Training Camp*. http://www.globalsecurity.org/military/world/iraq/camp-ashraf.htm (accessed January 10, 2009).

Greenburg, Jan Crawford, Howard L. Rosenberg, and Ariane de Vogue. *ABC News: Bush Aware of Advisers' Interrogation Talks*. April 11, 2008. http://abcnews.go.com/TheLaw/LawPolitics/Story?id=4635175&page=1 (accessed January 11, 2009).

Hajjar, Remi. "The Army's new TRADOC Culture Center." *Military Review* (November-December 2006).

Hashim, Ahmed S. *Insurgency and Counter-Insurgency in Iraq*. Ithaca: Cornell University Press, 2006.

Hoffman, Bruce. "Insurgency and Counterinsurgency in Iraq." *Rand National Security Research Division*. June 2004. http://www.rand.org/pubs/occasional_papers/2005/RAND_OP127.pdf (accessed January 10, 2008).

Holguin, Jaime. *CBS News: FBI Memos Describe Prison Abuses*. December 21, 2004. http://www.cbsnews.com/stories/2004/12/04/iraq/main659101.shtml (accessed January 11, 2009).

Holland, Keating. *CNN, Poll: Support for Bush, Iraq war dropping*. May 22, 2004. http://www.cnn.com/2004/ALLPOLITICS/05/14/bush.kerry/index.html (accessed December 12, 2008).

Human Rights Watch. "No Blood, No Foul." *Human Rights Watch*. July 2006. http://www.hrw.org/en/reports/2006/07/22/no-blood-no-foul-0 (accessed February 17, 2009).

Isikoff, Michael. "'We Could Have Done This the Right Way'." *Newsweek*, May 4, 2009: 18-21.

Iwicki, Lieutenant Colonel Steve. "CSA's Focus Area 16: Actionable Intelligence." *Military Intelligence Professional Bulletin*, January-March 2005: 51-53.

Jehl, Douglas. *Pentagon Will Not Try 17 G.I.'s Implicated in Prisoners' Deaths*. March 26, 2005. http://www.nytimes.com/2005/03/26/politics/26abuse.html?_r=1 (accessed August 24, 2009).

Kristol, William. *The Defense Secretary We Have*. December 15, 2004. http://www.washingtonpost.com/wp-dyn/articles/A132-2004Dec14.html (accessed August 20, 2009).

Kusnetz, Marc. "Torture on Trial – HRF Observes Court Martial of Army Officer Accused in Death of Iraqi Major General." *Human Rights First,* January 13-17, 2006. http://www.humanrightsfirst.org/us_law/etn/trial/welshofer-011706.asp (accessed March 20, 2009).

Lee, Wayne E. "From Gentility to Atrocity: The Continental Army's Ways of War." *Army History: The Professional Bulletin of Army History*, Winter 2006: 3-19.

Lopez, C. Todd. "Language Company First in Army." *ARMY.MIL/NEWS*. October 22, 2008. http://www.army.mil/-news/2008/10/22/13503-language-company-first-in-army/ (accessed April 27, 2009).

Meyer, Josh, and Gregg Miller. "Memos Reveal Harsh CIA Interrogation Methods." *Los Angeles Times*. April 17, 2009. http://www.latimes.com/news/ nationworld/ nation/la-na-interrogation17-2009apr17,0,5555846.story?page=2 (accessed April 21, 2009).

Moffeit, Mike. *Brutal Interrogation in Iraq*. May 19, 2004. http://www.denverpost.com/ search/ci_0002157003 (accessed August 24, 2009).

Riccardi, Nicholas. *Los Angeles Times: Interrogator Convicted in Iraqi's Death*. January 22, 2006. http://articles.latimes.com/2006/jan/22/nation/na-interrogate22 (accessed February 20, 2009).

Ricks, Thomas E. *Fiasco: The American Military Adventure in Iraq*. New York: The Penguin Press, 2006.

Schmitt, Eric. *The New York Times: Pentagon Study Describes Abuse by Units in Iraq*. June 17, 2006. http://www.nytimes.com/2006/06/17/washington/17formica. html?ex=1308196800& (accessed February 17, 2009).

Schmitt, Eric, and Carolyn Marshall. *New York Times: In Secret Unit's 'Black Room,' a Grim Portrait of U.S. Abuse*. March 19, 2006. http://www.nytimes.com/ 2006/03/19/international/middleeast/19abuse.html?_r=2&pagewanted=1 (accessed February 17, 2009).

Shamsi, Hina. "Command's Responsibility: Detainee Deaths in U.S. Custody in Iraq and Afghanistan." *Human Rights First*. Edited by Deborah Pearlstein. February 2006. http://www.humanrightsfirst.info/pdf/06221-etn-hrf-dic-rep-web.pdf (accessed March 20, 2009).

Shipman, Tim. *Sunday Telegraph: I blame myself for our downfall in Iraq*. June 10, 2007. http://www.telegraph.co.uk/news/worldnews/1554137/I-blame-myself-for-our-downfall-in-Iraq.html (accessed August 14, 2009).

Warden, Leon. *The Signal: Karpinski: Rumsfeld OK'd Methods at Abu Ghraib*. July 2, 2004. http://www.scvhistory.com/scvhistory/signal/iraq/sg070204.htm (accessed December 12, 2008).

White, Josh. "Documents Tell of Brutal Improvisation by GIs." *Washington Post*. August 3, 2005. http://www.washingtonpost.com/wp-dyn/content/article/2005/08/02/AR2005080201941_pf.html (accessed March 22, 2009).

Wright, Dr. Donald P., and Colonel Timothy R. Reese. *On Point II, Transition to the New Campaign: the United States Army in Operation IRAQI FREEDOM, May 2003 - January 2005*. Fort Leavenworth: Combat Studies Institute Press, 2008.

Zakaria, Fareed. "Pssst . . . Nobody Loves a Torturer." *Newsweek*. November 14, 2005. http://www.fareedzakaria.com/ARTICLES/newsweek/111405.html (accessed April 11, 2009).

Chronology

1949

8 Dec U.S. signs Geneva Conventions

1955

2 Aug U.S. Congress ratifies Geneva Conventions

1956

10 Aug Uniform Code of Military Justice signed into law

1992

28 Sep FM 34-52, *Intelligence Interrogation*, published

1994

21 Oct U.S. Congress ratifies "Torture Convention"

1996

29 Jul U.S. Congress passes War Crimes Act

1997

1 Oct Army Regulation 190-8, *Enemy Prisoners of War, Retained Personnel, Civilian Internees and other Detainees*, published

2001

20 Jan Inauguration of President George W. Bush
1 Aug FM 3-19.40, *Military Police Internment/Resettlement Operations*, published
11 Sep Al Qaeda terrorist attacks on America
Dec DoD General Counsel requests information regarding interrogation of detainees from JPRA

2002

19 Jan	Secretary of Defense Donald Rumsfeld memo to Joint Chiefs of Staff, "Status of Taliban and Al Qaeda," provides for withholding of Geneva protections for Taliban and al Qaeda detainees in the event of "military necessity"
7 Feb	President Bush's memo to National Security Advisors, "Humane Treatment of al Qaeda and Taliban Detainees," provides for withholding of Geneva protections for Taliban and al Qaeda detainees in the event of "military necessity"
16-21 Mar	Colonel Stuart Herrington inspects Gitmo
Jul	JPRA provides DoD General Counsel's office with SERE training extracts
14 Aug - 4 Sep	Colonel John Custer inspects Gitmo
11 Oct	Major General Michael Dunlavey, Gitmo commander, requests use of enhanced interrogation techniques at Gitmo
2 Dec	Rumsfeld provides blanket approval for the use of certain harsh interrogation techniques at Gitmo

2003

15 Jan	Rumsfeld rescinds blanket approval for the use of harsh interrogation techniques at Gitmo, providing for approval on a case-by-case basis
7 Feb	The 1AD is removed from the V Corps' invasion plan for Iraq
4 Mar	The 1AD is officially notified that it will be deploying to Iraq to relieve the 3rd Infantry Division
9 Apr	U.S. forces assume responsibility for Camp Freddy from British forces, renaming Iraq's first Theater Internment Facility "Camp Bucca"
14 Apr	U.S. DoD declares end of major combat operations in Iraq
16 Apr	Rumsfeld publishes memo that will be one of the primary source documents for CJTF-7's first interrogation policy
20 Apr	U.S. led invasion of Iraq
May	Red Cross sends report to U.S. Central Command alleging 200 cases of detainee abuse at point of capture and temporary holding facilities
1 May	Camp Cropper established at Baghdad International Airport
16-26 May	1AD assembles in Baghdad
29 May	1AD with attachments assumes military responsibility for Baghdad as "Task Force Baghdad"

14 Jun	CJTF-7 established with Lieutenant General Ricardo Sanchez as commander
22 Jun	Lieutenant Colonel Laurence Mixon assumes command of 501st MI Battalion, 1AD, from Lieutenant Colonel Kenneth Devan, and Devan assumes position of 1AD G2
30 Jun	Brigadier General Janice Karpinski assumes command of the 800th MP Brigade
Early Jul	Red Cross sends working paper to U.S. Central Command alleging 50 cases of abuse in the intelligence section at Camp Cropper
3 Jul	Ambassador Bremer approves use of Abu Ghraib Prison as a coalition holding facility
17 Jul	Major General Martin Dempsey assumes command of TF 1AD
21 Jul	TF 1AD Fragmentary Order published that criminalizes the abuse of detainees within TF 1AD
End of Jul	TF 1AD DIF established
26 Jul - 2 Aug	CJTF-7 conducts Operation Victory Bounty
4 Aug	Coalitional Provisional Authority official re-opens Abu Ghraib prison
7 Aug	Jordanian Embassy bombing in Baghdad
14 Aug	CJTF-7 Deputy J2X sends email out to G2X personnel requesting a "wish list" of interrogation techniques
19 Aug	United Nations Headquarters bombing in Baghdad
20 Aug	Lieutenant Colonel Allen West, Commander of the 2- 20th Field Artillery Battalion of the 4ID, fires a pistol near the head of a detainee during an interrogation
24 Aug	CJTF-7 publishes baseline order governing CJTF-7 detention and interrogation operations for OIF I
30 Aug	TF 1AD publishes baseline order governing TF 1AD detention and interrogation operations for OIF I
31 Aug - 9 Sep	Major General Geoffrey Miller, Gitmo Commander, leads a survey team on intelligence, interrogation, and detention operations in Iraq
14 Sep	CJTF-7 headquarters publishes first CJTF-7 interrogation policy
25 Sep	British forces reassume temporary responsibility for Camp Bucca
Oct - Dec	Most serious detainee abuses occur at Abu Ghraib
1 Oct	Lieutenant General Sanchez' deadline for closing main Camp Cropper detention facility and consolidating all CJTF-7 interrogation operations at Abu Ghraib
11 Oct - 6 Nov	Major General Donald J. Ryder, Provost Marshall General of the Army, leads an inspection of detention facilities in Iraq
12 Oct	CJTF-7 headquarters publishes second CJTF-7 interrogation policy

23 Nov	Iraqi Major General Abed Mowhoush dies during interrogation by CW3 Lewis Welshofer on Forward Operating Base Tiger

2004

10 Feb	Acting Secretary of the Army, R.L. Brownlee, directs Lieutenant General Paul Mikolashek to investigate detainee operations across the Army
14 Feb	Red Cross "Report on the Treatment by the Coalition Forces of Prisoners of War and Other Protected Persons by the Geneva Conventions in Iraq during Arrest Internment and Interrogation" published
6 Apr	TF 1AD relinquishes control of DIF to 1st Cavalry Division
15 Apr	Transition of Authority for Baghdad from TF 1AD to 1st Cavalry Division
28 Apr	CBS News breaks story of Abu Ghraib war crimes
13 May	Multi-National Force-Iraq issues interrogation policy requiring interrogators to use doctrinal approaches and techniques only
15 May	Multi-National Force-Iraq OPORD 04-01 inactivates CJTF-7 and activates Multi-National Force-Iraq and Multi-National Corps-Iraq
19 May	First two courts martial of the "Abu Ghraib Nine" begin; General John Abizaid, Lieutenant General Sanchez, Major General Miller, and Colonel Marc Warren testify before U.S. Senate Armed Services Committee about Abu Ghraib abuses
27 May	Taguba Report published
28 Jun	Coalition Provisional Authority dissolved
21 Jul	Mikolashek Report published
24 Aug	Schlesinger Report published
25 Aug	Fay/Jones Report published
10 Mar	Church Report published

2005

30 Dec	President Bush signs *Detainee Treatment Act of 2005* (also known as the McCain Amendment) into law

2006

Jan	Army activates first JIDC Battalion
1 Feb	Army's new Culture Center opens on Fort Huachuca
29 Jun	U.S. Supreme Court ruling, *Hamdan vs. Rumsfeld*
Sep	FM 2-22-3, *Human Intelligence Collector Operations*, published

17 Oct	President Bush signs Military Commissions Act of 2006 into law

2007

Apr	HUMINT Training Joint Center of Excellence established at Fort Huachuca
Sep	FM *3-19.40, Internment/Resettlement Operations,* published

2008

12 Jun	U.S. Supreme Court ruling, *Boumediene et Al v. Bush, President of the United States, et Al*

Glossary

Assign To place units or personnel in an organization where such placement is relatively permanent, and/or where such organization controls and administers the units or personnel for the primary function, or greater portion of the functions, of the unit or personnel. (FM 6-0)

Attach The placement of units or personnel in an organization where such placement is relatively temporary. (FM 6-0)

Battalion A unit consisting of two or more company-, battery-, or troop-sized units and a headquarters. (FM 3-90)

Battle Captain The shift officer in charge within a command post, associated by position and not rank. The battle captain is located in the operations section of a command post and oversees the conduct of command post operations during his shift. (FM 1-02)

Brigade A unit usually smaller than a division to which are attached groups and/or battalions and smaller units tailored to meet anticipated requirements. (FM 3-90)

Civilian Internees Individuals who are detained or interned in the United States or in occupied territory for security reasons or protection. (FM 3-19.40)

C/J/G/S2X The C/J/G/S2X is a staff element subordinate to the C/J/G/S2, is the primary advisor on HUMINT and CI, and is the focal point for all HUMINT and CI activities within a joint task force (J2X), an Army component task force (G2X) or a brigade combat team (BCT) (S2X). The 2X can be organic to the unit staff or can be attached or under operational control (OPCON) to the staff from another organization such as the theater military intelligence brigade. The C/J/G/S2X is part of a coherent architecture that includes organic HUMINT assets and HUMINT resources from national, theater, and non-DOD HUMINT organizations. (FM 2-22.3)

Command and Control The exercise of authority and direction by a properly designated commander over assigned and attached forces in the accomplishment of the mission. (FM 6-0)

Corps The Army's largest tactical unit and the instrument by which higher echelons of command conduct maneuver at the operational level. (FM 3-90)

Counterintelligence Information gathered and activities conducted to protect against espionage, other intelligence activities, sabotage, or assassinations conducted by or on behalf of foreign governments or elements thereof, foreign organizations, or foreign persons, or international terrorist activities. (FM 3-13)

Detainee The term "detainee" means any person captured, detained, held, or otherwise under the control of DoD personnel (military, civilian, or contractor). Detainees may also include enemy combatants (lawful and unlawful), retained persons, and civilian internees. It does not include personnel being held for law enforcement purposes, except where the United States is the occupying power. (FM 3-19.40)

Division A tactical unit/formation which combines in itself the necessary arms and services required for sustained combat, larger than a regiment/brigade and smaller than a corps. (FM 3-90)

Doctrine Fundamental principles by which the military forces or elements thereof guide their actions in support of national objectives. It is authoritative but requires judgment in application. (FM 3-0)

Document Exploitation The systematic extraction of information from documents either produced by the threat, having been in the possession of the threat, or that is directly related to the current or future threat situation for the purpose of producing intelligence or answering information requirements. This may be conducted in conjunction with human intelligence (HUMINT) collection activities or may be conducted as a separate activity. (FM 34-52)

Enemy Prisoners of War An individual or group of individuals detained by friendly forces in any operational environment who meet the criteria as listed in Article 4 of the Geneva Convention Relative to the Handling of Prisoners of War. (FM 34-52)

Forward Operations Base A base usually located in friendly territory that is established to extend command and control or communications or to provide support for training and tactical operations. (FM 100-25)

General Support That support which is given to the supported force as a whole and not to any particular subdivision thereof. [Note: the Army designates general support as a "support relationship."] (FM 101-5)

Human Intelligence A category of intelligence derived from information collected and provided by human sources. (FM 34-1.)

Human Intelligence Collector A person who is trained to collect information from individuals (human intelligence sources) for the purpose of answering intelligence information requirements. (FM 34-52)

Human Intelligence Source A person from whom information is collected for the purpose of producing intelligence. Human intelligence sources can include friendly, neutral, or hostile personnel. (FM 34-52)

Intelligence The product resulting from the collection, processing, integration, analysis, evaluation, and interpretation of available information concerning foreign countries or areas. (FM 34-1)

Interrogation Systematic effort to procure information by direct questioning of a person under the control of the questioner. (FM 34-52)

Law of War That part of international law that regulates the conduct of armed hostilities. (FM 27-10)

Lawful Combatants Lawful enemy combatants are persons entitled to protection under the Geneva Conventions, combatant immunity, or immunity from prosecution for their lawful acts as a belligerent. (FM 3-19.40)

Operational Control Operational control is the authority to perform those functions of command over subordinate forces involving organizing and employing commands and forces, assigning tasks, designating objectives, and giving authoritative direction necessary to accomplish the mission. (FM 3-0)

Operation Order A directive issued by a commander to subordinate commanders for the purpose of effecting the coordinated execution of an operation. Also called the five paragraph field order, it contains as a minimum a description of the task organization, situation, mission, execution, administrative and logistics support, and command and signal for the specified operation. (FM 101-5)

Operational Level of War The level of war at which campaigns and major operations are planned, conducted, and sustained to accomplish strategic objectives within theaters or operational areas. (FM 3-0)

Priority Intelligence Requirements Those intelligence requirements for which a commander has an anticipated and stated priority in his task of planning and decision-making. (FM 3-0)

Retained Persons A special category for medical personnel and chaplains because of their special skills and training. These individuals may be retained by the detaining power to aid other detainees, preferably those of the armed forces to which they belong. (FM 3-19.40)

Rules of Engagement Directives issued by competent military authority that delineate the circumstances and limitations under which United States forces will initiate and/or continue combat engagement with other forces encountered. (FM 3-07)

Screening As it applies to human intelligence operations, the process of evaluating and selecting human and document sources based on pre-established criteria for the prioritized collection of information in support of command intelligence requirements. While screening is not in itself an information collection technique, it is vital to the rapid collection of information. (FM 34-52)

Secret NOFORN Intelligence which is classified "Secret" and which cannot be shown to the citizens of any foreign country.

Signals Intelligence Intelligence derived from communications, electronics, and foreign instrumentation signals. (FM 34-2)

Source 1. A person, thing, or activity from which information is obtained. 2. In clandestine activities, a person (agent), normally a foreign national, in the employ of an intelligence activity for intelligence purposes. 3. In interrogation activities, any person who furnishes information, either with or without the knowledge that the information is being used for intelligence purposes. (FM 34-1)

Source Management Processes and administrative procedures used to control, orchestrate, and deconflict all actions pertaining to individuals utilized by human intelligence collectors and counterintelligence special agents to obtain information requirements. (FM 34-52)

Special Operations Forces Those Active and Reserve Component forces of the Military Services designated by the Secretary of Defense and specifically organized, trained, and equipped to conduct and support special operations. FM 100-25)

Stability Operations Operations that promote and protect U.S. national interests by influencing the threat, political, and information dimensions of the operational environment through a combination of peacetime developmental, cooperative activities and coercive actions in response to crisis. (FM 3-0)

Standard Operating Procedures A set of instructions covering those features of operations which lend themselves to a definite or standardized procedure without loss of effectiveness. The procedure is applicable unless ordered otherwise. (FM 6-0)

Strategic Level of War The level of war at which a nation, often as a member of a group of nations, determines national or multinational (alliance or coalition) strategic security objectives and guidance, and develops and uses national resources to accomplish these objectives. (FM 3-0)

Tactical Level of War The level of war at which battles and engagements are planned and executed to accomplish military objectives assigned to tactical units or task forces. (FM 3-0)

Task Force A temporary group of units, under one commander, formed for the purpose of carrying out a specific operation or mission. (FM 1-02)

Task Organization A temporary grouping of forces designed to accomplish a particular mission. (FM 3-0)

Techniques The general and detailed methods used to perform assigned missions and functions, specifically, the methods of using equipment and personnel. (FM 3-90).

Unconventional Warfare A broad spectrum of military and paramilitary operations, normally of long duration, predominantly conducted by indigenous or surrogate forces that are organized, trained, equipped, supported, and directed in varying degrees by an external source. It includes guerrilla warfare and other direct offensive, low visibility, covert, or clandestine operations, as well as the indirect activities of subversion, sabotage, intelligence activities, and evasion and escape. (FM 3-05.201)

Unlawful Enemy Combatants Persons who are not entitled to combatant immunity and engage in acts against the United States or its coalition partners in violation of the laws and customs of war during armed conflict. (FM 3-19.40)

Index

1st Armored Division, V Corps, 2, 66-81, 83, 85-86, 90-91, 95-96, 100-101, 103, 105-106, 112, 120, 135, 150-151, 155, 157, 159-160, 184-185, 196-197
    counterinsurgent operations of, 151,
    Division Interrogation Facility of, 71-75, 77, 105, 160, 184-185
    HUMINT operations of, 67, 70, 74-75, 80, 96, 104-106, 160
    HUMINT reporting of, 158
    Operation Iron Saber of, 89-90, 151
    pre-deployment HUMINT training of, 66-67
1st Brigade Combat Team, Task Force 1st Armored Division, 34, 38, 66, 80-90, 95, 97, 100, 114, 150, 155, 157
    1st Battalion, 36th Infantry Regiment of, 76, 81-82, 88-89, 95, 155
    2nd Battalion, 3rd Field Artillery Regiment of, 81, 88
    501st Forward Support Battalion of, 84-85
    Company A, 501st MI Battalion of, 71, 82-83, 92, 114, 121, 133 150
    counterinsurgent operations of, 81-82
    Forward Operating Base Provider of, 83-85, 88-89
    tactical HUMINT teams of, 83, 87
18th MP Brigade, Task Force 1st Armored Division 34, 68, 73,
    519th MP Battalion of, 76
2nd Brigade, 25th Infantry Division, 63-64
    Camp Honesty and, 63-64, 119
2nd Brigade, 82nd Airborne Division, Task Force 1st Armored Division, 68, 90, 151
2nd Brigade Combat Team, 101st Airborne Division, 55-60, 64
    1st Battalion, 327th Infantry, of, 56
    1st Battalion, 502nd Infantry, of, 56
    2nd Battalion, 44th Air Defense Artillery, of, 56
    Company B, 311th MI Battalion, of, 57-58
    counterinsurgent operations of, 97
    Strike Brigade Holding Area of, 14, 55-60, 63-64, 89, 119
2nd Brigade Combat Team, Task Force 1st Armored Division, 66, 73, 80, 93, 96-106, 135, 150, 152, 155, 160-162
    2nd Battalion, 6th Infantry Regiment of, 76, 97, 101, 103
    Camp Striker of, 101-103
    Company B, 501st MI Battalion, of, 71, 75, 92-94, 150, 153, 158, 160, 161, 196-197
    S2X of, 97-100, 104, 160, 197
    tactical HUMINT teams of, 80, 104
    use of informants by, 98-101, 103-104, 162
2nd Light Cavalry Regiment, Task Force 1st Armored Division, 68, 72, 151, 155
205th MI Brigade, Combined Joint Task Force 7, 27, 29, 32-33, 43, 113, 124, 126, 133-136
    223rd MI Battalion of, 40, 135, 136
    323rd MI Battalion of, 40, 136
    519th MI Battalion of, 27, 40, 44, 133, 136, 143
3d Armored Cavalry Regiment, 82nd Airborne Division, 2, 25, 51-54, 58, 63, 119, 144-146
    Al Asad Airfield Holding Area of, 52-53, 145
    Blacksmith Hotel Holding Area of, 52
    Forward Operating Base Tiger of 1st Squadron of, 51-52, 185

3rd Brigade Combat Team, Task Force 1st Armored Division, 34, 66, 68, 80, 90-97, 150-152, 157, 159
    1st Battalion, 13th Armor Regiment of, 90, 92, 95-96
    1st Battalion, 325th Infantry Regiment of, 90, 96
    2nd Battalion, 70th Armor Regiment of, 90, 94, 95-96, 150, 152
    4th Battalion, 1st Field Artillery Regiment of, 76, 90, 95
    Company C, 501st MI Battalion of, 71, 75, 91-95, 150, 158-159
    counterinsurgency operations of, 90
    Forward Operating Base Dakota of, 91-92
    tactical HUMINT teams of, 91
3rd Infantry Division, U.S. Army Forces Command, 39, 81, 150, 183-184
4th Brigade, Task Force 1st Armored Division, 66, 150
4th Infantry Division, III Corps, 2, 33-34, 61-63, 121, 124, 135, 149
    2nd Brigade of, 62
    Forward Operating Base Iron Horse of, 61-63, 119
501st MI Battalion, Task Force 1st Armored Division, 1-2, 67, 70-79, 93, 105, 150, 152-153, 158-159
    counterinsurgency operations and, 74-75
    detainee management within, 71-74, 77
    HUMINT Operations Cell of, 70, 76-77
    HUMINT reporting of, 71-72, 72, 77, 158
    pre-deployment training of, 60, 150,
    S3 Section of, 71, 77
501st MP Company, Task Force 1st Armored Division, 73
513th MI Brigade, Intelligence Security Command, 33
    202nd MI Battalion of, 40
    HUMINT operations of, 33
800th MP Brigade, CFLCC, 5, 10, 34, 37, 40, 124, 126, 184
    320th MP Battalion of, 43
Abizaid, General John, 8, 15, 25, 27, 46, 135, 185
Abu Ghraib (Baghdad Central Confinement Facility), Iraq, 1, 4-5, 8-10, 14-15, 17, 20, 25, 27-28, 34, 36-37 40-41, 43-47, 49, 50-52, 54, 58-59, 61, 63, 71-72, 87-89, 103, 107, 116-121, 124-126, 132-134, 137-138, 140-144
    "Abu Ghraib Nine" of, 8, 11, 185
    enhanced interrogation techniques, use of at, 14-15, 25, 44-47, 49, 63, 119, 142-144
    scandal from, 4-5, 20, 44, 58, 116, 119-120, 132-133
Afghanistan, 6, 20-21, 24-28, 42, 44, 46-47, 58, 60, 64, 110, 119, 125-126, 132, 143
    Bagram Airfield in, 25, 44, 142
    enhanced interrogation techniques, use of in, 24-28, 42, 44, 47, 58, 60, 119, 132-133
Al Habbaniyah, alleged use of enhanced interrogation techniques at, 51-52
Al Sadr, Muctada, 81, 89, 197
Alexander, Matthew, 4, 79, 118
Anderson, Lieutenant Colonel Curtis, 84-85
Aussaresses, General Paul, 6
Baghdad Central Collection Facility, Iraq, see Abu Ghraib
Baker, Colonel Ralph, 97-100, 102-103, 106, 155, 162
Becker, David, 21
Behavioral Scientists, 18, 20, 22, 26, 110
Bell, Captain William, 99
Bremer, Ambassador Paul, 30, 40, 184
Brownlee, R.L., 5, 124, 185

Buehring, Lieutenant Colonel Charles, 100
Bush, President George W., 1, 4, 19, 22-23, 28, 118, 132, 182-183, 185-186
> administration of, 7, 9-10, 18-23, 48, 108, 130
> alleged formal approval of use of enhanced interrogation techniques by, 23, 132
> approval of discussion of enhanced interrogation technique by, 19, 132
> exception to Geneva Conventions provided by, 22

Camp Ashraf, Iraq, 34, 40, 120, 139
Camp Bucca (Camp Freddy), Iraq, 34, 40-43, 120, 138, 141, 183-184
Camp Cropper, Iraq, 34, 40-43, 49, 51, 63, 119, 134, 140-142, 183-184
> alleged use of enhanced interrogation techniques at, 42-43, 49, 63, 119, 134, 142
> high value detainees at, 34, 36, 40, 42

Camp Nama, Iraq, alleged use of enhanced interrogation techniques at, 27, 42-43, 63
Camp Whitford, Iraq, 34, 39-40, 120
Central Intelligence Agency, 5, 18, 21-23, 26, 52-53, 61, 87, 110, 118-119, 130, 132, 146, 149
> use of enhanced interrogation techniques by, 52-53, 118-119, 130, 146, 149

Civilian Internees, 12, 35-36
Church, Vice Admiral Albert T, 5, 126
Church Report, 5, 15, 27, 43, 46, 50, 55, 75, 128, 132-133, 138, 142, 144, 185
Coalition Force Land Component Command, U.S. Army, 31-32, 34, 44, 126, 138
Coalition Provisional Authority, 30, 36, 43, 89, 97, 185
Combined Joint Special Operations Task Force Arabian Peninsula, use of enhanced interrogation techniques by, 47
Combined Joint Task Force 180, 24, 28
Combined Joint Task Force-7, 2, 7-8, 16, 27, 29, 31-49, 51-54, 68-71, 74-75, 78, 80, 86, 89, 93, 98, 113, 119-120, 123-126, 129, 137-138, 142-144, 152, 158, 160, 183-185
> counter-insurgency operations of, 31-33
> detention procedures of, 35-39, 137-138
> headquarters of, 8, 27, 29-33, 35-36, 46, 137
> HUMINT section of, 2, 61-62
> HUMINT operations of, 19, 21, 32-34, 48
> promulgation of enhanced interrogation techniques by, 27, 45-49, 52, 54, 61-62, 69-70, 86, 93, 119, 124, 142-144, 152, 158, 183-184

Cotell, Lieutenant Colonel Robert, 24-25
Counterintelligence Force Protection Source Operations, 83-84, 86-87, 92-93, 96, 99-101, 104-105, 111-112, 114, 162
Criminal Detainees, 36-37, 39, 43
Criminal Investigation Division, 36, 44, 88, 55, 59, 101, 125, 145, 148
Crisman, Lieutenant Colonel Mark, 34, 91-92, 94, 152, 158-159
Custer, Colonel John, 14-15, 183
Dalton, Navy Captain Jane, 23
DeBatto, David, 29, 134-135
Dempsey, Brigadier General Martin, 68-69, 71-72, 78, 86, 89, 106, 151-152, 184, 196
Detainees,
> corrective training (exercise and stress positions) of, 56, 69-70, 93-94, 103, 106, 147, 152, 158-159, 162
> database management of, 37, 71, 97-98, 138

Devan, Lieutenant Colonel Kenneth, 70, 184
Division Artillery, Task Force 1st Armored Division, 68, 150
> 1st Battalion, 4th Air Defense Artillery of, 76

Document Exploitation, 33, 48, 74, 78, 85, 93-94, 97-98, 104, 106

Dunlavey, Major General Michael, 21, 23, 183
Enemy Prisoners of War, 9-12, 22, 34-37, 39-40, 46, 67, 99, 138, 140
Fay, Major General George, 4, 44, 124-126
Fay-Jones Report, 16, 46, 124, 185
Fast, Brigadier General Barbara, 31-33, 37, 124, 137
Federal Bureau of Investigation, 21, 23, 26, 98, 104, 131-132
    advocacy of "soft" interrogation approaches of, 21
Formica, Brigadier General Richard, 47
Formica, Colonel Michael, 80
Fort Riley, Kansas, 66, 90, 150
Fredman, Jonathan, 22-23
French-Algerian War, 6
Geneva Conventions of 1949, 9-12, 14, 18-22, 28, 42, 46, 58, 71, 95, 106, 127-128, 130-131, 143, 182-183, 185
    Common Article 3 of, 10, 17, 19, 22, 128, 149
    Convention I of, 9
    Convention III of, 9-10, 12, 22, 36, 45, 130
    Convention IV of, 9-12, 18, 22, 36-37, 44, 106, 130
    Protocols 1 and II of, 130-131
Giefer, Chief Warrant Officer 3 Joel, 71, 158
Godsil, Lieutenant Colonel Russell, 38, 80, 82, 84-88, 107, 112-114, 152
Gold, Colonel Russell, 91-92
Groseclose, Chief Warrant Officer 2 John, 71, 75, 92-96, 115, 150, 152, 158-159
Guantanamo Bay, Cuba, 19
    national internment facility (Gitmo) at, 6, 14-15, 19-28, 42, 44-45, 61, 64, 119, 125-127, 131, 143, 183-184
    use of enhanced interrogation techniques at, 21-28, 46-47, 93, 118, 130-133
Guzman, Luis, 71
Haynes, II, William, 23-24, 131
Herrington, Colonel Stu, 15, 42, 74, 183
Hill, General James, 23
Hipwell, Colonel Robert, 37
Hoepner, Major Nathan, 1-2, 4, 6, 70-71, 73, 105, 119, 123, 152, 158-159, 162, 197
Huff, Fred, 137
HUMINT operations, 80, 109, 111-113
    Division-level organization for, 113
    HUMINT Operations Cells and
    manning within brigades for, 111-112, 120
    training of soldiers for, 110, 114-116
Hussein, Saddam, 2, 151
    Special Security Organization of, 40
Hussein, Uday, 81
    Saddam Fedayeen of, 29, 101
III Corps, U.S. Army, 31
International Committee of the Red Cross, 10, 41-44, 51-52, 55, 61, 68, 74, 85, 92, 102, 139, 142, 152, 183-185
Interrogation approaches, doctrinal, 12-14, 25, 78-79, 87-89, 93, 132, 185
    ambiguity during OIF I of, 14, 18, 69, 129
    Direct approach use as one of, 12
    Fear Up (Harsh) approach use as one of, 2, 12-14, 24, 47, 52, 58, 62, 93, 132

       Incentive approach use as one of, 13, 24, 47, 109, 127, 143
       Mutt and Jeff approach use as one of, 24, 45-46
       Pride and Ego Down approach use as one of, 13-14, 24, 132
Interrogation approaches, rapport-based, 20-21, 61, 79, 111
Interrogation, Lines of Questioning, 78, 86
Interrogation Rules of Engagement:
       at Abu Ghraib, 14, 45, 128-129
       at Strike Brigade Holding Area, 14, 58, 128-129
Interrogation Techniques, Enhanced or SERE, 7, 19, 22-27, 41-42, 44-45, 47, 49-52, 54-56, 58-60, 63-64, 68-70, 78, 86, 88, 93, 95, 108, 118-120, 131-132, 142-144, 149, 159, 183
       Close Confinement Quarters technique use as one of, 2, 52-53, 108
       Dietary Manipulation or Food Deprivation technique use as one of, 12, 24-25, 27, 45-47, 59, 108, 143
       Electric Shock technique use as one of, 2, 12, 62-64, 108
       Environmental Manipulation or Extreme Temperatures technique use as one of, 20, 27, 45-47, 56, 58-60, 108, 146
       Females to Create Discomfort technique use as one of, 24, 58,
       Forced Nudity or Removal of Clothing technique use as one of, 14, 19-20, 24-25, 27, 44, 47, 52, 66, 108, 134, 143
       Isolation technique use as one of, 19, 24, 26-27, 42-45, 53, 61, 149
       Loud Music and Flashing Lights technique use as one of, 20, 23, 25, 27, 45-46, 52, 55-56, 58, 108
       Military Working Dog technique use as one of,2, 12, 14, 23-27, 44-45, 47, 52, 58-59, 93, 108, 143-144, 148
       Mock execution technique as one of, 12, 22, 66, 95, 108
       Multiple Interrogators technique as one of,26
       Pressure Point Manipulation technique as one of, 2
       Putting Hoods on Subjects' Heads technique as one of, 20, 24, 56, 108
       Slapping or Punching the Face and Body technique as one of, 2, 20, 24, 27, 42, 52, 54, 56, 59-60, 66, 76, 95, 101
       Sleep Adjustment, Management, or Deprivation technique as one of, 2, 12, 14, 20, 23-27, 44-46, 52, 54, 56, 58-60, 108, 128, 132, 143-144
       Stimulus or Sensory deprivation technique as one of, 2, 23-25, 27, 62
       Stress or Safety Positions technique as one of, 14, 20, 23-27, 42, 44-45, 52, 58-59, 62, 86, 108, 144, 158-159
       Threat of Transfer technique as one of, 25, 42
       Waterboarding technique as one of, 19-20, 54, 60, 108, 132, 146
Iraq
       Al Anbar, province of, 2, 51, 63
       An Najaf, city of, 40, 197
       Al Qaim, city of, 52, 145
       Baghdad, city of, 2, 4, 8, 23, 27, 29-30, 34, 40, 67-68, 70-72, 76, 80-81, 87, 89-90, 96-97, 106 123, 136, 138, 151, 153, 160, 183-185, 196
       Baghdad airport in, 2, 27, 40, 72, 76 136, 160, 183
       Green Zone in, 97-98, 103-104, 160
       insurgency within, 1-2, 4, 20, 30-31, 50, 54, 81, 89-90, 97, 100-103, 114, 135, 151
       Karbala, city of, 90
       Mosul, city of, 14, 55, 58-61, 63-64, 89
       Shiites of, 81, 90, 151
       Sunni Triangle of, 2
       Sunnis of, 1-2

Tikrit, city of, 2, 29, 61, 63, 136
Um Qasr, city of, 41
Jameel, Lieutenant Colonel Abdul, death of, 53-54, 145
Johnson, Major Brad, 96
Jones, Lieutenant General Anthony, 4, 15, 124-126
Jordan, Lieutenant Colonel Steve, 134
Karpinski, Brigadier General Janis, 10, 34, 37, 184
Kenami, Abu Malik, death of, 55-56
Kennedy, Senator Ted, 9
Kern, General Paul, 124
Kilbourne, Chief Warrant Officer 2 Kenneth, 50, 71, 83, 85-86, 100-101, 111, 115, 150, 155-156
Kleinman, Lieutenant Colonel Steven, 134
Korean War, enhanced interrogation techniques and, 20, 118
LaFlamme, Major Art, 33, 136
Lagouranis, Tony, 14, 50, 55, 57-59, 61, 128-129
Lauenstein, Captain Nicole, 70-71, 159
Law of War, see Geneva Conventions of 1949,
Lee, Lieutenant Colonel Natalie, 43, 134
Mansoor, Colonel Peter, 34, 66, 82, 85-88
Martin, Captain Craig, 82-84, 155
Mattis, Major General James, 1
McConville, Captain Amy, 197
McFadden, Robert, 21
McMaster, Colonel H.R, 51
McNeill, Lieutenant General Dan, 25
Meyer, Sergeant Amanda, 23, 83, 87, 121
Mikolashek, Lieutenant General Paul, 5, 185
Mikolashek Report, 5, 15-16, 48, 125, 185
Miller, Major General Geoffrey, 8-9, 15, 24, 41, 44-45, 127, 138, 143, 184-185, 196
Miller, Major General Thomas, 31
Mixon, Lieutenant Colonel Laurence, 70, 184, 196-197
Mohammad, Fashad, death of, 60
Mohammed, Khalid Sheikh, 21
Mora, Vice Admiral Alberto, 20
Mowhoush, Major General Abed, death of, 52-54, 146, 185
Mujahedin el-Khalq, 31, 40, 139
Muhalla 636 Gang, 100-101, 161
Myers, General Richard, 23
Navy Seal Team NSWRON-7, alleged use of enhanced interrogation techniques by, 55, 59-60
Obama, President Barrack, 118, 131
Odierno, Major General Raymond, 33-34, 135
Operation Desert Storm, 12, 15
Panama, Operation Just Cause, 12, 15
Pappas, Colonel Thomas, 47, 134, 136, 143
Petraeus, Major General David, 64
Philippine-American War, water cure use of in, 6-7
Pitts, Major Esli, 82, 155
Polygraphists, 98, 104, 110, 160
Raddatz, Martha, 132

Rangel, Jr., Major Frank, 61
Reagan, President Ronald, 28
Recruiting Command, U.S. Training and Doctrine Command, 114
Red Cross, see International Committee of the Red Cross,
Revolutionary War, American, and America's Founding Fathers, 6-7, 28, 119, 126
Ricks, Thomas E, 1, 123, 149
Robinson, Major General Fred, 68
Rogers, Major Elizabeth, 70, 151-152
Rommel, Field Marshall Erwin, 107
Rumsfeld, Donald, 1, 10, 21-29, 46, 48, 125-126, 131, 135, 183
    enhanced interrogation techniques and, 23-28, 46, 118, 131-133, 196
    exception to Geneva Conventions provided by, 21-22
Ryder, Major General Donald, 15, 184
Sanchez, Lieutenant General Carlos, 8-9, 25, 32, 39-40, 44-47, 49, 68, 119, 124, 137, 143-144, 158-159, 184-185
Schlesinger, James, 5
Schlesinger Report, 5, 14-16, 116, 125-127, 131, 142, 144, 185
Security Internees, 36-37, 39, 43, 46-47, 71
SERE Schools, 2, 20-23, 28, 52-55, 58, 60, 64, 69, 118, 130, 133, 147
    also see Interrogation Techniques, Enhanced or SERE
Soufan, Ali, 21
Special Mission Unit (Afghanistan), U.S. Special Operations Command, 25-26, 133
Special Mission Unit (Iraq), U.S. Special Operations Command, 26-27, 131, 133-134
    also see Camp Nama, Iraq
Taguba, Major General Antonio, 5, 15, 41, 124, 126, 139
Taguba Report, 124, 133-134, 139, 185
Ticking Time Bomb Rationale and Ends-Justify-the-Means Mentality, 6, 16-17, 54, 64, 118-119, 121
Torture, 1, 5-7, 10-12, 18-19, 21-23, 40, 50, 59-61, 64, 79, 108, 118, 132, 182
    Bush Administration's re-definition of, 7, 22, 108
    also see Interrogation Techniques, Enhanced or SERE
Tucker, Colonel Michael, 80-82
Unlawful combatants, 7, 9-11, 18, 21-22, 53, 130, 132, 149
U.S. Army,
    Battlefield Surveillance Brigades of the, 113
    counterinsurgency operations of the, 16, 48, 107
    Command and General Staff College of, 116
    cultural training within, 82, 115-116, 185
    ethics education within, 64-65, 106, 115-117, 121
    GWOT and, 5, 64, 78, 89, 106-107, 117, 120, 123, 158
    language training within, 15-16
    Special Forces of, 47, 52-53, 61, 63, 87-88, 145
U.S. Army Doctrine,
    access to medical records within, 18, 110
    command and staff interrogation responsibilities within, 17, 109
    contiguous versus non-contiguous battlefields within, 16, 109-110
    contract personnel within, 17-18, 110
    ethical decision-making tool ("Army Values") within, 16-18, 111, 116, 121
    military intelligence versus military police responsibilities within, 8-9, 15, 108-109
U.S. Army Military Occupational Specialties,

351E Human Intelligence Collection Technician among, 83, 114-116, 121
35M Human Intelligence Collectors among, 83, 111, 115-116, 121
96R Ground Surveillance Radar Specialists among, 77, 160
97B Counterintelligence Specialists among, 75, 83, 111
97E Interrogators among, 83, 111

U.S. Department of Defense,
- 2003 Working Group of, 24
- Joint Center of Excellence of, 115, 186
- Joint Interrogation Debriefing Center Battalions of, 113
- Joint Personnel Recovery Agency of, 20-22, 27, 130, 134, 182-183
- Office of General Counsel of, 20-23
- U.S. Central Command of, 24-25, 27, 31, 44, 46, 135, 143, 151, 183-184
- U.S. Southern Command of, 14, 23

U.S. Department of Justice, Office of Legal Counsel, 22

U.S. National Law,
- 1994 Torture Convention and, 10-11, 18, 22, 132, 182
- 8th Amendment, U.S. Constitution, and, 10, 132
- Detainee Treatment Act of 2005 and, 19, 107-108, 185
- Military Commissions Act of 2006 and, 9, 19, 186
- Uniform Code of Military Justice and, 8, 11, 18, 23, 41, 128, 132, 182
- War Crimes Act of 1996 and, 9, 182

U.S. Senate Armed Services Committee,
- hearings of, 8, 20-21, 46
- report on detainee treatment of, 43, 63, 125, 130-134, 142, 185

U.S. Supreme Court,
- Boumediene Et Al vs. Bush, case of the, 19, 129, 186
- Hamdan vs. Rumsfeld, case of the, 10, 19, 128, 185

V Corps, U.S. Army Europe, 19, 30-33, 48, 66-67, 137, 183
- also see Combined Joint Task Force-7

Vietnam War, 107
- My Lai and the, 4, 117, 121

Warren, Colonel Marc, 8, 37, 39, 47, 143, 185

Washington, President George, 7

Welshofer, Chief Warrant Officer 3 Lewis, 2, 25, 52-54, 58, 61, 119, 123, 144-146, 185

West, Bing, 4

West, Lieutenant Colonel Allen, 62-63, 119, 121, 184

Williams, Kayla, 58

Wilson, Lieutenant Colonel Larry, 80, 97-100, 102-104, 106, 152, 162

Winthrop, John, 6, 19, 28, 119

Wood, Captain Carolyn, 25, 27, 44, 133, 140, 142

Wolfowitz, Paul, 21, 48, 100

Zarqawi, Abu Musab, 4, 46, 79, 118

Zubaydah, Abu, 21

Captain Douglas A. Pryer (left center, behind guidon bearer) and First Sergeant Michael Quinn (right center, behind guidon bearer) stand with a portion of their company, Bravo Company, 501st Military Intelligence Battalion, in front of Al Faw Palace, downtown Baghdad, February 29, 2004

Two weeks after the publication of the infamous Abu Ghraib photos, Lieutenant General Bantz Craddock (left), Major General Geoffrey Miller (center), and Secretary of Defense Donald H. Rumsfeld (right) tour the Abu Ghraib Detention Center in Abu Ghraib, Iraq on May 13, 2004. (DoD photo)

At the TF 1AD Division Interrogation Facility, Brigadier General Martin Dempsey (Center) speaks with 501st MI Battalion leadership, Command Sergeant Major Christina Washington (left) and Lieutenant Colonel Laurence Mixon (Photo courtesy of Colonel Laurence Mixon)

The 501st MI Battalion Team at the TF 1AD Division Interrogation Facility. Lieutenant Colonel Laurence Mixon stands on the far right; Captain Amy McConville, facility commander, stands left center, back row. (Photo courtesy of Colonel Laurence Mixon.)

Captain Doug Pryer at An Najaf upon end of Muctada Sadr's 2004 rebellion. In the distant background is the golden dome of the Kufa Mosque.

Major Nathan Hoepner, 501st MI Battalion Operations Officer. (Photo courtesy of Lt. Col. Nathan Hoepner.)

About the author

Major Douglas A. Pryer was born and raised in Southwest Missouri. He graduated Summa Cum Laude from Missouri State University with a degree in English in 1989. Upon graduation, he taught college composition at the university for two years while enrolled in the school's graduate program as an English student.

Major Pryer enlisted in the U.S. Army in 1992 as a Psychological Operations Specialist. He attended Basic Training at Fort Jackson, South Carolina, and Advanced Individual Training at Fort Bragg, North Carolina. He then received training in Persian Farsi at the Defense Language Institute in Monterey, CA. Upon graduation, he returned to Fort Bragg, where he was promoted to sergeant and selected for Officer Candidate School. After receiving his commission in 1995, Major Pryer attended Military Intelligence Officer Basic Course. He was then assigned to the 3rd Brigade, 4th Infantry Division (Mechanized) in Fort Carson, Colorado, where he served as a Platoon Leader, Company Executive Officer, Battalion S-2, and Assistant Brigade S-2. Upon his promotion to captain, he attended the Aviation Advanced Course at Fort Rucker, Alabama.

After arriving in Germany in March 2000, Major Pryer was assigned to Headquarters Company, 1st Armored Division, as the Division's Intelligence Training Officer. After six months, he was assigned to the Division's 2nd Brigade Combat Team, as the Chief Intelligence Officer for the 1-35 Armor Battalion. As the Battalion's Intelligence Officer, he deployed to Kosovo from October 2000 to March 2001 and from June to August 2002. He was assigned to the 501st Military Intelligence Battalion as the Assistant Operations Officer in March 2003 and deployed to Iraq as part of Operation Iraqi Freedom in May 2003. In December 2003, he took command of Bravo Company, 501st Military Intelligence Battalion, in Baghdad. Eight months later, his Company redeployed from Iraq to Germany.

From January 2005 to July 2008, Major Pryer served in Milwaukee Recruiting Battalion, first as a recruiting company commander then as the battalion's executive officer. In August 2008, he moved to Fort Leavenworth, Kansas, to attend Command and General Staff College. In July 2009, he reported for duty as the Senior Intelligence Officer, 14th Signal Regiment, Wales, United Kingdom, where he now lives with his wife, Bhabinder, and their two children, Leo and Brooke.

Major Pryer is the recipient of numerous awards and decorations including the Bronze Star, Combat Action Badge and the Parachutist Badge. His original manuscript for *The Fight for the High Ground* earned the U.S. Army Command and General Staff College's 2009 Birrer-Brooks Award for the most outstanding Masters of Military Arts and Sciences (MMAS) thesis as well as the Arter-Darby Award for the most significant historical work for his graduating class.